Why Do You Need This New Edition?

The new edition of *Managing Business and Professional Communication* approaches effective communication in the workplace in consideration of the most advanced research available from national competency surveys, which identify communication understanding and skills expected by new and experienced employees and leaders in the workplace in the twenty-first century.

To best help you acquire the skills and competencies you need to succeed in your careers, new coverage includes organizational structures and leadership, social media and electronic communication, listening, interpersonal communication, interviewing, cultural diversity, managing conflict, leading groups and teams, making informative and persuasive public presentations, developing customer service and sales communication, as well as ethics and written communication. The appendices facilitate your self-discovery of career opportunities and offer brief overviews of communication topics such as change management for auditing and networking. Additional features to the new edition include the following:

1 New emphasis on social media and electronic communication, which will better prepare you for the realities of the contemporary professional environment.

2 A new and practical section on written communication, placed as an appendix, for your ready access to writing résumés, cover letters, proposals, and other frequent texts.

3 Extended examples and real-life case studies bring the concepts to life and help you relate this new material to your everyday life.

4 Numerous principles and examples of interviewing best practices will help improve your leadership performance.

5 Expanded coverage of ethics in the workplace, a distinctive quality organizations look for more than ever, equip you to make informed, ethical decisions about your communication in the workplace.

6 Entirely new chapter on listening with emphasis on personal performance and leadership encourage you to consider and apply this critical skill to all of your professional communication.

PEARSON

Managing Business and Professional Communication

Third Edition

Managing Business and Professional Communication

Carley H. Dodd

Abilene Christian University

Allyn & Bacon

Boston   Columbus   Indianapolis   New York   San Francisco   Upper Saddle River
Amsterdam   Cape Town   Dubai   London   Madrid   Milan   Munich   Paris   Montreal   Toronto
Delhi   Mexico City   São Paulo   Sydney   Hong Kong   Seoul   Singapore   Taipei   Tokyo

Senior Acquisitions Editor: *Jeanne Zalesky*
Editorial Assistant: *Stephanie Chaisson*
Associate Project Editor: *Corey Kahn*
Marketing Manager: *Blair Tuckman*
Supplements Editor: *Angela Pickard*
Media Producer: *Megan Higginbotham*
Project Manager: *Barbara Mack*
Project Coordination, Text Design, and Electronic Page Makeup: *Saraswathi Muralidhar/PreMediaGlobal*
Art Director, Cover: *Leslie Osher*
Cover Designer: *Ximena Tamvakopoulos*
Cover Photo: *Right Image/Alamy Images*
Manufacturing Buyer: *Mary Ann Gloriande*
Printer and Binder: *Edwards Brothers*
Cover Printer: *Coral Graphic Services, Inc.*

For permission to use copyrighted material, grateful acknowledgment is made to the copyright holders on page 397, which is hereby made part of this copyright page.

Library of Congress Cataloging-in-Publication Data

Dodd, Carley H.
  Managing business and professional communication / Carley H. Dodd. — 3rd ed.
    p. cm.
  Includes bibliographical references and index.
  ISBN-13: 978-0-205-82386-4
  ISBN-10: 0-205-82386-6
  1. Business communication.   2. Communication in management.   3. Communication in organizations.
4. Interpersonal communication.   5. Intercultural communication.   I. Title.
  HF5718.D63 2011
  658.4'5—dc22

                                                                                  2010049569

Allyn & Bacon
is an imprint of

www.pearsonhighered.com

1 2 3 4 5 6 7 8 9 10   EDW   13 12 11 10

ISBN-13: 978-0-205-82386-4
ISBN-10:   0-205-82386-6

CONTENTS

Appendices   337

PREFACE

In my various roles as a communication teacher, researcher, author, academic leader, and consultant-trainer, I have found it exciting to observe how communication principles and strategies contribute to the day-to-day functioning of organizations and their members. Since *Managing Business and Professional Communication* integrates the academic perspective with actual experience in business and the professions, it discusses not only tried-and-true topics from research and literature in the field but also real issues and events from the workplace.

Today's workplace is a complicated mix of values and needs, relationships and conflicts, and technology and people. Communicating in that environment is demanding, to say the least. At times, managers and leaders must present significant messages of policy and mission to large audiences of employees or board members. At other times, team members must form work groups, brief supervisors, and present reports at seminars. Finally, individuals must participate in interviews and meetings and manage interpersonal relationships all through the organization. To be successful in the workplace requires competence in all these areas.

NEW TO THIS EDITION

This Third Edition of *Managing Business and Professional Communication* identifies the principles and practices that are fundamental to communication competence in today's workplace. Presenting a calculated balance of scholarship and experience, the text blends both traditional and current topics in speech communication and illustrates them with a variety of real-world applications. Not only does a focus on organizations and leadership run throughout, but the text identifies the importance of relationships, listening, technology (including social media and electronic communication), and ethics. Also, this edition proudly debuts a precise summary of written communication needed in most workplaces by providing an extensive appendix on Written Communication, as well as a brand new chapter on Listening.

WORKPLACE COMMUNICATION IN THE INFORMATION AGE

Today's businesses and organizations function in the most powerful information explosion in history, a phenomenon comparable to what followed the invention of the printing press. The Information Age emerged unexpectedly and then grew rapidly. According to Peter Drucker (1999), surprising developments, intense competition, and a paradigm shift to technology have heralded an information revolution that has proven more remarkable than the print and electronic revolutions of the twentieth century. The information revolution has witnessed profound and unprecedented changes in global economies, e-commerce, entertainment diversity, and worldwide distribution of goods and services.

Drucker (1999) provides a human communication perspective, noting that the information revolution is less a product of electronic science than of cognitive science. He has outlined a vision of "knowledge-based industries" and "attracting, holding, and motivating knowledge workers" through inspiration, values, and "social recognition and social power" (p. 57). In short, there is a human component to the situation—a need for interaction, motivation, and inspiration. Thus, in this Information Age, the need for communication competence at all levels has broadened, not narrowed. Individuals in the modern workplace must be able to function as information workers, knowledge brokers, and technologists. This is the workplace foretold by futurist John Naisbitt (1982) in his now classic *Megatrends:* A World in which High-Tech needs High-Touch.

Butcher's (2006) report of the Employment and Training Administration (called the ETA Report) presents a competency model of attitudes, values, and skills needed in the twenty-first-century workplace. This research (along with that of other scholars) emphasizes topics such as organizational structure and leadership, interpersonal communication, listening, interviewing, cultural diversity, managing conflict, building teams, making group decisions, making informative and persuasive public presentations, and developing customer service as well as sales communication.

Butcher along with Altinoz (2009) make clear how scholars should address both the **knowledge** and skills needed in today's workplace. In *Managing Business and Professional Communication*, I refer to this knowledge and application set as competencies needed for effective business and professional communication. The competencies emerge in the text in four units: Foundations of Business and Professional Communication; Interpersonal Communication in Business and Professional Communication; Small Groups and Teams in Business and Professional Communication; and Public Presentations in Business and Professional Communication.

ORGANIZATION OF THE TEXT

The above research has been affirmed by the reviewers of this text and is organized as follows:

- *Foundations of Business and Professional Communication.* Chapter 1 provides a definition and model of business and professional communication and identifies the four contexts in which it exists: organizational culture, interpersonal communication, groups and teams, and public presentations. These four contexts provide the organization for the major units of this book.
- *Dealing with leadership and organizational culture.* Chapter 2 explores practical communication approaches to develop readers' future leadership skills using the metaphor of the *organizational culture.* Most organizations today see themselves as a complex blend of many aspects—hence, the term *culture.* The leadership summary is profoundly helpful summarizing trends and skills along with personal ethics needed to be an effective leader.
- *Managing interpersonal communication.* The nature of interpersonal communication in the workplace is the topic of Chapter 3. Among the skills discussed are the needs to expand information sharing, to be assertive, and to practice communication immediacy.
- *Managing listening communication.* The nature of listening communication in the workplace is the topic of Chapter 4. Among the skills discussed are the needs to expand information sharing, to not miss critical information, and to practice active listening and avoid listening barriers.
- *Managing nonverbal communication.* Chapter 5 looks at the importance of nonverbal communication in the workplace, identifying the rules that govern it and the functions it serves. A wide range of nonverbal behaviors are discussed as well—from eye movements and vocal characteristics to the use of personal space and timing.
- *Managing conflict.* Given that conflict is inevitable in any relationship, being able to manage it is essential. Chapter 6 on managing conflict communication provides the skills and strategies needed to address workplace disagreements and disputes. Understanding these principles and practices should also provide confidence in dealing with conflict.
- *Managing cultural diversity.* The modern workforce is made up of people from multiple cultures, racial and ethnic groups, and generations. Navigating the personal differences that diversity can create in the business and professional environment can be challenging.

Chapter 7 explores the nature of cultural differences and recommends how to avoid the potential barriers and embrace diversity.

- *Leading small groups; building and managing teams.* The use of small groups and teams is one of the most consistent trends in the current workplace. Chapter 8 discusses the importance of group communication and explores the principles and skills involved in building teams.
- *Managing interview communication.* This practical chapter (Chapter 9) discloses the types and structures of interviews and how to do well as either the interviewer or the interviewee. Included among the types of interviews are media interviews and videoconference interviews, topics that are unique to this text.
- *Managing public presentations.* Chapters 10 and 11 present the foundations of public speaking, covering such topics as speaker credibility and confidence, audience analysis, language style and delivery, and the use of visual aids (including PowerPoint presentations). Chapter 12 focuses on developing and delivering informative presentations—from longer speeches to shorter oral reports and news releases and briefings. Chapter 13 focuses on persuasive presentations, addressing the specific issues involved in developing and supporting an argument and motivating an audience to accept it or act upon it.
- *Managing customer service and sales communication.* This text is also unique in providing a practical chapter on customer service and sales communication (Chapter 14). Many managers inaugurate their careers with marketing and sales positions, and virtually all positions entail some type of selling. This chapter approaches selling from a customer-focused perspective in presenting strategies and practices for effective sales communication.
- *Other topics.* Of particular interest to students, an Epilogue describes the importance of communication competence in the workplace and identifies a wide range of careers in communication. Also, the appendices offer stimulating summaries of communication style, change management, communication networks, communication audits, and a very practical appendix on Written Communication. This appendix covers not only reports and proposals, but resumes (paper and electronic), letters, and email etiquette with several examples.

FEATURES OF THE THIRD EDITION

This text offers numerous opportunities for students to apply what they have learned. My students regularly express their desire to know how things work in the real world. And in my teaching and consulting work, I have realized the importance of offering hard-and-fast examples and explanations. I am pleased to say that the reviewers of *Managing Business and Professional Communication* have praised the level to which this text extends theories and principles into real-world practice. Several boxed features serve this purpose throughout the book:

- *Case Studies.* I believe that students improve their critical-thinking and communication skills when they see how successful people function in actual workplace situations. Thus, I have included many examples and illustrations in a series of boxes labeled Cases. Found in every chapter, these short examples make ideas come alive, particularly those that tell the success stories of individuals such as J. C. Penney and Sam Walton and the remarkable achievements of companies such as IBM and Ford. Other cases present problem/solution scenarios—some hypothetical and some real—and ask students to consider what they would do in the same situations.
- *Skills at Work.* In order to develop the skills needed for communication competence, students must understand their current skill levels—both strengths and weaknesses. Toward

Case 5.1

Reading a Troubled Coworker

Suppose that you enter your office after a meeting to leave your notes on your desk before going to lunch. When you arrive, you find your coworker sitting at her desk with her head in her hands. She doesn't look up or acknowledge your presence, and so you ask, "Is everything okay?" Still without looking up at you, she slowly nods her head and says, "Just fine." You mention something about the meeting, which gets no response, and then you leave for lunch. However, as you head out the door, you feel that your coworker is holding something back—that things aren't "just fine."

What about your coworker's behavior makes you skeptical? In particular, what about her nonverbal communication suggests that something is wrong? What would you do in this situation? Why?

FUNCTIONS AND RULES OF NONVERBAL COMMUNICATION

Functions of Nonverbal Communication

...eaning and significance of nonverbal communication provides a founda-... There are four major **functions of nonverbal communication**:

...t. Nonverbal communication may complement verbal communication; ...al behaviors may complete or reinforce what is said. When you slap some-...k while asking, "Hi, how are you?" these behaviors complement each other. ...Nonverbal communication may contradict what's said. For example, some-...n you are conversing may say, "It's really good to talk to you," but his or her ...contact will contradict that message. Similarly, your supervisor may say, "I ...your report," but considering that he or she is standing at a distance, with ...nd eyes downcast, you may get the opposite impression, a finding supported ...005) research.

...nverbal communication also serves a regulative function in terms of control-...conversation between two people. How do you know when it is your turn to talk ...n? The nonverbal behaviors of the other person—particularly, head nods, eye ...al inflection—will tell you. Many people know when a preacher is nearing the ...on because of changes in his or her vocal behavior, especially pitch patterns. In ...ther ways, nonverbal behaviors regulate or guide our interactions with others. ...Nonverbal messages may substitute for verbal messages in certain settings. ...ant that." In a noisy, ...o a meeting place in-..., nonverbal behavior

. Certainly, rules dic-**communication** are vior in an elevator.

WEB AT WORK 3.1
Interpersonal Communication

The Internet sources listed here include companies that offer consulting and training on this
topic, which may provide valuable information
about the role of interpersonal communication
in the workplace. However, you should probably start with the first of these entries to help
you gain personal insight into your own communication style.

- **www.psychtests.com** Psychological
  tests and educational materials that you
  can obtain and administer yourself.

- **www.teambuildersplus.com** Training
  in team building, leadership, and sales.
- **www.fastcompany.com** Good guide
  to principles of relationship.
- **www.uky.edu/~drlane/capstone/
  interpersonal/reldial.htm** Workbook
  from a communication course; click on
  "Interpersonal Communication."

USE SIGNPOSTS Many conversat...
technique of delineating the indivi...
thing happened or the three steps ...
that are used to mark these point...
"Another reason behind this is ..."
through the message, point by poin...

MANAGING SOCIAL NE...
INTERPERSONAL COMM...

This section of the chapter extend...
skills for improving interpersonal ...
networking affect us in the workp...
media platforms, along with e-mail ...
many people around the world. M...
one or how to look up a YouTube vi...
social media's use in organizations. ...
tion can influence your networking ...
climates in organizational use of so...
trates at least one important step i...
data that illustrate social media as ...
workplace.

Organizations Seeking IT a...

Companies not only use social ...
Johnson above, but organizations ...
methods between leaders and em...
65 percent of these companies p...
(Nancherla, 2010).

SKILLS AT WORK 2.1
Improving Communication Style in Organizations

The guidelines listed here are ways of improving
communication style. Think about the questions asked with each guideline to determine
the communication style of an organization you
belong to—say, your workplace or university:

1. Turn taking
   - Is there a balance between talking
     and listening?
   - Do some people regularly dominate
     conversations?
2. Information processing
   - How is secrecy addressed in sharing
     task information?
   - How much information is given at a
     time?
   - Is information best presented in small
     or large "bites"?
   - Is personal conversation encouraged
     or mostly task-oriented conversation?
   - How is constructive criticism offered?
   - How is potentially threatening infor-
     mation conveyed?
   - How are innovations communicated?
   - Is information filtered for some peo-
     ple, either by "dumbing it down" or
     by holding back certain portions?
3. High- and low-context cultures
   - How much information is embedded
     in the situation and expected to be
     communicated through intuition,
     experience, or guesswork?
   - Can the organizational culture be
     described as high context or low con-
     text? (Information is less evident in a

   high-context culture than in a low-
   context culture.)
4. Uncertainty and anxiety reduction
   - Is it acceptable to ask for
     information?
   - If so, to what degree?
   - If not, what other options are avail-
     able for finding things out?
5. Conflict
   - How is conflict handled?
   - Is conflict seen as instigated and de-
     structive or as inevitable and healthy
     in terms of providing opportunities to
     learn and grow?
6. Nonverbal communication
   - What types of facial expression are
     appropriate and accepted?
   - What is the comfortable social
     distance for conversation?
   - Does the arrangement of office furni-
     ture encourage conversation or
     productivity?
   - What are the ergonomic issues in the
     design of the office?
7. Language and code
   - What acronyms, jargon, and profes-
     sional language are appropriate in this
     organizational culture?
   - How does the organization's lan-
     guage or code match that of the pro-
     fession at large?
   - How are outsiders, such as clients,
     communicated with so as not to
     obscure meaning?

EXAMPLE

A department leader ordered a new computer. However, because the requisition for the computer did
not match with the closing of the company's fiscal end of year, the money was removed from the department's budget when the yearly records were closed out. Early in the next fiscal year, the computer
arrived and the payment for it came due. Unfortunately, there was no longer any money for this item
in the budget. The result was that the department lost $5,000 by turning back unused computer money
for one fiscal year and then had to come up with an additional $5,000 at the start of the next year.

that end, each chapter contains one or more Skills at Work boxes, which provide self-assessment instruments, checklists of guidelines and best practices, and other useful analytical tools that students can use to evaluate their own communication abilities. In addition to providing self-awareness, these boxes introduce future managers to the tools used in training and organizational development.

- *Web at Work.* Each chapter contains one or more boxes that identify websites pertaining to the topic at hand. For example, the section on résumés and cover letters includes Web at Work boxes on writing résumés, electronically posting résumés, and writing cover letters. These boxes serve several purposes: to provide students with additional information and to familiarize them with the computer technology and resources available in the field of workplace communication. In all fairness, however, let me point out that today's hot website may be nonexistent when you look it up on your reading of the text. Sorry, but technology changes fast!

Students are also asked to apply what they have learned by completing chapter-ending Discussion Questions and Exercises. In the Discussion Questions, students are asked not only to recall chapter content but also to frame it within their own opinions and life experiences. In the Exercises, students are asked to complete small projects, many of which involve team participation and going into actual workplaces to observe.

This book provides other useful study tools as well. Each chapter opens with a statement of content-specific objectives and a list of key terms. These terms are then highlighted where they appear within the text and defined in the glossary at the end of the book. The chapter-ending In Perspective section offers a succinct summary of the chapter content.

SUPPLEMENTAL RESOURCES FOR INSTRUCTORS

To assist instructors in using this text, a variety of supplementary materials are available:

- *Instructor's Manual and Test Bank.* The *Instructor's Manual and Test Bank.* This provides chapter outlines, additional Exercises and Discussion Questions, additional websites, teaching tips, and test-bank items.
- *MyTest Computerized Test Bank.* All of the test questions are also available electronically through our web-based, computerized testing system MyTest. The user-friendly interface enables instructors to view, edit, and add questions, transfer questions to tests, and print tests from any computer with internet access. Available at http://www.pearsonmytest.com (access code required).
- *PowerPoint*^{TM} *Presentations.* Over 250 colorful, well-produced slides present graphics, key terms and phrases, and major points to help instructors develop classroom lectures and discussions. The slides are developed with students' learning styles in mind and have a particular focus on Generation Y students. Instructors can access these slides at Allyn & Bacon's Instructor's Resource Center (www.pearsonhighered.com/irc).
- *A&B Business & Professional Communication Study Site.* This website features business and professional communication study materials for students, including flashcards, a complete set of practice tests for all major topics, and Web links to valuable sites for further exploration of major topics (www.abbpcomm.com).
- *A&B Business and Professional Communication DVD.* This unique DVD includes video clips in an easy-to-use DVD format. Each clip emphasizes the communication skills that are necessary for the work world. Students will have the opportunity to see a job interview, professional presentations, interviews with top executives, and more.

As a communication teacher, researcher, academic manager, and consultant-trainer, it has been my privilege to observe how knowledge of communication skills and strategies can benefit workers at all levels. My goal is to pass on that knowledge to a new generation of managers and to help them realize their own goals in business and the professions.

ACKNOWLEDGMENTS

A project like this is truly a team effort, and many people deserve my sincere thanks. To begin, I would like to thank the individuals who reviewed the manuscript for each edition and offered many helpful comments: Katherine Allen, Midland College; Carolyn Louise Clark, Salt Lake City Community College; Cathy Dees, Keller Graduate School of Management at DeVry University; Brenton Faber, Clarkson University; Shelley A. Friend, San Antonio College; Lydia Gardner, Borough of Manhattan Community College; Christine R. Helsel, Eastern Illinois University; Arthur Khaw, Kirkwood Community College; Robert Mild, Fairmont State University; Mary L. Mohan, SUNY Geneseo; Susan Opt, University of Houston–Victoria; Tushar Raman Oza, Oakland University; Eileen M. Perrigo, University of West Florida; Ken Robol, East Carolina University; Travis Russ, Fordham University; Joseph A. Willis, Midland College.

The editorial team and production department at Allyn & Bacon have been tremendous in contributing their talents and insights to this project. Project Editor Corey Kahn knows how to make it happen. I appreciate the hard work of the Marketing Manager, Blair Tuckman, and the sales staff for making the book available to so many potential users. Thanks as well to Barry Pupella, a freelance graphic artist from ACU, who shared his gifts and crafted wonderful models for use by the editorial team. Finally, Karon Bowers, the Editor-in-Chief, has been a source of enthusiasm, vision, and "can do" spirit. (Karon, your giftedness touches so many of us, so thanks from the heart!)

The Department of Communication at Abilene Christian University has been supportive as well. From that group, Kelly Branch wrote and developed most of the instructor resources. Kelly has since finished her advanced degree and is now herself a college instructor. Jordan Ziemer served at key junctions for research assistance.

Most of all, I am grateful to my now grown family—Jeremy, Matthew, Philip, and Jennifer—whose professional successes in business and their professions, advanced degrees, and committed families stand as more encouragement to me than they will ever know. My wife, Ada, has been a constant inspiration and a spirtual influence to talk over ideas and let me test some of the innovations. Her professional counseling practice as a Licensed Professional Counselor with university students and her wisdom and wonderful communication ability make her the perfect partner, given the long hours needed to develop a product such as this.

—C. H. D., 2011

References

Altınöz, M. (2009). An Overall Approach to the Communication of Organizations in Conventional and Virtual Offices. *International Journal of Social Sciences, 4*(3), 217–223. Retrieved from Academic Search Complete database.

Butcher, D. R. (2006). *ETA identifies necessary skills for future workforce.* ThomasNet.com. June 6.

Drucker, P. F. (1999). Beyond the information revolution. *Atlantic Monthly,* October, pp. 47–57.

McLuhan, M., & Power, B. (1988). *The global village: Transformations in world life and media in the twenty-first century.* New York: Oxford University Press.

Naisbitt, J. (1982). *Megatrends.* New York: Warner Communications.

MANAGING BUSINESS AND PROFESSIONAL COMMUNICATION

Introducing Business and Professional Communication

After reading this chapter, you will be able to do the following:

- Explain why professional communication in the workplace is important.
- Recognize the central role of communication in the workplace.
- Assess your own communication strengths and weaknesses.
- Identify the fundamental components of a communication model.
- Incorporate communication assumptions that guide communication assessments in the workplace.

Communication is a continual balance act, juggling the conflicting needs for intimacy and independence.

DEBORAH TANNEN

Managing ideas and factual information among individuals and groups in the workplace are vital functions within today's organizations. For that reason, communication principles and information management skills occupy an innermost place in business and professional life. These observations illustrate why human communication is so important in twenty-first-century employment performance:

- Executives must have excellent communication skills among other competencies (Rothwell & Wellins, 2004).
- Workplace competencies highlight communication skills, reported in twenty-first-century industrial competency reports.
- Workforce gaps in the future will engage communication technology for employee learning resulting in 40 percent less cost for training and a 30 percent gain in worker retention for this generation (North & Worth, 2004).

KEY TERMS

communication competencies
 (p. 5)
communication model *(p. 9)*
organizational communication
 (p. 9)
participants *(p. 10)*
message *(p. 10)*
message filtering *(p. 10)*
channel *(p. 10)*
noise *(p. 11)*
organizational culture *(p. 11)*
context *(p. 11)*
occasion *(p. 11)*
communication axioms *(p. 12)*
interpersonal communication
 (p. 14)
group communication *(p. 14)*
public presentations *(p. 14)*
workplace communication-
 competencies *(p. 15)*

- Nearly all job descriptions in the *Wall Street Journal* and *National Business Employment Weekly* include this message: "The person we seek must have strong oral and written communication skills."
- Classic studies of chief executive officers (CEOs) reported that communication yielded a 235 percent return on investment (McPherson, 1998); the trend continues to this day.

COMMUNICATION GAPS IN THE WORKPLACE

As these brief facts above testify, organizational problems usually correlate with stories of how improving human communication would make work and organizational life far more satisfying—and more productive. This conclusion comes from hearing about tens of thousands of daily critical incidents in organizations—all stories that speak to the need for improved communication.

One illustration to understand the importance of human communication in business and the professions emerges from Case 1.1, the first of many narratives in this book. This brief story is about Marty and her need for communication adjustment in a changing workplace.

Marty, whose story is real, represents numerous employees at all levels of leadership, whose need for better communication skills is primary for their continued success. Fortunately, Marty realized this need and modified her communication approach by listening and being more helpful to coworkers. She also realized that Lynn was a compassionate coworker who had worked hard to build a team and that she and her coworkers were more effective when they performed as a team. Even now, the company is progressing because of the communication insights and applications Marty, Lynn, and the CEO have provided.

Along with hundreds of students who now serve as effective leaders in various organizational positions and who witness deficits in communication style, I have seen profit and nonprofit organizations create unbelievable problems among employees. Companies lose revenue, waste money, and create chaos when they do not know or do not apply fundamental communication theories.

Case 1.1

Making Communication Adjustments

Marty has been with the same retail company for ten years but has performed a variety of jobs. She has served as buyer, creator of new market designs, store manager, trainer, and overall coordinator of inventory for the home office. Over the last year or so, the company has grown significantly, and Marty has felt the need to renew her place within it.

Marty has always thought of herself as being able to talk with anyone, but she has recently discovered major shortcomings in her ability to present ideas publicly. Her attempts to speak to the other managers at last month's semiannual managers' meeting were ignored, compounding an ongoing conflict. Her relationship with Maria, the new CEO, also has been strained. Moreover, when Lynn was hired two years ago to develop and promote the company's marketing strategy, Marty felt threatened. Since then, it has seemed that the CEO's vision of teamwork has failed to emerge, that conflict among staff has intensified, and that information sharing about common tasks has ceased.

What types of communication training are needed to address these problems? In particular, what communication skills does Marty need to work on? What relationships does she need to work on as well?

Which skills and competencies will be most critical for leaders as the workplace continues to evolve? How will future leaders, as many of you will become, address communication gaps and deficits? Expert voices answer. For instance,

- Improved human communication leads to (1) outcomes of job and information satisfaction in organizations and (2) saving the billions of dollars lost due to communication problems, ranging from faulty listening to information gaps between and within work groups (DeWine, 2001).
- Knowledge workers represent 40 percent of employees; since they engage in "distributive work," this new level of participation will lead to satisfied, productive employees (Ware & Grantham, 2005).
- Millennials are "digital natives" who expect instant information and social networking (McNamara, 2009).
- The National Career Readiness Certificate now expects workforce readiness to include oral language skills (McNamara, 2009).

When these common issues are placed in perspective, they spotlight a need for leaders who understand the significance and ever-increasing importance of communication competencies, such as the foundational competencies described in this book.

We have to wonder at the communication gap and ask for explanations. One reason that communication underperformance is so noticeable in some organizations is that important communication qualities are overlooked in hiring and in providing continuing education. Another reason occurs when organizations emphasize written or technological communication, often failing to notice oral communication competencies (Reinsch & Shelby, 1997), some of which are represented in Skills at Work 1.1. A third explanation of communication deficits in organizations occurs when organizations innovate models like flextime and telecommuting, which

Communication involves not only the exchange of ideas but also the creation of common meanings. A first step is to be sure that people know the message's purpose. Thus, you can reduce the uncertainty that people experience in a communication encounter.

SKILLS AT WORK 1.1
What Functions Does Communication Solve in Organizations?

The many sources the text identifies highlights the enormous time managers spend engaged in communication. Many writers argue for over 75 percent of executive time devoted to communication. What does this time commitment resolve? What does it accomplish? Altinöz (2009) answers with these communication functions in organizations:

- Communication breakdown and ineffectiveness are lessened.

- Provide information: large and small group meetings, writing and reading (hard copy and e-mails), social networking, and telephoning.
- Convincing and influencing.
- Training.
- Creating unification.
- Control and motivation: that is, creating accountability for duties while instilling loyalty for goals.

National Public Radio (NPR) indicated leads to productivity increases but often at the expense of team synergy and interpersonal communication (NPR.org, March 16, 2010). A fourth deficit recalls how employees and leaders are ill prepared to implement typical specialty communication tasks, as for example:

1. *Sales calls.* Customers and suppliers, particularly in smaller organizations, depend on being able to make successful sales calls.
2. *Meetings.* Small groups and teams need to get along to efficiently share information and make decisions.
3. *Oral briefings, presentations, and written communication.* Making an informative oral or written presentation or making a persuasive speech creates anxiety for many individuals.
4. *Managing conflicts.* Communicating to manage stress and disagreement is essential to accomplishing organizational objectives.
5. *Boss stress.* How supervisory communication represents a formidable obstacle for many workers.
6. *Bad news.* Information that will likely be perceived as negative or threatening can be presented effectively by applying communication principles of interpersonal communication, customer relations, and conflict communication.

It is no wonder that organizations often ask their recruiters to locate individuals who can meet their most challenging communication episodes. Increasingly, large organizations call for communication-trained employees, which can mean a huge payoff to individuals trained this way. One classic study established that improving communication skills yields nearly a 2.5 times return on investment (McPherson, 1998).

WHAT GENERAL COMPETENCIES ARE NEEDED IN ORGANIZATIONS?

The communication gaps noted earlier illustrate why communication competencies can resolve overarching information needs in organizations. To illustrate this principle, Emily Stover DeRocco of the U.S. Labor Department convened a group of researchers to study workforce-training issues.

This relevant and thorough effort, stated in Butcher's (2006) report of the Employment and Training Administration (called the ETA Report), presented a model that initiates our discussion of competencies needed in the workplace. Not all of the ETA Report is about communication competencies, but many of these following elements serve as a backdrop subsequently to discuss communication competencies (Ware & Grantham, 2005). The report includes the following:

- *Personal effectiveness competencies* consist of integrity, motivation, dependability/reliability, and willingness to learn, and to this list we will add self-confidence.
- *Academic competencies* include applied sciences, computational and measurement abilities, computer skills, business writing, information-finding skills, information presentational skills, and interpersonal communication skills.
- *Workplace competencies* such as business fundamentals, teamwork, adaptability/flexibility, marketing/customer focus, managing/organizing, problem-solving/decision-making skills, and applying technology.
- *Industry-wide technical competencies*, including manufacturing or processing for each industry/field, quality assurance, maintenance needed, and health and safety.
- *Industry-specific technical competencies* vary, but illustrations include specific computer software applications and particular knowledge such as how to prepare a customer satisfaction survey or how to conduct an employee survey if you lead or work in human resources.

Since this text addresses relevant communication competencies, our hope is that your time reading and studying will facilitate your communication education in business and professional careers. After all, if motivating, persuading; being able to make ideas clear; showing sensitivity to cultural diversity; having skills in conflict management, team building, and leadership; and overcoming communication anxiety are relevant at all, then we expect graduates of this course to be better prepared for business and professional communication competencies.

COMMUNICATION COMPETENCIES EXPECTED IN ORGANIZATIONS

Not all competencies needed in the workplace relate to communication, as we just saw in the section above. The model we can extract from this point presents a dynamic model of multiple competencies required. When you drill at a deep level, clearly communication *understanding* and *best practices* for self and others are essential.

What are the specific **communication competencies** needed for effective business and professional communication? Several scholarly summaries (DeWine, 2001; Zeremba, 2003; Butcher, 2006; Stefl, 2008; Altinöz, 2009) distill into the following fifteen communication competencies, which we group in four categories representing the major units for this textbook:

Managing Leadership Communication in Organizational Cultures

1. Understanding communication models, the importance of communication competencies, and how to understand alternatives to finding effective leadership structures and management styles.

Leadership in communicating is effective when the leader adapts the communication style to the level of employee receptivity. This ability to adapt, rather than engage the same approach, is the essence of contingency leadership.

Managing Interpersonal, Group, and Intercultural Communication in Business and Professional Situations

2. Manage interpersonal communication in both face-to-face and virtual teams and in social networks.
3. Creating active listening skills.
4. Understand and make effective use of nonverbal communication.
5. Understand and manage conflict and apply negotiation skills.
6. Identify intercultural communication and cultural diversity management opportunities in the workplace.
7. Deal effectively with customer and client relationships, including relating well with difficult people.

Small Groups and Teams in Business and Professional Communication

8. Manage group communication, group leadership, group decision making through communication knowledge and skills while developing high-performance face-to-face and virtual technology teams.
9. Manage interviews both in types and effective skills and practices within an organization.
10. Develop effective paper and electronic résumés and cover letters for interviewing.
11. Assess communication problems and derive effective solutions.

Public Presentations in Business and Professional Communication

12. Make clear, informative oral and written presentations to large and small audiences.
13. Overcome anxiety about communicating.
14. Present effective persuasive speeches to large and small groups.
15. Sell or create a plan that leads to sales.

A review of these competencies highlights the extent to which effective communication in the workplace is recognized as a major factor in organizational effectiveness. As you prepare yourself for a future in whatever field you choose, communication will play a central role in your success. A good way to begin this journey is to complete the assessment of your communication skills presented in Skills at Work 1.2.

SKILLS AT WORK 1.2
Self-Assessment of Communication Strengths and Weaknesses

In this two-part activity, you will identify which areas of communication are your strongest and which areas need improvement.

WRITE A NARRATIVE

Write a one-page narrative about a recent communication encounter that you recall with clarity and that had significance for you in terms of its outcome. Describe your purpose in going into this encounter and indicate what happened. Did you achieve your goal? Why or why not?

　　Your communication encounter could be one of these situations:

- Participating in a selection, evaluation, or information-gathering interview
- Participating in a sales interview
- Resolving a conflict
- Addressing a customer or client grievance
- Participating in a small-group discussion
- Being part of an appointed team on a short-term project
- Speaking on the telephone with a vendor or an order-supply person
- Making a written or an oral proposal
- Making an oral or written report or a briefing
- Meeting with your boss
- Meeting with the president of the company
- Socializing with clients
- Writing an e-mail or memo
- Making an informative speech
- Making a persuasive presentation

ASSESS YOUR STRENGTHS AND WEAKNESSES

Now, evaluate your narrative to identify your strengths and weaknesses. What do you do well? What do you need to work on? With these points in mind, review the following list of communication skills. For each skill you perform well, put a plus sign (+) on the blank line, and for each skill you need to work on, put a minus sign (−). If a skill is not relevant to the scenario described in your narrative, put an "NA" (not applicable) on the line.

COMMUNICATION SKILLS

———— 1. Manage impressions positively
———— 2. Listen well
———— 3. Demonstrate assertiveness
———— 4. Read effectively
———— 5. Write effectively
———— 6. Articulate ideas
———— 7. Have good verbal delivery
———— 8. Have good nonverbal delivery
———— 9. Can understand the problem
———— 10. Can develop a solution
———— 11. Avoid arguing
———— 12. Cooperate willingly
———— 13. Use appropriate technical language
———— 14. Help others feel satisfied with the conversation
———— 15. Control the outcomes of the situation
———— 16. Explain clearly
———— 17. Feel confident

　　Next, sort and rank these skills. List the numbers of all of the skills that you gave pluses to under the "Strengths" heading below in the order of how well you do them, starting with your best skill. Then list the numbers of all of the skills that you gave minuses to under the "Weaknesses" heading, starting with your worst skill. Skip over those skills that you gave an "NA" rating.

Strengths	Weaknesses
————	————
————	————
————	————
————	————
————	————
————	————
————	————
————	————

Given the total pluses and minuses, how would you describe what happened? Did you achieve your goal? Why or why not?

Source: Based on Downs (1988), Goldhaber (1993), and Reinsch and Shelby (1997).

This call for improved communication skills, even in the most technically challenging fields, underscores why this text will be helpful. Communication solutions that cross many situations and professions are presented in the chapters that follow. When faced with a similar real-life communication challenge, you will be able to draw from what you have learned and apply the skills you will learn regarding such areas as managing interpersonal relationships, learning about your conflict style, creating effective teams and meetings, improving interviewing, and facing cultural diversity. Other material will focus on solutions for making effective oral and written presentations. Furthermore, throughout the text, opportunities to consider technology and mediated communication will emerge.

One helpful way of understanding communication competencies is to represent them visually. A *communication model* displays the key components of communication, as discussed in the next section.

DEFINITION AND MODEL OF BUSINESS AND PROFESSIONAL COMMUNICATION

The understanding of communication has changed a great deal over the past few decades. The field has moved across views that define communication as straight-lined, or linear, to less static and more dynamic models that consider the give-and-take of most communication situations. By defining business and professional communication and presenting a beginning model you will enlarge a vision of the communication process.

Defining Communication in Business and the Professions

Communication in business and the professions is defined in this text as "participants interpreting information by interacting through sending and receiving messages across a channel in an organizational context." The components identified in this definition will be explained in the description of the model in the next section. For now, the point is that business and professional organizations present unique communication challenges and opportunities.

This definition of communication helps us make sense of the fact that when people interact, they understand and learn from each other simultaneously. Communication theorists classify this concurrent sharing and learning of a message as a *transactional approach* to communication. This and several other approaches, or models, will be discussed in the following section.

A Briefing on Models

In addition to the transactional model, there are two other common models. Theorists describe one of them as an *action model*, which represents communication as mostly linear. Namely, a source sends a message to a receiver in a kind of one-way system; feedback is delayed, if provided at all. Another type of model, labeled an *interaction model*, suggests that communication goes back and forth between the source and the receiver, as the source responds to feedback from the receiver and vice versa.

Again, the *transactional model* suggests that communication participants share information and discover meaning simultaneously. Communication theorist Em Griffin (2003) refers to this sharing as "a bond of union." According to the transactional model, several other factors also influence the communication process besides the participants' sharing of meaning.

A Communication Model Focusing on Components in Business and the Professions

A **communication model** identifies and visually presents the essential elements of communication. The model presented in Figure 1.1 illustrates how communication participants A and B (who can be individuals or groups) in an organizational culture send and receive messages through a channel (be it public speaking, interpersonal, group, or technology) and interact with the goal of creating meaning and understanding for the purpose of organizational effectiveness.

A model can also help identify the factors within communication interactions that may lead to breakdown. The following statements represent typical frustrations heard every day in organizations:

"When I issue a directive from my office, nothing ever changes. The information I try to communicate becomes distorted by the time everyone in the organization hears about it."

"When our first-line supervisor tried out a new system of operation, the entire crew was enthusiastic. However, after a while, the top brass learned about it and put a damper on the whole idea. Now the workers are slowing down production."

"Our dean assigns work to our department head, but the department head is so overloaded that the work never gets done."

"This organizational chart shows our communication channels, but it doesn't work. Our people don't pay attention to the chart."

"This is the worst place in the world to work. I actually hate coming to work in the morning. It is so different from my previous place of employment."

One way to improve the **organizational communication** conditions illustrated by these frustrated employees is to apply a communication model to assess the areas of breakdown. When you read the details of the model presented in the following, ask yourself what sorts of changes in communication would resolve the issues.

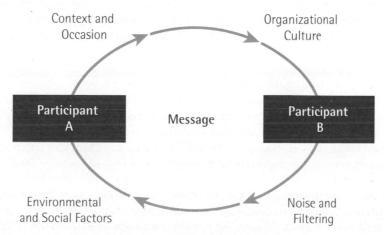

FIGURE 1.1 A Model of Communication in Business and the Professions

THE PARTICIPANTS   First, the participants can be coworkers, an employee and a boss, a team working to solve a problem, or one division of a company talking with another division. Sometimes the communication participants are representatives of an organization talking with the public outside the organization. Anytime people are talking and listening, human communication is under way. If we represent the **participants** in a communication model as A and B, a question becomes who are these individuals or groups who interact and interpret information in an organizational culture. From a speech communication perspective, A portrays the presenter and B the audience.

Although any model can suggest that these participants are independent in their sending, receiving, and interpreting of messages, in reality, they concurrently send, receive, and interpret information, as the word "transaction" implies. Furthermore and of great importance to managing ideas in organizations, A and B are resources of knowledge and experience. Finally, A and B not only share information or exchange knowledge, but they also treat one another with a give-and-take attitude. These mutual perceptions are significant, since on-the-job communication stems from correct or incorrect information regarding other people and their messages.

THE MESSAGE   The interpretation of messages highlights another of the many challenges in organizational communication. Communication theorists such as I. A. Richards emphasize that shared meaning occurs when participants understand the expectations of a situation, understand the other person or persons, and understand the symbols used in the interaction (Griffin, 2008). In the same way, your knowledge of an organization's structure, leadership style, interpersonal roles, team expectations, cultural diversity, and presentational requirements all contribute to your clear understanding of others in the work environment Obviously, the **message** and its interpretation represent a central component of communication. One key point to remember is the multifaceted nature of the message: it can be verbal or nonverbal. Technology-based information also can be interpreted based on personal or eccentric group frames of reference. Real-life organizational background requires communication participants to pay close attention to the interests, values, needs, and prior knowledge that other persons or groups may have about a certain topic. Their influence on each other results from feedback, which is information interpreted by each communication participant.

Message filtering exposes or denies important information to individuals or groups within an organization. For example, the case described in news sources during the spring of 2002—concerning executive shredding of the historically infamous Enron Corporation documents seemingly to avoid legal scrutiny—is an example of such filtering. From a communication view, detrimental corporate practices such as shredding can be traced to poorly operating information flow, inadequate group communication, faulty listening, and inadequate communication policy and feedback.

THE CHANNEL   The medium, or **channel**, of communication is yet another important part of the communication model. There are two types of channels. A *face-to-face channel* features live interpersonal conditions, as is the case in an interview, a meeting, a client visit, or a public presentation. Technology-mediated conditions characterize a second type of channel, which includes communication using the telephone, e-mail, Internet, written memos, and teleconferences. Are these *mediated channels* less interpersonal? Yes and no. Some chat rooms, e-mails, Skype connections, phone interactions, and virtual team conferences offer a close, interpersonal feel. Yet a teleconference screen can appear jerky, a cell phone conversation can be disconnected, and an Internet connection can be interrupted during a chat session.

Thus, while several similarities can be identified between face-to-face and mediated channels of communication, several differences should be noted as well. First, interruptions in communication due to technology are an ever-present possibility. Second, face-to-face types of communication offer the most immediate and clearest interaction and feedback, particularly in terms of nonverbal dimensions. This allows the speaker, for instance, to adapt to a changing communication environment. Moreover, during an interpersonal interview, the participants can immediately adjust their questions and answers to accommodate the assessment under way.

For these reasons, Timmerman (2002) underscores the advantages of using what he calls *rich media* (such as interpersonal communication, meetings, and voicemail) at certain times and *lean media* (such as the Web, memos, and less immediate feedback opportunities) at other times.

NOISE   Another component of the communication model is **noise**, which can be defined as interference with the message interaction process between A and B. There are two types of noise. *Physical interference* affects accurate message processing. The sound of an air conditioner, inadequate room temperature, outside sights and sounds, and pervasive odors are examples of auditory, kinesthetic, visual, and olfactory causes of message distortion. *Psychological noise* includes human causes of inaccurate message perception, such as fatigue and emotional distress.

Noise is present in most communication settings, and people usually adjust to it unconsciously. In some cases, however, it is best to pause and make whatever correction allows maximum information flow.

ENVIRONMENTAL AND SOCIETAL FACTORS   The environmental component of the communication model addresses the role of external influences on organizations and their employees. Environmental factors manage to control many of the attitudes and practices of organizations. It is easy to recognize how civil law, public opinion, resource availability, and the perception of moral law all influence corporate actions. Less obvious are the influence of powerful individuals or groups outside the organization, changes in economic and competitive conditions, and scarcity of assets.

You can envision the effectiveness of a presenter who has considered these environmental factors. Conversely, imagine the embarrassment of presenting a case for an organization's growth after never having considered environmental factors in the argument supporting the proposal.

CONTEXT AND OCCASION   Business and professional communication takes place in the context of the workplace, which usually centers on procedures, norms, and structures. In other words, tasks are to be accomplished, schedules are to be kept, and policies are to be enforced. Even the language used in workplace messages may be full of commonly known acronyms or codes that frequently apply to talking and listening on the job. Collectively, these unique features of the workplace are what communication experts refer to as an **organizational culture** described in detail in Chapter 2. Like any culture, the workplace has its own expectations in terms of achieving a unity of purpose and vision.

The **context** is the physical location or setting in which the message is delivered. You might have to deal with a crowded room, for example, or perhaps the opposite problem: a meeting of three people in a room designed for three hundred. When the company president speaks to employees at an outdoor picnic, the context as well as other environmental factors should influence not only what he or she says but also the length of the message.

The **occasion** is the reason for a communication event. Each occasion leads to certain participant expectations. The same company president speaking at the employee picnic would normally do well to keep the tone of the speech light and to emphasize, for instance, the fun of the occasion, the opportunity to forge new relationships, and the delight of crossing departmental lines in conversations. The president would likely be less effective if he or she leveraged the occasion to motivate productivity, announce new personnel policy, or indicate downsizing. The occasion calls for the communicator to understand the unspoken communication culture of appropriateness. When such expectations are violated, the organization can be affected in untold ways.

Finally, the appropriate match between the occasion and the group's expectations involves an understanding of delivery, language and code, and topic choice. A humorous speaking occasion, such as an after-dinner speech, requires specific preparation, a certain delivery and vocal style, and so on. Thus, a speech delivered on a required topic in a classroom setting is not the same as a motivating message to rally volunteers in a nonprofit organization.

ORGANIZATIONAL CULTURE   Another factor in the model for business and professional communication is the powerful influence of the organization's culture. As detailed in Chapter 2, the metaphor "culture" refers to a group where people develop norms, attitudes, beliefs, and procedures as they interact. These, in turn, influence how people communicate with each other. The collection of these qualities in an ongoing group is called an *organizational culture.*

ASSUMPTIONS ABOUT COMMUNICATION: A WORD ON AXIOMS

A long-standing tradition in the study of communication relies on fundamental assumptions, called axioms, to describe a fundamental framework. While social scientists envision several of these axioms (Watslawick, Beavin, & Jackson, 1967), the four **communication axioms** presented in this section best explain the nature of business and professional communication. While the communication model explains the "big picture," these four axioms provide specific guidance on how communication works. (Also, see Web at Work 1.1, which provides several resources for online materials.)

Communication Is Unavoidable

No matter how hard you try, it is nearly impossible *not* to communicate as if to say, "You cannot not communicate." Even if you fall asleep during a meeting or sit through it looking dazed and fatigued, you are still exhibiting behavior that others will interpret as a message, whether or not you intend it. If a coworker says, "Tell me about the big meeting with the boss," your silence or attempt to avoid giving a straight answer will inevitably prompt your coworker to read between the lines.

A good rule of thumb is that people generally do not read your intentions but rather your actions. All too unfortunate is how they respond based on those actions. It is therefore

---

WEB AT WORK 1.1
Business and Professional Communication

For a sampling of the online resources available about business and professional communication, access these websites:

- **www.work911.com** This consulting firm provides a collection of work-related articles and ideas on all aspects of the workplace.

- **www.ceoexpress.com** CEOExpress claims to "connect busy executives to information that matters."
- **www.thinkmanagers.com** Think Managers offers insight into the introduction to business communication.

no surprise that communication in the workplace is riddled with confusion, omission, and misunderstanding.

Communication Is Irreversible

Human communication is permanent. That is, once you say something, you can't take it back. Attempts to indicate "I didn't mean it" or "Let me try that again" often are ignored. As Beebe, Beebe, and Ivy (2001) express it well, "Once created, communication has the physical property of matter; it can't be uncreated" (p. 17). The framework is set, and normally the process of changing what you said takes time along with consistent behavior to prove otherwise. This second quality also explains why communication in the workplace is at times characterized by suspicion, mistrust, and low credibility.

Communication Involves Content and Relationship

One of the most damaging areas of communication in organizations is a frequently obscure point to many employees, managers, and leaders. Stated as a formula, the idea behind this axiom is as follows:

Communication = Content + Relationship

This concept implies that when an idea is spoken or facts are provided, it comprises only half the message. The illusion is that by saying or writing something, the message settles all understanding. This view limits communication to *what* is said, or the content of the message. Addressing the other half of the formula, the *relationship,* creates a more complete view of communication—namely, *how* something is said directs the message at the relationship. This idea is so powerful that health-care leaders now require "relationship management" as an essential component defining effective competency (Stefl, 2008).

For instance, your directing an employee "Get this report done now—and I mean it!" illustrates the relationship aspect of the message. In this case, it signifies power, raw emotion, and perhaps a negative attitude about another person. Voice quality, body movements, posture, and eye movements are major conveyors of these relationship features in communication. Again, even if you do not intend to convey a negative view, others will read into your message a relationship dimension. It is no wonder that so many business and professional interactions lead to uncertainty, fear, and low morale.

Communication Is Rule Governed

Every culture has a set of norms, procedures, codes, appearances, attitudes, and general expectations that are expressed in the communication of its members. When communication occurs with these expectations in mind, rules govern the expression. Thus, the communication within an organization usually follows a set of conventions or guidelines. Some are highly refined and articulated, whereas others are expected but ambiguous. Here are some examples of rules in organizations:

EXAMPLES

"All ideas must be shared."

"We are a team, like a family."

"Innovation and creativity are expected every week. What have you done today?"

"Watch your backside."

"Don't keep secrets."

"Support the organization at all costs."

Clearly, some of these rules present a challenge to effective communication. For that reason, knowing the explicit and implicit rules of an organization can provide a comfortable edge for your communication efforts. As such, this fourth communication axiom explains the powerful influence organizations hold over employees: they create the potential for stress and conflict as well as the potential for achievement and great satisfaction.

BUSINESS AND PROFESSIONAL COMMUNICATION IN FOUR CONTEXTS

The variety of communication competencies and axioms discussed thus far suggests the need to condense the most effective components of knowledge and practice into four main areas. The chapters in the rest of this book will explore the competencies introduced in detail, offering knowledge and skills to enhance communication performance in these contexts. The first of these contexts is an understanding of organizations.

Organizational Culture

The first context is the organizational culture mentioned earlier. This context involves expected structures, leadership styles, reporting authority, lines of formal and informal communication, expected procedures of teamwork, crisis approaches, and decision-making procedures. Chapter 2, which rounds out Unit I on foundations of business and professional communication, examines these issues.

Interpersonal Communication

The second Interpersonal Communication in Business and Professional Communication involves **interpersonal communication**, or sharing information, creating ideas, working with difficult people, and so forth. Topics in this unit area include the nature of verbal and nonverbal communication, listening and assertiveness skills, conflict management, managing cultural diversity, and dealing effectively with customer relationships.

Groups and Teams

Unit III organizes the third context, which examines the principles and skills related to **group communication which includes team building**. The procedures for conducting an effective meeting are presented, as well as principles for achieving balance in group communication and exercising productive leadership skills. The concept behind building teams are also covered, and guidelines are provided for how to adapt the message to varying people and conditions. Finally, interview communication is described as a two-person group involving specialized communication procedures.

Public Presentations

The fourth context includes principles and skills in making **public presentations** as discussed in Unit IV. One type of presentation is informing, which may include making a speech or writing to a group or individual in order to explain or define. Presenting oral reports and briefings is sometimes similar to informative speaking. Another presentational aspect relates to persuasive speaking, in which the goal is to convince the audience of the validity of a certain attitude, belief, behavior, or policy, perhaps to the point of adopting it. Sales communication is considered as well, given the many times an idea or product is presented with the goal of managing change with information. The context of a public presentation may be face-to-face or mediated with technology.

In Perspective

The research findings about business and professional communication covered in this chapter should enhance your confidence in communicating in a wide variety of speaking and listening situations. You can get the job, take care of the customers, be more persuasive, evaluate fairly, make the sale, be a great team member, and get your ideas across clearly and forcefully.

To perform competently as a communicator in business or the professions begins with understanding the link between communication and organizational effectiveness. Communication competencies, as well as communication deficits, can be uncovered and clarified in an organizational setting. In addition, when the principles of effective communication are applied, the image presented is one of employee quality and competence expected in most businesses and professions.

A communication model illustrates the components of the communication process, including the participants; their interpersonal perceptions of each other; the message and its interpretation; the channel, noise and filtering; societal/environmental influences; the context and occasion; and organizational culture.

The present text distills the communication literature and relevant experiences to condense the most important competencies needed in business and professional communication. The principles related to **workplace communication competencies** are the basis for the material in Managing Business and Professional Communication. Consequently, you will read common-sense principles and examples regarding organizational topics such as organizational structure and leadership, interpersonal communication, listening, interviewing, cultural diversity, managing conflict, building teams, making group decisions, making informative and persuasive public presentations, and developing customer service as well as sales communication. The many appendices provide additional practical guidelines on topics ranging from self-assessment to managing change strategies in organizations. Learning from these theories and experiences will help jump-start the careers of future managers like you. Over the years, many students have explored the benefits of communication principles applied on the job. Now, to that experience can be added an array of concepts reported in an efficient and easy-to-use textbook, which applies solid research and experience to the real-world situations future leaders will encounter.

Discussion Questions

1. Why is it important to study business and professional communication?
2. What is unique about workplace communication compared to other areas of communication in your life? What is similar?
3. How does the model presented in Figure 1.1 illustrate the "big picture" of communication? What would you add to the model? Why?
4. How do the four communication axioms presented in this chapter help explain why communication breakdown occurs?

5. What aspects of business communication can you link with the competencies covered in this chapter? For instance, interpersonal communication is a competency and one of the four major areas covered in this textbook. What examples of business communication fit into interpersonal communication?

Exercises

1. Take another look at Skills at Work 1.2, in which you assessed your communication strengths and weaknesses. Discuss what you learned about yourself with a trusted individual: a teacher, a parent, or a friend, for example. What does this individual say about your self-assessment? Does he or she agree or disagree with your conclusions?
2. With a team, develop your own model of business and professional communication. What would you add to or

take away from the model presented in this chapter? Produce a drawing, a physical model, or some other product that expresses communication in the workplace.

3. Is it true that "you cannot not communicate"? Do a brief survey of two or three friends, asking each for his or her response to the idea. What do they say? What examples do they provide to back up their opinions?

4. Interview the leaders of an organization. Ask each person to state his or her five most difficult areas of leading and managing. What is the role of information management or communication in his or her answer? Present your findings to the class, and start a group discussion about the challenges of hiring and training employees today.

5. If you could illustrate your experience as an employee or think ahead to your time as a future manager, what single object would you display to illustrate your self-perception? Explain this idea in an "object" speech to your group, in which you state "My work life is like this object. Here is why . . ."

References

Altınöz, M. (2009). An overall approach to the communication of organizations in conventional and virtual offices. *International Journal of Social Sciences, 4*(3), 217–223. Retrieved from Academic Search Complete database.

Beebe, S. A., Beebe, S. J., & Ivy, D. K. (2001). *Communication principles for a lifetime.* Boston: Allyn & Bacon.

Butcher, D. R. (2006). *ETA identifies necessary skills for future workforce.* ThomasNet.com. June 6.

DeWine, S. (2001). *The consultant's craft: Improving organizational communication.* Boston: Allyn & Bacon.

Downs, C. W. (1988). *Communication audits.* Glenview, IL: Scott, Foresman.

Goldhaber, G. (1993). *Organizational communication.* 6th ed. Madison, WI: Brown and Benchmark.

Griffin, E. (2008). *A first look at communication theory.* 7th ed. New York: McGraw-Hill.

McNamara, B. (2009). The Skill gap: Will the future workplace become an abyss. *Techniques: Connecting Education & Careers, 84*(5), 24–27. Retrieved from Academic Search Complete database.

McPherson, B. (1998). Student perceptions about business communication in their careers. *Business Communication Quarterly,* 61, 68–79.

North, A., & Worth, W. (2004). Trends in selected entry-level technology, interpersonal, and basic communication SCANS skills: 1992–2002. *Journal of Employment Counseling, 41*(2), 60–70. Retrieved from Academic Search Complete database.

Reinsch, L., & Shelby, A. N. (1997). What communication abilities do practitioners need? Evidence from MBA students. *Business Communication Quarterly,* 60, 7–29.

Rothwell, W., & Wellins, R. (2004). Mapping your future: Putting new competencies to work for you. *T+D, 58*(5), 1–8. Retrieved from Academic Search Complete database.

Stefl, M. (2008). Common competencies for all healthcare managers: The healthcare leadership alliance model. *Journal of Healthcare Management, 53*(6), 360–374. Retrieved from Academic Search Complete database.

Timmerman, C. E. (2002). The moderating effect of mindlessness/mindfulness upon media richness and social influence explanations of organizational media use. *Communication Monographs,* 69, 111–131.

Ware, J., & Grantham, C. (2005). Which skills and competencies will be most critical for leaders as the workplace continues to evolve?. *Leadership in Action, 24*(6), 15. Retrieved from Academic Search Complete database.

Watslawick, P., Bevin, J., & Jackson, D. (1967). *Pragmatics of human communication.* New York: W. W. Norton.

Zaremba, A. J. (2003). *Organizational communication: Foundations for business and management.* Mason, OH: South-Western.

CHAPTER 2

Managing Leadership Communication in Organizational Cultures

After completing this chapter, you will be able to do the following:

- Identify diverse management structures and leadership styles.
- Develop your personal communication style in the context of leadership and management.
- Identify the influence of organizational culture on communication and performance.
- Describe the elements of organizational culture.
- Communicate more effectively with units by considering the mutual effects of systems thinking.

KEY TERMS

organizational culture *(p. 17)*
leadership communication *(p. 17)*
leadership alternatives *(p. 17)*
scientific management
   perspective *(p. 29)*
human relations perspective *(p. 32)*
human resources perspective *(p. 33)*
systems communication
   perspective *(p. 35)*
total quality management
   (TQM) *(p. 37)*
contingency leadership *(p. 39)*

Leadership and learning are indispensable to each other.

JOHN F. KENNEDY

As discussed in Chapter 1, business and professional communication affects many aspects of organizational performance and employee satisfaction. Effective workplace communication also enhances a group's image outside the organization, bringing benefits ranging from profit to prestige. Clearly, competent communication offers many benefits to organizations.

This chapter seeks to help readers know the importance of **organizational culture** and **leadership communication** as fundamental competencies for effective business and professional communication. Both organizational culture and **leadership alternatives** help us understand organizational roles, organizational design, and communication expectations. In one sense, organizational culture represents a unifying platform on which workplace communication competencies stand. In another sense, organizational culture is the audience of business and professional communication. Either way, organizational culture comprises a complex web of values and relationships within a given organization. This collective thought and action reverberates throughout most courses of action within an organization, including its procedures and policies, whether or not formalized.

Future managers who grasp this view of organizations as cultures, along with leadership alternatives, will be prepared to create competent messages, share information, interpret decisions, interview others, and provide leadership. Thus, understanding organizational culture provides a means to make sense of communication in organizations—and in turn, enhances your knowledge competency. In examining organizational culture, we will consider its influence on forming messages and communication styles, its role in maintaining hierarchy and structure, and its significance for leadership expectations.

ORGANIZATIONAL CULTURE AS A CONTEXT FOR COMMUNICATION

The metaphor "culture" refers to a group where people develop norms, attitudes, beliefs, and procedures as they interact. These, in turn, influence how people communicate with each other. The collection of these qualities in an ongoing group is called an *organizational culture.*

Borrowed from anthropology and intercultural communication, the term *culture* implies a common set of values, language, and behaviors. Like a tribe, an organization cultivates and encourages uniform attitudes and actions among its members, usually resulting in unity and consistency. Consequently, effective communicators try to fulfill cultural expectations about information needed and how that information should be presented and actions implemented. Such expectations galvanize the organization's system of rules (policies, procedures, and practices), language, beliefs, values (areas of supreme importance, including valued people), and mission. These simple but profound elements of organizational life can be stated or unstated—in fact they often are part of the hidden rules in organizations. In either case, identifying these perspectives in typical organizational communication situations is important to success.

This contemporary view of organizational culture contrasts to historical views in organizational studies, which defined organizations in narrower terms, mostly emphasizing structure and hierarchy. Now, this holistic approach encourages the study of communication as dynamic interactions, something unachievable by traditional hierarchical models. By understanding communication from an organizational culture viewpoint, future managers will be able to make sense of the many communication episodes they will encounter.

Knowing an organization's culture during an employment interview, for instance, is vital to assessing a candidate's viability to carry out goals and tasks. Walmart's customer-friendly policy regarding returns and exchanges represents the norms of its organizational culture and its leaders, who insist on adherence to this policy. This may explain, in part, why Walmart is the largest revenue-producing corporation in the United States. Internal influences not only affect customers and clients in businesses and professional organizations, but the organizational culture also motivates and persuades employees to act and think in one direction or another.

To demonstrate the importance of understanding organizational culture, consider the classic example that Case 2.1 presents is regarding the story of two large companies—Uniroyal and Goodrich—and the clash of cultures resulting from their merger. Sadly, this scenario occurs repeatedly throughout the business world—not only with titans of industry but also with medium and small companies, as well as nonprofit organizations.

Addressing the concerns in this culture clash story, communication specialists have seized upon the rich metaphor of *culture* to examine the many complexities of talking and listening in

Case 2.1

A Clash of Cultures

In 1986, two giants in the tire industry announced their merger. The partnership between Uniroyal and Goodrich brought together two highly established and profitable companies. But much to the surprise of company leaders and industry analysts, customers canceled orders and profits soon dried up. How could this have happened?

Market forces certainly played a role. Auto manufacturer General Motors (GM) experienced lower car sales, which led to a 20 percent drop in tire sales industrywide. However, more was involved in the case of Uniroyal and Goodrich. A range of corporate culture issues also emerged, including how to mesh production systems, harmonize cost-accounting systems, blend policy differences, and implement competing management styles. In short, Uniroyal and Goodrich had very different ways of doing things—something company leaders seemed to fail to realize when they struck the merger.

In this classic clash of two organizational cultures, collapse seemed inevitable until the new Uni-Goodrich company was compelled to pull together to fight a common enemy: company buyout efforts. They were not successful in this fight. By 1990, Michelin had bought the still struggling Uni-Goodrich. But in the end, this buyout made the original venture profitable.

What issues of corporate culture do you think company leaders should have considered before the merger? How about after the merger?

organizations. This metaphor illustrates how effective communication within *organizations* represents a communication context that is much broader than that of individual competence. Consequently, organizational culture assumes that humans as social beings need to connect with one another through a variety of communal networks (Conrad & Poole, 2002).

Not only is culture a network phenomenon, but the metaphor of culture underscores how organizations nurture *shared values* that identify what is important to the members of that group. When values go all the way through a group, individuals communicate and act in ways to line up with those values. For instance, when the sales staff of a car dealership aligns with the value of integrity, future negotiations in selling a vehicle enhance future customer trust of that company. Accordingly, the ability to promote values in organizations sets expectations for the group to engage in communication that is applied to resolving negotiation and having relevant group network members totally informed.

FEATURES OF ORGANIZATIONAL CULTURE

One way to discuss organizational culture is to identify basic factors. These clusters or factors represent qualities such as an organization's mission and goals, values and beliefs, procedures and rituals, scope and space, roles and relationships, methods of reward and recognition, language and communication style, leadership design and approach, and identity and image (Scott & Stephens, 2009). Furthermore, analyzing the stories, metaphors, and behaviors of the organization's members become efficient ways to undercover an organization's culture (Moran, Harris, & Moran, 2007; Taylor & Trujillo, 2001).

Mission and Goals

An organization's *mission* is its driving force—that is, its central belief of purpose. *Goals* are the actions or steps taken to accomplish the mission. For example, these slogans serve as mission statements for several real organizations:

EXAMPLES

This university serves its students by educating for service, scholarship, and leadership throughout the region.

Satisfaction of customers is our main business.

Doing it right the first time is what we stand for.

We won't provide any product for your home we would not put in our own.

None of these slogans would likely win the prize for best-worded mission statement, but each serves a valuable purpose: it captures a key point about the organization's purpose. Organizations typically galvanize their beliefs, attitudes, and behaviors around a central theme. In turn, this theme becomes the group's mission, guiding its business practice and providing a standard for measuring group performance.

Values

Values are topics of worth and importance—things an organization holds dear. Regardless of whether an organization's values are articulated, they usually influence its members' behavior and attitudes. These illustrations show how some organizations communicate their values to employees and customers:

EXAMPLES

Texas Instruments asks for daily innovation developments.

Delta emphasizes a family feeling.

Maytag boasts of product reliability and its employee work ethic.

Ford changed its values to focus on quality and teams.

PeopleSoft uses language that conveys individual growth, valued-added customer service, integrity, and relationships.

Of course, for values to have meaning, they must show up in actions—something that does not always happen. For example, the Enron Corporation espoused strong values about productivity and creativity. Despite these espoused values, Enron executives evidently deceived and manipulated messages and documents for their advantage concerning developing products and services. Even their finest speeches about integrity values seemed to fall on deaf ears among the upper ranks.

Case 2.2

Accepting Company Values

The owner of a new car dealership believed that four principles were the cornerstones of the company's previous success, and those core values influenced hiring and training. In a managerial training session, the trainer was conducting team building and routinely confirmed the company's core principles by quizzing new managers regarding their acceptance of these values. After two days of training, one of the new sales managers admitted his lack of confidence in the principle that dealt with integrity in providing customer service. He argued that adhering to this value was not possible in the car business and that trying to do so would damage his ability to sell cars and win bonuses. That day, he resigned.

Why did the new manager resign from a job he had just started? If he hadn't quit, how well do you think he would have performed his job?

Beliefs

Beliefs are the truths that an organization holds about relevant topics—the things it knows to be true or real. For instance, most organizations believe in what they feel are the best ways to produce, lead, compete, communicate, and invest. Company manuals, newsletters, and meetings often reinforce formal beliefs. Moreover, when employees accept an organization's beliefs (and for that matter, its mission and values), they are more likely to fit with the organization. This situation points to the importance of stating beliefs in a direct and tangible manner, something not all organizations do. Case 2.2 presents an interesting story about employees accepting (and not accepting) the values of their employer.

Procedures and Rituals

As we noted earlier about the context of networking and values, organizational culture enriches a framework for organizational members to understand the group's *procedures*. Procedures often appear as rules or policies. For instance, an expense report illustrates reimbursement policy. Similarly, procedures to request a merit raise or to purchase equipment demonstrate rules or policies. From a business and professional communication standpoint, where unclear procedures leave doubts or when uncertainty persists, employee productivity and satisfaction suffer. Without clear information, how does a person know what is expected or how to perform the job?

Rituals are the routine activities performed within an organization. Illustrations include designating Friday as office dress-down or casual day, holding holiday parties, and celebrating events such as promotions and retirements. The rituals that are part of an organization's culture may surprise new employees. Thus, part of socializing employees into an organization involves introducing them to the rituals, as well as the procedures, relevant to their roles.

Scope

Most organizational cultures also make assumptions about their *scope*—that is, the boundaries of space and size that delineate its service territory. First City Bank, for instance, may define its primary service area as the immediate local area. However, Citicorp and Bank One clearly cover a global service area.

Case 2.3

Taco Bell's Organizational Culture

During the 1980s, the leadership of Taco Bell viewed the company as competing in the *Mexican* fast-food business. Rapid changes took place when the leadership changed its focus and saw the company as competing with *all* fast-food chains, including pizza and hamburger restaurants. The next expansion occurred when Taco Bell redefined itself as being "in the business of feeding people." Finally, the company extended its store hours and expanded its delivery channels to include convenience stores, schools, airports, and so on. In all, these changes resulted in a rise in market sales worth billions from 1983 to 1993.

How would you evaluate the roles of customer service, scope, and mission in this example? What, if any, has been your own experience with Taco Bell?

The scope that an organization claims relates to the breadth and quality of its services. For example, for many years in the state of Texas, Blue Bell Ice Cream was available only in limited areas—those that the company could reach with its delivery system and still ensure product freshness and quality. When the company envisioned covering a larger territory and expanded its delivery system to do so, the engineering and manufacturing departments responded with new ways to continue producing a quality product. In other words, Blue Bell expanded its scope successfully by holding onto the quality taste that made the company famous in the first place while adding innovations in preservation and delivery.

Expanding scope and space was one of the factors that led to a period of rapid growth for the Taco Bell chain. Evaluate this and other factors of organizational culture by reading Case 2.3.

Roles

Roles refer to prescribed or expected models of organizational behavior and activity. Individual roles usually relate to positions and people's performance in those positions. As the safety engineer, for instance, what does the organization expect from Susan? Her role within the organization she works for may be similar to but also different from the same role in another organization. As a marketing analyst, what is Jeff expected to do to fulfill his role expectations? His education and previous experience may serve him well, but he will likely need to adjust his behavior to meet the specific expectations of his current employer's organizational culture.

Roles also refer to how organizations identify key individuals, such as the president or the expert. The positive outcome to roles in this sense is to clarify who can expect to act or make decisions. However, leadership roles go beyond the formal boundaries to various informal leadership roles. These subtle roles, rarely identified in an organization, have a powerful influence. Examples include individuals who hold a lot of social influence, who always know the latest office rumor, and who have extensive or unique job knowledge.

One technique communication professionals apply in achieving competency is to clarify roles. Whether realized through initial employee orientation or through later training, such instruction helps people throughout the organization by identifying relevant information sources and means to accomplish tasks.

Relationships

The *relationships* in an organizational culture are the associations and interactions among its members. These are the networks referred to in the introduction of this discussion. Relationships refer not only to feelings about fellow employees but also to shared assumptions between associates, such as what they value and believe about organizational topics. Clearly, status and hierarchy also define relationships. For instance, some associates have equal status and power, whereas others are in different positions within the organizational hierarchy (e.g., a manager and the people who report to him or her). Defining relationships, including their relative hierarchical positions, is important to the stability of the organizational culture and is an important communication knowledge competency.

Reward and Recognition

Reward and recognition addresses how employees receive merit and advance themselves within an organization. What are the obvious versus hidden ways of acknowledgment? What qualities define success, and how do individuals document and present their performance? What paths exist for advancement? How do individuals know when they deserve reprimand? What written and oral formats facilitate reward? This area of organizational culture provides many opportunities in which business and professional communicators can achieve competence.

Language and Communication Style

Language refers to the code or jargon associated with an organizational culture, which may not make sense to someone outside that culture. For instance, the military's frequent use of acronyms illustrates the difficulty of interpreting meaning without knowing about the language of this organizational culture.

Communication *style* refers to an organization's traditional processes for and approaches to information sharing. An analysis of communication style identifies three key elements: what is said, how it is said, and through what channel it is said.

WHAT IS SAID   The first element of communication style is the *content* of the message. What is the topic? How much information does someone present, and how specific is it? In addition, how relevant is the information?

In some cases, information sharing occurs in direct ways, leaving little doubt about the content of the message. At other times, the approach is indirect, which may make people wonder about what the content is. In these situations, people may feel they missed the point or did not comprehend the details of a certain task, project, or proposal.

A related content issue is *information availability*. Is information freely available to everyone, to certain individuals, or to no one? If information is available, how do people access it? Finally, what *response processes* are available? For example, suppose you received news via your employer's website that it was introducing a new product next month. How would you clarify the implications of that news?

In considering content, it is helpful to assess the agenda of the communication participants as it influences stating their goals. To do so, we must listen and carefully attend to the matter of understanding *what* is said.

HOW IT IS SAID   The second element involves the emotions that play a role in our interpretation of messages. Recall from Chapter 1 the third communication axiom: *Communication involves content and relationship.* The relationship between communicators occurs by taking in what we interpret as the emotional side of the information, which is usually conveyed by voice, body position, eye contact, and other nonverbal behaviors.

Thus, a good approach to understanding communication style is to observe what emotive communication qualities occur during information sharing. Is the exchange friendly and open, or is it confrontational? Is it task-oriented or people-oriented in style? How does this person share good versus bad news? What level of emotional expression is encouraged, tolerated, or discouraged? Does the organizational culture promote friendliness and fun, or is the expectation to remain reserved in expressing communication? Are people encouraged to talk candidly about problems, or are they supposed to be subtle, talking around the issue or even deflecting it through humor and off-the-topic stories?

THROUGH WHAT CHANNEL IT IS SAID The third element of communication style is the *channel* that appears appropriate for a specific topic—for instance, a face-to-face conversation, a phone call, a written memo, an e-mail, and so on. To discuss a new idea with his or her manager, does an employee need to make an appointment, or can he or she just drop in? What topics work best to discuss via interpersonal channels, and what topics warrant an e-mail or other written communication?

Before moving on, evaluate the communication style of an organization you belong to by answering the questions in Skills at Work 2.1.

Stories/Narratives

The literature of an organizational culture focuses on its *stories* or *narratives*. These stories are extremely valuable both in terms of being interesting in and of themselves and in providing a means to understand the values and norms of the organization. As LaGuardia argues, organizational culture is interpretive, a point which makes stories all the more important to understand as to their actual meaning (LaGuardia, 2008). Some stories comprise rumors and half-truths, but others intentionally reinforce a theme or make a point. Such stories include hero stories, rules and procedures stories, and leadership expectation stories.

HERO STORIES *Hero stories* tell about personal achievements and thus define organizational success by accentuating the model qualities of outstanding employees. As such, these stories also reinforce the organization's values and its expectations from its members. Two examples will illustrate the nature of hero stories:

EXAMPLE

For years, J. C. Penney store managers motivated employees in sales and customer service by sharing traditional stories about the company's founder. In particular, managers' motivational speeches, usually presented at a store meeting, described Penney's strong work ethic and integrity. The implication was that the company appreciated and recognized those employees who emulated these values. The founder of Walmart, Sam Walton, motivated employees with his speeches about the need for maintaining low prices while enhancing customer service. Stories are told about Walton's views on low prices and quality service, about how he made unplanned inspections of stores, and about the old truck he drove and the old jeans he wore. In today's retail industry, Walton's vigilance regarding customer service is legendary.

RULES AND PROCEDURES STORIES *Rules and procedures stories* tell memorable and thought-provoking tales of horrible mistakes as well as remarkable victories that resulted from doing things the "company way." These classic rules stories provide powerful, reinforcing messages for following company rules and procedures:

SKILLS AT WORK 2.1
Improving Communication Style in Organizations

The guidelines listed here are ways of improving communication style. Think about the questions asked with each guideline to determine the communication style of an organization you belong to—say, your workplace or university:

1. Turn taking
   - Is there a balance between talking and listening?
   - Do some people regularly dominate conversations?
2. Information processing
   - How is secrecy addressed in sharing task information?
   - How much information is given at a time?
   - Is information best presented in small or large "bites"?
   - Is personal conversation encouraged or mostly task-oriented conversation?
   - How is constructive criticism offered?
   - How is potentially threatening information conveyed?
   - How are innovations communicated?
   - Is information filtered for some people, either by "dumbing it down" or by holding back certain portions?
3. High- and low-context cultures
   - How much information is embedded in the situation and expected to be communicated through intuition, experience, or guesswork?
   - Can the organizational culture be described as high context or low context? (Information is less evident in a high-context culture than in a low-context culture.)
4. Uncertainty and anxiety reduction
   - Is it acceptable to ask for information?
   - If so, to what degree?
   - If not, what other options are available for finding things out?
5. Conflict
   - How is conflict handled?
   - Is conflict seen as instigated and destructive or as inevitable and healthy in terms of providing opportunities to learn and grow?
6. Nonverbal communication
   - What types of facial expression are appropriate and accepted?
   - What is the comfortable social distance for conversation?
   - Does the arrangement of office furniture encourage conversation or productivity?
   - What are the ergonomic issues in the design of the office?
7. Language and code
   - What acronyms, jargon, and professional language are appropriate in this organizational culture?
   - How does the organization's language or code match that of the profession at large?
   - How are outsiders, such as clients, communicated with so as not to obscure meaning?

EXAMPLE

A department leader ordered a new computer. However, because the requisition for the computer did not match with the closing of the company's fiscal end of year, the money was removed from the department's budget when the yearly records were closed out. Early in the next fiscal year, the computer arrived and the payment for it came due. Unfortunately, there was no longer any money for this item in the budget. The result was that the department lost $5,000 by turning back unused computer money for one fiscal year and then had to come up with an additional $5,000 at the start of the next year.

LEADERSHIP EXPECTATION STORIES In short, *leadership expectation stories* tell employees how to treat the boss. Books on organizational culture are replete with stories about leaders as heroes and villains. For instance, Sypher's (1990) casebook on organizational communication reports many incidents about GM management. John DeLorean (himself a rising GM star at one time) repeated the following organizational story in speeches:

EXAMPLE

A particular regional manager always expected his GM subordinates to stock his hotel room with plenty of cold refreshments for him and his guests. This meant that a large-sized refrigerator was always needed for these occasions. During one visit, the hotel could not accommodate the refrigerator request, so the car dealers in that city went to great expense and trouble to bring in a large refrigerator and thus please the visiting manager. Unfortunately, the room entrance could not accommodate the refrigerator's size. With time running out, a quick-thinking zone manager hired a crane and operator, knocked out a set of windows in the hotel suite, and lowered the oversized refrigerator into the room through the newly formed hole.

What values does this story teach? What does it tell you about the organizational culture that was typical three decades or more ago? DeLorean told the story to ridicule this culture of deference to high-level executives. He also refused to pick up his boss from the airport, as was normally expected among subordinates in his day, perhaps further demonstrating his disdain for the cultural ritual.

Leadership Style

Another category of organizational culture is *leadership*. Specifically, what style do leaders follow, and what do they expect in return? These questions involve leaders' philosophy of the importance of people versus tasks and expectations about sharing of and access to information. Later in this chapter, we will explore leadership styles, and you will have the opportunity to analyze your own leadership style.

Organizational Identity and Image

The narratives, slogans, phrases, and words used by an organization also indicate something about the group's *identity and image*. In one study, Lovas (1999) analyzed a number of corporate websites to uncover the hidden identities conveyed by their language and themes. Interestingly, the study disclosed two types.

One organizational type values *people*. The language used in these organizations reflects this attitude, as demonstrated by the use of key words such as *nurturing, people-oriented, fun, learning, communication, interpersonal, team, together,* and *collaborate*. For instance, the website for PeopleSoft, Inc. (that is, people.com) contains attractive messages about people and personal values, all of which speak to relationships and communication.

A second organizational type values *things*. In these organizations, themes of power and technology overshadow personal themes. Not surprisingly, Lovas found the word "you" hardly ever used in this second type of organization. The Exxon–Mobil website has a link to a page entitled "Working at Exxon–Mobil," which contains this language: "Exxon–Mobil is a valued global partner due to our technical skills, our financial strength, our experience managing major projects, and our dedication to environmental leadership and good corporate citizenship." Not even their use of the editorial "we" obviates what remains unsaid; namely, how technical and financial themes appear to over-shadow employee welfare and customer service, themes often underscored by people-oriented companies.

A review of organizational websites and other literature also demonstrates how language and graphics convey organizational image. One way to enhance competent communication is to use words and images to attract employees who fit the company's culture. If you are a "people person" and searching for a job, will you be happy working for a company that values technology and products? Conversely, if you are a "task person," will you be happy working in an environment that promotes a person-oriented culture?

If you find yourself in a human resources situation to improve the fit between people and the culture, you might enjoy these ten communication strategies to build an organizational culture (Lovas, 1999; Trice & Beyer, 1993):

1. Articulate the primary mission and values with an overarching metaphor.
2. Develop an employee orientation program to emphasize mission and values.
3. Develop a common image or template for all messages, websites, speeches, and meetings.
4. Match employee self-interests with organizational goals.
5. Provide opportunities for employees to be heard.
6. Change elements in the culture as needed, taking a gradual but continual approach.
7. Demonstrate trust by doing what you say you will do.
8. Support innovation and accept the risks of temporary failure.
9. Be flexible and adaptable in communication style.
10. Empower others by listening to and encouraging them.

In closing this section of the chapter, an important case example will provide a useful reminder of how communication principles can help you implement skills in developing organizational culture (see Case 2.4 on the next page).

LEADERSHIP IN ORGANIZATIONAL CULTURES: STRUCTURES AND STYLES

As noted in the previous section, organizational culture provides the context for business and professional communication. Competent business and professional communication clearly involves understanding leadership alternatives as well. Leadership and management approaches presented in this section center around communication principles applied within organizational cultures.

Organizational communication theorists Conrad and Poole (2002) describe leadership paradigms as "organizational designs." This idea reminds us that organizational culture is seen as a system in which each part influences other parts (McNamara, 2006).

It also reminds us that you need to grasp how leadership is structured and what styles are expected. Competent communication involves astute recognition of organizational designs and expectations. In real-life organizations today, we actually see a blended, multidimensional approach, which makes up most organizational cultures (Scott & Stephens, 2009). Some organizations are highly bureaucratic in structure, as evidenced by qualities such as formal authority, ingrained procedures, personal accountability, and even scrutiny. Other organizations are more loosely structured and thus less formal and more participatory. Each kind of organizational design presents challenges for communicators—the big headline is being able to adapt to varying organizational designs.

Case 2.4

Developing Ethics in Communication Strategies

Midwestern Services, Inc.*—a large nonprofit counseling organization—experienced a large growth in client load over a decade, and most clients reported satisfaction with the timing, quality, and availability of Midwestern's services. Then things changed.

On one Monday afternoon, Tricia, the divisional manager of operations (that is, accounting, scheduling, and logistics), was overheard making negative comments to a subordinate about the recent performance of Jeff, the divisional manager of direct services (counseling, community relations, client relations). Within a few days, this conversation made its way back to Jeff, who was enraged.

Jeff confronted Tricia angrily, remarking that she had no right to criticize him to a subordinate and that what she had said was untrue anyway. Tricia shot back that Jeff's performance was so bad that *someone* needed to call attention to it. Furthermore, she argued that under the circumstances, confiding in the company's comptroller seemed both professional and reasonable to her.

Tricia's comments, along with her stiffened resolve, further enraged Jeff. The confrontation escalated into an episode just short of a fight. Other managers and employees witnessed part of the scene and spent the next week or so debriefing, taking sides, and creating defense strategies among themselves.

At the next company meeting, the chief executive officer (CEO), Charles, invited participants to express their feelings about what had happened and where the organization was at that point. Images of rockiness, storms, confusion, and anger came pouring forth. One employee who had witnessed the scene and felt loyalty to Tricia remarked, "I've felt like I've had an elephant in the living room for the last week," meaning that the high level of tension and emotion was obvious throughout the organization.

By actively soliciting and then listening to people's sentiments, Charles created a climate of openness, which is a fundamental principle of successful organizational communication. He applied a second basic principle in closing the meeting with a speech in which he acknowledged people's hurt feelings and positive intent and explained how conflict could be an opportunity for growth. In the final point of his persuasive speech, Charles reaffirmed key relationships, offered a metaphor of unity, and realigned the organization's mission.

Charles's communication helped the organization to move forward. Participants reported feeling relief and restored confidence in the company. They also indicated their positive feelings about Charles's listening to them (principles from Chapters 3 and 5) and showing empathy for their concerns. After the meeting, people let go of the hurt and apologies thus leading to healing. Today, the organization continues to flourish.

In this case, what would you do to resolve the companywide conflict that followed Tricia and Jeff's confrontation? How did Charles's listening play a role? What other leadership strategies seemed to help?

*To ensure confidentiality, the name of the organization and all individuals' names in this case are fictitious.

The following sections invite your careful attention first to some management traditions and styles followed by more recent models of management and leadership. As a future leader, you may discover fragments from several of these designs, and with this reading, you will be able to recognize what you will experience.

Scientific Management Perspective

The study of management goes back to the late 1800s and early 1900s, when leadership pioneers such as Max Weber (the father of the classical theory of management) adopted a military hierarchical model and applied it to the burgeoning manufacturing enterprises of the day. From this start, the **scientific management perspective** emerged.

By 1915, the scientific management approach spawned additional concepts, which by today's standards resemble *efficiency engineering* and *ergonomics*. Frederick Taylor, one of the leaders of this movement (sometimes called *Taylorism*), conducted research on a number of concepts still in use today: time-and-motion studies, motivation of workers, organizational structure, and lines of formal authority as viewed in tall and flat organizations.

TIME-AND-MOTION STUDIES AND EFFICIENCY   Members of the scientific management school reasoned that if human work could be isolated into its smallest units, then improved work processing or timesavings would reduce the effort needed to complete certain jobs. These *time-and-motion studies* provided a baseline from which to estimate the productivity of a given worker. In this sense, scientific management viewed human beings like machines that were capable of producing more or less work, depending on the tools and equipment provided and the degree of reward available.

For example, Taylor's study of coal shoveling at the Bethlehem Steel Works revealed that in a given timeframe, a worker could load significantly more coal with a small shovel (about 21 pounds) than with a large shovel (that could hold 38 pounds). Changing the shovel size used to load various materials eventually resulted in more output.

Communicating in the workplace offers challenging but satisfying opportunities for personal growth and development.

MOTIVATION   Closely tied to the time-and-motion studies was the period's theory of human *motivation*. The reasoning went like this: since motivation is economic in nature, it stressed a "carrot-and-stick" philosophy. Consequently, sufficient financial reward resulted in achieving peak productivity. Often, the rewards showed up as piecework systems and bonuses. Employees who did not fulfill output expectations suffered verbal abuse, if not dismissal.

A more recent application of this concept involves a salesperson from a Fortune 500 electronics company, who bragged about how the company scientifically managed its sales force by attracting candidates through the promise of high bonuses. However, the less obvious dimension of this approach, according to this salesperson, occurred when the company periodically raised the sales quota and simultaneously reduced the size of the sales territory. This company continues to attract extremely capable salespeople, but its turnover is high.

ORGANIZATIONAL STRUCTURE   Another major tenet of the scientific management perspective emphasized *organizational structure* in order to group employee units and prescribe communication responsibility. Having structure meant that organizational tasks and divisions of labor flowed through formal, hierarchical channels of communication. Often intentionally designed to increase efficiency, a structural approach to leadership limited communication to mostly linear, one way, top down, and related to the task at hand.

Some of these organizational structures defined years ago by scientific management theorists are found today, such as these organizational roles:

- **Boards and policymakers.** This role is usually limited to policy. For example, the board of directors for a bank might vote to increase interest rates, but management will still decide who qualifies for loans.
- **Upper management.** Upper management has the responsibility of overseeing everyday operations, often illustrated by the CEO and/or the president and various vice presidents and other individuals considered top executives. Illustrations of additional roles include chief operations officer (COO), chief financial officer (CFO), chief information officer (CIO), and other high-ranking employees in production, research and development, marketing, quality control, and human resources. Each of these groups may consider itself part of the direct functioning of the organization (for example, research and development), or it may define itself as providing a support function (for example, human resources). Designations such as *direct* and *support* do not necessarily imply significance, since all units function to assist the whole organization.
- **Middle management.** In classical terms, middle managers provide an important link between the bottom and the top of the organizational hierarchy. In particular, middle managers (including first-line supervisors) serve as the channel of communication between upper management and workers. Unfortunately, in this central role—sandwiched between the top and bottom echelons—middle managers often experience high levels of alienation and stress.
- **Supervisors.** This level of management, sometimes called *lower management*, serves as the direct link to workers. Titles may include *directors, front-line leaders, team leaders,* and *coordinators.*
- **Support staff.** Staffs such as administrative assistants, associate directors, assistant coordinators, and secretaries play a supporting role within the organization.
- **Front-line employees.** Also called *production workers* in classical terms, these employees are the front-line, direct-task producers. In a factory, front-line employees work on the assembly line. In a medical clinic, these employees are the nurses, doctors, and other health professionals who perform direct patient services.

ADAPTATIONS TO STRUCTURE: TALL AND FLAT ORGANIZATIONS   A commonly understood approach today with origins in Taylorism is a way of describing formal organizational structure known as the *organizational chart*. Two basic types of charts describe formal communication channels (see Figure 2.1): a tall organization and a flat organization.

A *tall organization* illustrates a traditional hierarchy, with many vertical levels of decision making and communication. The potential advantage of this type of structure is that employees receive more attention, since the coordinator or division head at each level has fewer employees than would be the case if there were fewer vertical levels. The primary disadvantage of a tall organization is information distortion, since each division may choose to filter upward and downward communication:

- *Downward communication* refers to the process in which information that is generated from the upper levels in an organization is passed down through successively lower levels. (The accuracy of information communicated this way can be reduced by as much as 20 percent per layer.)
- *Upward communication* refers to the process in which information that is generated primarily from the lower levels is passed up through successively higher levels.

In contrast to a tall organization, a *flat organization* has a central person to whom many employees report. Without a hierarchical structure, such an organization has fewer managers above employees, which offers the potential advantage to reduce costs. Another advantage of a flat structure is that there is less information distortion. Its primary disadvantage is that the central person must maintain a large set of interpersonal relationships. This can lead to potential information overload, low-quality relationships, and high stress.

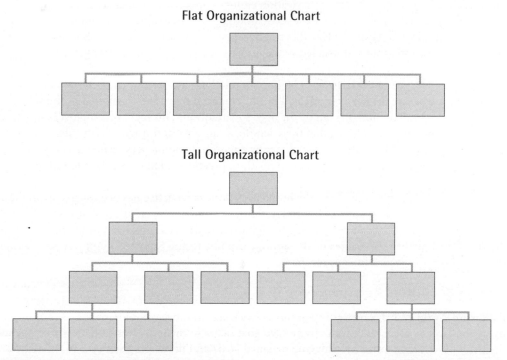

Flat Organizational Chart

Tall Organizational Chart

FIGURE 2.1 Flat and Tall Organizational Charts

Advocates of other management approaches today recommend a more people-oriented approach than is characteristic of the traditional production-oriented approach of the scientific management school. Such a shift in focus occurred in the later 1920s and resulted in the development of the human relations perspective, to which we now turn. This change in views opened up the subject of management to an investigation of employee motivation and communication. In reading further, also notice what developments occurred in leadership approaches.

Human Relations Perspective

The **human relations perspective** emerged from a series of trials examining the effects of working conditions and other environmental factors on workers' productivity. The evidence led to surprising discoveries, namely that workers were hungry for management attention as a cause to productivity—a concept called the Hawthorne effect.

HAWTHORNE EFFECT   During the 1920s, a series of experimental studies at the Cicero, Illinois, Western Electric Hawthorne plant effected a change in the managerial perspective away from the scientific management approach and toward the human relations approach. These now famous Hawthorne studies were part of the National Academy of Science's campaign to examine the effect of lighting levels on manufacturing productivity. The researchers reasoned that as the level of lighting went down, productivity would go down correspondingly. However, to everyone's surprise, just the opposite happened. Productivity actually increased with a decrease in lighting, only falling at the point when barely any light was available.

This unexpected finding, called the *Hawthorne effect*, was explained in terms of the increased attention that workers received. In other words, the sheer fact that management was paying attention to their needs seemed motivation enough for workers to increase their output. This finding also marked for the first time the recognition of the value of upward communication and listening to employees. Thus, the Hawthorne effect had a significant impact on how leaders managed employees, and as such, it ushered in the human relations school of management.

EMPLOYEE-FOCUSED ATTENTION   The human relations framework characterizes humans as social beings who are primarily motivated not by financial incentives (assumed in the scientific management school of thought) but by the need for attention. This focus on employees was quite innovative, especially considering that the scientific management framework considered humans as "cogs in the wheel." Increasing productivity by attention to employees seemed an easy strategy. Unfortunately, insincere attempts at human relations practices led many workers to feel they were being manipulated.

Although its zenith was short, the human relations perspective has been surfacing in many organizational leadership approaches today. Critics of the approach argue that research never produced convincing data showing that paying more attention to employees would increase productivity and quality. Advocates of the approach point to the reported employee satisfaction resulting from this leadership approach.

Human Resources Perspective

Following World War II, a new group of theorists viewed employee development and responsibility as the keys to increased productivity. The goal of these theorists was to help workers reach their full potential in terms of achieving personal goals and developing self-esteem. In addition, the organizational payoff was to produce creative, motivated employees.

In other words, the assumption was that when a matrix of social and achievement needs was met, these needs balanced and promoted production concerns. Contributors to this **human resources perspective** made impressive contributions to organizational and managerial theory. For instance, the pioneering work of Henri Fayol and later Elton Mayo in the 1930s underscored the motivational and deep psychological concerns of people. Their ideas illustrated how employees could reach across the rigid boundaries of departments and thus communicate horizontally. Fayol's idea, known as *Fayol's bridge*, was an early prototype for network analysis, which portrays inter-locking communication patterns and sharing information through interpersonal linkages forged across organizationally created divisional lines.

MASLOW'S HIERARCHY OF NEEDS   Another social scientist concerned with theories of human needs and motivation, Abraham Maslow wrote that motivation occurs when a person's needs are met—beginning with fundamental, broad-based needs and including levels of increas-ingly more abstract social and individual needs. The adaptation of Maslow's (1954) *hierarchy of needs* shown in Figure 2.2 reveals this pattern.

The first, most basic level of need is *sustenance and nurturance*, or physiological need. In terms of motivation, it is certainly difficult to imagine employees being motivated to work when they are hungry, thirsty, or homeless.

When this need is met, the second level of need emerges, *safety and security.* You can prob-ably think of advertising that appeals to this basic need for security, such as the Michelin tire campaign showing a happy baby seated inside a tire, and the accompanying slogan asking viewers to consider safety. In terms of the workplace, when people feel secure in their jobs and within their environment, their motivation increases.

The third level is the social need for *affiliation and acceptance.* This powerful force drives us toward friendship and group membership. Organizational retention studies offer convincing data that group identification contributes to employee longevity (Scott & Stephens, 2009).

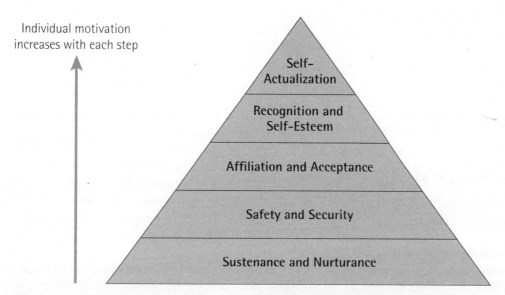

FIGURE 2.2   Maslow's Hierarchy of Needs   *Source:* Based on Maslow (1954).

The fourth level of Maslow's hierarchy is the need for *recognition and self-worth*. Once we belong to a group and feel accepted by it, we also want appreciation and respect for what we do. Communicating with others on the job is one important way to cause acceptance and self-worth. Thus, communicating with rituals and using symbols of recognition in organizational culture encourages employees to equate performance with enhanced self-esteem.

The fifth level (and the most difficult to achieve) is *self-actualization*. At this level, people satisfy their needs by fulfilling their individual potential, often by intrinsic values and experiencing personal pride about one's work.

HERZBERG'S HYGIENIC AND MOTIVATING FACTORS   Another development in human resources leadership resulted from the historical research of Herzberg (1968). His hygienic and motivating factors define two distinguishing elements of work leading to dissatisfaction or satisfaction:

1. *Hygienic factors* include elements of the work environment, such as company administration and policies, supervision, relationships with coworkers, work conditions, personal life, salary, status, and security. These factors do not necessarily increase people's motivation, but without them, people experience dissatisfaction.
2. *Motivating factors* include elements of what people do on the job, such as achievement, the work itself, responsibility, advancement, and growth. These factors bring people satisfaction and contribute to performance.

Here are the levels of dissatisfaction and satisfaction that come from specific hygienic and motivating factors, respectively:

Hygienic Factors		Motivating Factors	
Company policies/administration	36%	Achievement	42%
Supervision	19%	Work itself	31%
Relationship with supervisor	10%	Responsibility	22%
Work conditions	10%	Advancement	21%
Salary	8%	Growth	12%
Relationship with peers	6%		
Personal life	5%		
Relationship with subordinates	5%		

Based on Herzberg's original work, researchers continue to prove that enjoyment of the work itself, along with salary, is among the primary reasons for people's job satisfaction. As considered in Skills at Work 2.2, job enrichment is an important method of communicating responsibility and growth for positions. The *job enrichment technique* (*JET*) brings employees responsibility and personal significance.

THEORY X AND THEORY Y   Another way to understand the human resources emphasis on employees and philosophies of management is to explore McGregor's (1967) *theory X* and *theory Y*. These contrasting theories of management pivot on two philosophies about the nature of employees:

SKILLS AT WORK 2.2
Rethinking Herzberg and Applying Ethics

Should employers communicate incentives and rewards to their employees?

When used alone, incentive programs can actually *diminish* employee satisfaction. A study by Annas (1973), which was years ahead of its time, found that of 80 sales and compensation arrangements across a broad range of companies, well-educated, secure, salaried salespeople reacted less favorably to sales contests because they viewed them as "gimmickry." Rather, these individuals were motivated by the work itself and by productivity, according to the study.

A number of years ago, Black & Decker reported that the company's job enrichment program was based on salary, growth potential, self-development, training, communication, responsibilities, and recognition. These job enrichment factors helped contribute to Black & Decker's 15 percent annual average growth in net earnings during a significant point in its history. It's important to keep in mind, however, that these results were achieved over the long term. In the short term, marketing strategies can create peak-and-valley sales cycles, diverting the sales force from balanced selling.

What do you think about incentive programs and their effectiveness in motivating employees? If you were a manager today, how would you use Herzberg's two factors? What ethical principles are involved?

- *Theory X* views employees as lazy, in need of supervision and discipline, and as lacking competence.
- *Theory Y* views employees as creative, wanting to work, and willing to grow, all of which can be achieved with the right motivation. In this view, the work itself is considered motivating.

In fact, both approaches are useful at certain times. The nature of the work and the history of a particular organizational culture will likely determine which theory works best. Some leaders find a need to use a blend of X or Y, depending on the situation. Moreover, leaders responsible for recruiting employees often find this role as an opportunity to select employees who are likely to match the organization's prevailing leadership style.

Before moving on to the next section, apply what you have learned about the human resources perspective by analyzing the scenario in Case 2.5 on the next page.

Systems Communication Perspective

Tracing its origins to the biological sciences, the *systems theory* uses the metaphor of a *system* to explain the ecological interconnectedness found in natural habitats—hence, the modern use of the term *ecological systems* or a **systems communication perspective** emerged a few decades ago.

The metaphor of a system is particularly appropriate when you remember that leadership in an organizational culture is by nature systemic with norms, relationships, and patterns of interaction. The seminal idea is that each component within a system—say, an individual, a team, or a department—affects the other components. Thus, a communication system engages a set of mutually influencing units, or it meets as a web of networks forged through daily interaction. The implications are colossal for relationships and for making a product or accomplishing a task.

Leadership, according to this perspective, balances a concern for people with a concern for tasks. In this view, employees influence leaders just as leaders influence employees because of the assumption that components of the system are mutually influential. The following model illustrates this principle.

Case 2.5

Incentives and Performance

The experience of IncenSoft LLC, an electronic manufacturing firm, is not too different from that of many other companies that seek a team orientation and self-directed workers. As summed up by the company president, "It is not just the money that motivates sales employees. Recognition is just as important as money."

Given this awareness, IncenSoft uses incentives to address the employee issues of low motivation, poor performance, and high turnover. Rather than merely throw cash bonuses at employees, the company has set these goals:

- Create a self-motivated, team-oriented environment.
- Unify employees under a common mission and set of strategic goals.
- Communicate goals and performance results frequently to employees.
- Establish a link between incentive rewards/employee performance and the company's overall performance; that is, reward the group's performance as well as the individual performances.

How successful do you think IncenSoft will be in achieving these goals? What do you feel is the link between incentives and performance? How would you communicate to reward people? How would you prevent dissatisfaction among employees? What would you communicate to inspire job satisfaction and promote excellence in performance?

BLAKE AND MOUTON'S MANAGERIAL GRID   Blake and Mouton's (1985) approach to leadership, although close to a human resources perspective, is systemic in nature. One reason is a leader's managerial communication style choice affects a team or individual's performance. As you will see next, a manager may emphasize task, relationship, or both.

Figure 2.3 illustrates Blake and Mouton's *managerial grid*, which is composed of two axes. The horizontal axis reflects a manager's concern for the task, which is a productivity measure ranging from 1 to 9. The vertical axis reflects a manager's concern for people, which also ranges from 1 to 9. The grid is formed by finding the midpoint of each axis and drawing intersecting lines. The resulting model shows four quadrants describing a managerial style:

- Quadrant 1 (9, 9) is the *team management* style, which reflects a high concern for both task and people.
- Quadrant 2 (9, 1) is the *authority management* style, reflecting a high task concern but a low people concern.
- Quadrant 3 (1, 1) is the *impoverished management* style, which reflects a low concern for both task and people.
- Quadrant 4 (1, 9) is the *country club management* style, reflecting a low task concern but high people concern.

The figure also includes the middle-of-the-road *organizational person management* style, which reflects moderate concern for both task and people. Communicators using this style experience a great deal of give-and-take and compromise.

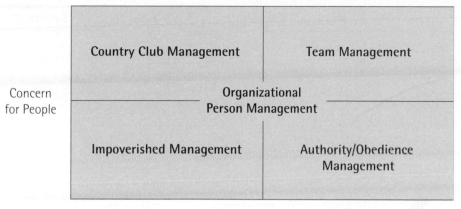

FIGURE 2.3   Blake and Mouton's Managerial Grid   *Source:* Adapted from Blake and Mouton (1985).

LIKERT'S FOUR SYSTEMS   Another system model is Rensis Likert's (1961) *group performance model* which describes four levels of individual involvement across six major tasks typically executed in organizations:

1. Leadership
2. Motivation
3. Communication
4. Decisions
5. Goals
6. Control

As Figure 2.4 illustrates, a manager's profile is determined by answering several questions within each task category. The System 1 profile is one extreme of a continuum shown as top down and centralized and maintaining high control. Its opposite, System 4, presents a profile characterized as being more participatory, involving communication and interaction with employees.

As you review the questions and responses in the figure, notice how communication-based practices play a dominant role in determining which profile a person uses. This suggests that future managers can adapt their communication strategies to the organizational culture of their employer and the needs of their employees.

TOTAL QUALITY MANAGEMENT (TQM) MOVEMENT   Over the past two decades, a movement known as **total quality management (TQM)** has strongly influenced leadership practices. Not just a single theory, TQM is a collection of ideas based on values important to leaders: quality without errors, value-driven outcomes, market-driven responses, and continuous improvement. From a TQM perspective, the elements of successful management include maintaining great service and producing a great product. In addition, employee involvement and vigorous training are keys (Walton, 1991).

	System 1	System 2	System 3	System 4
Leadership				
Can leaders trust their subordinates?	Never	Sometimes	Usually	Always
Can subordinates talk to leaders and have their ideas accepted?	Rarely	Sometimes	Usually	Always
Motivation				
Is fear or reward used to motivate employees?	Both occasionally	Fear sometimes	Reward sometimes	Accountability is based on a group's set goals
Where is responsibility felt for achieving the organization's goals?	Mostly at top	At the top and middle	Between the top and all levels	At all levels
Communication				
How much communication is aimed at achieving organizational objectives?	Very little	Some	Quite a bit	A lot
What is the direction of information flow?	Downward	Mostly downward	Downward and upward	Downward, upward, and sideways
Decisions				
What is the formal level of decision making?	Mostly at top	Policy at top	Broad policy at top but some delegation	Throughout and well integrated
What is the level of subordinate decision making?	Never involved	Occasionally involved	Generally involved	Always involved
Goals				
How are organizational goals established?	Orders are issued	Orders are issued; some comment is invited	Orders are issued after discussion	By group action (except in crisis)
Control				
How concentrated are review and control functions?	Highly concentrated at top	Fairly concentrated at top	Moderate delegation to lower levels	Widely shared throughout
Is there an informal organization resisting the formal one?	Yes	Usually	Sometimes	No; both have same goals
What are cost, productivity, and other control data used for?	Policing and punishment	Reward and punishment	Reward and some self-guidance	Self-guidance and problem solving

FIGURE 2.4   Likert System Profile   *Source:* Adapted from Likert (1961).

The popularity of TQM stems in part from its wide application during the mid-1970s in the Japanese automobile manufacturing business. At the time, new U.S. autos had an average defect rate of 27 percent, whereas new Japanese autos had less than a 3 percent defect rate. This remarkable difference in quality was attributed to the Japanese focus on the core values of TQM.

General Motors (GM) was able to resolve some serious problems in one of its U.S. plants by applying some TQM principles—namely, asking employees for input, setting up strong expectations and rules, and conducting regular meetings to discuss complaints and efficiency. Within a matter of months, employee absenteeism went from 7 to 2.5 percent and the number of employee grievances decreased from 2,000 to 30.

One example of how communication is adapted based on the TQM perspective comes from a consulting analysis showing which skills can boost TQM to help management achieve improved results (McCormack, 1994). Work in this areas has been distilled into the best six skills to make TQM work for you:

1. Commit to mission, vision, and action-centered values.
2. Foster and train self-directed teams, with everyone assuming leadership and passionate responsibility.
3. Focus on results that pull rather than push.
4. Commit to continuous learning and improvement.
5. Create job evaluations based on innovation, creativity, and change.
6. Give earned praise freely.

Thus, TQM offers a framework not only for organizational design but also for leadership communication strategies.

CONTINGENCY LEADERSHIP   A final systems communication perspective is **contingency leadership**, which refers to *situational leadership* as communication writers Hersey & Blanchard (1988) describe. Like most of the theories of leadership and organizational culture, this theory has

Contingency leadership matches leadership style with employee ability and motivation.

evolving uses. Generally, the word "contingency" refers to the idea of adapting communication to the situational information needs and maturity levels of employees. Like audience analysis skills to prepare for a public speech, contingency leadership requires matching a sender's style with a receiver's needs.

The typical situational leadership model from Hersey and Blanchard (1988) matches four communication styles, S1 through S4, with four receiver styles, R1 through R4. The resulting four leadership styles are as follows:

- *S1: Directing.* The leader uses telling and deciding.
- *S2: Problem solving.* The leader uses selling and coaching along with listening to employee input.
- *S3: Developing.* The leader uses participating and supporting to develop employees.
- *S4: Delegating.* The leader uses delegating to offer employees increasing levels of responsibility.

The four receiver styles are based on employee readiness to perform (defined as competence + motivation):

- *R1: Low-performance readiness*
- *R2: Moderate- to low-performance readiness*
- *R3: Moderate-performance readiness*
- *R4: High-performance readiness*

What makes this leadership model effective is the matching between communication style and employee readiness. The dynamics flow means that as R1 presents itself, the leader would utilize an S1 style and so on. However, as employees progress to higher R levels, say from R1 to R2, then the leader adapts to an S2, and so on through the combinations. It is called situational because employee abilities and motivations are not constant, changing according to each task or for other reasons. This critical step ensures that leaders adaptively communicate with their followers adjusting across a range of alternatives (see Figure 2.5).

In some cases, the employee's performance potential is so low (R0) that he or she needs retraining, reassignment, mentoring, or some sort of redirection. This is the recommendation of the consulting company known as the Oak Charter Group in its version of contingency leadership.

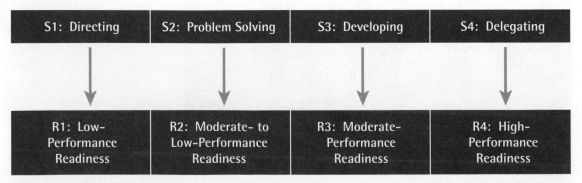

FIGURE 2.5 Model of Contingency Leadership

Recap of Leadership Communication Perspectives

Most communication experts today agree that identifying mission and vision, applying empowerment strategies, encouraging employees to participate in goal setting and decision making, and developing teams are associated with effective and growing organizations. However, at times the situation demands flexible, adaptive communication applied to task or to relationship needs. No single approach will work across complex management situations. For instance, on one hand, exerting too much control might make you so authoritarian that employees will comply but remain unmotivated. On the other hand, giving up control and failing to provide direction might suggest that you have low expectations and leave employees frustrated and dissatisfied. Keep in mind, however, that a good rule of thumb in today's management environment is that empowering employees—either individually or in teams—along with expecting accountability is the most effective approach in terms of maximizing both morale and productivity.

Overall, the leadership communication perspectives described in this chapter center on two key variables: the degree of involvement from employees as contrasted with the control of the leadership. It will be your responsibility as a manager to choose from among the perspectives in forging your own style and approach. Clearly, your choices must work in concert with the structures and leadership options of the organization to which you belong. To evaluate your own leadership qualities, take the short quiz in Skills at Work 2.3.

See Web at Work 2.1 on the next page for online sources of information about organizational culture and leadership in the context of communication. Many of these sources will lead you to significant ideas for further research and interest. Happy hunting!

SKILLS AT WORK 2.3
What Are Your Qualities as a Leader?

Answer the following questions to get an idea of what leadership qualities you possess.

	No	Uncertain	Yes
1. Do I encourage others' participation?	____	____	____
2. Do I have realistic goals?	____	____	____
3. Am I confident about the decisions I make?	____	____	____
4. Am I aware of team effort and loyalty?	____	____	____
5. Do I work with a group before effecting innovation?	____	____	____
6. Do I provide enough information to teams?	____	____	____
7. Can I tolerate ambiguity and frustration?	____	____	____
8. Can I share success with others?	____	____	____
9. Can I not get my way without being resentful?	____	____	____
10. Do I control the impulse to get even?	____	____	____

Clearly, the more "Yes" responses, the better your score in terms of your being an effective leader. What qualities do you need to work on? Which of these are ethically oriented principles, in your view?

WEB AT WORK 2.1
Organizational Culture and Leadership

Explore these websites to learn more about the communication-based aspects of organizational culture and leadership:

- **www.inc.com** The website for *Inc.* magazine.

- **www.hoovers.com** Offers valuation regarding company information, business news, and more.
- **www.marketresearch.com** A well-known selection of market research.

In Perspective

The discussion of leadership in this chapter follows from the context of organizational culture as a central metaphor for competent knowledge regarding organizations. Understanding an organization's culture means knowing about its mission and goals, values and beliefs, procedures and rituals, scope, roles, relationships, language and communication style, stories, leadership style, and identity and image—all of which affect the nature of effective leadership communication within that organization.

In this context of organizational culture, competent business and professional communicators recognize the advantages and applications regarding major perspectives on leadership communication examined in the chapter: scientific management (or classical theory), human relations, human resources, and systems communication (including Blake and Mouton's grid, Likert's Four System, total quality management, and contingency leadership). Understanding these various perspectives will help you make sense of their implications for various organizational cultures. In addition, understanding the evolution of these approaches, collectively and individually, provides useful insight about their successful application. Many of these principles are ethically based, as well.

In sum, these approaches to leadership communication boil down to two variables: employee involvement and leadership control. As a future leader, your job is to choose from among the perspectives to forge your style. When that choice applies to the organizational culture of which you are a member, you will be able to adapt to their needs.

Discussion Questions

1. What qualities of organizational culture have you observed in, say, a previous job or at your college or university? What effect did these qualities have on you personally?
2. Describe two of the major ideas associated with the scientific management perspective. Can you think of an organization that uses this classic approach to leadership?
3. How are the human relations perspective and the human resources perspectives similar? How are they different?
4. Describe two of the major ideas associated with the systems communication perspective. Can you think of an organization that uses this contemporary approach to leadership?
5. Think about Maslow's hierarchy of needs in terms of your own life. Where would you place yourself along the hierarchy? In other words, what needs have been met and what needs have not?
6. Which of the Likert management profiles is most appealing to you? Why?

Exercises

1. Make a list of popular slogans from businesses and other organizations, past and present. What does each indicate about the organization and its culture? How do the organizations compare in terms of what they value or hope to achieve?

2. Draw an organizational chart of your school or another organization you are involved with. Identify whether it is a tall or flat organization. How could the structure of the organization be changed to increase the effectiveness and timeliness of communication?

3. Do some research on a failing company, learning as much about it as you can. How would you change the organization using the total quality management (TQM) approach? How would doing so fix the organization's problems?

4. Look again at your responses in Skills at Work 2.3, which asked you to assess your leadership qualities. In particular, consider the qualities you need to work on. List three to five actions you can take this week to begin improving these areas.

5. With a classroom team or individually, identify someone whom you consider a good leader. Why is he or she a good leader? What is his or her approach to managing people?

References

Annas, J. W. (1973). Profiles of motivation. *Personnel Journal,* March, pp. 205–208.

Blake, R. R., & Mouton, J. S. (1985). *The managerial grid: The key to leadership excellence.* Houston, TX: Gulf.

Conrad, C., & Poole, M. S. (2002). *Strategic organizational communication in a global economy.* 5th ed. Fort Worth, TX: Harcourt College.

Hersey, P., & Blanchard, K. (1988). *Management of organizational behavior utilizing human resources.* 5th ed. Englewood Cliffs, NJ: Prentice Hall.

Herzberg, F. I. (1968). One more time: How do you motivate employees? *Harvard Business Review, 46,* 53–62.

LaGuardia, D. (2008). Organizational culture. *Training and Development, 62*(3), 56–61. Retrieved from Academic Search Complete database.

Likert, R. (1961). *Patterns of management.* New York: McGraw-Hill.

Lovas, M. (1999). *Beyond wave marketing.* Dallas, TX: About People Press. Available online: aboutpeople.com/CredibilityMarketing.

Maslow, A. (1954). *Motivation and personality.* New York: Harper.

McCormack, S. P. (1994). TQM: Getting it right the first time. *Training and Development,* June, 42–47.

McGregor, D. (1967). *Professional manager.* New York: McGraw-Hill.

McNamara, C. (2006). *Field guide to consulting and organizational development—A collaborative and systems approach to performance, change and learning.* Minneapolis: Authenticity Consulting, LLC. Retrieved March 17, 2010, http://managementhelp.org/org_thry/culture/culture.htm#anchor1160179.

Moran, R. T., Harris, P. R., & Moran, S. V. (2007). *Managing cultural differences.* 7th ed. New York: Elsevier.

Scott, C., & Stephens, K. (2009). It depends on who you're talking to...: Predictors and outcomes of situated measures of organizational identification. *Western Journal of Communication, 73*(4), 370–394. doi:10.1080/10570310903279075.

Sypher, B. D., ed. (1990). Case studies in organizational communication. New York: Guilford.

Taylor, B., & Trujillo, N. (2001). Qualitative research methods. In *The new handbook of organizational communication,* ed. F. Jablin & L. L. Putnam, 173–185. Thousand Oaks, CA: Sage.

Trice, H. M., & Beyer, J. M. (1993). *The cultures of work organizations.* Englewood Cliffs, NJ: Prentice Hall.

Walton, M. (1991). *The Deming method.* New York: Houghton Mifflin.

Managing Interpersonal Communication in the Workplace

KEY TERMS

After reading this chapter, you will be able to do the following:

- Discuss the principles of how relationships are perceived and categorized.
- Be aware of the communication climate.
- Develop the skills needed to enhance communication in relationships.
- Improve the openness of communication.
- Ask for and give feedback.
- Acquire appropriate assertiveness and immediacy behaviors.
- Use clear language and improve verbal style to increase effectiveness.
- Avoid communication omissions.

People ask you for criticism, but they only want praise.

WILLIAM SOMERSET MAUGHAM

Communication studies in business and the professions have shown that relating to people is essential to successful organizations. Simply put, the development of effective workplace relationships can result in gains in productivity and morale. By contrast, isolation and alienation among coworkers can breed dissatisfaction.

INTERPERSONAL COMMUNICATION PRINCIPLES IN THE WORKPLACE

Interpersonal communication in the workplace refers to sending, receiving, and interpreting messages between individuals or groups. The application of interpersonal communication principles can resolve many of the problems and opportunities experienced in the workplace when it is intentional and when participants understand interpersonal communication.

The Pygmalion Effect and Self-Fulfilling Prophecy: Managing Expectations

The Greek mythology character Pygmalion carved a figure of a woman and subsequently fell in love with his creation. His intense desire for the woman to become real, as the myth goes, compelled the goddess Venus to turn the lifeless form into a living, beautiful woman. Thus, Pygmalion's wish became a reality.

This notion of wishing something to be true has been carried down into a modern principle known as the *Pygmalion effect*, which states that expectations influence relationships. Namely, your **expectations** of other people form self-fulfilling predictions of how those people will actually respond. An employer, for example, who expects his or her employees to perform poorly will likely observe performance consistent with those low expectations.

Educational studies have had similar findings, demonstrating that students perform according to what is expected of them. In various experiments, half of a class was told about their superior performance on a bogus assessment, while the other half was told that their performance was average or below average. In reality, no differences existed between the two groups, since the students had been assigned randomly to one condition or the other. However, later performance assessments revealed that the positive expectation condition usually improved performance. That is, the students who had previously been told that they did well actually did well. The average to below-average group also performed as expected. When the findings of these studies were revealed to instructors, they were shocked to discover how their beliefs about the bogus assessments inadvertently influenced students' performance. Apparently, teachers' positive and negative beliefs communicate a message that influences students' success.

How are messages like this communicated? Beyond spoken words, such communication features as tone of voice, body posture, and eye contact can reveal positive expectations along with negative feelings. And despite our best efforts to control our thoughts and actions, messages conveying expectations often get through. The power of this expectation principle should make us consider how our actions and words consequently affect others. In particular, communicating encouraging language and expressing positive actions can generate effective results.

Interpersonal Attribution: I "Know" Why You Do That

Research has also studied **interpersonal perception**, or how we categorize others' motives. In doing so, we create a kind of mind map—a judgment of sorts—about who someone is and what we think of that person. This private interpretation in turn influences communication through a sorting process during **interpersonal attribution**.

Interpersonal attribution begins when we form an early impression about a person's general character or some specific quality. We often do this without having all the facts. Yet despite these gaps in knowledge or experience, we build up a consistent and holistic narrative about the person. We then use this story, or personal narrative, to interpret what we observe about the person's behavior. Thus, we might attribute certain causes or motivations to explain what he or she does or does not do.

For instance, if Mary is late for work, the other people around the office may draw on their stored narratives about her to explain this behavior. One person might think, "She worked all night on a report for the boss" (which is obviously a positive interpersonal attribution), whereas another might think, "She is so slow during the day that she has to work overtime just to stay caught up" (a negative interpersonal attribution). Mary's coworkers will interpret her behavior by framing her actions with their own private stories.

As it happens, attributions toward others have internal and external causes:

- *Internal attributions* explain a person's behavior in terms of his or her character. For instance, low performance may be attributed to laziness, fragility, or incompetence.
- *External attributions* explain a person's behavior in terms of causes beyond his or her control. For example, low performance may be the result of family anxiety. In the case of Mary, caring for her ten-year-old son, who had the flu, is what made her unavoidably late that morning.

We also make *self-attributions* to explain our own successes and failures. Typically, the pattern works like this: we attribute our successes to internal causes and our failures to external causes. In other words, we take credit for our successes but blame our failures on things beyond our control. A late report, for instance, is explained by the lack of departmental support: "Nearly everyone turned in their information late, and I had to hound them for it." By contrast, a successful report is credited to genius and hard work: "I worked for weeks to find just the right sources and worked late last night to add the finishing touches." As you might expect, this self-protection tendency is noticeable more when we deal with private issues than when passing on information as Johnson's (2009) data reveal.

In light of this theory of attribution, it would seem that to become better interpersonal communicators, we must reframe our perceptions of those people about whom we have created negative stories. By doing so, we create a nonjudgmental climate (a point explained later in this chapter) and open ourselves up to discover more positive qualities about these individuals. Put simply, we give them the benefit of the doubt. Competent communicators look beyond the surface and try to understand the positive intent associated with every communication participant (Dainton & Aylor, 2002).

The next principle carries this idea a step further and calls on our resources to manage the interpersonal perceptions that we have of others and that others have of us.

Managing Interpersonal Perceptions: Impression Formation

Another interpersonal communication theory suggests that we can evaluate and manage our misperceptions and faulty attributions and thus control our communication. A significant amount of the information that we learn about others comes from our initial encounters. That means that these encounters are often where impressions and misperceptions between communication partners transpire.

Research in this area conducts what are commonly known as *first impression experiments*. In these studies, participants are told to accept the earliest message they are given about another person as an attitude guide. These first impressions usually have a powerful influence on participants' interpretations of subsequent messages about that individual. For example, a typical experiment involves giving one sample of participants a list of positive and negative adjectives describing someone. Another sample is presented with the same adjectives but listed in reverse order. In each sample, the adjectives listed first wielded the greatest influence, whether positive or negative. To see impression formation in action, refer to Skills at Work 3.1.

FOUR-MINUTE BARRIER   First impressions are typically so strong that they are formed in a short period of time. The *four-minute barrier*, identified years ago but still relevant (Brooks, 1978), describes the limited timeframe in which people form their interpersonal impressions of others. Within the first two minutes, Brooks suggests, we tentatively fix on a positive or negative attitude

SKILLS AT WORK 3.1
Impression Formation in Action

Suppose someone tells you that Jim is *intelligent* and *energetic* and that you should guess whether an accurate third trait is *bold* or *timid*. Which word would you choose to describe Jim? *Bold* is the likely choice because it is a positive characteristic and thus goes with the other positive characteristics you were given about Jim.

What if someone told you that Mary is *distracted* and *slow*. For a third trait, would you select *intelligent* or *stupid*? Most likely, you would choose *stupid*, given the negative tone of the first two characteristics.

How do you see this principle operating in the workplace? How do our impressions of others—even impressions based on incomplete and subjective information—affect our interpersonal communication with them?

---

toward a communication participant. During the next two minutes, we internally deduce the future direction of the relationship: that is, whether to continue or discontinue interpersonal contact.

Although we may or may not take exactly four minutes to size up another person, the point is that we form a strong impression fairly soon after initial contact (MacGeorge, 2001). Moreover, on the basis of that impression, we make a decision about the future of our relationship with that individual. This phenomenon proves why the need to manage impressions early in relationships is so important. To do so, we can use strategies to enhance impression development, such as immediacy communication.

IMMEDIACY COMMUNICATION   Skills for managing interpersonal communication also include what researchers call **immediacy communication** (Richmond & McCroskey, 2000). This type of communication involves behaviors that create a sense of closeness and personal identification with the people with whom we communicate. Simple recommendations for achieving immediacy are as follows:

- Establish a positive tone early in the communication. That is, emphasize the positive aspects of the relationship by finding common ground, paying compliments, or exploring future plans that will benefit you both.
- Practice greeting skills, such as shaking hands firmly, keeping eye contact, smiling, and having an alert posture and listening well.

Social Equity Theory

Another principle of interpersonal communication suggests that people tend to evaluate relationships by taking into account a ratio of their rewards to their costs. Interpersonal experts refer to this ratio as social equity (Galvin, Bylund, & Brommel, 2007) in which a person is either *overbenefitted* or *underbenefitted*. Organizational communication writers Modaff and DeWine (2002) develop helpful implications of this theory for the workplace.

For instance, if the rewarding, advantageous messages between coworkers outweigh the costly, disadvantageous messages, then individuals will feel overbenefitted and make a positive evaluation of the relationship. In addition, the communication itself will more likely be considerate and persistent. Conversely, when the negative messages outnumber the positive (and the costs

SKILLS AT WORK 3.2
Social Equity Theory at Work

Write down the names of five people with whom you work, whether at a job or perhaps at school. For these persons, list the things about your relationship with each of them that you consider benefits or rewards: for instance, providing helpful information, being cooperative or agreeable, and feeling good around them. Then list the things about your relationship with each person that you consider drawbacks, or costs: for instance, being ill prepared or undependable, and complaining a lot.

Now look at your lists for these five individuals. Which relationship seems to bring you the greatest rewards? Which seems to have the greatest costs? What accounts for the reason someone is at the top of your list? the bottom?

thus outweigh the rewards leading to a feeling of being underbenefitted), the communication will likely be characterized by avoiding, blaming, and distrusting.

Applying social equity theory to work relationships can lead to insightful conclusions. See Skills at Work 3.2, which has you consider several such relationships in terms of their cost versus reward ratios.

Some relationships have to do with status benefits, self-esteem, or communication satisfaction. Those relationships that cost you more are likely to dissipate over time, but those that are rewarding are more likely to endure. Therefore, to enhance important relationships, think about ways that you can heighten the perceived rewards they bring.

MANAGING INTERPERSONAL COMMUNICATION SKILLS

This section of the chapter extends the principles outlined thus far and identifies several basic skills for improving interpersonal communication. The skills presented range from influencing the communication climate to developing an awareness of your own personal communication style. The case of James and Matt, presented in Case 3.1, illustrates the significance of interpersonal communication skills in the workplace.

Case 3.1

The Effects of Unresolved Conflict

The relationship of two coworkers, James and Matt, had been spiraling downward for some time. The situation became critical one day when in a meeting among all team members, James refused to work with Matt on a project. Even when they were assigned unrelated job duties—for instance, when Matt planned and scheduled projects and James carried out the ordering—tension soon escalated, frustrating the other team members. Work suffered, morale declined, people chose sides, and animosity spread among the entire group. A dark cloud seemed to hover over the team. Clearly, James and Matt were hypercritical of one another and unresponsive to their supervisor's and coworkers' attempts to bring about their reconciliation.

Given this brief snapshot of the situation, what problems in communication can you identify? How do systems contribute to these issues? What communication skills would you focus on if you were training this team?

Focus on a Positive Communication Climate to Build and Maintain Relationships

At one time, communication scholars emphasized the *message* more than other elements in communication. It was realized, however, that despite how important the message is, merely saying the right words isn't enough. Recall from Chapter 1 that many elements are involved in the communication process. One of those elements is the overall context of communication, such as the organizational culture described in Chapter 2.

A contextual element specific to interpersonal communication is the **communication climate** established between people. The communication climate refers to those conditions in the immediate communication context that influence the feeling of acceptance and other emotions regarding the relationship. This formula may be helpful to remember:

Communication = Content + Relationship

Researchers Vangelisti and Crumley (1998) have examined how people respond to hurtful messages, such as these:

EXAMPLES

Silence:	"I became silent and was jealous."
Crying:	"It made me cry."
Attack:	"I can't believe you said that. You are so insensitive!"
Defend:	"I didn't do it on purpose."
Sarcasm:	"Great [sarcastically]! Thanks a lot!"
Ask for explanation:	"What do you mean by that?"
Ignore:	"I blew it off and did something else."
Concede:	"Fine, I'll leave." "Whatever."

Obviously, if you want to see relationships in your communication environment flourish, it is important to develop good communication skills. Research shows that by enhancing others' self-esteem, and offering positive support, you are engaging **relationship maintenance** factors. Simply stated, experiments have concluded the importance of the following elements:

- *Assurance giving.* Offer support and inclusion and shows loyalty (MacGeorge, 2001). For example, in the case of Matt and James in Case 3.1, if even one of them had gone out of his way to help the other in a task, the vicious cycle of suspicion and mistrust would likely have begun to break down.
- *Positive, affirming communication.* Attempt to make conversations enjoyable, cooperate in handling disagreements, and be courteous, patient, and forgiving. Burgoon, Berger, and Waldron (2000) recommend being "mindful," or intentional, as a way of fostering understanding.
- *Networking.* Focus on common friends and include people that others like.
- *Spontaneity.* Lively and dynamic communication is much more effective than stilted and overly formal methods. To be spontaneous, use a lively tone of voice, make eye contact, smile, and take turns with your communication partner. Turn taking also implies moving on to new conversational topics that are relevant to others, rather than enforcing

Interpersonal communication builds trust in a supportive communication climate.

your favorite topics. For example, if Shaun wants to improve his interpersonal communication skills, he should learn to listen carefully and then speak using less "canned" language. Also, by sounding less dogmatic and more open to suggestions from others, Shaun may find that his coworkers respond differently to him, as the next point suggests.

• *Openness.* Being outgoing and relaxed as you encourage others to share their thoughts and ideas as you also respectfully disclose relevant ideas (Paulsel & Mottet, 2004). It is important to do this without evaluation or judgmental attitudes toward the other person, as the following examples show.

EXAMPLES

Communicating mostly feelings: "Shaun, you are a loudmouth in meetings."

Communicating mostly observations: "Shaun, you talk like you know everything. Part of the problem is that everything sounds like you stayed up all night rehearsing exactly what to say. That makes me feel like I have nothing to add."

Communicating more behaviors than observations: "Shaun, when we are in a group, you may not be aware of how much your voice rises in volume and pitch. That can make others and, at times, me uncomfortable when you talk so loudly."

Not only does this final example make good use of observations, but it also illustrates the use of *I-messages* or *I-statements*, in which you state how things appear from your point of view. In doing so, you assume responsibility for your own perceptions but attempt to minimize personal judgments. The result is to avoid blaming and attacking.

Whereas dogmatic communication introduces negative elements into the communication climate, erecting barriers between participants, being open-minded and receptive to innovation contributes to a successful communication climate. To maintain openness and avoid dogmatism, one suggestion is to use so-called *cushion statements*, which make dialogue less abrupt and more sensitive. These examples illustrate the use of such cushion statements:

EXAMPLES

"Let me see if I understand this right. I think I hear you saying ..." *instead of* "I already understand."

"I don't have all the answers, but it seems to me that there are three things we should consider ..." *instead of* "Everyone, now listen to my three answers."

"On balance, it looks as if we have a trend worth pursuing ..." *instead of* "Obviously, here's the only direction we can go."

Cushioning your remarks doesn't mean that you can't say what you intend. Rather, it means that you are aware of people's comfort levels when disagreeing or agreeing with them (Dainton & Aylor, 2002).

Expand Awareness

By its nature, interpersonal communication involves two areas of awareness: *awareness of self* and *awareness of others*. One way to represent the awareness factor is through the *Johari window*, in which each person is depicted as having known and unknown areas of awareness (Luft, 1970). In addition, there are areas of awareness known and unknown to other people. As shown in Figure 3.1, these known and unknown areas of the self and others compose the four quadrants of the model.

One quadrant is labeled the *Open Self*, which is known to you and to others. For example, your title and job description fall into this category. The area known to you but unknown to others is called the *Hidden Self*. An example of understanding in this area is the knowledge of a bad annual review that you share only with your supervisors. The third area, which is unknown to you but known to others, is called the *Blind Self*. For instance, you may not be aware of your own diminished performance on some task, but others may have recognized your reduced speed. The fourth quadrant, labeled the *Unknown Self*, is unknown to you as well as others. For example, no one, including you, may know why your progress on a task has slowed.

Significant communication functions activate changes in these quadrants. As new information is shared with you through feedback, you enlarge the Open Self quadrant and reduce the Blind Self quadrant. As you share that information with others, the Hidden Self quadrant is diminished and

	Known to Self	Unknown to Self
Known to Others	Open Self	Blind Self
Unknown to Others	Hidden Self	Unknown Self

FIGURE 3.1   The Johari Window   *Source:* Based on Luft (1970).

again the Open Self quadrant is expanded. In either case, you and others in the workplace have disclosed more information about each other. As long as the information is appropriate (and not just office gossip), this opening up of yourself and others can promote business and professional task development. Other positive consequences of healthy, appropriate disclosure include trust, liking, and reciprocity.

It may be especially useful when you encourage disclosure form another person in situations in which it is difficult for him or her to talk by using affirmation—for example, "Kim, I appreciate the way you explained the barriers you are overcoming on this project." This affirming communication may help Kim evaluate her message less as risk taking and more as contributing.

Another way to improve information sharing is to initiate affinity-seeking communication behaviors in relationships, as discussed in the next section.

Initiate Affinity-Seeking Communication

Affinity-seeking communication refers to developing connections or establishing bonds in relating to others on the job. Communication scholars Lakey and Canary (2002) have recognized that the way coworkers present themselves in terms of their partners' goals and desires for achievement is a major determinant in their relationships. Thus, never overlook the importance of greetings and other means of initiating conversation. Even simple greetings such as "How are you?" and "How is that project you've been working on so hard coming?" recognize others and establish a sensitive link in forming interpersonal relationships.

In a research study as your author I conducted for the Xerox Corporation, an analysis of executive telephone messages revealed that one purpose of exchanging interpersonal messages was to maintain friendly ties. In fact, Xerox was one of the first companies to recognize how the various communication technologies in use today serve another function beyond conducting their specific tasks. That is, these technologies provide the opportunity to maintain influential social networks.

Develop Assertiveness Skills

Communication scholars believe that developing basic **assertiveness skills** will improve interpersonal communication and relationships. *Assertiveness* on the job is defined as the ability to state your expectations as you work toward achieving goals. Assertiveness differs from *aggressiveness*, which is an overpowering use of force, coercion, and physical or verbal abuse as a means of achieving goals. Finally, assertiveness can be understood by contrasting it with *nonassertiveness*, or the avoidance of communication in reaching goals.

To illustrate, contrast these different responses to the simple question of where to go to lunch:

EXAMPLES

Assertive response: "There are two or three places I would really like to go, but I'm open to talk it over."

Aggressive response: "We're going to Pizza Hut, or I'm not going."

Nonassertive response: "I'll go anywhere you want—whatever you say" (when this person actually has several preferences).

Assertive people feel comfortable offering their feelings and opinions even when they know others may disagree, including authority figures like teachers (Myers, Martin, & Mottet, 2002). At the same time, assertive people feel comfortable receiving others' feelings and opinions even when those others disagree. Thus, assertive people are not guided by threats or fears of rejection, nor are they obnoxious bullies who are careless with the feelings of others. Being assertive means courageously sharing your own thoughts while respecting those of others.

Being assertive brings a number of advantages in interpersonal communication, as identified in this list by consultant Dr. Clyde Austin (1992):

1. *Provides energy.* Being assertive makes individuals feel stronger and more confident. Being unassertive, in contrast, leads to becoming discouraged and literally tired.
2. *Improves relationships.* When important issues are opened up and discussed, relationships remain honest and healthy. In particular, when disagreements are resolved, people feel they have engaged in a common task and develop a bond with one another.
3. *Promotes developing solutions.* Assertive people get their tensions and questions out in the open and thus off their minds. As a result, they feel better and can better focus on the task at hand. Not surprisingly, assertive people deal constructively with ideas and listen actively. As a result, they feel emotionally satisfied.
4. *Achieves results.* When people know what to expect of one another and what individual needs are involved in reaching a solution or making a decision, then results can be achieved with a minimum of time or effort. When people hide their feelings and no one knows what is needed or wanted, task outcomes will remain elusive.
5. *Improves decision making.* Under assertiveness conditions, so-called half-baked ideas are examined and revealed for what they are. Providing a complete critique allows full discussion and encourages more input. Also, the loudest voice is not the only one heard.

To enjoy these benefits yourself, do what you can to improve your assertiveness skills with these **five keys to better assertiveness**:

1. *Avoid emotional presentations.* Adding emotion to your message will not usually be as effective as being assertive. Crying and pouting, as well as using silence and anger, are common emotional strategies. Instead, be factual, clear, and direct.
2. *Deal with one issue at a time.* In discussing one issue, many people also raise unresolved issues from last week or last month or even last year. Again, doing so tends to cloud communication. It's better to discuss and resolve one issue at a time.
3. *Avoid steamrollering.* Some people get into a discussion and intend to get what they want through sheer communication control. This type of manipulation in communication has been labeled *steamrollering*. Assertive individuals clearly state their position, but they do not become domineering or use power to achieve those results. Rather, they use reason and seek mutually agreeable solutions.
4. *Be solution focused.* When you are wrong, say so and admit error. In this way, you can move forward. Assertive persons are willing to seek the truth, to not merely defend their positions, but to cope focusing on solutions.
5. *Make I-statements.* As noted earlier, making *I-statements* refers to owning your feelings. Rather than accuse another person using language like "You really don't care about me," express your own feelings that have resulted from the other person's actions, perhaps saying "When you ..., I feel like you don't care about me." The primary value of this strategy is that it takes the pressure off the other person to defend him- or herself. Moreover, by taking responsibility for just your own feelings, the discussion can be an objective one, not an accusatory one.

Practice Communication Immediacy

Communication immediacy refers to perceived nearness or closeness in talking and listening. If someone is practicing communication immediacy, he or she is likely to demonstrate acceptance, smile frequently, look directly at the other person, use a variety of vocal expressions, and appear relaxed. Lack of immediacy can explain communication failures and breakdowns and show why some professionals are less successful in their workplace relationships (Richmond & McCroskey, 2000).

The formula stated in this book—that is, Communication = Content + Relationship—operates in this case, too. When people feel they are communicating with someone who is warm and accepting, this emotional perception enhances the meaning derived from the message. In their study of immediacy in the learning context, Messman and Jones-Corley (2001) reported significantly higher levels of learning when instructors applied immediacy in both interpersonal and lecture contexts. This suggests that every time you practice immediacy, whether one-on-one with a coworker or while giving a speech to a large group, you may develop better attention and relationship skills.

You can check your own practice of communication immediacy. Heightened interpersonal communication skills take into account some of the behaviors indicated in the assessment found in Skills at Work 3.3.

SKILLS AT WORK 3.3
Immediacy Assessment

The 14 items below were found to correlate significantly with motivation and learning outcomes in the classroom. In other words, when a teacher or any communicator practices immediacy behaviors (as indicated by the scale items), he or she will generally be more successful in achieving learning and motivation outcomes.

With a particular teacher in mind, respond to each of the following statements with one of these answers:

1 = Strongly disagree   2 = Disagree
3 = Neither agree nor disagree
4 = Agree   5 = Strongly agree

Write the appropriate answer on the line preceding each statement below. Also note that the asterisked (*) items are reverse scored (i.e., 1 = 5, 5 = 1, etc.). Then total your answers at the bottom after you have finished.

_____ 1. Sits behind the desk when teaching.
_____ 2. Gestures when talking to the class.
_____ 3. Uses a monotone/dull voice when talking to the class.
_____ 4. Looks at the class when talking.
_____ 5. Smiles at the class as a whole, not just at individual students.
_____ 6. Has a tense body position when talking to the class.

_____ 7. Touches students in the class.
_____ 8. Moves around the classroom when teaching.
_____ 9. Sits on a desk or in a chair when teaching.
_____ 10. Looks at the board or notes when talking to the class.
_____ 11. Stands behind a podium or desk when teaching.
_____ 12. Has a relaxed body position when talking to the class.
_____ 13. Smiles at individual students in the class.
_____ 14. Uses a variety of vocal expressions when talking to the class.
_____ **Total Score**

A teacher whose total score is less than 36 can be described as "Low Immediacy"; one whose score is 37–48 can be described as "Moderate Immediacy"; and one whose score is 49 or higher can be described as "High Immediacy."

What score was earned by the teacher you observed? Does this seem a reasonable assessment of his or her immediacy behaviors? Given what you've learned, how do you think you would score if you completed an assessment like this one? Why?

Source: Adapted from Richmond (1990).

Apply Improved Verbal and Language Style

A special set of **verbal skills** is related to the use of language in interpersonal communication. These skills, which are commonly discussed in communication literature, present efficient ways of handling verbal interaction in terms of how we arrange words in messages and the vocal emphasis we apply to those messages.

When language is not handled so efficiently, we fall into what can be called *language traps*. They can be devastating to interpersonal communication and thus contribute to breakdowns in business and professional life. A sampling of language traps are discussed in the following sections.

THE TALKING-DOWN TRAP   Have you ever felt small because of how someone else talked down to you? This should not be confused with downward communication, in which information sharing occurs in an organizational hierarchy. Rather, *talking down* means to communicate in a manner that conveys superiority. Here are some expressions and mannerisms involved in the talking-down trap:

EXAMPLES

Expressions

> "I know you don't know this, so let me say ..."
>
> "You probably didn't realize this, but ..."
>
> "Hi, Bill. I'm Dr. Smith."

Mannerisms

> Standing back from people
>
> Standing with folded arms
>
> Putting a hand on the other person's shoulder
>
> Breaking eye contact and looking away while talking

As you think about these expressions and mannerisms (and possibly think of others you might add), you will likely recognize the high level of control involved in talking down to someone. By asserting his or her superior knowledge, presence, status, and so on, the speaker is attempting to intimidate the other person and thus take control of the situation.

THE POWER COMMUNICATION TRAP   Closely tied to talking down is *power communication*, which comprises using both verbal and nonverbal communication to maintain control of a person or situation. Whereas some of these power moves may be unconscious, many others are not. Some people deliberately use power communication, as illustrated by these examples:

EXAMPLES

> Interrupting
>
> Increasing vocal volume
>
> Making verbal putdowns, such as "You can't be serious!"
>
> Making pronouncements with a tone of superiority

Overusing jargon and technical language

Being silent

Withdrawing affection

THE EITHER/OR LANGUAGE TRAP   Given the nature of language, it is easy to create a set of polar opposites in describing an event, person, or situation. For example, if someone is not *tall*, then is he or she *short*? If an event was not *exciting*, then was it *boring*? For nearly every adjective, an opposite quickly comes to mind. Too often, these polarizations seem efficient.

But what if you're trying to describe some middle ground—a person of *medium* height, for instance, or an event that was *satisfying* or *pleasant* or *thought provoking*? Doing so clearly involves more thought and more effort. It's easier to fall into the *either/or* trap: it's either this or that.

These examples from business and professional settings illustrate how *either/or* language can, in fact, alienate people in interpersonal relationships by jumping to extremes:

EXAMPLES

"Bill's proposal is not logical."

"The technology team's proposal is not functional."

"This portfolio analysis is not synchronized with the risk analysis formula."

"This account needs to be aligned with our other accounting procedures."

"The Zebra team needs to include logistical planning in its proposal."

Identify the key words in these sentences—the ones that seem unnecessarily harsh and that would sting a bit upon hearing them. Is Bill's proposal really not logical, or does the individual who made this statement simply not understand or agree with part of it? Is the Zebra team's proposal actually incomplete, when, in fact, it led the evaluator simply to request improvement?

THE LABELING TRAP   Another language trap is using descriptions that involve labels, whether technical or personal. Many labels convey negative impressions and stereotypes. Sexist and racist terms obviously fit into this category. Yet, even subtle instances of labeling can transport the wrong message, as illustrated by these examples from business settings:

EXAMPLES

"Uh-oh. The guys in the Big House are making changes again."

"The Big Enchilada is coming for your evaluation this afternoon."

"The top dog in the sales staff this month will get two days in Dallas."

"This junky piece of equipment really doesn't show who we are."

"The PDM format for team input looks like snake oil to me."

"These fire-eating evangelists really turn me off."

"I can't meet my weekly goals in this kind of watchdog atmosphere."

"Kris and that obstructionist attitude of hers will block these changes."

"Wow, I can't believe her narcissistic outlook on this project! She should go back to L.A."

"The sales pitch is way too thin. Let's see a beefier pitch next time."

By avoiding negative labels, we can interpret coworkers' actions more accurately and achieve common task goals.

THE JARGON TRAP   Almost every organizational culture or group has a set of private code or jargon for expressing certain group-related ideas. Sometimes the code is familiar to everyone who reads it or hears it. Alternatively, the code can serve either as a private language that's intended for use mostly by an in-group to streamline communication or, in some cases, to impress others. For instance, the code used in Internet chat rooms will exclude anyone who is unfamiliar with it but convey significant meaning to those who learn it. At any rate, organizational jargon can save time by providing a sort of shorthand for communication.

Sometimes the use of jargon can lead to ambiguity and frustration. Judge for yourself the following samples, determining how clear each message will be to an average listener. These are actual messages provided for general audiences. Which ones use too much private code? Do any try to be impressive?

EXAMPLES

"We had anticipated being ready to roll out Corporate Time to replace Schedule+. During our testing within information technology, we discovered a significant problem with the Palm sync that will delay rolling this out. We currently have about 65 to 75 Palm users. Steltor, the vendor, is working on a new version for syncing with a Palm. We will have more information in July. At that time, we will reassess the status of the project."

"The SAC report from Washington subsumes the MAC readiness risk factor capabilities and concludes optimal logistical projection within the DOF parameters."

"Any report or extract job, including FOCUS jobs, should be submitted to the appropriate SCT batch-processing queue and not run as an interactive job. If a report or extract job is found running interactively and appears to be utilizing an excessive amount of processing resources, the job may be set to a low priority or terminated at the discretion of the system administrator. The job's owner will be notified in the event of a job termination."

"The beta weights of the regression analysis clearly indicate the variable hierarchy. While the line of best fit underscores the average and its special quality of providing a variable estimate, the total regression beta analysis offers an accurate prediction."

As you might expect, some of these messages make little or no sense to many individuals. You might try to reread them and figure out how to reword them for clarity.

Many employers of individuals who are straight out of college complain about jargon of a specific type: young adult slang. Consider the following samples from generations past:

EXAMPLES

"Sweet, man, really sweet"

"Cool stuff, guy"

"Whatever ..."

"Buff"

"Awesome"

Verbal pauses, such as "Like and ...," "Really," "You know?" and "Uh"

Although such language may clearly be useful in a personal and social context, it is not appropriate in a professional context. Workplace supervisors sometimes complain about the lack of professional precision in the language use of new hires. Besides, restricted codes such as slang terms change quickly; today's favorite will be gone tomorrow.

THE WORD COMPLEXITY TRAP   Some communicators eagerly attempt to sound articulate or otherwise try to impress by using big and important-sounding words. Yet, when the meaning is extracted, the actual content yields little information. Using unfamiliar words in a presentation or a conversation almost guarantees your meaning will be obscured. And in terms of impressing others, using overblown language will boost your image only if your listeners are impressed by such language, which is a rare occurrence.

Years ago, I read a classic article by Larry Tucker, who was then editor of the *Kansas Daily Sun* (Neodesha, Kansas), and it prompted me to create a model based on his notion of combining so-called *buzz words* (that is, newly created or coined words that sound important) and putting them together in strings to create nonsensical language that sounds good. In any order, a word from column 1 can be combined with one from column 2 and then one from column 3:

Column 1	Column 2	Column 3
Interactive	Focused	Analysis
Systematic	Holistic	Prediction
Synchronized	Strategic	Resources
Variable	Regressive	Parameter

At times, strategic ambiguity has a place in communication. That is, talking without saying anything—or as communication writers commonly state, using *doublespeak*—is a valuable skill on occasion. For instance, perhaps more time is needed before a decision can be reached or to allow listeners to draw some sort of conclusions about the message. More often, however, the goal in communication is to be clear, not to confuse.

Take a moment before moving ahead to think about the language traps that you may fall into from time to time. Complete the assessment in Skills at Work 3.4 and then reflect on your answers to determine the areas in which you need improvement.

SKILLS AT WORK 3.4
Verbal Communication Skills Assessment

Use this list of questions to evaluate your communication style:

1. *Do you assume your viewpoints are universal?* That is, because you know and understand something, do you assume that everyone knows and understands it equally well?
2. *Do you interrupt?* It may be hard to identify this fault in yourself if you are chronic interrupter, so ask one or more good friends for a straight answer.
3. *Do you give positive feedback?* Engaging in dialogue and providing affirmations to your communication partner both show that you care enough to respond. It's possible to say good things about another person's presentation or work without being obsequious.
4. *Do you ask for information and feedback?* You will not know if your ideas are workable or clear unless you ask for feedback, too.
5. *Do you convey an ego threat?* By implying a punitive theme in your message, you will be conveying your own sense of having been threatened. Also keep in mind that appeals based on fear work best when used sparingly.
6. *Do you paraphrase and summarize?* Throughout dialogue, it is useful to pause periodically and offer a summary or restatement of what someone else has said. Doing so not only demonstrates that you are paying attention but also allows the opportunity to clear up any misunderstanding on that point.
7. *Do you cope or avoid?* Does your typical response pattern show you to be a coping, decisive person or an avoiding, procrastinating person?
8. *Do you use "gunny sacking"?* That is, do you store up emotional hurts and then dump them unexpectedly on your communication partner? Clearly, it's best to address issues as they arise, rather than let them build up until some sort of confrontation is inevitable.
9. *Do you use silencers?* Silencers are techniques that tend to quiet other people, such as emotional outbursts and sarcasm. The immediate effect is to dampen the conversation, but ultimately, using these techniques may result in people avoiding you.
10. *What are your nonverbals?* Analyze the nonverbal things you communicate, whether intentionally or otherwise, such as volume and tone of voice, body language, eye contact, and personal space.

How did you do? Which areas seem to be your strengths versus your weaknesses? How do you think your communication style affects your interpersonal relationships?

Improve Efficiency and Clarity

USE INCLUSION LANGUAGE   An important concept in workplace communication is *inclusion*: How do we make people feel wanted and part of the team? How do we drive people away?

Inclusion language invites people in. Words such as *we, our, and team*, which convey connection, reliance, trust, empathy, and belonging, all signify inclusion. Inclusion language goes beyond word choice, however, to include conversational habits such as turn taking, inviting alternative points of view, showing empathy, and listening attentively and other appropriate nonverbal behaviors, such as showing interest and providing affirmation through body language, eye contact, and facial expressions. Obviously, conversations that exclude another gender or ethnic group do not convey inclusion. Doing random acts of kindness such as sending interesting information, dropping by to speak to someone, inviting someone to lunch or coffee, and other invitational actions also convey inclusion. The impact of inclusion is to reduce cross-cultural misunderstanding and to increase commitment (Burgoon, Berger, & Waldron, 2000; Rocca, 2004).

BE AWARE OF THE PRAISE TO CRITICISM RATIO   The *praise to criticism ratio* is a comparison of the number of statements of praise or confirmation with the number of statements of criticism or disagreement. For example, a ratio of 8 to 2 would demonstrate that four times as many positive statements were made as negative during the session that was observed (that is, 8 versus 2, respectively).

Over time, whether in a single conversation or during the course of several conversations or even a relationship, people remember the emotion behind a message more than the content. Thus, being the recipient of an abundance of negative statements will likely set the tone of the relationship. Many relationships are defined by this ratio problem, in which more criticism than praise is provided, yet it is one of the most overlooked issues in the workplace and in marital communication as well.

In their best-selling book *The One-Minute Manager*, Blanchard and Johnson (1982) describe a variation of the praise/criticism ratio. When a manager needs to reprimand or offer constructive advice to an employee, he or she takes two steps. First, the manager visits face-to-face with the employee and gets to the immediate and precise problem. Then, after a brief pause, the manager confirms his or her belief and trust in the employee to solve the problem and to continue to excel in the company. This approach does not suggest a ratio of praise versus criticism, but clearly, the manager is expected to follow up over time with confirming statements. Unlike typical approaches, which delay the correction stage until a formal meeting, this technique relies on quick, informal, and efficient communication encounters.

Although different researchers have made their own observations, a praise/criticism ratio of 5 to 1 or higher is considered vital to maintaining a good relationship (Galvin, Bylund, & Brommel, 2007). Other guidelines for improving communication in leadership are presented in Skills at Work 3.5.

USE MORE POWERFUL SPEECH   Many communication textbooks make a case for using more powerful speech by eliminating verbal vagaries and disqualifiers. For example, try to avoid expressions of uncertainty ("I guess so"), inadequate one-word answers ("yes," "no"), self-critical statements ("I'm not very good at this"), and strings of intensifiers ("That's a really great, terrific, and truly phenomenal idea"). All of these practices undermine effective communication.

SKILLS AT WORK 3.5
Improving Interpersonal Communication in Leadership

One of the hallmarks of a good leader is having strong interpersonal communication skills. These 20 guidelines provide useful suggestions for improving your own skills in both communication and leadership:

1. Return phone calls promptly.
2. Empower others.
3. Improve your oral communication skills.
4. Praise in public, but criticize in private.
5. Spell and pronounce people's names and titles correctly.
6. Cut down on the number of memos by using more face-to-face communication.
7. Place your own telephone calls.
8. Network with people outside your field.
9. Train supervisors in effective interviewing techniques.
10. Be an active listener.
11. Offer to mentor someone on the way up.
12. Don't be a slave to technology.
13. Be truthful and forthcoming when dealing with the media.
14. Be on time for appointments.
15. Start and end meetings on time, and stay on track by using a written agenda.
16. Offer praise and criticism in a specific and timely manner.
17. Focus annual performance reviews on the goal of constructive improvement.
18. Apologize when you are wrong.
19. Ensure that planning includes both top-down and bottom-up perspectives.
20. Remember that the customer or client is the most important part of any organization.

Source: Adapted from Anderson (1995).

Don't be afraid to state what you want or what you feel. Be specific, rather than general, in your comments:

EXAMPLES

General statement: "I guess you don't like my programming report."

Specific statement of feeling: "I sense that you are concerned with one or two points in my programming report. Is that accurate? Which points would you like to discuss?"

Specific statement of want: "I would like to know where you feel the programming report can be improved and what you suggest to make the improvements."

If you feel people do not take you seriously enough, use more powerful language. Say what you are going to do and then do it. Credibility is earned not only through demonstrating competence but also through having the confidence to declare a plan and move forward. Teams are inspired by vision and competent follow-through.

AVOID STATEMENTS OF ALL-NESS All-ness statements use terms such as *all, always, nothing,* and *never* to suggest the extremes of a situation or simply to be dramatic. Yet most people know that few things *always* or *never* happen, which raises issues of credibility and accuracy. Even in the most certain of situations, it's better to talk about probabilities and likelihoods, avoiding statements of extremes.

WEB AT WORK 3.1
Interpersonal Communication

The Internet sources listed here include companies that offer consulting and training on this topic, which may provide valuable information about the role of interpersonal communication in the workplace. However, you should probably start with the first of these entries to help you gain personal insight into your own communication style.

- **www.psychtests.com** Psychological tests and educational materials that you can obtain and administer yourself.

- **www.teambuildersplus.com** Training in team building, leadership, and sales.
- **www.fastcompany.com** Good guide to principles of relationship.
- **www.uky.edu/~drlane/capstone/ interpersonal/reldial.htm** Workbook from a communication course; click on "Interpersonal Communication."

USE SIGNPOSTS   Many conversations, briefings, and oral reports are enhanced by the simple technique of delineating the individual points that are being made—say, the four reasons something happened or the three steps in a process. *Signposts* are the numbers and transition words that are used to mark these points—for instance, "The first step in team building is ..." and "Another reason behind this is ..." When used effectively, signposts guide listeners and readers through the message, point by point.

MANAGING SOCIAL NETWORKING AS INTERPERSONAL COMMUNICATION

This section of the chapter extends the principles outlined thus far and identifies several basic skills for improving interpersonal communication by emphasizing how social media and social networking affect us in the workplace. Facebook, MySpace, Twitter, LinkedIn and other social media platforms, along with e-mail, blogs, and text messages, clearly have become a way of life for many people around the world. Most of you don't need a textbook to tell you how to text someone or how to look up a YouTube video. What is of interest in a book like this is the findings about social media's use in organizations. In that vein, the concepts and practices presented in this section can influence your networking understanding and perhaps improve various communication climates in organizational use of social media. The case of Johnson and Johnson in Case 3.2 illustrates at least one important step in using social media in business. We hope to show even more data that illustrate social media as an extension of interpersonal communication skills in the workplace.

Organizations Seeking IT and Social Media

Companies not only use social media to advertise, illustrated in the case of Johnson and Johnson above, but organizations are envisioning innovative ways to improve communication methods between leaders and employees. Recently, data from 328 companies revealed that 65 percent of these companies plan to increase their use of social media in the workplace (Nancherla, 2010).

Case 3.2

Johnson and Johnson Want More of the Social Media Pie

The Johnson and Johnson company using social systems like Facebook and YouTube. They also are inviting mothers to testify to their products and targeting online users with "mommy bloggers" who seem excited about the J&J lineup of products these moms enthusiastically use for their kids.

Like Johnson and Johnson, other corporations are beginning to realize the power of social media activities. What better sources than actual users to provide realism and unbiased and truthful opinions about a product? After all, if the users are happy, the company is, too. The messages are customized and influential. So does this mean that the folks at Johnson and Johnson recognize a good thing when they see it (as far as marketing goes), or do they want more exposure in the social arena? Or both?

Food for thought: is Johnson and Johnson doing a good thing? Do you see any value in offering this type of incentive for the users? Or, is all the benefit for the company only?

From Business Communication Headline News, in a report from March 3, 2009, support@businesscommunicationblog.com; http://adage.com/digital/article?article_id-135588

EXAMPLES

Reasons why Social Networking is Important

Relationship:	"Social isolation does not build an organization."
Satisfaction:	"Any mean of relationship within the organization, traditional or electronic, helps us form community."
Total Communication:	"The effective companies integrate social media as part of their total communications programs."
Meeting Productivity:	"There is a strong correlation between companies that have effective communication and those that meet their financial targets."

Obviously, social media are not the only means of communicating in organizations, but as you can see, professionals view them as central to a total program of communication. In fact, the expenses associated with heavy reliance on mediated communication on the job are viewed as return on investment (ROI), not simply as expenses.

With this kind of importance on various forms of IT and social media, why would organizations not engage such innovations? Simply stated, here are the top reasons, according to data reported by Nancherla (2010):

- *Limited staff:* Insufficient people resources to implement social media.   45%
- *Limited knowledge of social media:* Not enough information about this innovation   40%
- *Lack of IT support:* Not enough technical capability.   36%
- *Lack of CEO or senior management support:* It takes top leadership involvement.   33%
- *Lack of employee access:* Employees do not have social media tools.   32%
- *Lack of impact measures:* Insufficient metrics to measure social media impact.   32%
- *Legal restrictions:* Legal department imposes restrictions.   19%

Is There Harm in Unconnected Employees?

Surveys of employees who either do not have good interpersonal communication or those who choose to remain isolated are called "unconnected employees." If the reason were introversion, experts project there may be as many as half of employees on average who are disconnected interpersonally. Of this group, most are younger employees, those whose networks have been disrupted by layoffs or reorganizations, international employees, or those who have a hard time feeling appreciated or included (Baber & Waymon, 2010).

EXAMPLES

Unconnected Employees' Statements

> *New to the organization:* "I've not been here long enough to know anyone."
>
> *Shy people:* "I just don't like being around people when I have work to do or don't know them."
>
> *International or diverse cultures:* "I feel unfamiliar with U.S.-style relationships; at times it make, me uncomfortable when you talk so loudly."
>
> *No one cares about me:* "I feel like no one notices my hard work and if they did, they wouldn't care anyway."

The preceding comments are even more concerning when researchers ask the question, "Do you have the network you need," and only 20 percent answer "yes." Since networking and relationships appear to be correlated with higher performance in organizations and achieving group goals, organizational leaders are making employee connections a priority (Baber & Waymon, 2010). That is exactly where social media intersections with traditional interpersonal networking and communication forms. If productivity is served, the question is how does an organization boost connectivity? We extrapolate from Baber and Waymon's (2010) analysis to develop key social networking competencies. There are several examples to illustrate:

EXAMPLES

1. Clarify ROI benefits of social media among employees and dispel negative attitudes.
2. Expect training using various media.
3. Create virtual teams to reduce travel and time.
4. Create metrics to measure the effects of networking.

Many employees like the idea that power differentials can be reduced using mediated communication along with the opportunities for trust and interaction. This advantage of mediated communication is particularly appealing with the unconnected-risk employee mentioned earlier. In a study regarding trust and power in the workplace, Panteli and Tucker (2009) cite the importance of power shifting and trust in order to produce higher productivity. In turn, they offer intriguing statements where more comprehensive communication systems such as virtual teams can reverse power and trust differentials:

> *"We could avoid individual political needs and view the customer as the central focus. This worked well in the majority of situations as everybody could easily relate to meeting the customers' needs."*

> *"My approach is definitely to focus on the fact that we both work for the same corporation and ultimately need to be making the best decisions in the interest of maximizing profits."*

Case 3.3

Twitter Has Uses in Education and Organizations

Twitter has enlarged beyond personal networking to be used increasingly in education and in business and other organizations. Here are a few of the uses for Twitter to open up lines of communication.

In the Classroom

1. Direct tweet from professor to students as well as between students.
2. Collaborate on projects.
3. Get to know your classmates: use a class Twitter.
4. Take a survey—a good learning tool for class discussions.

As a Future Professional

1. Get started on your career by a personal Web presence—Twitter can help.
2. Follow your occupation—find tracking opportunities.
3. Follow your target company.
4. Use Twitter job-hunting opportunities, such as:

   Twitterjobcast. Search for jobs posted on Twitter by keyword or geographic location with this tool.
   TweetMyJobs. This job search tool allows job seekers and employers to find each other via Twitter.
   follow@jobhunting. This Twitter feed offers tips from recent college grads.

From Business Communication Headline News, in a report posted June 8, 2009, support@businesscommunicationblog.com

---

With these factors in mind, we can also point to data which reveal that on average the high increase of Internet communication and blogs has fostered a sense of ethics in these forms of communication. *Science Daily* (2009) delineates high expectations of ethics, credibility, and accountability among online community members. Exceptionally large groups of diverse linked users may not always follow such ideas, but increasingly high expectations accompany virtual communities.

In Perspective

By understanding the principles that influence interpersonal communication, we can learn skills for improving communication in business and professional relationships. Our interpersonal relationships are formed, developed, and maintained in part by our expectations of others, a principle called the *Pygmalion effect*. Accordingly, our perception of another person's motivation or performance will depend on what we initially expected of that individual.

Interpersonal attribution begins when we form an early impression about a person's general character or some specific quality, often without having all the facts. Yet despite these gaps in knowledge or experience, we build up a consistent and holistic narrative about the person. In practicing attribution, we attribute motivations and reasons to the behaviors of others.

A significant amount of the information we learn about others comes from our initial encounters.

It is in these encounters that impressions and misperceptions between communication partners often are formed. Research has shown first impressions to be unusually strong. The use of immediacy communication is one means to manage the impressions we make on others.

The selectivity principle suggests that we choose to listen to ideas and messages that reinforce what we already know, believe, or like. We filter communication through selective exposure, selective attention, and selective retention. In addition, social equity theory suggests that we evaluate relationships by weighing their advantages and disadvantages and considering a ratio of the rewards compared with the costs.

A variety of skills are essential to managing interpersonal communication: developing a positive communication climate, sharing information to create awareness, building affinity with others, avoiding communication omission, being assertive, communicating with immediacy, and using an appropriate verbal and language style. In addition, these skills are basic to improving language efficiency and clarity: using inclusion language, being aware of the praise/criticism ratio, owning your ideas, using more powerful speech, avoiding statements of all-ness, and using signposts. The chapter closes with opportunity to consider social media in the workplace. More than personal tools, social media are correlated with morale, social relationships, productivity, and time/cost savings such as using virtual teams.

Discussion Questions

1. How do we go about categorizing others? Why do we do this?
2. How can you develop a positive communication climate? What are the benefits of doing so? What are the disadvantages, if any?
3. How can you achieve communication immediacy? What are the advantages of doing so? What are the disadvantages, if any?
4. How are affinity-seeking communication and immediacy communication similar? How are they different?

5. Among the language traps discussed, which two are you most susceptible to? Why? What can you do to avoid these traps in your interpersonal communication? Study business and professional communication?
6. How can you encourage a social media community? What are the advantages of such a community applied to satisfaction or productivity?

Exercises

1. Go back to Skills at Work 3.2, in which you evaluated the costs and rewards of five work-related relationships. Review the qualities you attributed to these individuals and how you weighted these qualities in rating the five relationships. Look for patterns in your responses. What qualities seem to be especially important to you? What qualities seem unimportant?
2. Make a master list of communication skills that are based on the concepts of affinity seeking and immediacy communication. Select three skills that you believe will improve your communication, and describe how you can go about developing them.
3. Find examples from your own communication or the communication of people around you that demonstrate the three aspects of selectivity: selective exposure, selective attention, and selective retention. Discuss whether people generally seem aware of the filtering they do or whether this is an unconscious process.

4. Collect four or five newspaper articles that describe some sort of conflict between individuals or groups. For each, determine what communication skills seem lacking and perhaps contribute to the conflict. If you were an interpersonal communication consultant or trainer, what would you recommend to solve each conflict? Why?
5. Interview two or three friends and get their impression of the praise/criticism ratio. Do they believe a 5 to 1 ratio is sufficient for maintaining a healthy relationship? Should different ratios be considered appropriate for different types of interpersonal relationships? If so, how?
6. Create a class blog or social network among your classmates. Use this experience for your personal skills, or use it to advance a research project such as a survey.

References

Anderson, R. (1995). Tips for managers. *The Rotarian,* October, pp. 18–19.

Austin, C. (1992). Advantages for assertiveness. In *Human communication.* 2nd ed., ed. C. H. Dodd & M. L. Lewis. Dubuque, IA: Kendall-Hunt.

Baber, A., & Waymon, L. (2010). The CONNECTED employee: The 8 networking competencies for organizational success. *Training and Development, 64*(2), 50–53. Retrieved from Academic Search Complete database.

Blanchard, K., & Johnson, S. (1982). *The one-minute manager.* New York: Berkley Books.

Brooks, W. (1978). *Speech communication.* 3rd ed. Dubuque, IA: Wm. C. Brown.

Burgoon, J., Berger, C., & Waldron, V. (2000). Mindfulness and interpersonal communication. *Journal of Social Issues, 56*(1), 105–128. Retrieved from Academic Search Complete database.

Dainton, M., & Aylor, B. (2002). Routine and strategic maintenance efforts: Behavioral patterns, variations associated with relational length, and the prediction of relational characteristics. *Communication Monographs, 69,* 52–66.

Galvin, K. M., Bylund, C. L., & Brommel, B. J. (2008). *Family communication.* 7th ed. New York: Longman.

Johnson, A. (2009). A functional approach to interpersonal argument: Differences between public-issue and personal-issue arguments. *Communication Reports, 22*(1), 13–28. doi:10.1080/08934210902798528.

Lakey, S. G., & Canary, D. J. (2002). Actor goal achievement and sensitivity to partner as critical factors in understanding interpersonal communication competence and conflict strategies. *Communication Monographs, 69,* 217–235.

Luft, J. (1970). *Group process: An introduction to group dynamics.* Palo Alto, CA: National Press.

MacGeorge, E. L. (2001). Support providers' interaction goals: The influence of attributions and emotions. *Communication Monographs, 68,* 72–97.

Messman, S. J., & Jones-Corley, J. (2001). Effects of communication environment, immediacy, and communication apprehension on cognitive and affective learning. *Communication Monographs, 68,* 184–200.

Modaff, D. P., & DeWine, S. D. (2002). *Organizational communication: Foundations, challenges, misunderstandings.* Los Angeles: Roxbury.

Myers, S. A., Martin, M. M., & Mottet, T. P. (2002). Student's motives for communicating with their instructors: Considering instructor socio-communicative style. *Communication Education, 51,* 121–133.

Nancherla, A. (2010). Don't delete the E-messenger: Companies are thinking of innovative ways to improve communication methods between leaders and staff. *Training and Development, 64*(2), 26. Retrieved from Academic Search Complete database.

Paulsel, M., & Mottet, T. (2004). Interpersonal communication motives: A communibiological perspective. *Communication Quarterly, 52*(2), 182–195. Retrieved from Academic Search Complete database.

Richmond, V. P. (1990). Communication in the classroom. *Communication Education, 39,* 188.

Richmond, V. P., & McCroskey, J. C. (2000). The impact of supervisor and subordinate immediacy on relational and organizational outcomes. *Communication Monographs, 67,* 85–95.

Rocca, K. A. (2004). College student attendance: Impact of instructor immediacy and verbal aggression. *Communication Education, 53,* 185–195.

Vangelisti, A. L., & Crumley, L. P. (1998). Reactions to message that hurt: The influence of relational contexts. *Communication Monographs, 65,* 173–196.

CHAPTER 4

Managing Listening Communication in the Workplace

KEY TERMS

After reading this chapter, you will be able to do the following:

- Identify the principles that influence listening between supervisor and employees.
- Be aware of how listening influences the organizational climate.
- Develop the listening skills needed to enhance relationship communication.
- Improve the openness of communication through active listening applications.
- Use active listening for accuracy, paraphrasing, and feedback.
- Avoid communication omissions.

When people talk, listen completely. Most people never listen.

ERNEST HEMINGWAY

Effective communication centers much more than on merely expressing yourself clearly. It also expects effective listening, a skill set that will improve your communication and make you a stronger leader. Studies in business and the professions have shown that relating to people is essential to successful organizations. Simply put, the development of effective workplace relationships can result in gains in productivity and morale. By contrast, isolation and alienation among coworkers can breed dissatisfaction and poor information sharing. As you will observe in the examples in this chapter, listening in organizations has powerful effects, ranging from improved morale to boosting productivity. Without attention, listening may become a lost communication skill necessary to accomplish business and professional activities.

THE SIGNIFICANCE OF LISTENING IN ORGANIZATIONS

Relationships are built and maintained in organizations through listening communication processes. This theme echoes in scholarly and applied literature. Even in some of the earliest days of speech communication studies experts recognized the value of discovering why people don't listen and what skills would be more effective (Rankin, 1930; Nichols & Stephens, 1957). In other words, for several decades business professionals and communication scholars have emphasized how desirable listening skills are in the workplace. Over the years, groundbreaking insights showed that paying attention to people's feelings matters to validate others and to genuinely seek to understand.

Listening is part of a complex set of communication competence variables such as social cognition ability that researchers like Sypher (1984) identify. Even though listening is central to competence, its neglect in practice and in significant ongoing research is startling, as Flynn, Valikoski, and Grau (2008) observe. One reason may be that it is viewed as a "soft skill" and appears to not be taken seriously at times.

Collections of major principles can be distilled into how listening is actually a significant management skill in today's the workplace (Flynn, Valikoski, & Grau, 2008). These next pages document some of the issues, practices, and outcomes surrounding listening in the workplace.

Managers' Use of Listening

Leaders spend 80 percent of their time communicating. This figure breaks down as 45 percent listening, 30 percent speaking, 16 percent reading, and 9 percent writing. In fact, top executives and senior management spend about twice as much of their time listening as other employees. Perhaps for this reason, general managers ranked listening first out of eight communication behaviors. There is reason to believe that listening along with general oral communications skills plays an important role in hiring decisions (Flynn, Valikoski, & Grau, 2008; Brown, 2009).

Organizational Outcomes Associated with Listening

We have collected several studies concerning organizational outcomes related to listening in the workplace. Among the scholarly and anecdotal findings, we choose to emphasize these that are best described in articles by recent scholars who have done significant summaries of business and professional contexts (Flynn, Valikoski, & Grau, 2008; Brown, 2009; Nicholson, 2007; Bruner, 2008). We'll get to the practice part of listening later in this chapter, but here are more of the research findings:

- Listening is a key management skill
- Listening is a neglected skills in organizations
- Listening improvements among employees yield higher performance in these ways:
  - Relationships improve
  - Change is easier
  - Customer service and sales increase

Furthermore, a listening environment in the workplace has been linked with the following:

- Job satisfaction
- Increased productivity
- Lowered absenteeism (Flynn, Valikoski, & Grau, 2008)

CONCEPTS THAT EXPLAIN LISTENING DEFICITS

Selectivity in Listening to Information

Another principle of interpersonal communication explains why messages seem to be ignored. Even messages that share work-related information among coworkers seem not to get through at times, as shown in Case 4.1.

One reason for such breakdowns is the **selectivity principle**, which suggests that people choose to listen to ideas and messages that reinforce what they already know, believe, or like. It takes creative repetition and competent listening skills to move forward—beyond these initial perceptions. This helpful principle explains the limits of interpersonal communication in terms of three areas:

1. *Selective exposure.* Studies have shown that individuals open themselves up to information and ideas consistent with their existing knowledge, beliefs, and tastes. For instance, the primary listeners to religious messages are themselves religious, the participants at political rallies tend to be party members, and those who attend meetings about fund-raising efforts for, say, a college or university tend to favor that school.

2. *Selective attention.* Once people are exposed to certain issues or topics, they tend to pay attention to or to perceive only the things they already know, believe, and like. For

---

Case 4.1

Separate Conversations

Pablo and Shaun work in the technology support department for a medium-sized advertising agency. When the two tried to talk about a particular problem they have been experiencing, the dialogue went like this:

PABLO: We never should have installed the SPSS-PC without first checking on a central server opportunity. It eats up too much RAM and is causing problems for the marketing researchers.

SHAUN: I like SPSS-PC, since it allows each person to manage the data better.

PABLO: With connections to a central server, they can still manage data and, in fact, incorporate a lot more information and not overstress their individual computers.

SHAUN: SPSS corporate support says they're coming out with a new version that doesn't take up as much space, depending on how you reconfigure the hard drive.

PABLO: I'm telling you, we need to go to a centralized server—that's it.

SHAUN: I want to learn more about PC versions. I love statistics.

Shaun and Pablo seem to be having two separate conversations. Shaun continues to recycle his initial positive attitude about PC versions of SPSS, while Pablo insists on the need for a centralized version of the product. Neither asks questions of the other, offers feedback to acknowledge what the other has said, or calls for an investigation of the facts. What needs to happen to make this a productive discussion?

Case 4.2

Processing Bad News

The meeting about downsizing the unit was going nowhere. On the one hand, Robert and Kathy continued to repeat their hope that the position vacated with Ken's transfer would not be permanently lost—that funding would be available next year. On the other hand, Kyle, Lara, and Charles assumed that the position was being eliminated for good, which meant the unit needed to decide how to move forward with limited staffing. And so for the next hour, each group recycled their view (and deep-seated desire) about the status of the position.

No one wanted to lose the position, but until they could agree on whether that was actually going to happen, they couldn't go forward. Not until the company vice president stepped in to clarify an executive decision did everyone finally hear the same message: There would be no funding in next year's budget. The position had been lost for good.

Selective attention was clearly at work here. Why might processing bad or at least disruptive news exacerbate the problem of selective attention?

↳ you don't actually deal with the problem

instance, when listening to a speech, you likely take notice of those topics that concern you the most or toward which you are favorably predisposed. If the speaker develops a topic, a point that you do not particularly like, or understand, chances are that your attention will drop. This *filtering* process is particularly relevant for interpersonal communication among coworkers and team members. Pablo and Shaun, from the previous case, continued to filter one another's messages from their own initial positions. Also, consider the example in Case 4.2, which involved a meeting among unit members to discuss downsizing.

3. *Selective retention.* A final aspect of selectivity is that people tend to remember mostly those topics or points they already know, believe, and like. Thus, they may retain old information and ignore new information. Memory, too, can have a filtering effect, preventing new information from getting through. In Case 4.2, even after hearing the company vice president state clearly that the position would be lost, Robert and Kathy persisted in further conversation about the renewed position, not wanting to accept the reality of the situation. Feedback, restatement of positions, and skills in communicating conclusive decisions are vital in overcoming the effects of selective attention.

Overall, the principle of selectivity regards information like a funnel. First, only certain information is even recognized because of selected exposure. Then, the perceptual mechanism of selective attention operates to filter information so that it fits a preconceived framework (which is perhaps based on legitimate needs but is interpretive in any case). Finally, selective retention serves to replay the interpretive conditions.

Unfortunately, such a model limits opportunities for information growth and even for interpersonal associations. In addition, since these limitations often are subtle, conscious effort is needed to examine communication pathways and to correct communication habits. That means taking full advantage of changing venues for meetings (for instance, eating lunch at a different spot) and experiencing new people (perhaps sitting at a different table with unfamiliar individuals). What's more, individuals must be open to new ideas and avoid making impulsive judgments about information and people that they otherwise might avoid.

Enhance Information Sharing

Griffin (2008), among others, summarizes how the scarcity of information resources contaminates efficiency and morale in the workplace. Thus, to promote competent **information sharing**, these guidelines are practical:

1. Be sure of your facts and what you intend.
2. Clarify the components of your message—for instance, "The five major reasons for this change have been decided by recent court cases. Each one is important, so let's review them individually."
3. Use examples to back up what you say.
4. Ask for feedback and then listen to others' responses and understanding.

How to improve this organizational deficit remains an intriguing area of research in the business and professional communication context. One way to improve information sharing is to initiate affinity-seeking.

Avoid Communication Omission

Communication omission involves filtering out or eliminating significant information in relating ideas to others in business and professional settings. Since such a large percentage of time in the workplace is spent in various communication activities, it is not surprising that communicators sometimes lose focus and omit information. Paying attention to when and how this omission happens alerts communicators to the ways they can provide the information needed in various interactions.

The brief case of Kristine and Debbie, two friends who are staff members in a midsized organization, illustrates the need to prevent communication omission (see Case 4.3).

The following reasons account for most of the communication omissions people like Kristine and Debbie experience in organizations:

1. *Assuming that being there ensures the sharing of information.* One of the most frequent errors made in organizational communication is assuming that being present at a meeting or in a conversation allows everyone to know relevant information. In some cases, being

---

Case 4.3

Overcoming Omission

Debbie and Kristine had worked together for nearly ten years and had become good friends in the meantime. But in fact, over the years Debbie had frequently neglected to share with Kristine the details of client-centered projects they were working on together. Finally, one day, Kristine erupted angrily at Debbie, accusing her of deliberately withholding information on critical dates about meetings with clients. Debbie was taken aback by Kristine's charges, particularly given their history of working together, not to mention their friendship. It seemed that the long series of incidents involving missing or incomplete information had left some deep wounds.

What successful communication lesson might Debbie and Kristine, along with the rest of the office, learn from this incident? In particular, what should they learn about communication omission?

Case 4.4

"Any Questions"

A small manufacturing company in Oklahoma made valves and piping. Upon receiving a special, urgent job for some 1,000 valves, the supervisor assembled the machinists for the project and explained what they were going to do. After telling them how important the project was to the company, he then asked if any of the workers had any questions. After a long silence, the supervisor ended the meeting with the advice to work hard and quickly.

Later that day, the company leaders inspected the early work that had been done and, to their horror, discovered that many of the valves had been made incorrectly. They ended up scrapping thousands of dollars worth of parts, not to mention the cost of labor and the delay that resulted from having to start over.

What seems to have gone wrong? What would you have done if you were one of the employees or the supervisor? the company leadership?

met with silence is similarly interpreted as meaning being understood. For instance, one small manufacturing company lost several thousand dollars in just a few hours due to a communication lapse between the supervisor and workers in a machine operations plant (see Case 4.4).

2. *Ignoring uncomfortable messages.* Another reason for the omission of information is discomfort. Some employees remove information from memos, e-mails, team meetings, and conversations if it is perceived as potentially disagreeable or threatening. Screening information in this way prevents it from reaching everyone for whom it was intended.

3. *Viewing disagreement as a personal attack.* Disagreement is a normal aspect of interpersonal communication and should be viewed as such. Doing so can be difficult, however, as the sense of missed expectation can overcome the best of intentions for understanding. For instance, a major part of Kristine and Debbie's breakdown involved the perceived tone of attack, rather than simple disagreement. Until that point, Kristine had not made her feelings clear to Debbie, despite the series of miscommunications that had occurred over the years. Debbie had not been aware there was a problem—or at least, she had not realized Kristine's level of upset until the blowup.

4. *Interrupting.* Allowing the other person to finish what he or she wants to say is basic to effective communication, for several reasons. Namely, it's important to allow a full hearing of ideas in any exchange—to get everything "on the table," so to speak. It's also an important show of respect and consideration to allow someone to speak without interruption.

5. *Not providing affirming nonverbal cues.* Nodding your head, looking at the other person, smiling, and leaning forward are a few of the positive nonverbal cues that make any interaction more inviting and thus more productive. Conversely, not to provide these affirming gestures is counterproductive and even damaging to communication. For instance, deliberately refusing to look at someone when he or she is speaking to you will indicate that you are closed off to communication due perhaps to anger or disinterest.

6. *Not providing feedback or paraphrase.* Providing feedback or asking someone to clarify what he or she has said shows your interest in the topic—for instance, "Larry, I understand your main point, but I didn't get all your reasons. Could you summarize them for me?"

Paraphrasing, or providing a gentle repetition of what was just stated, also clarifies understanding, showing the other person your attention to his or her needs.

7. *Making ego threats.* Under the guise of honest communication, some individuals blame, accuse, and attack others. These remarks usually have the effect of silencing or at least startling the people against whom they're directed. And depending on the severity of the attack, it may be difficult to resume communication at a later point.

Clearly, these are all attitudes and practices that you want to avoid and that can be overcome by building interpersonal communication skills. For example, practicing assertiveness, as discussed next, will help you avoid common omissions and misunderstandings.

How did you do? Which areas seem to be your strengths versus your weaknesses? How do you think your communication style affects your interpersonal relationships?

SKILLS AT WORK 4.1
Listening Skills Assessment

1. *Do you assume your views are shared by everyone?* Because you know and understand something, do you assume that everyone knows and understands it equally well?

2. *Do you interrupt?* It may be hard to identify this fault in yourself if you are a chronic interrupter, so ask one or more good friends for a straight answer.

3. *Do you give positive feedback?* Engaging in dialogue and providing affirmations to your communication partner show that you care enough to respond. It's possible to say good things about another person's presentation or work without being obsequious.

4. *Do you ask for information and feedback?* You will not know if your ideas are workable or clear unless you ask for feedback, too.

5. *Do you convey an ego threat?* By implying a punitive theme in your message, you will be conveying your own sense of having been threatened. Also keep in mind that appeals based on fear work best when used sparingly.

6. *Do you paraphrase and summarize?* Throughout dialogue, it is useful to pause periodically and offer a summary or restatement of what someone else has said. Doing so not only demonstrates that you are paying attention but also allows the opportunity to clear up any misunderstanding on that point.

7. *Do you cope or avoid?* Does your typical response pattern show you to be a coping, decisive person or an avoiding, procrastinating person?

8. *Do you use "gunny sacking"?* That is, do you store up emotional hurts and then dump them unexpectedly on your communication partner? Clearly, it's best to address issues as they arise, rather than let them build up until some sort of confrontation is inevitable.

9. *Do you use silencers?* Silencers are techniques that tend to quiet other people, such as emotional outbursts and sarcasm. The immediate effect is to dampen the conversation, but ultimately, using these techniques may result in people avoiding you.

10. *What are your nonverbals?* Analyze the nonverbal aspects of your communication, whether intentionally or otherwise, such as volume and tone of voice, body language, eye contact, and personal space.

> ### WEB AT WORK 4.1
> **Listening Communication**
>
> The Internet sources listed here include companies that offer consulting and training on this topic, which may provide valuable information about the role of interpersonal communication in the workplace. However, you should probably start with the first of these entries to help you gain personal insight into your own communication style.
>
> - **http://www.learningthroughlistening. org** This site offers K–12 listening skills and teaching ideas.
> - **http://www.mindtools.com/ CommSkll/ActiveListening.htm/** Lists
>
> and ideas for training, leading, and self-developing.
> - **http://www.selfgrowth.com/ listening_skills.html/Self-development.** Sponsored, but has practical skills.
> - **http://www.web-strategist.com/ blog/2009/11/10/evolution-the-eight-stages-of-listening/** Excellent listing of strategies for creating better corporate listening training and policies.

HOW TO IMPROVE LISTENING SKILLS

Listening has been recognized as a simple yet significant means of improving communication in the workplace, resulting in a better work environment and more competent and knowledgeable workers. It is not unusual to see measures of productivity and human resources go up after training on listening has been conducted among an organization's workforce. As stated by former Chrysler CEO Lee Iacocca and ABC television anchor Diane Sawyer, listening lies at the heart of a successful work experience:

> *"I only wish I could find an institute that teaches people how to listen. Business people need to listen at least as much as they need to talk. Too many people fail to realize that real communication goes in both directions."*
>
> —LEE IACOCCA

> *"I think the one lesson I have learned is that there is no substitute for paying attention."*
>
> —DIANE SAWYER

Another factor that points to the importance of listening is that it accounts for most of a professional person's communication time. As indicated earlier, experts agree that almost half of leadership time is spent listening.

What do we mean by good listening skills? The many voices on this topic boil down to examples of several skills (Bruner, 2008):

- Not interrupting
- Being an active listener (nodding, taking notes, making comments when appropriate)
- Giving your full attention and blocking out background noise
- Keeping an open mind and taking time to think about what's been said before responding
- Asking for clarification if something is unclear

Moreover, listening behavior can be categorized by types:

1. *Evaluative listening* involves attending to information or critical analysis or perhaps expecting an informed response. Examples include listening in a meeting, on the phone, or in a face-to-face conversation.
2. *Empathetic listening* occurs when one person attends to the feelings of another, perhaps to console him or her or to understand his or her circumstances. Often in such cases, listening occurs with the intent of helping or making suggestions.
3. *Enjoyment listening* occurs when people listen for entertainment—for instance, to a talk-show host, to music, or to a friend in a conversation. A person may suspend critical thinking and the evaluative dimension of listening in order to enjoy the content or stimuli more completely.

The approach to listening that's most advocated in business and the professions goes beyond these types. That is, listening in the workplace should be *active listening*.

ACTIVE LISTENING

Active listening means to listen with a "third ear." By going beyond physical hearing to attend to such qualities as feedback and paraphrase, turn taking and responsiveness, nonverbal eye contact, and a host of positive interactive qualities, the speaker-listener relationship is enhanced. The communication process is sometimes described as moving to a higher dimension. Philosopher Martin Buber once described this form of deeper connection as a *duologue* rather than a *dialogue*.

Strategies for Active Listening

PARAPHRASE THE SPEAKER'S MEANING   One strategy is to provide feedback to the other person in a conversation. By paraphrasing, the listener offers a summary or restatement of content back to the speaker as an accuracy check. Consequently, this summary or restatement can be rejected or accepted as a valid measure of the communication fidelity.

> *"Just being available and attentive is a great way to use listening as a management tool. Some employees will come in, talk for twenty minutes, and leave having solved their problems entirely by themselves."*
>
> —NICHOLAS V. LUPPA

EXPRESS AN UNDERSTANDING OF THE SPEAKER'S FEELINGS   While paraphrasing focuses on the speaker's content, expressing awareness focuses on the speaker's feelings. Most people want to be understood, or as Stephen Covey (1989) has stated in *The 7 Habits of Highly Effective People*, "Seek first to understand and you will be understood.":

> *"So when you are listening to somebody, completely, attentively, then you are listening not only to the words, but also to the feeling of what is being conveyed, to the whole of it, not part of it."*
>
> —JIDDU KRISHNAMURTI

> *"The most basic of all human needs is the need to understand and be understood. The best way to understand people is to listen to them."*
>
> —RALPH NICHOLS

"To say that a person feels listened to means a lot more than just their ideas get heard. It's a sign of respect. It makes people feel valued."

—DEBORAH TANNEN

"I would say that listening to the other person's emotions may be the most important thing I've learned in twenty years of business."

—HEATH HERBER

To express an understanding of the speaker's feelings, do the following:

1. Ask questions of the speaker.
2. Give the person your undivided attention.
3. Avoid distractions from others and filter out unwanted noises.
4. Give positive nonverbal attention, such as nodding your head, leaning forward slightly, and avoiding blocking behaviors such as crossing your arms or leaning away from the speaker.

ENGAGE IN THE FACTS AND JOIN IN   Active listening also involves the listener's logical/analytical response to the speaker. Thus, listening has a *cognitive* side as well as an *affective* side. To explore the cognitive side, follow these suggestions:

1. Take notes and identify facts.
2. Ask for clarification.
3. Offer responses and facts in return.
4. Take your turn.

It's worth elaborating on this final point. Most communication involves the type of turn taking that characterizes everyday conversation. Even in formal settings such as job interviews and question-and-answer sessions following news briefings, offering a response to what the speaker has said is responsible communication (as long as it follows the norms for the setting, of course).

"I remind myself every morning: Nothing I say this day will teach me anything. So if I'm going to learn, I must do it by listening."

—LARRY KING

"Of all the skills of leadership, listening is the most valuable—and one of the least understood. Most captains of industry listen only sometimes, and they remain ordinary leaders. But a few, the great ones, never stop listening. That's how they get word before anyone else of unseen problems and opportunities."

—PETER NULTY

Steps in Effective Listening

One of the hallmarks of listening theory is that it has defined listening as a process and identified the steps involved. These steps are not necessarily linear but provide a general structure for the process. The very act of recognizing these steps can lead to improvement in listening:

1. *Hear.* Hearing is the *physical* dimension of listening. That means that the first step in improving listening is to assess if any type of hearing impairment is involved.

FIGURE 4.1   Chinese Representation of *To Listen*.

2. ***Attend.*** Attending to a message involves filtering out distracting messages and focusing on just one. Providing this undivided loyalty makes listening skills improve dramatically.
3. ***Understand and remember.*** Understanding occurs when the listener grasps the sense of a message. To understand, the listener should ask "What is the speaker's point?" and "What subpoints are relevant to the presenter's thesis?"
4. ***Respond.*** As noted earlier, responding consists of giving observable feedback. It can be content oriented, such as asking for more information, or behaviorally oriented, such as making affirmative head nods.

Speakers who want to make sure they get listener feedback use devices such as that shown in Skills at Work 4.2, a listening evaluation for a seminar or workshop.

Barriers to Effective Listening

SPEAKER MANNERISMS   A number of speaker mannerisms can distract the listener and thus obstruct the listening process. Some of those distracting habits are listed here to serve as a friendly reminder to speakers to avoid them:

1. Fidgeting (for instance, with your hair, fingernails, ears, pockets)
2. Speaking too loudly or too softly, too quickly or too slowly
3. Pacing
4. Avoiding eye contact
5. Using mistimed, inappropriate, too few, or ineffective gestures
6. Wearing distracting clothing or jewelry or having a distracting hairstyle

Listeners are cautioned to overlook these behaviors (as much as possible). Regardless, speaker mannerisms should not be used as an excuse to tune out.

POWER AND STATUS DIFFERENCES   Real or imagined differences between a speaker and an audience, between two groups, or between two people can block effective listening. This perceived imbalance forces attention away from the ideas and misdirects the energy it takes to listen actively.

SKILLS AT WORK 4.2
Listening Evaluation for a Seminar or Workshop

There are times you need to evaluate a presentation, seminar, or workshop. This simple evaluation is direct and useful in those cases.

"We hope you enjoyed the time in our workshop today! We would like to hear your comments concerning our presentation. Please circle the most appropriate number for each question according to the following scale:"

1 = Poor   2 = Needs Improvement
3 = Average   4 = Good
5 = Excellent

1. The presenters were prepared.   1 2 3 4 5
2. The presentation was informative.   1 2 3 4 5
3. The materials followed the lecture format.   1 2 3 4 5
4. The activities and illustrations were relevant to the topic.   1 2 3 4 5
5. Your overall opinion of the workshop.   1 2 3 4 5

If you rated any factors as "Needs Improvement" (2) or "Poor" (1), please provide an explanation and suggestions.

DIFFERENCES IN COMMUNICATION STYLE   Elements of the speaker's communication style may also obstruct listening—for instance, if the speaker is quite casual and the audience expects a formal presentation. Other potential issues involving communication style are as follows:

1. Cultural differences (stereotyping a speaker or discovering the organizational approaches are different)
2. Unmet expectations of the purpose of the speech
3. Mismatch of logic, humor, or emotional expectations

LANGUAGE DIFFERENCES   Obviously, problems with understanding word meanings, jargon, slang, and technical language can obscure listening. Alternatively, providing too much detail may result in deemphasizing the main point.

BORING OR UNINTERESTING TOPICS   If the topic appears irrelevant or boring, listening will surely be more difficult. In these situations, commitment and dedication to the task of listening becomes hard work but worth doing.

THOUGHT SPEED EXCEEDS SPEAKING SPEED   Humans typically think at 450 to 500 words a minute—even faster, if you are a visual learner. Contrast that speed with the average speaking rate of 175 words per minute, and it's easy to understand why listening can be difficult at times. By moving with the speaker's points, you can stay focused. Slowing down by taking notes or keeping an outline in your head may also help you track the presenter and not get too far ahead.

LISTENER FATIGUE   The most obvious barrier of all is listener sleepiness. Obviously, we can all come up with ways to remain alert.

Great Quotes on Listening

"The ear of the leader must ring with the voices of the people."

—WOODROW WILSON

"Many a man would rather you heard his story than granted his request."

—PHILLIP STANHOPE, EARL OF CHESTERFIELD

"Effective questioning brings insight, which fuels curiosity, which cultivates wisdom."

—CHIP BELL

"Silence is a source of great strength."

—LAO TZU

"Let a fool hold his tongue and he will pass for a sage."

—PUBLIUS SYRUS

"History repeats itself because no one listens the first time."

—ANONYMOUS

"Conversation: a vocal competition in which the one who is catching his breath is called the listener."

—ANONYMOUS

"One advantage of talking to yourself is that you know at least somebody's listening."

—FRANKLIN P. JONES

"The opposite of talking is not listening. The opposite of talking is waiting."

—FRAN LEBOWITZ

"Marge, it takes two to lie. One to lie and one to listen."

—HOMER SIMPSON

"A good listener is a good talker with a sore throat."

—KATHERINE WHITEHORN

In Perspective

This chapter introduces the importance of listening in the workplace where productivity, morale, relationship and team building, and customer service are affected when listening skills are missing. The reasons why organizations don't pay as much attention to listening as they should range from too much trouble to simply lack of awareness of the benefits of improved listening skills. Also, listening deficits can occur for a lot of reasons, such as personality habits of interrupting, lack of openness, or from a theory perspective of theories like selectivity and information omission. Whatever the reasons, the chapter documents a significant number of listening skills that can make employees and future managers better prepared for today's workplace communication demands.

Discussion Questions

1. How do we go about misunderstanding others because of faulty listening habits? Why do we do this?
2. How can you develop an organizational listening climate? What are the benefits?
3. How can you achieve improved listening skills? Why is that important?
4. How are selectivity and information omission similar and how are they different?
5. What do you think are your biggest listening strengths and weaknesses? What can you do to enhance skills?

Exercises

1. Go back to Skills at Work 4.4, in which you saw costly listening problems. What seems most important to you? If you were training with the company, what list of the top three things would you teach?
2. Make a master list of listening skills that are based on the concept of active listening.
3. Find examples from your own communication or the communication of people around you that demonstrate the three aspects of selectivity: selective exposure, selective attention, and selective retention. Discuss whether people generally seem aware of the filtering they do or whether this is an unconscious process.
4. Collect four or five newspaper articles that describe how listening caused interpersonal conflict. What would you recommend to solve the conflict?
5. Interview two or three friends and get their impression of the why people don't listen. Does your list match what you are reading in the book? How could you validate the principles indicated in this chapter?

References

Covey, S. (1989). *The 7* New York: Simon and Schuster.

Brown, W. (2009). Listen up. *Professional Safety, 54*(4), 8. Retrieved from Academic Search Complete database.

Brunner, B. (2008). Listening, communication & trust: Practitioners' perspectives of business/organizational relationships. *International Journal of Listening, 22*(1), 73–82. Retrieved from Academic Search Complete database.

DeVito, J. A. (2008). *Human communication.* 10th ed. New York: Longman.

Flynn, J., Valikoski, T., & Grau, J. (2008). Listening in the business context: Reviewing the state of research. *International Journal of Listening, 22*(2), 141–151. Retrieved from Academic Search Complete database.

Galvin, K. M., Bylund, Carma, & Brommel, B. J. (2007). *Family communication.* 7th ed. New York: Longman.

Griffin, E. (2008). *Communication theory.* 7th ed. New York: McGraw-Hill.

Nichols, R. G., & Stevens, L. A. (1957). *Are you listening?* New York: McGraw-Hill

Nicholson, N. (2007). Listening and learning. *Communication World, July,* p. 2. Retrieved from Academic Search database. Rankin P. T. (1930). Listening ability. Its importance, measurement, and development. *Chicago School Journal, 12,* 177–179.

Sypher, B. D. (1984). The importance of social cognition abilities in organizations. In *Competence in communication,* ed. R. Bostrom, 103–128. Beverly Hills, CA: Sage.

CHAPTER 5

Managing Nonverbal Communication in the Workplace

KEY TERMS

After reading this chapter, you will be able to do the following:

- Understand the meaning and importance of nonverbal communication.

- Recognize the functions of nonverbal behavior and the rules that govern it.

- Enhance your communication by using various nonverbal behaviors.

- Interpret the nonverbal behaviors of others with greater understanding and clarity.

- Apply nonverbal communication effectively in the workplace.

Do not let your deeds belie your words.

ST. JEROME

Did you ever leave a conversation feeling uneasy because you heard one thing but felt another? Maybe you sensed the other person thinking, "I'm not really interested in what you have to say" or "Please hurry up and finish so I can leave." Perhaps he or she expressed compliments and liking, but you weren't so sure he or she really meant it. It wasn't anything the person said, but there was something about how the person acted.

Most of us can relate to this example of the subtle influence of nonverbal communication. Whether the nonverbal behavior is deliberate or unconscious, we feel its effects when we attempt to make sense of what has been communicated to us—verbally and otherwise. Understanding nonverbal communication and its place in organizations will help us fine-tune our own communication and better comprehend that of others.

DEFINING NONVERBAL COMMUNICATION

Verbal communication involves the study of communicating meaning when we are perceiving what has been written or said in a face-to-face situation. **Nonverbal communication** can be thought of quite simply as "communication without words" (Remland, 2000). A deeper view, however, indicates the complexity of nonverbal communication. For instance, many communication writers, such as Richmond and McCroskey (2004), describe nonverbal communication as occurring primarily when a receiver interprets a behavior. Writers such as Remland (2000) orient us to a broader view of nonverbal communication—one that includes a wide range of interactions.

Whatever the case, members of organizations regularly perform nonverbal communication behaviors, including eye contact, facial expressions, body movements, and vocal utterances, such as sighs and laughs. For example, coworkers interpret their supervisor's tone of voice and manner, not just the words he or she speaks. A team leader conducting a planning meeting senses who among the group is paying attention based on behaviors such as posture and eye contact. The speaker at a large-group presentation considers how to emphasize certain words and phrases and even when to pause in order to make certain points more effectively.

However you choose to define nonverbal communication—emphasizing that it received nonverbal behavior or that it comprises a wide range of interactions—it involves behaviors that are interpreted as having meaning during face-to-face communication. Moreover, the meanings of those behaviors must be considered in different relationships and contexts.

IMPORTANCE OF NONVERBAL COMMUNICATION IN THE WORKPLACE

Research on interpersonal relations reveals that early in interactions between individuals, nonverbal behaviors lead them to form initial impressions about one another's attitudes and moods and the meaning of their conversation. These impressions, when studied in workplace situations, are reported to be powerful ways of conveying leadership people skills (Morand, 2001). For instance, a statement that is followed by a laugh and a smile is likely to be interpreted differently than one followed by folded arms and a glare.

Nonverbal behavior is a significant area of communication study for at least two main reasons (Garner, 1992): it conveys meaning and it reflects the unspoken.

Conveying Meaning

According to research, nonverbal communication accounts for a large amount of the meaning we derive from conversation. The historic work of Mehrabian (1981) indicates that as much as 93 percent of the emotion and meaning in a conversation is conveyed nonverbally: 38 percent through the tone of voice and 55 percent through the face. Even more conservative data than this classic work suggest that over two-thirds of meaning is nonverbal. Such high percentages do not represent all situations, but even at that, experts remind us that at least two-thirds of our nonverbal behavior accounts for our meanings (Gentry & Kuhnert, 2007).

Moreover, people tend to believe nonverbal communication more than verbal communication. Our behaviors often bypass the cognitive processing of information that is involved in spoken language and communicate their own meanings and feelings, which may or may not support the words that are spoken. An example comes from a conversation between two coworkers regarding a supervisor:

EXAMPLE

COWORKER 1: "Did you see what she just did [rolling of eyes]? I can't believe it [said with a chopping gesture]!"

COWORKER 2: Yeah, but you should have been here yesterday and heard how she laid out the schedule for next week. You'd think we were all in trouble [said with eyes up and sarcastic tone of voice]."

Whatever the supervisor did—say, made a gesture or had a certain look on her face—it would seem that she lacks effective immediacy communication skills (see Chapter 3). Regardless, the coworkers' attribution was framed from her nonverbal interactions related to other recent encounters (again, see Chapter 3). The tone of voice and any gestures accompanying this conversation remind us of powerful filters through which we interpret verbal messages. Whether or not you believe the supervisor's nonverbal communication was intentional, it has been interpreted with suspicion and perhaps even anger.

Reflecting the Unspoken

Nonverbal communication is also significant because it is sometimes considered a spontaneous reflection of unspoken thoughts and feelings. In this way, nonverbal behaviors are outward expressions of inward mental activities. Some areas of nonverbal communication, such as pupil dilation, are a type of reflex action and thereby virtually uncontrollable. Other types of nonverbal communication show up as "leakage," including eye contact, facial expressions, and hand and foot movements. In the workplace, this idea emerges in studies designed to detect how one's ability to read emotions affects how people might perceive you. As an example of this kind of research, one study shows that when managers accurately perceived nonverbal emotions, their supervisors and subordinates rated them higher in performance and in supportiveness (Byron, 2007). Another study underscores how when nonverbal cues match the recipient, the message "feels right" and is effective. This effect, known as *regulatory-fit theory*, helps us understand the powerful effects matching nonverbal with an intended communication partner—that is nonverbal matching with receivers yields perceived message effectiveness (Cesario & Higgins, 2008).

Even when we attempt to control these kinds of behaviors, our resulting expressions may appear unnatural. For example, have you ever had to fake a smile for a photograph? Your smile and the resulting picture probably didn't look quite right; rather, they looked strained or posed. When we try to mask our feelings, they may seep out in other more subtle mannerisms. Even accomplished liars unknowingly emit subtle nonverbal cues.

Hence, because we know that nonverbal communication is spontaneous and not easily manipulated, we tend to believe it, even if it contradicts the verbal communication. Doing so involves our "reading" others, as illustrated in Case 5.1. The *cognitive* content of this encounter consists of what the interactants plainly stated. The *affective* content is the conveyance of feeling, a feature primarily observed through nonverbal behavior.

Case 5.1

Reading a Troubled Coworker

Suppose that you enter your office after a meeting to leave your notes on your desk before going to lunch. When you arrive, you find your coworker sitting at her desk with her head in her hands. She doesn't look up or acknowledge your presence, and so you ask, "Is everything okay?" Still without looking up at you, she slowly nods her head and says, "Just fine." You mention something about the meeting, which gets no response, and then you leave for lunch. However, as you head out the door, you feel that your coworker is holding something back—that things aren't "just fine."

What about your coworker's behavior makes you skeptical? In particular, what about her nonverbal communication suggests that something is wrong? What would you do in this situation? Why?

FUNCTIONS AND RULES OF NONVERBAL COMMUNICATION

Functions of Nonverbal Communication

Understanding the meaning and significance of nonverbal communication provides a foundation for its usefulness. There are four major **functions of nonverbal communication**:

1. *To complement.* Nonverbal communication may complement verbal communication; that is, nonverbal behaviors may complete or reinforce what is said. When you slap someone on the back while asking, "Hi, how are you?" these behaviors complement each other.
2. *To contradict.* Nonverbal communication may contradict what's said. For example, someone with whom you are conversing may say, "It's really good to talk to you," but his or her wandering eye contact will contradict that message. Similarly, your supervisor may say, "I absolutely love your report," but considering that he or she is standing at a distance, with crossed arms and eyes downcast, you may get the opposite impression, a finding supported by Houser's (2005) research.
3. *To regulate.* Nonverbal communication also serves a regulative function in terms of controlling the flow of conversation between two people. How do you know when it is your turn to talk in a conversation? The nonverbal behaviors of the other person—particularly, head nods, eye contact, and vocal inflection—will tell you. Many people know when a preacher is nearing the end of the sermon because of changes in his or her vocal behavior, especially pitch patterns. In this and many other ways, nonverbal behaviors regulate or guide our interactions with others.
4. *To substitute.* Nonverbal messages may substitute for verbal messages in certain settings. For example, a small child may point to a toy instead of saying "I want that." In a noisy, crowded place, you may wave to the friend you are meeting and point to a meeting place instead of yelling that information to him or her. In both these instances, nonverbal behavior serves a substitution function.

Rules Governing Nonverbal Communication

Nonverbal behavior is very much a rule-governed system of communication. Certainly, rules dictate all our communication behaviors, but the **rules governing nonverbal communication** are very much evident. One obvious example is the rules governing behavior in an elevator.

You probably can come up with them without much thought: (1) don't talk, (2) don't look at the other people, (3) move to the back of the elevator, (4) don't touch anyone, (5) don't take up more room than necessary, and (6) find something to focus on, like the buttons or the floor panel. Even though these rules are unwritten and unspoken, they are very real. (If you are not too sure about that, try breaking them and note the response.)

Nonverbal behaviors occur in a variety of cultural and social contexts, all with their own sets of rules and definitely not written. Rather, they are understood in light of the cultural context of the situation and because people have been socialized into that culture (see Chapter 7). These types of cultural rules, or *norms*, help communicators identify what is considered acceptable or appropriate behavior for a given situation.

For example, at a professional conference, several rules typically determine the role of communicators. One rule is to use ritualistic greetings when interacting with fellow colleagues, regardless of whether they are friends or strangers. As one colleague approaches another, they must be careful not to catch one another's glance too soon. They are supposed to look down or straight ahead until they are within an acceptable greeting range. Then they make eye contact, smile politely, and say something like "Well, hello, Jack!" or "Good to see you!" Once the greeting has been acknowledged and eye contact is broken, the ritual is over.

Professional and business settings govern still other subtle rules. For instance, eye contact can be too much or too little. In some settings, touching a coworker may be taboo; in others, only a mild touch on the arm or a handshake may be acceptable. Since these rules vary from one setting to another, it is important to understand what is considered appropriate for a given workplace. In any case, these rules direct many interpersonal interactions.

ELEMENTS OF NONVERBAL COMMUNICATION

Researchers have identified a range of elements of nonverbal communication. Commonly discussed elements include communication with the body, the face, the eyes, and the voice. However, the elements of touch, space, time, and objects are also included in nonverbal communication. Certainly, many categories of nonverbal communication could be explored (Leathers, 1997). Our intent in this discussion is to identify those nonverbal behaviors that influence workplace communication.

Personal and Organizational Space

In organizations, individuals communicate through their use of **personal and organizational space**. The roots of human spatial behavior developed from a territorial instinct, or a need to claim and defend space. The study of spatial relationships between people and the objects in their workspace is called *proxemics*.

Think about your own sense of territoriality. Do you usually sit in the same place in a class? Do you feel somewhat protective of your desk or computer at work? Are you protective of your personal space?

PERSONAL SPACE   *Personal space* is an imaginary buffer of space surrounding an individual—a sort of comfort zone that an individual prefers to maintain while interacting with others. That buffer can vary among individuals according to certain factors, such as gender, age, and status. In addition, culture is a factor in identifying what is a comfortable or acceptable personal space.

Violating an individual's personal space—that imaginary buffer surrounding a person—causes discomfort of varying degrees.

In some cultures, it is acceptable for people to stand quite close, while in others, people prefer to allow more space while interacting.

Personal space is not necessarily spherical or equal on all sides of the individual. If we were to view several people from above and see three-dimensional outlines of their respective space zones, they would probably all be different. Some people have a larger front zone than rear zone. Others have a larger zone at the head than at the feet. Moreover, each person's space zone may expand and contract, depending on several things.

Most experts still agree with the pioneering work of Hall (1973), who observed differences in personal space based on relational differences. Generally, the more informal and intimate the relationship, the less the distance. These general categories describe relational differences in personal space:

- *Intimate:* Touching to 18 inches
- *Personal:* 1½ to 4 feet
- *Social:* 4 to 12 feet
- *Public:* 12 feet or greater

(Note that these distances refer to the U.S. context and are typically larger or smaller spaces in other cultures.)

An extension of the concept of personal space is the study of *crowding*. Specifically, what happens when someone is exposed to repeated invasions of personal space over a long period? Although studies of human overcrowding have not provided definitive results, there does seem to be a correlation between crowding and aggression and negative attitudes. Obviously, some people deal with high-density situations better than others do. Regardless, issues of personal space affect work and communication.

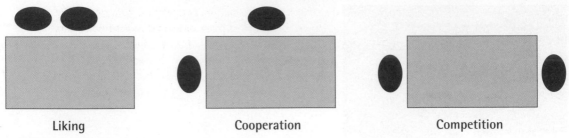

FIGURE 5.1 Seating Arrangements and Perceptions.

SEMIFIXED SPACE   Communication scholars use the term *semifixed space* to refer to how an organizational culture uses its space and organizes objects in that space as well as how that usage affects employees. Some organizations provide their employees with more office space than others. The type of furniture and other objects in the space can also send conscious and unconscious messages. Some employees find significant meaning in the semifixed spaces in which they work.

In studies related to semifixed space, seating behavior affects people's attitudes and processes. For instance, when people were seated across a table from one another, they felt competitive; when they were seated side by side, they felt a liking for one another; and when they were seated around a corner, they felt cooperative (see Figure 5.1). Given these insights, it seems that we should manage seating arrangements that appear to affect interviews and meetings.

In addition, office furniture can be arranged to seclude or include participants. For example, the chairs in the waiting area of a doctor's office are typically arranged in rows along walls so that the interaction pattern focuses outwardly, thus discouraging people from interacting. However, in a counseling office, the chairs might be grouped and otherwise positioned to encourage interaction.

In other words, the use of space makes it possible to encourage or discourage communication. Unfortunately, the effects may be subtle and go unnoticed, such that communication may be inadvertently quashed or that participants will not even be aware of what's happening. Thus, future managers should take note of the importance of interaction cues facilitated by these arrangement patterns.

OTHER SPACE-RELATED ISSUES   In addition to the traditional semifixed features of spaces, other environmental arrangements influence communication and information processing in organizational settings. Various studies (e.g., see Knapp & Hall, 1997) have conducted ratings of objects and even people in varying conditions, such as in an ugly room or a beautiful room. Typically, respondents rate objects such as pictures more negatively in an ugly room. Subsequent research has confirmed the impact of such factors as lighting, color, and furnishings on people in the workplace (Jones, 1997). Think about places in which you felt immediately uplifted or cheerful upon entering. Conversely, have you ever entered a room and felt sad or anxious?

Finally, researchers also consider spatial factors in such fields as marketing and retail sales. According to many studies (e.g., Underhill, 1999), the effective positioning of products in stores and other locations in which products are sold offers a marketing advantage. Theories about the spatial aspects of marketing propose the idea of *zones of interaction*. Namely, customers usually view items by moving from left to right—say, down the aisle in a store or even down a row of cars in a car lot. Customers are more likely to buy the item at the end, or the far right. Thus, stores tend to place higher-profit products at the ends of aisles and in the middle shelves of displays.

Other techniques of "nonverbal persuasion" used in retail sales include the following:

- Well-placed signs identifying items on sale or new to the store
- Slanted shelves that allow customers to see more of the product
- Interactive kiosks that feature specialty items
- Point-of-purchase displays at cashiers and checkouts
- Nearly silent cash registers
- Baskets and carts for carrying items
- Atmospheric touches, such as complimentary lighting and relaxing background music

Body Movements

KINESICS AND GESTURES   The study of communication and **body movements**, called *kinesics*, encompasses a wide area of research (Ekman, 1985). Research on gestures, in particular, reveals their significant meaning during communication. While the research is expansive, here are some types of gestures commonly used in business and professional interactions:

- *Emblems* have direct verbal counterparts and can be substituted without sacrificing meaning. Americans' use of the gesture for "OK" is an example of an emblem, as are the "V" for victory sign and the "thumbs up" for winning sign.
- *Illustrators* are gestures that complement spoken words—for example, indicating a position by pointing to it or showing an emotion with a gesture that enhances its meaning.
- *Regulators* include gestures, hand movements, and shifts in posture that are used to control the flow of conversation. By using them ourselves and observing others' use of them, we know when to speak and when to yield to others.
- *Adaptors* are behaviors that help accomplish various physiological needs. Examples include holding your hand over your mouth when you cough and shielding your eyes in bright sunlight.

POSTURE   What most parents seem to know intuitively about posture, nonverbal researchers have been validating empirically. As researchers such as Knapp and Hall (1997) suggest, different postures convey various interpersonal messages in U.S. culture. Here are several messages commonly communicated in the workplace:

- *Relationships.* Two people who lean toward each other and whose bodies are turned toward each other display a positive, open relationship. Conversely, disinterest or even conflict is communicated when people turn away from one another and maintain an upright, even stiff posture.
- *Status.* Individuals of equal status assume like postures. Individuals of lower status display tense postures, while those of higher status are more relaxed.
- *Gender differences.* In U.S. culture, male posturing and body positioning is more expansive, taking up greater space, than female posturing and positioning (Woods, 2001).
- *Emotional state.* Clinical data suggest that clients with certain emotional states—such as aggression and alienation—can be recognized by their postures.

Case 5.2

Sending Unintentional Messages

Kimberly, a twenty-eight-year-old highly educated, and intelligent professional, changed careers and moved to a new location. She was very excited about the move and confident in her ability to do well in her new career. During her first week or so on the job, her coworkers became impressed with her task competence and obvious expertise. Before long, however, they started to wonder about her demeanor and whether she liked her new job.

People had observed that Kimberly rarely looked at anyone, even when she was talking to them. She was also quite serious and rarely smiled or laughed; in their words, she seemed "angry about something." The more Kimberly's coworkers talked about these observations, the more uncomfortable they became with her. Kimberly picked up on this tension immediately and became even more withdrawn and somber. She knew something was going on, but she couldn't figure out what or why.

In discussing the situation with a close friend one day, Kimberly realized that her nonverbal behaviors had been misinterpreted. Her friend pointed out that Kimberly's typical lack of eye contact and serious expressions were having an alienating effect on her coworkers. Of course, the friend knew that these behaviors were rooted in Kimberly's upbringing in a conservative family and living in a crime-ridden neighborhood, where looking at people carries the risk of potential violence. Kimberly's new coworkers didn't know these things about her, and so they drew their own conclusions based on what they did know.

What can Kimberly do to change her coworkers' perception of her and thus ease the tension in the workplace? If you were her good friend, what would you suggest she do? Why?

Facial Expressions

Another nonverbal communication behavior commonly observed in the workplace is **facial expressions**. Some of the universal facial expressions include those that depict anger, disgust, fear, happiness, sadness, and surprise. Whereas factors such as gender, culture, and age may affect how a receiver interprets certain facial expressions, emotions clearly correlate with this type of nonverbal behavior (Ekman, 1985). An example of how facial expressions and other types of nonverbal communication can be misperceived in the workplace can be seen in the case of Kimberly (see Case 5.2).

Eye Movements

Another area studied by nonverbal communication researchers, called *oculesics*, is the study of **eye movements**. Again, age, culture, gender, and other factors affect how this type of nonverbal behavior is interpreted by receivers. However, some key principles describe the meanings conveyed by eye movements that are relevant in the workplace.

One of the strongest beliefs about eye contact is that it relates to perceptions of submission and dominance. In many cultures, lowering the eyes signals submission. By contrast, staring at someone can be considered a dominant or even an aggressive behavior. A humorous observation of eye contact reviewed driving behavior at stoplights. In one condition, the pedestrians crossing the street at a crosswalk stared at the drivers stopped behind them. In the second condition, a motorcyclist pulled up next to the drivers and stared at them while they were stopped at a light.

Nonverbal communication represents over 75 percent of total communication, a notion that explains why paying attention to one's bodily and facial communication is so important in the workplace. Respecting personal boundaries is very important in communicating with others through touch.

In both conditions, the drivers accelerated away significantly faster after the light turned green than did drivers in the control condition (in which no staring individuals were involved).

Throughout the history of research on nonverbal communication, eye contact has been demonstrated to convey physiological interest in a person or a topic (Knapp & Vangelisti, 2000). Specifically, enlarged pupils signal interest. In fact, realizing this fact, magazine editors sometimes intentionally enlarge a model's pupils in advertising photos. By capturing a highly desirable look (at least in some cultures), in which eye behavior signals interest or arousal, they are more successful in selling their product.

Eye behavior also serves to regulate conversation. With a glance, we can draw others into conversation or cut them off. Studies of conversation show the close relationship among gazing, mutual gazing, and conversational flow. When viewed in context with the face and eyebrows, the eyes are quite expressive of emotional state. They can show the sort of relationship we have or wish to have with someone.

Finally, in U.S. culture, eye contact is associated with trust and credibility. The many communication studies that have examined credibility have found that appropriate eye contact is considered a positive attribute (Remland, 2000).

Touch

Haptics is the study of **touch** in human communication. From intimacy studies to clinical studies involving patients in therapeutic environments, touch is significant in human interaction.

As with other types of nonverbal behavior, rules or norms dictate what is and is not appropriate. Detailed studies have been made of touching norms in the United States, indicating great variation in the frequency of touch based on the area of the body and the kind of relationship. Not surprisingly, norms regarding touch also convey status messages. For instance, a high-status person initiates touching with a low-status person, not the other way around (Knapp & Hall, 1997; Leathers, 1997).

In general, people touch for a variety of reasons:

- To express love or friendship
- To express a greeting or simply to be polite
- To provide care or assistance (such as caring for a baby or someone who is sick)
- To fulfill a job requirement (as in various health and medical professionals)

Obviously, touching that involves these innocuous, warm, and caring purposes is at the very foundation of interpersonal relationships. However, in business and professional settings, touch can convey different meanings and thus be subject to a different set of rules or norms. As already noted, touch often signals status and power in the workplace—that is, the person who initiates the touching has greater status and power. When touch is experienced in this way, feelings of inequality and powerlessness may arise, greatly influencing the ability to have effective business and professional communication.

Second, touching in the workplace can be perceived as inappropriate sexual advancement, or *sexual harassment*. Most laws today that govern interaction in the workplace indicate verbal and nonverbal actions that constitute impropriety. Unwanted touch may be grounds for a lawsuit. Moreover, not only the offending toucher but also his or her supervisor and even employer can be named as defendants, if it can be established that inappropriate behavior was tolerated or somehow allowed to continue in the workplace.

People who like to touch but intend nothing improper in doing so are perhaps vulnerable to being misperceived or even wrongfully accused. They would be wise to reconsider how they show friendship and affirmation, particularly in the workplace, and should perhaps select behaviors that express their sentiments in ways that are safer and culturally appropriate.

Respecting personal boundaries is very important in communicating with others through touch.

Vocal Characteristics

Vocal characteristics include qualities of voice such as accent, volume, pitch, and rate along with *paralanguage* (i.e., vocal utterances that have meanings but are not words, notably, *ah, uh-huh, ooo*). Several studies document how paralinguistic (sometimes called vocalic) utterances along with delivery formats influence the communication process. For instance, Messman and Jones-Corley (2001) identified how delivery (with vocalic changes) influences not only feelings of warmth and caring but also how people learn new ideas. This suggests how powerful our voice qualities are.

First, the voice regulates the flow of conversation (Hickson, Stacks, & Moore, 2004). Shifts occur as the dialogue moves from speaker to listener and back again. This turn taking in conversation is regulated by the vocal cues of the participants, such as (1) by uttering various vocalized pauses (such as *uh* and *um*), (2) by altering voice rates, and (3) by manipulating voice pitch at the ends of sentences.

For example, if you want to keep talking in a conversation, you might speak at a faster rate and simply not let your vocal pitch go down at the end of the sentence or paragraph. This behavior will indicate to your conversational partner that you are not through talking yet, and he or she will likely let you continue. When you are ready to give up the floor, you can slow down your vocal rate and lower your pitch.

Vocal characteristics are also inherent to the semantic process of interpreting oral communication. When you emphasize a word or phrase by increasing your volume, use a whispering voice to share news with a friend, or argue with someone in a monotone, you are using your voice to add special meaning to your message. Given this ability, oral communication is uniquely different from written communication.

Unfortunately, the meanings that we intend to convey through vocal characteristics are not always interpreted accurately, which is a particular issue in workplace communication. Managers and employees make errors in judging emotions such as excitement versus anger by considering factors such as increased volume, intensity, and rate. On one hand, you may feel sympathetic toward a coworker whose low-key vocal features you interpret as sadness. On the other hand, you may feel joy based on your communication with a person who speaks with a modulating pitch, a normal vocal rate, and an appropriate use of pausing at the end of sentences.

Timing

As discussed earlier, individuals who interact successfully practice synchronized, well-timed verbal and nonverbal behaviors. *Chronemic research*—the study of how people communicate using time—has identified the value of appropriate **timing** in business and the professions.

How an individual deals with time involves issues of respect and credibility and cultural norms as well. For example, in U.S. culture, a habitually late person is seen as inconsiderate, lazy, or incompetent. In this sense, time is a valuable commodity. In the world of customer service and sales, *wait time* refers to the amount of time a customer will remain patient while waiting in a line or on the phone.

Underhill (1999) has estimated that the average tolerated wait time in American retail sales is only three minutes. If the wait time exceeds that amount, the customer's perception of the actual wait time appears exponentially longer. This wait time principle alters judgments significantly, including interpersonal perceptions. For example, an individual who waits a significantly long time to see someone may feel insulted if the wait seems too long.

To improve interpersonal relationships, communicators may choose to realign their priorities based on time. For instance, ensuring the delivery of a product on time could make or break a huge contract. Clients make major judgments about trust and competence based on behavior as simple as managing to meet a deadline. The last-minute, late-night calls that professors get regarding assignments raise similar questions about individual students' time management and responsibility.

Objects and Clothing

An individual's clothing and jewelry, hairstyle and make-up, and body art and body piercings are all elements of nonverbal communication and thus influence his or her interactions with others. Research in this area is labeled *objectics*.

Some selections of **objects and clothing** are made to intentionally project a certain image; in other instances, these choices may reflect mood. In any case, each organizational culture has a unique interpretation of what is considered appropriate for that organization. It is unlikely that such information will be stated formally, as in a dress code, but cultural norms will communicate what is and is not acceptable. Understanding those expectations is vital for an individual's success within an organization. For good or bad, people attribute to others motivations and qualities based on appearance.

USING NONVERBAL COMMUNICATION IN THE WORKPLACE

One axiom of nonverbal communication stands out clearly in the minds of professionals who work in sales: *Actions speak louder than words.* A number of sales-training seminars promote the use of nonverbal techniques to help participants increase sales, boost closing rates, improve productivity, and otherwise gain an edge. Traditional sales training alone is believed to be insufficient. When you are trying to sell, words are only 7 percent of the effort!

Don Rosenthal, of Gant & Donald Communications, asks key questions of his clients when teaching them skills for nonverbal communication and sales (see Skills at Work 5.1). His

---

SKILLS AT WORK 5.1
Nonverbal Communication and Sales

Review the following list of questions, which come from a sales-training program. What points do they raise about the importance of understanding nonverbal behavior in trying to sell something?

1. How would you approach a client who is ten years older than you? How about a client who is ten years younger than you?
2. What five nonverbal body language indicators do you use to send signals to the client, and vice versa?
3. How do you know when to stop talking because the client is honestly evaluating what you have said?

4. Why is the worst place to conduct a business transaction over a desk?
5. How do you know when a client is giving you a dishonest versus an honest answer?
6. How do you decide when to stop your sales presentation because you have hit an emotional "hot button" and the client wants to interrupt you?
7. What nonverbal body language says the client disagrees with you but is reluctant to verbalize it?
8. How can a simple handshake tell you if a client is dominant, passive, or cooperative?

Source: Adapted from Rosenthal (2000).

approach is to read the customer's body language, which requires a comprehensive understanding of nonverbal behaviors.

Rosenthal's approach to sales training supports what others have found about the importance of nonverbal communication in work situations, including sales and interviewing. Consider the following strategies for improving communication:

1. *Shaking hands.* In every culture, making the proper greeting is essential. In U.S. culture, that means shaking hands firmly and directly—for women and men. This ritual is so significant that an improper handshake is seen as a potential weakness or even a sign that one person can dominate the other. Some claim that by drawing the other person's hand toward you just slightly, you gain a small amount of control. Manipulative as this may seem, it points to the importance of the business ritual.

2. *Making eye contact and smiling.* Although making deliberate eye contact and smiling intentionally may seem awkward at first, they are both important in personal interaction. Recall from the earlier discussion that these behaviors affect the sharing of information and the exertion of influence. To understand this point more clearly, consider the effect of the opposite behaviors: looking down or away and appearing stern or worried. These behaviors simply do not evoke trust.

3. *Emerging from behind the desk.* Using office space creatively during interviews with clients and in sharing information with colleagues is important. Furniture that creates an obstruction can inhibit communication by creating a symbolic barrier. Conversely, eliminating the obstacles can create openness and improve listening. Even moving your chair closer to someone (without violating his or her personal space, of course) suggests your interest in and desire to communicate with him or her. Issues of space are critical in business settings, given that information exchange can lead to important decisions.

4. *Attending to vocal qualities.* Many of the people who study communication and want to enhance their public presentations and interpersonal relationships are concerned with how they sound. The first rule of thumb in this area is to vary your pitch, volume, and rate. Second, when in someone else's workplace, try to match his or her pitch, volume, and rate so as to avoid violating his or her expectations and customs. You will rarely go wrong by imitating someone, unless he or she is unable to hear or otherwise does not communicate well.

5. *Being on time and timing.* Obviously, being punctual is important in many organizational cultures. The subtle use of the monochronic and polychronic order may also be helpful in improving communication.
   - *Monochronic order* is linear and involves dealing with one issue at a time.
   - *Polychronic order* is associated with the "big picture" and thus involves dealing with several things at a time and in no particular order.

A good rule is to match the style of the client or participant. Doing so will help others understand your presentation in the way they like best. Interestingly, recent brain research points to information storage and retrieval based on learning styles similar to the monochronic and polychronic styles (Dilts, Bandler, & Bandler, 1990). To see which type of style you are most comfortable with, complete the assessment in Skills at Work 5.2 on the next page.

6. *Nodding your head.* A large body of research developed over the last two decades, called *neurolinguistic programming,* or *NLP* (Dilts et al., 1990), has identified the value of affirmative gestures such as nodding your head. During negotiations, for instance, gently nodding your head is a subtle way of showing agreement or support.

SKILLS AT WORK 5.2
Monochronic and Polychronic Style Assessment

To determine your style for dealing with information and relating to people, respond to each of the following statements with one of these answers:

1 = Strongly agree   2 = Agree
3 = Neither agree nor disagree
4 = Disagree   5 = Strongly disagree

Write the appropriate answer on the line preceding each statement below. Also note that the asterisked (*) items are reverse scored (i.e., 1 = 5, 5 = 1, etc.). Then total your answers at the bottom after you have finished.

_____ **1.** I usually feel frustrated when I try to do too many things at once.

_____ **2.** I tend to finish one thing before moving to something different.

_____ **3.** In meetings, I feel irritated when someone brings up a new item before we have finished with the item we are currently discussing.

_____ **4.** I usually need to focus on one task at a time in order to finish things.

_____ ***5.** At work, it doesn't bother me to talk with several people at a time.

_____ ***6.** I find it stimulating to think about several ideas at a time.

_____ ***7.** I like working on several tasks at a time.

_____ ***8.** When I am talking with others, I don't mind being interrupted in the middle of one conversation to pick up and start another conversation, as needed.

_____ **Total Score**

How did you do? A total score of 4 to 24 indicates a monochronic style of communication, and a total score of 25 to 40 indicates a polychronic style. Consider, too, that there may be some overlap between the two styles. If your score is in the 20s, you likely are comfortable with both styles and capable of communicating either way.

Source: Adapted from Phipps' (1998) scale reported in Dodd (1998).

7. *Avoiding nervous gestures.* No doubt, there are differences in cultural and individual indications of nervous behavior. But in general, playing with your hair, stuffing your hands into your pockets, rubbing your hands on your face, and picking at your ears are interpreted as signs of being nervous. Most of us want to express confidence in meetings and interviews, and clearly, distracting behaviors such as these undermine that goal.

8. *Listening.* When asking for a sale, it's important to know when to stop talking and listen. In exchanging information or making a sales presentation, you will heighten the impact of what you say by stopping and asking for questions or listening to the responses of others. With that feedback, you can go back and address objections or clarify a point that seems unclear.

9. *Going low and slow.* When dealing with an emotional client, try to lower the volume and slow down the pace of the dialogue. In a situation in which emotions are running high, ease into this interchange, at first matching the participant's volume and pace but not the other vocal and gestural aspects of his or her communication. Then gradually tone things down. This low-and-slow strategy was designed to take control of an interview situation, for controlling the conversational climate has been shown to facilitate increased information processing.

WEB AT WORK 5.1
Nonverbal Communication

Use these websites to get you started in finding out more about nonverbal communication:

- **www.content.monster.com/ articles/3485/17685/1/home.aspx** An overview of research on nonverbal communication.

- **www.acjournal.org** *American Communication Journal:* Source of scholarly materials on nonverbal communication.
- **www.allbusiness.com/management/ 443058-1.html** Articles on marketing and sales.

Applying these strategies will depend on your expectations and styles as well as the situation in which you are communicating. Nonetheless, through the purposeful use of these nonverbal behaviors you will create a professional presence. They will become part of your repertoire of interpersonal skills and with continued and careful use will strengthen your overall communication.

To find online sources of information about nonverbal communication, consult the websites in Web at Work 5.1. You might also use various search engines to look further into this vital topic.

In Perspective

Nonverbal communication functions in four primary ways with spoken language: to complement what is being said, to contradict what has been said, to regulate speech, and to substitute behaviors for words or concepts. Like all communication, rules govern the use of nonverbal behaviors in specific cultures, such as those of workplaces. Regulatory-fit theory reminds us that a speaker's nonverbal "match" to a receiver yields perceived message effectiveness.

Nonverbal communication consists of a variety of elements or behaviors. One of those factors is personal space: an imaginary buffer of space surrounding an individual. Levels of personal space range from intimate to personal to social to public. Semifixed space refers to how an organizational culture uses its space and organizes objects in that space as well as how that usage affects employees and clients.

A second element of nonverbal communication is body movements. Research on gestures and postures, in particular, has identified the various interpersonal messages such movements convey in U.S. culture. Culture is also a factor—along with age, gender, and other characteristics—in how receivers interpret facial expressions and eye movements.

Touching, another nonverbal behavior, can be performed for a variety of purposes, including to express love or friendship or to greet someone. As with other types of nonverbal behavior, rules or norms dictate what is acceptable in certain situations. In the workplace especially, communicators should pay attention to the meaning of touch and be aware of what is and is not appropriate.

Additional elements of nonverbal communication include vocal characteristics, timing, and objects and clothing. Vocal characteristics include qualities of voice such as accent, volume, pitch, and rate along with paralanguage (that is, vocal utterances). Timing addresses issues of synchronized, well-timed verbal and nonverbal behavior, including its cultural and relational dimensions. Finally, an individual's clothing and jewelry, hairstyle and makeup, and body art and body piercing are all elements of nonverbal communication and thus influence one's interactions with others.

Applying the principles of successful nonverbal communication in the workplace has obvious ramifications in the areas of sales and interviewing. Being able to use strategies such as extending a firm handshake, smiling and making eye contact, and nodding your head in agreement, not only enhances communication but creates a professional presence. They should become part of your repertoire of interpersonal skills.

Discussion Questions

1. What general guidelines should be followed for making eye contact in business and professional settings?
2. What advice would you give a coworker who is a toucher? In particular, how might his or her behavior make others uncomfortable (especially nontouchers), and what risks does he or she run in today's workplace?
3. How does the arrangement of space, including the positioning of furniture, affect personal interaction in the workplace? Use examples to support your point.

4. What would be the benefits of doing an audit of individuals' nonverbal communication in your organization? What might you learn that would enhance communication among members?
5. In an emotional conversation, what vocal characteristics might easily be misinterpreted? For instance, talking at a fast rate might signify what different emotional states? What about talking loudly? Give examples.

Exercises

1. Conduct a nonverbal communication audit of an organization in which you can observe its members. Begin by making a list of the major nonverbal behaviors listed in this chapter. Then, as an individual or a team, go into the organization and make observations regarding members' nonverbal behaviors. Report your findings in class or in a short report.
2. Visit a variety of retail organizations to see how retailers position products. After noticing some patterns, interview the stores' managers about the principles of positioning that they follow. In particular, determine how positioning influences sales.
3. Interview a sample of members in an organization regarding the use of time and various timing issues in their group. How do these issues influence the satisfaction of

employees? worker productivity? the organizational climate?
4. Take some of Rosenthal's ideas about effective selling behaviors (see Skills at Work 5.1) and use them to create role-play scenarios for an in-class presentation or video. Have class members comment on how effective these nonverbal behaviors might be in a real sales interview.
5. Give the monochronic/polychronic assessment (see Skills at Work 5.2) to a few friends to determine their preferred styles. How does each person score? Does this assessment identify possible areas of conflict or agreement in your communicating with him or her? With whom do you seem to have the most in common in terms of your own score?

References

Byron, K. (2007). Male and female managers' ability to 'read' emotions: Relationships with supervisor's performance no space—connect with next phrase ratings and subordinates' satisfaction ratings. *Journal of Occupational & Organizational Psychology, 80*(4), 713–733. Retrieved from Academic Search Complete database.

Cesario, J., & Higgins, E. (2008). Making message recipients "feel right": How nonverbal cues can increase persuasion. *Psychological Science, 19*(5), 415–420. doi:10.1111/j.1467-9280.2008.02102.x.

Dilts, R., Bandler, R., & Bandler, R. C. (1990). *Neuro-linguistic programming.* Vol. 1. Capitola, CA: Meta Publications.

Dodd, C. H. (1998). *Dynamics of intercultural communication.* 5th ed. New York: McGraw-Hill.

Ekman, P. (1985). *Telling lies.* New York: Norton.

Garner, P. (1992). Nonverbal communication. In *Human communication.* 2nd ed. ed C. H. Dodd & M. L. Lewis. Dubuque, IA: Kendall/Hunt.

Hall, E. T. (1973). *The silent language.* New York: Anchor Books.

Hickson, M. L., Stacks, D. W., & Moore, N. J. (2004). *Nonverbal communication.* 3rd ed. Los Angeles: Roxbury.

Jones, S. L. (1997). A guide to using color effectively in business communication. *Business Communication Quarterly, 60,* 76–88.

Knapp, M. L., & Hall, J. A. (1997). *Nonverbal communication in human interaction.* 4th ed. New York: Harcourt Brace.

Knapp, M. L., & Vangelisti, A. (2000). *Interpersonal communication and human relations.* 4th ed. Boston: Allyn & Bacon.

Gentry, W., & Kuhnert, K. (2007). Sending signals: Nonverbal communication can speak volumes. *Leadership in Action, 27*(5), 3–7. Retrieved from Academic Search Complete database.

Houser, M. (2005). Are we violating their expectations? Instructor communication expectations of traditional and nontraditional students. *Communication Quarterly, 53*(2), 213–228. doi:10.1080/01463370500090332.

Leathers, D. G. (1997). *Successful nonverbal communication.* 3rd ed. Boston: Allyn & Bacon.

Mehrabian, A. (1981). *Silent messages.* 2nd ed. Belmont, CA: Wadsworth.

Messman, S. J., & Jones-Corley, J. (2001). Effects of communication environment, immediacy, and communication apprehension on cognitive and affective learning. *Communication Monographs, 68,* 184–200.

Morand, D. (2001). The Emotional Intelligence of managers: Assessing the construct validity of a nonverbal measure of "People Skills." *Journal of Business & Psychology, 16*(1), 21–34. Retrieved from Academic Search Complete database.

Phipps, C. (1998). Monochronic and polychromic communication styles between U.S. and Mexican nationals. Honors thesis, Abilene Christian University, Abilene, TX.

Remland, M. S. (2000). *Nonverbal communication in everyday life.* New York: Houghton Mifflin.

Richmond, V. P., & McCroskey, J. C. (2004). *Nonverbal behavior in interpersonal relations.* 5th ed. Boston: Allyn & Bacon.

Rosenthal, D. (2000). Nonverbal selling. Available online: www.nonverbal-sales-seminars.com/body_language.html.

Underhill, P. (1999). *Why we buy: The science of shopping.* New York: Simon and Schuster.

Woods, J. T. (2001). *Gendered lives.* 4th ed. Belmont, CA: Wadsworth.

CHAPTER 6

Managing Communication Conflict in the Workplace

After reading this chapter, you will be able to do the following:

- Define conflict.
- Identify the causes and types of conflict.
- Understand the theories of conflict in the workplace.
- Develop skills for managing conflict.
- Understand the different styles of conflict communication.
- Know how to receive and give criticism.
- Develop skills for managing negotiation.
- Understand the principles of negotiation and negotiation styles.

If knowledge can create problems, it is not through ignorance that we can solve them.

ISAAC ASIMOV

In the fall of 1842, Abraham Lincoln was a respected attorney in Springfield, Illinois, and a well-known Republican state legislator. Yet without identifying himself, he wrote several satirical "open letters" in the local newspaper that criticized James Shields, a Democratic politician, whose policies conflicted with his own. Upon learning that Lincoln had supposedly written the letters, Shields challenged him to a duel.

Although both men's associates negotiated back and forth, trying to seek release from the challenge, it was to no avail. Lincoln finally was forced to accept the challenge. The date for the duel was set, and, perhaps due to honor or integrity, both men prepared for what seemed an inevitable death. At the last minute, however, the parties involved reconciled their differences and the duel was called off.

We can conclude that Lincoln learned two great lessons from this ordeal: not to write anonymous letters and not to underestimate the value of mediation and conflict resolution (Scheske, 2000).

CONFLICT IN THE WORKPLACE

Defining Conflict

In general terms, **conflict** occurs when two or more people clash over an issue about which they have different beliefs or values. On a more advanced level, Hocker and Wilmot (2001) describe conflict as "an expressed struggle," in which at least two parties perceive very different goals, scarce resources, and no help from others in achieving their goals.

Organizational conflict specialist Brenton (2000) describes conflict as a "clash between two or more people over their perceptions." Moreover, she identifies the objects over which the clash occurs as "scarce resources, incompatible relational or content goals, unfulfilled needs, imbalances of power, and loss of face" (p. 2). For example, when two people have to share a printer and they are hurried, you can see how this illustrates scarce resources.

Causes of Conflict

Again, in general terms, conflict occurs when individuals or groups either misunderstood one another or have understood correctly but are dissatisfied with the result. Beyond that, a number of specific **causes of conflict** can be identified, as discussed in the following sections (Rau-Foster, 2000).

DIFFERENT GOALS   One source of conflict results from a clash in expectations or goals related to a certain task. You may know from experience that it is difficult to work and feel good about an outcome when you and a coworker or classmate view your work in dramatically different ways. You may want one thing, and he or she may want something else. When a content difference is the issue, it will be helpful to discuss matters to clarify understanding and reconcile the direction in which you're headed. However, when the difference is symptomatic of deeper, unresolved issues—say, long-term budget or hiring plans—finding a resolution will be more complicated.

METHODS OF REACHING GOALS   Sometimes people agree on the goal but differ on how to achieve the goal. Two team members may both want to complete a report by 4:00 PM Friday, but one may feel they should work individually on parts of the report and then assemble it, whereas the other might feel they should work together, side by side, in developing the entire report.

SCARCITY OF RESOURCES   Conflict can also result from competition over limited resources— that is, the finances, personnel, and facilities needed to complete a task. Such conflicts often involve issues of boundaries and territory. For example, suppose Bill wants the entire office to move up to a more expensive but more powerful computer network. Bill's supervisor, Lynnette, agrees this is desirable but must veto the purchase because the budget cannot support it. Rather than avoid the issue altogether or expect that one or the other proposal will win out, Bill and Lynnette should try to compromise: to buy a few computers now, to reduce the maintenance contract, and to pursue a five-year plan for ongoing technology replacement.

RELATIONSHIP DIFFERENCES   Another underlying cause of conflict is relationship differences. The issue may be any of several differences, some quite subjective—for instance, "just the way he is!" More objectively, differences in information processing and communication style may be involved. Many conflicts stem from basic differences such as these:

- A win-lose versus a win-win outlook
- A task versus people orientation

- A lack of perceived competence
- A lack of trust
- A perception of extreme dissimilarity
- Jealousy

UNEQUAL POWER DISTRIBUTION   When people perceive power differences in relationships, conflict can easily result. For instance, suppose that Jana is promoted to a managerial position, but her friend Angela, who has similar experience and qualifications, is not promoted. Now, when they meet, Angela constantly compares her performance against Jana's. To reciprocate, Jana refers to her new position and tries to persuade Angela to leave the company, citing exaggerated information about future changes. Jana has vengefully created these changes, which are not true.

The general principle is that power is a resource that can be used for influence. Determining just how power is used and for what influence depends on the type of power:

1. *Positional power.* This type of power refers to the authority someone is commonly accepted as having in terms of being able to decide, influence, and lead. People such as supervisors, managers, teachers, and chief executive officers (CEOs) have positional power.
2. *Reward or punishment power.* Someone who has the ability to offer rewards or mete out punishments has this type of power. Understandably, people with positional power often have reward or punishment power, too. Nonetheless, this latter type of power can be exercised by people who have a considerable amount of influence as a result of seniority, experience, or manipulative ability.
3. *Informational power.* This type of power rests on a communicator's ability to present meaningful information. Namely, the person who can present information in an effective and competent manner attains power because he or she enables others to conduct business or pursue tasks. In this case, knowledge is power.
4. *Persuasive power.* The ability to influence or persuade others also creates power. For example, trainers have persuasive power because they can influence employees in ways that bring about greater quantity or quality—things that are deemed important. Similarly, people who are good at negotiating have persuasive power. This type of power is not related to a personal position or the ability to serve out reward and punishment; rather, it lies in someone's ability to convince others to change or comply.

UNCLEAR ROLE EXPECTATIONS   Some conflicts are caused by unclear role expectations, again, likely involving issues of boundaries and territories. Kim, a member of a proposal development team, understood that she alone was interviewing executives in the senior management group as part of their research. Jason, her team member, thought this was his exclusive responsibility. By discussing this misunderstanding early on, Kim and Jason avoided an extended conflict.

Their experience matches what conflict in the workplace experts defined as establishing systems that define roles and manage conflict. For instance, Lipsky, Seeber, and Fincher (2003) trace conflict in the workplace back to a "social contract" that appeared after World War II, whereby organizational systems with clearly defined roles worked out their conflicts. This situation appears to have changed, giving rise to alternative dispute systems, extreme negotiations, and missed expectations in a litigious society.

LACK OF INFORMATION   Conflict may also result when people lack the information needed to make a good decision or understand why something happened. Lulofs and Cahn (2000) identify uncertainty as one major cause of conflict in the workplace. For example, Marc never got the word that Kanesha's training program had undergone significant changes since he had last sent new employees to her. If he had known about the changes, he would have discussed them with Kanesha and found out what the new training involved before automatically sending his new hires to her. This conflict was definitely related to a lack of information.

DIFFERENT VALUES   Because values underlie people's beliefs and attitudes about what is worthwhile and acceptable, differences in values often result in conflict. In a moral conflict, for instance, people have different outlooks on what is the right or the wrong way to think or act. Conflicts over rules and procedures can be common in the workplace, as rules, procedures, standards, and the like are basic elements of corporate culture.

FACE-SAVING   Asserting one's identity and needing to "save face" is another potential cause of conflict. Someone who has experienced real or imagined shame or embarrassment will want some sort of resolution or even retribution, setting the stage for conflict. Similarly, someone who is unsure of his or her identity or position, particularly in regard to others, may create conflict in attempting to find clarification.

Case 6.1 presents a real-world illustration of a business conflict that was ultimately identified and resolved. Consider how this matter was handled before going ahead to the next section on types of conflict.

Case 6.1

The Day the Committee Came

Jackson and Lorraine, both senior management partners, had known from previous evaluations that the divisional training unit had some problems. Participants had had some complaints about the training program and the manager of the divisional training unit, Sonja. Jackson and Lorraine had asked Sonja about these complaints on several occasions over the last eighteen months, but her answers had always been consistent: "I'm working on a new project," "We have had major team changes," and "My personal health situation hasn't been good."

Looking back, Jackson and Lorraine had simply failed to be specific with Sonja and had allowed things to continue. They were forced to deal with the problems when some dozen training recipients and several divisional managers came in for a two-hour meeting. In the meeting, numerous details emerged about the training program and Sonja's role in running it.

With this information in hand, Jackson and Lorraine went to work with Sonja: summarizing the issues, offering feedback, and helping her improve her communication skills. To her credit, Sonja continued to disagree with several philosophical points about the training protocol, but she made major shifts in the format of the training and her role in it. In the end, the training program got back on track, and the level of complaints went down to zero.

Based on what you've learned so far in this chapter and the information provided in this case, what causes of conflict might be involved? Why?

Types of Conflict

Conflict is a multifaceted phenomenon. Not only are there multiple causes of conflict, but there are multiple **types of conflict** as well, ranging from simple disagreement to outright hostility. Lulofs and Cahn (2000) have identified four categories of conflict: (1) disagreements, (2) misplaced conflicts, (3) nonsubstantive conflicts, and (4) substantive conflicts.

DISAGREEMENTS   A *disagreement* is a mild conflict and usually involves issues that are not necessarily related to the relationship. For instance, Bill and David may disagree over the layout and design of an advertisement program, but they can talk out their differences and come to some sort of agreement. If they don't reach agreement and the matter goes unresolved, it may ultimately become more serious, particularly if failure to resolve matters becomes a pattern of communication. At that point, what began as a disagreement could lead to a conflict.

MISPLACED CONFLICTS   Sometimes what is presumed to be the topic of conflict is not the true source. A *misplaced conflict* is one in which one or both of the parties fail to recognize the real issue and instead engage someone or something else. Three types of misplaced conflict can be identified:

1. In a *false conflict,* one person thinks there is a conflict only to discover there is not. In this example, Sarah's false conflict was based on her expecting the worst:

EXAMPLE

"I managed to foul up royally on the data analysis, and after I fixed it, I was four days late in turning in my report. I was sure my boss would kill me. Instead, after I explained what had happened, he thanked me for my hard work and said he understood how we all make mistakes. I was floored! All that anxiety for nothing!"

2. *Displaced conflict* occurs when one person wrongfully attributes a problem or issue to another person, ultimately blaming and perhaps punishing him or her. Jeff experienced displaced conflict in this example:

EXAMPLE

"What a day! First, I had car problems on the way to work. Then, when I got there, I found out that I had been turned down for my promotion. After that, my wife called, telling me our basement was full of water again. I was so stressed out that when I met with my coworker Jonathan, that afternoon, I unloaded on him with both barrels. I told him how stupid his ideas were and that I was tired of doing all the work. We bickered for a while and then stopped for the day. The next day, I apologized to Jonathan, explaining that he had nothing to do with why I was so mad."

3. In a *substitution conflict,* people argue about an issue, but it's not the one at the center of the problem. For instance, when people argue over money and other resources, often the real issue is one of competition or popularity or some unresolved conflict. By substituting the issue in this way, people can avoid addressing the real issue, intentionally or otherwise. Laurie, a patient-relations manager in a large hospital, realized she had a substitution conflict with Angie, another manager.

EXAMPLE

"I couldn't wait for my ten o'clock meeting with Angie, the customer account manager. Then, only minutes into the meeting, we engaged in a heated discussion about the many complaints we'd received from patients in the last two months. It took an hour or more, but we both finally realized that the issue of patient complaints was rooted in our lack of coordination in dealing with patients. That was the major source of our conflict."

NONSUBSTANTIVE CONFLICTS   *Nonsubstantive conflicts* are rooted in personal habits and styles, not specific topics or issues (except perhaps attacking another person or attacking the system in general). Nonsubstantive conflicts involve behaviors such as complaining and whining, bickering, being verbally or physically abusive or aggressive, and being competitive and jealous.

SUBSTANTIVE CONFLICTS   *Substantive conflicts* involve real issues and thus have real substance. Examples include not only specific topics, such as social and political issues, but also processes and methods, relationships and role expectations, morals and values, and other topics about which people might disagree. Like any significant conflict, a substantive conflict must be addressed using solution-oriented communication.

Levels of Conflict and Tension in Organizations

Organizational conflict occurs when policies, decisions, or directional shifts create resistance between individuals who feel others are blocking their efforts or those of their group. That these conflicts will occur is inevitable. In fact, some level of conflict actually has performance benefits. As George and Jones (1999) explain, as conflict increases, the level of performance increases up to an optimal point. Thus, when managed properly, organizational conflict can create enough motivation to cause improvement. Beyond the optimal point, however, conflict not only ceases to be beneficial but creates major obstacles.

Some of the causes of organizational conflict were identified earlier in this chapter. Additional causes include the following (Cloke & Goldsmith, 2000; George & Jones, 1999):

- Differences in functions and outcomes
- Status inconsistencies
- Overlapping authority
- Scarcity of resources
- Incompatible evaluation methods

Whatever the cause, conflict can develop to the extent that it creates dysfunctional behavior in an organization. Specifically, Siburt (2000) has interpreted three levels of conflict, which develop incrementally and represent increasing degrees of tension:

- *Level 1: Problem identification.* At this level of conflict, individuals identify a problem and move toward a solution. Their focus is on the problem, not the relationship between the individuals involved. The risk taking is minimal, and openness is encouraged in terms of sharing information, communicating interpersonally, and so on. The conflict will escalate and tension will grow, for instance, if not all of the information is presented or if what is presented is inaccurate. Trust will begin to break down, depending on how effectively issues are dealt with and how well relationships are developed or ignored.

- *Level 2: Advocacy.* At this heightened level of conflict, the purpose of problem solving has changed from consensus building to debating and providing proof. There is now a position to advocate and individuals take sides, no longer seeing themselves as having a mutual cause. Consequently, there are increases in self-protective actions, turf wars, distortions of information, and expressions of tension and uneasiness in verbal and nonverbal communication. At this level, individuals often attempt to gain power by forming cliques and coalitions, which may be accomplished through bargaining.
- *Level 3: Winning.* At this most extreme level of conflict, winning is the goal, and it may be pursued at all costs. At this point, the conflict may escalate into a fight. Negative and hurtful behaviors are common, and a "seize and destroy" mentality prevails. One party may withdraw or ask the other party to withdraw.

For more information about conflict, go online and access the websites identified in Web at Work 6.1.

Theories of Conflict in the Workplace

We will consider four **theories of conflict** as it occurs in the workplace: (1) phase theory, (2) conflict avoidance cycle theory (3) chilling effect theory (which are both cycle theories), and (4) escalation theory.

PHASE THEORY   Proponents of phase theory believe that conflict occurs in predictable patterns, progressing through a series of identifiable stages or phases. One possible sequence of phases is as follows (see also Figure 6.1):

1. Some source initiates the conflict; it is brewing, though not fully manifested.
2. People become aware of the conflict and sense the difficulties associated with it.
3. Strategies are attempted to resolve the conflict.

WEB AT WORK 6.1
Conflict at Work

Conflict is a much-studied topic in the field of workplace communication. To learn more, consult the following:

- **http://edis.ifas.ufl.edu/hr024.** University of Florida's extension service of key causes of workplace conflict.
- **http://www.allbusiness.com/ human-resources/workforce- management-conflict-resolution/ 12260-1.html.** This site offers major tips for handing workplace conflicts and developing skills.
- **http://www.businessknowhow.com/ manage/resolve.htm.** Site offers a simple set of reasons for conflict between people in companies, but this site appears to be commercial.
- **http://www.workplaceissues.com/ arconflict.htm.** This site offers articles by a nurse who is also an attorney explaining the nature of conflict and mediation in the workplace.
- **www.managementhelp.org** A great management library with numerous topics including conflict.
- **www.alaskachd.org** Has a section on advocacy as well as special needs populations.

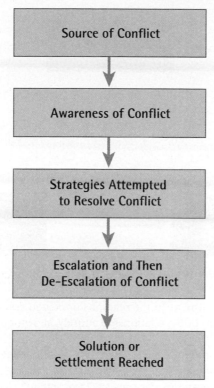

FIGURE 6.1   Phase Theory of Conflict   *Source:* Based on Lulofs and Cahn (2000).

4. The conflict first escalates and then deescalates.
5. A solution or settlement is reached.

A logical consequence of phase theory is being aware of how to prevent or at least derail conflict (George & Jones, 1999; Lulofs & Cahn, 2000). That is, if conflict inevitably follows this pattern, it should be possible to develop solutions or otherwise intervene to thwart the pattern. This possibility could set the tone for future conflict management.

CONFLICT AVOIDANCE CYCLE THEORY   Another way to look at conflict is to analyze the avoidance tendencies that cause us to put off dealing with it. According to this view, there is a **cycle of conflict** that involves a series of steps, as shown in Figure 6.2 on the next page. For instance, upon realizing that the conflict is bad, we may become nervous and avoid dealing with the issue as long as possible. Usually, the conflict will get worse the longer we avoid it, perhaps to the point that it gets out of control and must be confronted. Lulofs and Cahn (2000) describe this cycle, along with several others, as having an unhappy ending unless the pattern is altered.

CHILLING EFFECT THEORY   Another type of conflict cycle, called the *chilling effect* (Lulofs & Cahn, 2000), ultimately results in the death of the relationship. This cycle view of conflict often begins with unresolved anger, a point articulated in McClure's writings (2000). At the start of the cycle, we anticipate the negative effects of conflict on the relationship, which makes us afraid of losing it. In anticipation of this negative outcome, we simply avoid communication, which leads

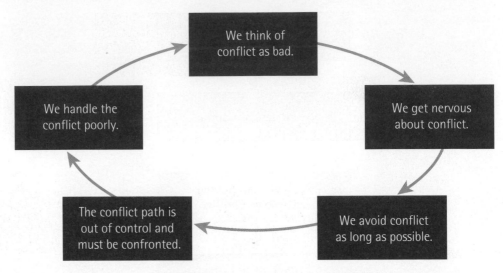

FIGURE 6.2 The Cycle of Conflict *Source:* Based on Lulofs and Cahn (2000).

to a decreased level of commitment to the relationship. Upon realizing that the conflict is not worth the effort, we may let go of the relationship entirely, allowing it die (see Figure 6.3).

ESCALATION THEORY Avoidance leads us to the illusion that the conflict will go away. However, the cycle theories of conflict just discussed suggest that when conflict goes unresolved, it tends to become worse and even resurface at a level worse than before. This notion can be called *escalation theory* (see Figure 6.4).

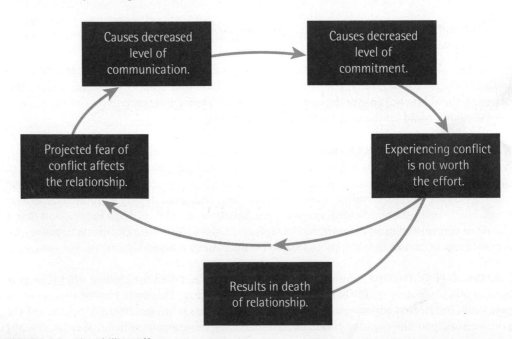

FIGURE 6.3 The Chilling Effect

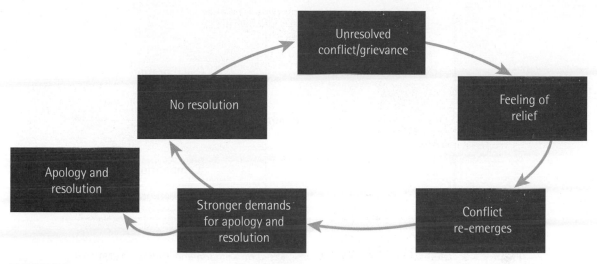

FIGURE 6.4 Escalation Theory

A good metaphor of how conflict escalates when it is ignored is to imagine an armed submarine. It lies under the surface of the water, waiting and ready for action. Then, when it's least expected, the weapons on the submarine are discharged and deliver a serious destructive blow. And in most cases, no one saw it coming, let alone anticipated the damage it would do.

Certainly, more than one organizational leader has been "torpedoed" by an unresolved issue, grievance, or conflict. Conflict's refusal to go away typically surprises a person, which only feeds the vicious cycle. Other consequences of ignoring conflict include increased speculation and gossip among coworkers and employees, personal embarrassment and anxiety, and perhaps even episodes of anger and threatening behavior.

COMMUNICATION SKILLS IN MANAGING CONFLICT

Understanding Conflict Communication Styles

There are five basic approaches or styles for managing conflict, according to research by Kilmann and Thomas (1975). As shown in Figure 6.5 on the next page, their classic work establishes two axes—concern for task and concern for people—which, upon intersection, form four quadrants and a central midpoint region. These five regions represent five **conflict communication styles**:

1. *Competition.* This style is marked by a high assertiveness in terms of accomplishing the task but a low concern for people and relationships. Consequently, this person exhibits a win-lose orientation, or what can be summed up as "My way."
2. *Collaboration.* The person with this style has a high task orientation and a high concern for other people. This is a win-win orientation, reflecting "Our way."
3. *Accommodation.* This style is characterized by wanting to please others, as shown by a high concern for people and relationships, but being less concerned for achieving goals and tasks. As a lose-win orientation, this can be described as "Your way."

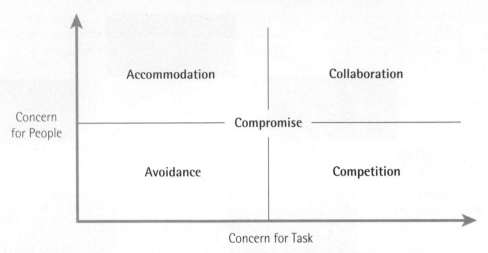

FIGURE 6.5   Orientations to Conflict   *Source:* Based on Kilmann and Thomas (1975).

4. *Avoidance.* This style is marked by showing little concern for either the task or the people. This lose-lose orientation puts work and relationships at risk and can be summed up as "No way."

5. *Compromise.* The person with this style realizes the need to give up one of his or her goals in order to meet the goals of someone else. This halfway orientation, which focuses equally on the task and the people, can be described as "Some way."

Rather than categorizing an individual according to one of these styles of managing conflict, it is more accurate to think of how each person uses a variety of styles, depending on the situation. Certainly, each of us has a leading or primary style as well as a style we use infrequently. Which style we align with in a given situation depends on the task, our experience, and the people with whom we are working.

In addition, we can be more effective in managing conflict if we understand when each style is most appropriate. At times, one style or another should surface in a team, for instance, in order to resolve questions or move in a certain direction (Brenton, 2000; Kilmann & Thomas, 1975; Lulofs & Cahn, 2000). Here are some basic guidelines:

1. The *competition* style works well when a quick decision is needed, when an emergency arises, or when an unpopular issue must be decided.

2. The *collaboration* style works well when commitment has been obtained from all parties, when maintaining the relationship is important, or when time is not a constraint.

3. The *compromise* style works well when accomplishing the goal is not as important as maintaining the relationship, when the opposing parties have extremely different positions, or when collaboration or competition does not work and a fallback position becomes necessary.

4. The *accommodation* style works well when preserving harmony is more important than achieving the goal, when working in a culture that expects this style (for instance, some Asian cultures), or when you are wrong.

5. The *avoidance* style works well when people need to cool down and gain perspective or when more information is required.

In order to enhance your own communication skills development, complete the assessment in Skills at Work 6.1 and determine which style of conflict management seems most characteristic of you. Perhaps ask friends to give you an honest evaluation, as well, based on the definition of each style.

Communication Skills for Handling Criticism

All members of organizations receive and provide feedback, both positive and negative. Supervisors expect to evaluate their employees, employees expect to develop personal goals and be evaluated against them, and executives expect to receive criticism from their board of directors and clients. Given this ongoing exchange of feedback, how can we ensure that the information we provide is constructive criticism?

SKILLS AT WORK 6.1
Conflict Style Assessment

What is your preferred or natural style for managing conflict? To find out, respond to each of the following statements with one of these responses:

> 5 = Strongly agree   4 = Agree
> 3 = Neither agree nor disagree
> 2 = Disagree   1 = Strongly disagree

Write the appropriate answer on the line preceding each statement below. After you've finished, total your answers following the directions provided.

_____ **1.** I try to integrate everyone's concerns in solving a conflict.

_____ **2.** I try to win and get approval for my position in solving a conflict.

_____ **3.** In conflict situations, I try to find the middle ground and reach a compromise solution.

_____ **4.** I work hard in conflicts to soothe other people's feelings and reduce tensions.

_____ **5.** I try to avoid creating unpleasantness for myself in managing conflict.

_____ **6.** Merging the insights of people with different perspectives is something I work toward in resolving a conflict.

_____ **7.** When I know I am right, I press my point very hard in resolving a conflict.

_____ **8.** I usually propose a middle position in a conflict to help the group move forward.

_____ **9.** In resolving a conflict, I am more concerned with how people feel than with solving the problem.

_____ **10.** I do what is necessary to avoid tension in conflict situations.

Rather than produce a total score, add the numbers to produce a score for each of the five styles:

Collaboration style (add items 1 and 6) _____

Competition style (add items 2 and 7) _____

Compromise style (add items 3 and 8) _____

Accommodation style (add items 4 and 9)

_____

Avoidance style (add items 5 and 10) _____

The style for which you have the highest score can be considered your preferred style in many situations, and that for which you have the lowest score can be considered the style you like least or are least comfortable using. Are you surprised by the results of this assessment? Why or why not?

Some people view criticism negatively. Thus, many employees are afraid to receive criticism, and many supervisors are reluctant to provide it. However, researchers in communication have discovered that it is possible to put a positive spin on criticism. This can occur when we learn how best to give and receive criticism and how to stay in control emotionally during the criticism process.

GIVING CRITICISM   Obviously, handing down a raw critical evaluation can be destructive. So how can we improve this vital task? In her extensive work in education, training, and consulting, communication scholar Brenton (2000) has identified some useful guidelines for giving criticism:

1. Ensure that the setting in which the criticism will be delivered is nonthreatening and that the timing is appropriate. The conversation should be private. (Never reprimand or criticize someone in a situation in which others might hear.)
2. Get to the point and describe the person's actual behavior. In doing so, provide objective data, not hearsay or private interpretations that lack objectivity. Also, avoid attributing motives to the other person (see Chapter 3 on making attributions).
3. Make sure the change you are requesting is something with which the person can comply. For example, don't raise an individual performance issue that is rooted in an office or system policy and is thus beyond the individual's control.
4. Work out a plan for change, stating the desired outcomes and when each should be accomplished. Make sure reasonable assessments apply reasonably to the outcomes expected.

RECEIVING CRITICISM   Some helpful ideas for receiving criticism also apply in situations involving organizational conflict (Larson, 2009):

1. Ask for a description or example of the behavior in question. Avoid becoming defensive, even if the person criticizing you communicates using negative emotions.
2. Listen to the criticism as delivered to you, and then paraphrase it back to the person who delivered it. Make sure you both agree on what is said.
3. Admit when you are wrong and acknowledge that conflict is important.
4. Ask how you can improve, be open, and support others in the conflict.

Imagine the additional aspects of handling criticism that might be involved in a family business—and the good advice that might come from people in such businesses. That's the topic of Case 6.2.

COMMUNICATION SKILLS FOR MAINTAINING EMOTIONAL CONTROL   A problem many communicators experience during conflict is controlling their emotional responses. Obviously, the goal is to remain calm and composed. Having an emotional outburst or otherwise losing your composure will cloud your judgment and thus limit your effectiveness in dealing with the issue at hand. Allowing the situation to become emotional can also derail successful communication and thus block completion of the conflict resolution process.

Follow these principles to maintain emotional control during conflict (Galvin, Bylund, & Brommel, 2008; Hocker & Wilmot, 2001):

1. Accept that conflict is normal. In fact, conflict can provide the opportunity for growth and change, which could be to everyone's benefit.
2. Clarify by listening actively. Then repeat back, or paraphrase, what you understand the other person has said.

Case 6.2

Running a Family Business

Susan and Peter Glaser, who own the consulting firm Glaser & Associates, in Eugene, Oregon, have realized the challenges of open communication in running a family business. As is the case in most families, members develop strong emotional responses to each other and pick up easily on even subtle nonverbal behaviors, such as a particular glance or tone of voice. Mixed messages are also common among family members. The Glasers tell of a father who wondered why his son didn't want to take over the family business and a son who heard his father tell him, "You can't do anything right."

The Glasers offer two pieces of advice, which are relevant to people in all business situations, not just family businesses: (1) respond to criticism without getting defensive, and (2) learn how to raise sensitive issues without making others defensive. Can you think of any other useful suggestions?

Source: Based on Reeves (2000).

3. Ask for more information when you need it—for example, "I'm not sure I understand this. How did you arrive at this conclusion? Tell me more."
4. Show that you understand the situation and, when necessary, that you accept the other person's emotions—for example, "This affects our whole group, and I, too, would not want this to happen. I understand how you must feel about it."
5. Ask for suggestions about how to solve the problem collaboratively. Keep the conversation moving forward and focus on a solution.

Before moving ahead with the discussion of managing negotiation, apply what you've learned about managing conflict to the scenario depicted in Case 6.3 on the next page.

The conflict management process is enhanced when people seek to understand and cooperate rather than compete or avoid.

Case 6.3

Supportive and Defensive Climates

Here's the situation: Pat, a technician, has been called in for a meeting with Chris, the new departmental manager. Pat arrives for the scheduled meeting at 2:00 PM and then waits for Chris to complete a prior meeting before finally being ready for Pat at 2:20 PM.

CHRIS (THE MANAGER): I'm pleased to meet you, Pat. Please call me Chris. I'm trying to meet each staff member and get acquainted so we can establish an effective working relationship from the beginning.

PAT (THE TECHNICIAN): I'm certainly glad to see you taking such a personal approach to the job, Chris.

CHRIS: Well, I've been told that this department has been run pretty loosely in the past, so it seems a lot of discipline will be needed to get things back on track.

PAT: Who told you *that?*

CHRIS: It's pretty common knowledge among management.

PAT: I see. Well, most of us who work in this department are like a family, and we're proud of the work we do.

CHRIS: We are a *lab*, Pat, not a *family*. At any rate, I'm certain you'll work with me in making improvements.

PAT: Certainly. We *all* want to work with you.

CHRIS: Fine. First, we want to establish a climate of discipline and respect, so I'm establishing a dress code for all our employees. From now on, we will not allow jeans or shorts. Men must wear ties. Women must wear nylons when they wear dresses, and when they wear pants, they must be tailored pants.

PAT: Is all that necessary for the laboratory? We all do our work, and we don't have that much contact with patients. Why does it matter what we wear?

CHRIS: You know, Pat, that's the kind of thinking that has given this department such a bad reputation. I'm sure the staff won't want to cross me over this issue.

PAT: No one wants to be uncooperative, Chris. But you might get further by making requests and explaining the reasons behind them instead of just giving orders.

Based on what you've learned about managing conflict, what do you think of each person's behavior in this scenario? What did each person do well? What did each person do not so well? In particular, look for behaviors that indicate defensiveness and closing down communication.

Source: Based on Brenton (2000).

COMMUNICATION SKILLS IN MANAGING NEGOTIATION

Defining Negotiation

Negotiation means moving two parties from opposite positions to a common position over some resource that is desired by both. The practice of negotiation can apply to a wide range of transactions—from a billion-dollar corporate buyout to buying a car. The basic principles in any successful negotiation remain the same.

Approaches to Negotiation

Communication researchers and legal experts have identified a variety of theories and **approaches to negotiation**. In the following sections, we will discuss the principled negotiation model of Fisher and Ury (1981), Lowry's (2000) concept of positional conflict management, and Moran, Harris, and Moran's (2007) successful negotiator qualities.

PRINCIPLED NEGOTIATION   Fisher and Ury's (1981) frequently applied model of *principled negotiation* identifies four key elements that are involved in any negotiation: people, interests, options, and criteria. By examining each element individually, we can understand both the process and the outcome of negotiation:

1. *People.* Separate the people from the issue. Attempt to find common ground by working with your opponent on the problem, not by attacking him or her. In terms of dialogue, consider the message sent by each of the following examples:

EXAMPLES

> *Bad:* "You always get us off track. I can't trust you with anything."
>
> *Better:* "Our group may be straying a bit, and so we may be repeating our efforts."

---

2. *Interests.* Focus on you and your opponent's shared interests, not your separate positions. Avoid stating an initial position and sticking with it, no matter what.

The common thread that runs among the various approaches to negotiation is the need to find common ground—some topic or area of interest on which the two parties can agree.

EXAMPLES

> *Bad:* "This is my bottom line and I'm not changing it, so don't expect anything."
>
> *Better:* "I was hoping we could . . ." or "What would you like to see happen?"

3. **Options.** Come to the negotiation with a variety of options. Doing so will not only ensure that a good decision will be reached, but it will also present you as being open and reasonable.

EXAMPLES

> *Bad:* "Okay, we know enough about this. Let's just get it done."
>
> *Better:* "Let's consider all the possibilities before moving ahead."

4. **Criteria.** Good decision making follows from practices and standards that both parties have already accepted. By laying the groundwork and then honoring what has been established, you will demonstrate fairness and equity.

EXAMPLES

> *Bad:* "I don't care about what was decided last time. This is what we want now."
>
> *Better:* "This solution doesn't meet the criteria we agreed on earlier" or "Based on the national insurance codes, we can . . ."

POSITIONAL CONFLICT MANAGEMENT   Randy Lowry (2000), director of the Pepperdine Law School Strauss Institute for Dispute Resolution, argues that *positional conflict management* offers a unique approach to negotiation. Namely, not only are the opposing parties' positions considered; their interests, as well as the issue itself, are also considered in an attempt to find common ground. This approach has four elements (see Figure 6.6):

1. **Issue.** First, the presenting issue is articulated. The opposing parties have several options when they become aware of the conflict: to ignore it, to resolve it, to allow it to escalate, or

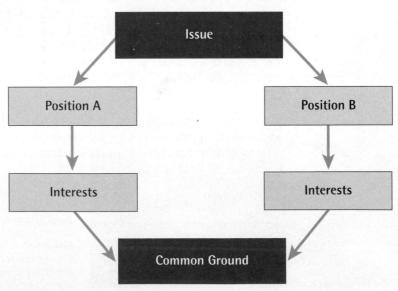

FIGURE 6.6 Positional Conflict Management   *Source:* Based on Lowry (2000).

to turn it over for mediation or arbitration. (See the section later in this chapter called "Alternative Dispute Resolutions.")

2. **Positions.** Each party articulates his or her position in the dispute. This is an advocated structuring of the message.

3. **Interests.** Underneath each party's stated position is that party's interest in the issue, which Lowry (2000) defined as "something that needs to be satisfied in order to complete a negotiation." Interests are not usually stated and may even be abstract. However, their significance in resolving a conflict lies at the foundation of Lowry's model.

4. **Common ground.** Once the opposing interests have been uncovered and accredited, the negotiation process can seek a solution by establishing common ground.

Lowry suggests that once a negotiation goes below the surface of the opposing parties' stated positions and uncovers their interests, then a serious search for common ground can occur. That common ground is what Lowry calls the *zone of agreement*, which starts with examining reasonable, credible offers. The key word here is *reasonable*, which means these offers are not insulting to either side but represent middle-of-the-road agreements.

For example, suppose a car dealer is asking $30,000 for a vehicle. After researching the features of the car and ascertaining the dealer's cost plus a reasonable profit, you decide on what you feel is a reasonable offer: $25,000. Given the $5,000 difference between your own and the dealer's opening offers, you would both negotiate by coming toward the middle, perhaps agreeing on $27,500 for the car. For you to offer $20,000 at the start would likely have been considered insulting in U.S. culture, and so the dealer may not have been willing to negotiate with you.

Skills at Work 6.2 on the next page asks you to participate in a group decision-making activity that may mean survival for you and your classmates. As explained in the box, you may be stranded on the moon and must work with your fellow astronauts to determine the importance of fifteen items in supporting your survival. Put your negotiating skills to the test by trying to rank the items in an order that everyone can agree to at least somewhat.

SUCCESSFUL NEGOTIATOR QUALITIES   Moran, Harris, and Moran (2007) identified qualities that make some negotiators successful and others only average in terms of their ability to resolve a conflict and come to an agreement. While their work stems primarily from an intercultural management perspective, their findings pertain to many business and professional situations. Compare these lists of negotiator qualities:

Successful Negotiators	Average Negotiators
Presented more options	Presented fewer options
Identified three times as much common ground	Paid less attention to common ground
Made more comments about long-term factors	Paid less attention to long-term factors
Covered more range in terms of upper and lower limits	Worked from a fixed point, making little use of range
Did not present issues as necessarily sequential or linked	Presented issues as sequential or linked
Made few immediate counterproposals	Made counterproposals quickly
Identified a few solid reasons to support	Identified many reasons to support

SKILLS AT WORK 6.2
Space Survival Exercise

PART 1: INDIVIDUAL ACTIVITY

You are a member of a space crew that was originally scheduled to rendezvous with a mother ship on the lighted surface of the moon. Due to mechanical difficulties, your ship was forced to land at a spot some two hundred miles from the rendezvous point. During the landing, much of the equipment aboard your ship was damaged. And since your survival will depend on being able to reach the mother ship, you must identify the most critical equipment for making the two-hundred-mile trip.

The 15 items listed below are all that was left intact and undamaged after the landing. Your task is to rank them in terms of their importance to helping your crew reach the rendezvous point. Place the number 1 by what you feel is the most important item, the number 2 by the second most important item, and so on through number 15. Give this ranking serious thought, as you will likely have to defend your choices later!

PART 2: GROUP ACTIVITY

Join the members of your group, your individual rankings in hand, to reach agreement in ranking the 15 items. Either vote on the items or reach a group consensus. Certainly, not every ranking will meet with everyone's complete approval. Try, as a group, to make each ranking one with which all group members can at least partially agree. Take only ten minutes to complete this activity.

How well did your group do in reaching a consensus about each item? How did your initial list of rankings compare with the final list agreed on by your group? Which items generated the most discussion or were the most difficult for group members to agree on? Which items were easiest to agree on? What did you learn about negotiation in completing this activity?

DECISION-MAKING WORKSHEET

Individual Rankings	Group Rankings	Items
_____	_____	Box of matches
_____	_____	Food concentrate
_____	_____	50 feet of nylon rope
_____	_____	Parachute silk
_____	_____	Portable heating unit
_____	_____	Two .45 caliber pistols
_____	_____	One case dehydrated Pet Milk
_____	_____	Two 100-pound tanks of oxygen
_____	_____	Stellar map (of the moon's constellation)
_____	_____	Life raft
_____	_____	Magnetic compass
_____	_____	5 gallons of water
_____	_____	Signal flares
_____	_____	First aid kit containing injection needs
_____	_____	Solar-powered FM receiver/transmitter

Source: Based on an exercise from the National Aeronautics and Space Administration (NASA).

The implication for future managers is to identify and then apply those communication skills that have been proven useful in a negotiation context. The more you express commonality, collaboration, and firm evidence, the more likely you will be successful in negotiating.

ALTERNATIVE DISPUTE RESOLUTIONS The negotiation process can take many forms in working toward the goal of resolving a dispute. Depending on the culture of the organization, including its level of formality in terms of procedures and channels of communication, any of the following approaches might be used:

- *Open-door policy.* Management has an "open door" in terms of welcoming employee discussion and suggestions. This approach is effective with small, informal organizations but not large, formal ones. It expects a lot of employees but little of management.
- *Peer review.* Complaints are heard by a panel of employees and supervisors, who then issue some sort of decision. A review is usually initiated after an employee has an unsuccessful discussion with a supervisor.
- *Ombudsman.* An independent office is established within the organization for the purpose of investigating and resolving problems. This approach is used by perhaps five hundred to a thousand U.S. organizations, most of which have five hundred or more members.
- *Union management model.* This is the most well-established and familiar approach to negotiation. Both parties (typically, labor and management) forgo short-term advantages to obtain long-term stability and thus less loss (for instance, no labor strikes or management lockouts).
- *Employer-run dispute resolution procedures.* Organizations that are not union "shops" use this approach as a precursor to litigation. That is, any employee with a dispute must follow these procedures before taking the dispute to the courts.
- *Mediation.* A neutral party serves as an impartial channel for communication and judgment in reaching a voluntary compromised agreement. The neutral party may come from within or outside the organization.
- *Mediation/arbitration.* As an extension of mediation, a third party, or *arbiter*, is brought in to help reach a settlement. He or she can give advice as to what an arbitrated decision would be and ask for an agreement.
- *Arbitration.* A third party is brought in exclusively to decide a matter. He or she acts as an impartial decision maker and has binding authority in handing down a resolution.
- *Fact finding.* A third party hears both sides' positions, studies the dispute, and then issues a decision that is not binding on either side. Sometimes called *advisory arbitration*, the goal is to get the opposing parties to reach a mutual decision themselves.

Before moving ahead, take a moment to consider a real-world case involving a family's donation of land to a local university. What elements of successful conflict management and negotiation can you identify in Case 6.4 on the next page?

Understanding Negotiation Styles

As you have probably realized from reading the cases and other examples presented in this chapter, people have individual styles of managing conflict and negotiation. Moran, Harris, and Moran (2007) identified four **negotiation styles**: intuitive, normative, analytical, and factual.

INTUITIVE STYLE   The key characteristic of the intuitive style is creativity—namely, "Imagination can solve any problem." The communication behaviors associated with this style include making relational statements, affirming others, using polychronic order, deriving conclusions quickly, and sometimes getting the facts a bit wrong.

NORMATIVE STYLE   The normative style implies a view that everything can be bargained for, or as Moran, Harris, and Moran state, "Negotiating is bargaining." Communication behaviors include developing messages that evaluate facts from a set of personal values, approving and disapproving language, offering bargains, proposing rewards and incentives, using language appealing to feelings and emotions to reach a "fair" deal, and recognizing and responding to how others are reacting.

Case 6.4

The Jones Family Land Case

The Jones family* wanted to give a parcel of land to the local university. Although others had already donated thousands of acres of farm- and ranch land to this particular school for a variety of building and development projects, the Jones family wanted to ensure that their twenty-five acres would be preserved, allowing only recreational use. They did not use the term *nature preserve* in describing this intention, but they did reason that urban development unnecessarily disregarded land preservation. Furthermore, the Jones family wanted to respect the university and its needs with this donation while also honoring the long-time family patriarch, Abijah Jones.

The university accepted the twenty-five acres with the family's perceived understanding that the land would be kept in some natural state or developed minimally for recreational purposes. A conflict soon arose, however, when the new chief financial officer (CFO) in the university administration saw a need for more student housing and proposed to use the Jones's land. The CFO reasoned that the family's intent was far less restrictive than previous administrators had perceived and that the university could legitimately use the land for his proposed purpose.

When this proposal became known to the Jones family, they were outraged. The new CFO's interpretation of their agreement with the university was clearly not what they had intended. A dispute quickly developed, and plans for any use of the land were stalled for ten years. The conflict was intense, and repeated attempts at negotiation were unsuccessful. On several occasions, the family refused even to talk with the university.

Finally, a breakthrough occurred when a new mediator was brought in. He listened more intently than previous mediators had listened and realized that the Jones family's primary interests were to have their name live on and to have their view against urban development acknowledged. With these significant insights, the new mediator immediately went to work on a plan.

The new proposal began with language not about the need to erect buildings but the need to elevate lasting values. The proposal prominently paid tribute to the Jones family, who honored such values and whose name should be remembered. The new plan sought to develop the land for a youth program building, a recreational site for hiking, a small golf course, and housing for young married couples and families. The landscape design featured nature trails, protected animal habitats, and environmentally friendly recreational sites. Moreover, it would incorporate badly needed buildings to house people who would enjoy these natural benefits. The people using these facilities would appreciate the Jones family's traditions, it was argued. Following this line of reasoning, the proposal asked, "How could we honor the Jones family's land and their values while incorporating people and buildings on the property, yet maintaining it as nature preserve?" Finally, Abijah Jones's name was to be featured in naming the new buildings.

The proposal worked—but why? What did the new mediator discover that seems to have brought the Jones family back to the negotiating table? What skills did the mediator have that ultimately brought about success in negotiating this proposal?

ANALYTICAL STYLE   The fundamental notion behind the analytical style is that "logic leads to the right conclusions." That is, communication behaviors correspond to linear reasoning and argumentation, analyzing situations for cause and effect, identifying the part and the whole, organizing, and weighing the advantages and disadvantages.

FACTUAL STYLE   The factual style can be summed up by the axiom "The facts speak for themselves." Communication behaviors include pointing out facts in a neutral way, keeping track of what has been said, indicating the complete details of a proposal, exhibiting low-key reactions, and expecting a lot of proof and documentation.

Which of these negotiation styles best fits you? To find out, complete the assessment in Skills at Work 6.3. Keep in mind that your responses should reflect your normal behavior in day-to-day interactions.

SKILLS AT WORK 6.3
Negotiation-Style Assessment

For each statement below, provide the most appropriate answer from these choices:

> 1 = Never or rarely   2 = Occasionally (less than most people)
> 3 = Sometimes (like most people)
> 4 = Frequently (more than most people)   5 = Very frequently (much more than most people)

Write your answers on the Score Sheet provided on the next page. (Note that the numbering of items goes across the page, not down.) Base your responses to these items on what you believe you do when interacting with others in typical day-to-day activities. Also be as frank as you can.

1. I focus on the entire situation or problem.
2. I evaluate the facts according to a set of personal values.
3. I am relatively unemotional.
4. I think that the facts speak for themselves in most situations.
5. I work in bursts of energy with slack periods in between.
6. I focus on what is going on between people when interacting.
7. I tend to analyze things very carefully.
8. I am pragmatic.
9. I derive a conclusion very quickly
10. I look for common ground and compromise.
11. I use logic to solve problems.
12. I know most of the details when discussing an issue.
13. I follow my inspiration of the moment.

14. I am sensitive to other people's needs and feelings.
15. I am good at using a step-by-step approach.
16. I document my statements.
17. I project myself into the future.
18. I try to please people.
19. I am very systematic when making a point.
20. I like to use the inductive method (from facts to theories).
21. When others become uncertain or discouraged, my enthusiasm carries them along.
22. I let my decisions be influenced by my personal likes and wishes.
23. I look for cause and effect.
24. I do not trust inspiration.
25. I often switch from one idea to another.
26. I offer bargains.
27. I weigh the pros and cons.
28. I am perceived as a down-to-earth person.

SCORE SHEET

Enter the response that you chose for each statement (1, 2, 3, 4, or 5) in the space provided. Again, note that the numbering progresses across the page from left to right. After you have responded to all of the statements, add up the scores vertically to attain four totals. Enter each total in the blank indicated. (Insert a 3 in any number space left blank.)

(Continued)

SKILLS AT WORK 6.3 *(Continued)*
Negotiation-Style Assessment

1. _____	2. _____	3. _____	4. _____
5. _____	6. _____	7. _____	8. _____
9. _____	10. _____	11. _____	12. _____
13. _____	14. _____	15. _____	16. _____
17. _____	18. _____	19. _____	20. _____
21. _____	22. _____	23. _____	24. _____
25. _____	26. _____	27. _____	28. _____
_____	_____	_____	_____
Intuitive Total	*Normative Total*	*Analytical Total*	*Factual Total*

NEGOTIATION-STYLE PROFILE

Take your four total scores from the Score Sheet and plot them on the table below, aligning each score with the appropriate style type. Then connect the four points to form your profile.

	Low Use	**Moderate Use**	**High Use**
Intuitive			
Normative			
Analytical			
Factual			

0 2 4 6 8 10 12 14 16 18 20 22 24 26 28 30 32 34

Review the graph you created to determine which style you use the most and the least. What seems to be your preferred or dominant negotiation style? Does this seem reasonable to you? Why or why not?

Source: This 28-item scale (which has an alpha reliability of 0.71) is based on an 80-item version in Moran, Harris, and Moran (2007-Teacher Manual). That 80-item version was based on the original Interactive Style Questionnaire in *Training for the Cross-Cultural Mind* (Washington, DC: SIETAR, 1979).

GUIDELINES FOR NEGOTIATING WITH PEOPLE WHO HAVE DIFFERENT STYLES   It may already be obvious to you that in order to be a successful negotiator, you must adapt your style to that of your opponent. That is, if he or she has an intuitive style, you must tailor your approach to deal with that style. Consider the following guidelines for doing so:

To negotiate with someone who has an intuitive style:

- Focus on the situation as a whole.
- Look for opportunities by thinking ahead to the future.
- Tap the imagination and creativity of your partner.
- Move quickly, even if you appear to be jumping from one idea to another.

To negotiate with someone who has a normative style:

- Establish a sound relationship at the start of the negotiation.
- Listen carefully and use feedback with purpose.

- Identify your opponent's values and adjust to them accordingly.
- Be ready to compromise to reach a fair solution.

To negotiate with someone who has an analytical style:

- Look for logic, especially causes and effects.
- Analyze the parts of the complete problem or situation.
- Be patient.
- Analyze options based on their advantages and disadvantages.

To negotiate with someone who has a factual style:

- Be precise in presenting your facts.
- Look to the past to review what has already been tried and learned.
- Know your proposal well, including all its details.
- Document what you say.

Before closing this chapter, put your knowledge to the test by working on another case study. Case 6.5 presents another real-world scenario, this one involving a dispute between two managers of different departments in a hospital. In reading this case, note that in addition to a section of background information on the issue, each manager's perspective is also described in a separate section. Finally, see the series of questions at the end of the case.

Case 6.5

Conflict at City Hospital

Background

The CEO at City Hospital has a difficult conflict that has been simmering and recently boiled over. Dr. Smith, the hospital's medical director, and Ms. Jones, the director of nursing in the emergency department, are at war. In recent weeks, each has come to the CEO independently with an ultimatum that he or she will quit if the other individual isn't fired. He is wanting negotiation to work. So, what would you do?

Personnel problems are diminishing the effectiveness of the emergency department which now has 75 percent turnover, a 40 percent absenteeism rate, a huge number of employee grievances, and two malpractice suits filed in the past year.

The CEO has ensured that you will have complete access to everyone in the emergency department and to other resources that will provide the information you need. The CEO has encouraged you to mediate a resolution between the two managers, if possible, or to make a recommendation on the matter if resolution is not possible.

Perspective of the Medical Directors

Dr. Smith was brought in two years ago to take over a troubled department and was given the mandate to make the changes necessary to help the department get accredited within one year. The department made it through the accreditation review but just barely.

When you sat down with Dr. Smith, she told you that she took the job with the clear understanding from the CEO that she would be completely in charge of the department and could make any changes she felt were necessary. Yet according to Smith, the nursing staff opposed almost every change she has tried to make.

(Continued)

Case 6.5 *(Continued)*

For example, she tried to change the assignment patterns of emergency room personnel. Previously, nurses were assigned to individual patients, but Smith felt it would be efficient to have nurses responsible for certain areas. The staff objected, refusing to cover assigned areas. The staff also opposed Smith's plan to ensure that security was available to emergency room personnel. Finally, they refused to use new charting methods typical of other hospitals.

Dr. Smith told you that the nurses at City Hospital are spoiled and lazy, compared to those she has worked with elsewhere, and that they have been allowed to get by with mediocre standards. A large part of the problem, in Smith's view, is the director of nursing, Ms. Jones. Smith feels that Jones generates unrest among the nursing staff and works against her efforts to initiate changes. The situation is complicated by the fact that Jones reports directly to the director of nursing for the hospital, rather than to Smith.

In sum, Smith feels strongly that she is trying to do the job she was hired to do: improve the quality of the department. She is tired of fighting direct and indirect opposition from Jones and her nurses, and she wants Jones fired.

Dr. Smith is a woman in her late forties. She has never married and currently lives with her elderly mother, for whom she is the primary caretaker. Smith has an excellent reputation in the field of emergency medicine and has published widely. She has been the medical director of two other emergency departments at other major hospitals. This conflict is taking its toll on her, however. She reports that she is unable to sleep and has experienced symptoms of depression during her brief tenure at City Hospital.

Perspective of the Director of Nursing of the Emergency Department

Ms. Jones has been director of nursing in the emergency room at City Hospital for eight years. During that time, she has worked under three different medical directors. Her favorite was Dr. Larkin, who was Dr. Smith's immediate predecessor. Larkin was a warm and caring man who granted autonomy to and fostered loyalty among the staff.

When you spoke with Jones, she told you that Smith showed no respect for the nursing staff. When you asked for examples of Smith's lack of respect, Jones came up with several cases of changes that had been implemented without any involvement of the staff. Jones admitted that some of Smith's ideas were good, but she criticized Smith for making decisions completely on her own. For instance, Smith had announced major changes in policies and practices without even conferring with Jones. Moreover, Smith reportedly became defensive when asked questions about the changes.

Jones continued with more examples: Smith had decided on methods of improving operations without ever asking the staff for their ideas. And when the staff did offer ideas for changes they saw as critical, such as improving outdated equipment, Smith ignored them. The new patient charts Smith had proposed included no space for nurses' comments (which any nurse could have told Smith was a problem, "if she had ever asked!"). And the new method of assigning nurses to areas rather than patients jeopardized the continuity of care and assigned staff to areas for which they were not suitably trained.

According to Jones, the nurses' respect for Dr. Smith had been further undermined by their interaction with her in the emergency room, where she worked as attending physician two days a week. Most of the nurses felt Smith's skills were poor—both her medical expertise and her interpersonal skills with patients and coworkers. In fact, Smith often raised her voice and cursed

Case 6.5   *(Continued)*

at the nursing staff, which had made it increasingly difficult to get staff to work during her shifts. Jones also cited two occasions when Smith had made serious medical mistakes and noted that the hospital was lucky not to have been sued. Jones said she personally had lost respect for Smith after seeing her alter a patient's record, which was a clear lapse of ethical and legal standards.

Jones confirmed Smith's statement that she reported to the hospital's director of nursing, not to Smith. The hospital had intentionally developed this reporting structure in order to ensure the autonomy of effective nursing practice. Jones said that the incident involving the altered patient's record validated the wisdom of such an arrangement. She had gone to the CEO of the hospital only recently to confirm that she was not required to report directly to Smith, and she had been assured that that was still the case—that nothing had changed. Jones felt that Smith was threatened by her autonomy.

Ms. Jones is in her early fifties and has been a nurse for thirty years. She has been married for twenty-eight years to the same man—a doctor at a local dermatology clinic—and together they have raised three children, all of whom are now living on their own. She has an active social life outside the hospital, enjoying activities with her family and friends. While she loves her job, she has considered quitting. She has stayed primarily because of the loyalty she feels for her nursing staff and the patients in the emergency room. She feels that she is the only buffer protecting these individuals from the autocratic rule of Dr. Smith.

Questions for Analyzing This Conflict

1. What are the main issues in this conflict?
2. Categorize the issues according to the main conflict types:
   Disagreements:
   Misplaced conflicts:
   Nonsubstantive conflicts:
   Substantive conflicts:
3. What role do power and control play in this conflict? Explain using examples.
4. Is this a person-based conflict or a system-based conflict? Why?
5. Can these two individuals solve the conflict on their own? Why or why not?
6. As the mediator hired to resolve this conflict, what would you do? Outline a plan from start to finish.
7. What could have been done at an earlier stage to have prevented this conflict from becoming so serious?

Source: Based on Brenton (2000).

In Perspective

Conflict occurs when two or more people clash over an issue about which they have different beliefs or values. Causes of conflict include different goals or methods for achieving those goals, scarcity of resources, relationship differences, unequal distribution of power, unclear role expectations, lack of information, value differences, and need to save face. There are four types or categories of conflict: disagreements, misplaced conflicts, nonsubstantive conflicts, and substantive conflicts.

Organizational conflict occurs when policies, decisions, or directional shifts create resistance between individuals who feel others are blocking their efforts or those of their group. The occurrence of conflict is inevitable, and it can develop to the extent of creating dysfunctional behavior in an organization. Four theories explain the development of conflict in the workplace: phase theory, conflict avoidance cycle theory, chilling effect theory, and escalation theory.

There are five basic approaches or styles for managing conflict, each of which is some combination of a concern for task and a concern for people: competition, collaboration, accommodation, avoidance, and compromise. Rather than categorizing an individual according to one style, it is more accurate to think of how each person uses a variety of styles, depending on the situation. We can be more effective in managing conflict if we understand when each style is most appropriate. Similarly, we can learn how to handle criticism by understanding how best to give and receive it and how to maintain emotional control.

Negotiation involves moving two parties with opposite positions to a common position for attaining some desired resource. The model of principled negotiation identifies four key elements that are involved in any negotiation: people, interests, options, and criteria. In applying the positional conflict management approach, not only the opposing parties' positions but also their interests, as well as the issue itself, are considered in an attempt to find common ground.

Finally, research has identified qualities that make some negotiators successful and others only average. The study of communication patterns has identified four styles of negotiation: intuitive, normative, factual, and analytical. In order to be a successful negotiator, you must adapt your style to that of your opponent.

Discussion Questions

1. Why does conflict occur? Given your own experience, which causes of conflict seem most relevant? Provide examples to support your answer.
2. What are the basic types of conflict? Which of these types have you experienced? Again, provide examples.
3. Of the models of conflict discussed, which do you think best describes the course that conflict seems to follow? Why?

4. What elements seem essential to successful negotiation? If you were a professional negotiator, what basic plan would you follow in approaching a conflict? How would this fit your preferred negotiation style?
5. How can you identify another person's negotiation style through talking with him or her? What can you do to adapt to his or her style—or should you adapt to that person's style? Why or why not?

Exercises

1. Visit the supervisor or manager of some organization or a department within an organization. Ask him or her to identify the most common reasons for conflict in the workplace. What makes the list?
2. Share your list from Exercise 1 with the lists of your classmates. How are they similar and different? How do they match the information about types of conflict presented in the chapter?
3. Assess your own conflict communication style and then the styles of one or two friends. What styles do you have? Do these findings agree with your perceptions of each other? If so, discuss what the assessment confirmed about each of your communication skills. If not, what did the assessment seem to miss?
4. Develop several role-playing scenarios in which you and one or more classmates portray negotiators at work: some successful negotiators and some not so successful. Use the cases and other examples in this chapter to help you create conflict situations for these negotiators to work on.
5. What is your preferred negotiation style? What are the negotiation styles of one or two classmates? Discuss among yourselves whether you agree with these assessments and why. Specifically, what does the assessment say about each individual?

References

Brenton, A. L. (2000). Conflict management for Christian leaders. Seminar presented at the Abilene Christian University Conference on Conflict, Dallas, TX.

Cloke, K., & Goldsmith, J. (2000). *Resolving conflicts at work.* San Francisco: Jossey-Bass.

Fisher, R., & Ury, W. (1981). *Getting to yes.* New York: Houghton Mifflin.

Galvin, K. M., Bylund, C. L., & Brommel, B. J. (2008). *Family communication.* 7th ed. Boston: Allyn & Bacon.

George, J. M., & Jones, G. R. (1999). *Organizational behavior.* 2nd ed. Boston: Addison-Wesley.

Hocker, J., & Wilmot, W. (2001). *Interpersonal conflict.* 6th ed. New York: McGraw-Hill.

Kilmann, R., & Thomas, K. (1975). Interpersonal conflict handling behavior as reflections of Jungian personality dimensions. *Psychological Reports, 37,* 971–980.

Larson, P. (2009). Tips for resolving workplace conflict. In *workplaceculture.suite101.com/article.cfm/tips_for_resolving_workplace_conflict.*

Lipsky, D. B., Seeber, R. L., & Fincher, R. D. (2003). *Emerging systems for managing workplace conflict.* San Francisco: Jossey-Bass.

Lowry, R. (2000). Negotiating church conflict. Seminar presented at the Abilene Christian University Conference on Conflict, Dallas, TX.

Lulofs, R. S., & Cahn, D. D. (2000). *Conflict: From theory to action.* Boston: Allyn & Bacon.

McClure, L. (2000). *Anger and conflict in the workplace.* Manassas Park, VA: Impact Publications.

Moran, R. T., Harris, P. R., & Moran, S. V. (2007). *Managing cultural differences.* 7th ed. New York: Elsevier. (See also accompanying Teacher Manual for Negotiation.)

Rau-Foster, M. (2000). Conflict in the workplace. In *worplaceissues.com/arconflict.htm.*

Reeves, F. (2000). Open communication is the key to family business. *Abilene Reporter News,* March 31, p. 4-c.

Scheske, J. J. (2000). The law and church based conflict resolution: Will it be guns or knives or will it be wine and roses? Seminar presented at the Abilene Christian University Conference on Conflict, Dallas, TX.

Siburt, C. (2000). How conflict progresses. Seminar presented at the Abilene Christian University Conference on Conflict, May, Dallas, TX.

CHAPTER 7

Managing Intercultural Communication in the Workplace

KEY TERMS

cultural diversity *(p. 128)*
culture *(p. 128)*
intercultural communication
    (p. 129)
ethnocentrism *(p. 131)*
prejudice *(p. 131)*
stereotyping *(p. 132)*
in-groups and out-groups *(p. 132)*
gender issues *(p. 135)*
strategies for intercultural
    communication *(p. 138)*
low-context and high-context
    cultures *(p. 138)*
task-oriented and people-oriented
    cultures *(p. 139)*
culture shock *(p. 142)*
cultural adaptation *(p. 142)*

After reading this chapter, you will be able to do the following:

■ Understand the nature of cultural diversity.

■ Understand the nature of intercultural communication and its impact on communication in the workplace.

■ Identify the cultural differences that create barriers to understanding.

■ Recognize the importance of managing cultural diversity in the workplace.

■ Use intercultural communication strategies that promote unity and cultural adaptation.

Think like a wise man but communicate in the language of the people.

WILLIAM BUTLER YEATS

In the previous chapters, we examined a range of specific organizational and interpersonal reasons as to why coworkers misunderstand information and fail to develop supportive relationships. In addition, we examined a range of strategies for managing these various issues, essentially using effective interpersonal communication.

In this chapter, we will focus on the misunderstanding and conflict that occurs because of **cultural diversity**: differences in group identity, ethnic or national origin, religious belief or practice, gender or sexual preference, and economics. In addition, to ensure a mutual understanding of what is meant by the term **culture**, we will use this definition: a set of beliefs, attitudes, customs, rules, activities, and communication patterns of an identifiable group of people. While not everyone in a culture thinks or acts alike, many themes are consistent across the group. Thus, the collection of attitudes, actions, themes, and patterns that constitute a culture provide us with a holistic way to picture a certain group.

Communicating in a culturally diverse workplace necessitates understanding and working with people of many backgrounds.

When cultural differences emerge in the workplace, the response must be to manage them through improved understanding and communication. Moreover, while the principles and skills explored in earlier chapters will still be applicable, additional strategies are needed to address the cultural context of these issues.

Such strategies stem from communication-based theories that probe the unique relationship between culture and communication. By understanding this relationship, you will add to your growing repertoire of communication skills. In addition, given the increasing globalization of the world economy, along with the growing cultural diversity of the United States, it is essential that workers in the twenty-first century be competent in intercultural communication.

DEFINITION AND MODEL OF INTERCULTURAL COMMUNICATION

The specialized segment of communication studies that considers the relationship between culture and language is **intercultural communication**. The phrase *communication with strangers,* used by Gudykunst and Kim (2003), is descriptive in suggesting the issues that arise, for example, when someone feels isolated or alone in relationships at work because of perceived group differences. Unfortunately, despite many advances in U.S. communities, schools, and other organizations, perceived cultural differences continue to create misunderstanding and even conflict.

A model of intercultural communication offers insight into how perceived differences affect communication in the workplace (see Figure 7.1 on the next page). Interacting participants—say, from Cultural Group A and Cultural Group B—may or may not perceive significant group or cultural differences. However, when they do, their comfort level will drive them to reduce their uncertainty or anxiety by creating harmony with others. That need ideally leads to communication that is characterized by openness, listening, understanding, respect, and friendship. This ideal, positive result represents a *functional outcome.* By contrast, a *dysfunctional outcome* is possible as well, including instances of negative stereotyping, ethnocentrism, communication avoidance, lack of cooperation, and even hostility (Dodd, 1998).

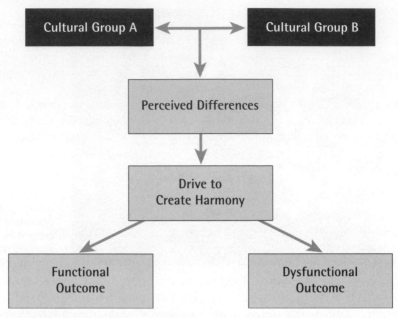

FIGURE 7.1 Model of Intercultural Communication

Such a dysfunctional outcome occurred in a work-related incident involving Samuel, a Nigerian emigrant. He experienced rejection from his coworkers in the form of communication avoidance, when they frequently left him out of the loop regarding significant work-related information. Some three months into the job, Samuel noticed that several key coworkers avoided communicating with him, among other things ignoring his requests and suggestions. In addition, he was not notified about significant meetings until the last minute. These behaviors not only alienated Samuel in terms of forming interpersonal relationships but also affected his ability to do his job.

We'll examine dysfunctional outcomes, along with strategies for dealing with them, later in this chapter. You should also consult the sources in Web at Work 7.1, which contain information about intercultural communication.

WEB AT WORK 7.1
Intercultural Communication

Some of these sites represent companies that specialize in training, while others explore ideas and practices related to cultural diversity in organizations:

- **www.jobweb.com** Search here for potential intercultural questions related to international jobs.
- **www.communicaid.com** Reveals intercultural communication insights and skills.

- **www.questia.com** Have to dig further to find cultural diversity issues.
- **www.communicationideas.com** Shows communication principles and skills across cultures.
- **www.tmaworld.com** Helpful and solid material on intercultural relationships.

UNDERSTANDING CULTURAL DIVERSITY

Again, *cultural diversity* is characterized by the presence of groups with different and sometimes opposing values and loyalties, whether due to ethnic or national origin, religious belief or practice, gender or sexual preference, economic or educational status, and so on. When people fail to understand or respect such differences, the result is dysfunction, as noted earlier.

We will look at a range of dysfunctional outcomes in this section, along with elements of cultural diversity that commonly create misunderstanding and intolerance. Understanding these elements will provide a foundation for knowing how to manage and resolve the issues related to cultural diversity.

Ethnocentrism

Ethnocentrism is a sense of egotism and selfishness about a person's own culture, whereby he or she elevates that culture to a status above all other cultures. Thus, ethnocentrism is at the root of many unkind behaviors toward people from other countries and often underlies expressions of hostility and anger.

For example, when Samuel, introduced earlier, first came to work at his current employer, a midsized company of 150 employees, he thought little about being one of only two African workers. The same was true of the company's owners and managers. Clearly, they hired Samuel because he was highly qualified and competent. They had also welcomed him, in part, because of their desire to emerge into a global marketplace. But they were perhaps naïve in their failure to anticipate possible issues of diversity. Therefore, when it became apparent that Samuel's coworkers were isolating him, management was somewhat taken aback. This was not a simple problem, they realized, but the primary cause seemed to be ethnocentrism. When subsequent discussions opened up the lines of communication, Samuel's fellow employees exhibited a sense of superiority. Their actions had served to marginalize an international employee like Samuel.

Prejudice

Prejudice occurs when people have preconceived attitudes toward the members of a particular cultural group, leading to bias, unfairness, intolerance, and even injustice. Individual beliefs, social attitudes, and organizational policies can all reflect prejudice. Examples of prejudicial organizational policies appear in these cases from recent news reports:

- Minorities are passed over for promotion at the Federal Bureau of Investigation (FBI).
- Auto manufacturer Nissan allegedly discriminates in promotion practices in its U.S. plant.
- Women are not promoted to executive positions, hitting the *glass ceiling*.
- A millennial generation employee claims a conflict with her older boss because of differing values.
- Shootings in high schools stem from intolerance to academic, athletic, and social diversity.

Prejudicial behavior does not necessarily manifest itself in overt discrimination. Rather, it can have many faces and emerge in many forms (Brislin, 1993; Dodd, 1998; see also extensive articles in Landis, Bennett, & Bennett, 2004). The following types of prejudice are listed in order from most to least overt:

1. *Intense prejudice.* At this most extreme level, prejudice comprises believing or acting in ways that designate members of certain groups as outcasts. Behaviors include devaluation,

ignoring, withdrawal, and other actions that demean others and perpetuate negative perceptions of them.

2. *Symbolic prejudice.* This form of prejudice involves devaluing others not because they are believed to be inherently inferior but because they are seen as blocking certain desired cultural goals. Many times, the targets of prejudice are not individuals themselves but rather what they represent in terms of group identity. For example, they may be seen as troublemakers or as disrupting the status quo.

3. *Tokenistic prejudice.* In this more subtle form of prejudice, people make small gestures so as to appear unprejudiced—for example, making a small donation or volunteering for a bit of charity work. In the workplace, hiring decisions that clearly target members of specific groups, such as women and racial/ethnic minorities, are sometimes attributed to tokenism.

4. *Arms-length prejudice.* This final form of prejudice characterizes those individuals whose public actions are not prejudicial but whose private actions are. For example, people who adhere to policies about cultural diversity in the workplace and yet tell racist or sexist jokes among their closest circle of friends may represent this form of prejudice.

Stereotyping

Related to ethnocentrism and prejudice is the practice of **stereotyping,** or having a set mental picture of a particular group and arbitrarily attributing the traits of that group to someone who belongs to it. Stereotypes often are based on incomplete information and limited exposure to members of groups. For that reason, they are deficient, unrefined assumptions that lead to errors in judgment and communication. (See Case 7.1 later in this chapter, which addresses some of the costs that can result from stereotyping in the workplace.)

In-Groups and Out-Groups

Research in the field of intercultural communication has demonstrated that, as individuals in social groups, we characterize our relationships in two ways: as **in-groups and out-groups**. First, we seek balance and harmony through contact with people who match our own identities, or share our beliefs, values, language, religion, and so on. These associations are *in-groups.* The attachment to our cultural group is understandable, in that it provides a comfortable zone of interaction. Similarity and liking explain bonding experiences.

The second type of relationship is with *out-groups:* those who are perceived as different from us and the people with whom we strongly identify. Given the strength of that identification and the comfort that comes from in-group identification, we may have a cliquish outlook that makes us avoid or at least fail to connect with people who are different from us. The concept of routine exclusion of out-groups is called *marginalization.*

Regardless of the reasons behind marginalization, the filtering that it creates leads to enormous consequences in organizational communication. The perception that others are "not like me" underlies many misunderstandings in the workplace (Gudykunst & Kim, 2003).

Communication Style Expectations

Individuals' preferences regarding styles of conversation or methods of interaction may stem from personal likes and dislikes or group identification. In either case, when one person's communication fails to meet another person's expectations, frustration will likely ensue.

For instance, Raul has been with a small company in Texas for six years and competently performs his job. In fact, he has been promoted several times—the last time, to the position of manager of his department. Despite his overall success, Raul occasionally experiences conflicts with coworkers who feel that he wastes time on the job by talking too much and showing too much concern for chronic employee complaints. These behaviors stem from his cultural identity as Hispanic. One part of his culture values personal relationships and therefore encourages friendliness, small talk, and hospitality among other things. From Raul's point of view, communication on the job should involve interaction that makes people feel comfortable. His non-Hispanic coworkers do not easily accept this view, however.

Raul and his coworkers likely have different approaches to handling conflict as well. As with communication style in general, conflict style can be unique to each person or associated with a culture. For example, when working on projects with their Japanese counterparts, some American managers have described misunderstandings and occasional frustration with differences. Americans often misunderstand the Asian use of silence, the emphasis on group, and the significance of saving face (Gudykunst & Ting-Toomey, 1992). Conversely, Americans advocate "putting their cards on the table" and "letting happen what will happen," both of which are philosophies that do not fit with the Japanese focus on saving face.

One study (Kume, 1985) looked at the differences in how Japanese and American managers perceive doing business. American managers shared these perceptions:

"American companies usually have a definite line of decision making, but Japanese decision making is not clear."

"In most American companies, executives set company policy. But employees have access to that policy and access to a process to change or implement policy. That all seems unclear among the Japanese managers."

"American meetings are generally more rapid—discussion, response, discussion—while Japanese meetings go on and on."

Moreover, here is what Japanese managers had to say about the American way of doing things:

"American people work individually. The quality control people in manufacturing departments seldom hold meetings. They don't think it necessary to hold cross-departmental meetings."

"I think it is better not to make a snap judgment or a quick decision, but to think about it a little bit, and get someone else involved."

"Americans take it for granted that 2 or 3 percent of the total number of products will be defective, but the Japanese managers really try to make sure that not a single product will be defective. Of course, the Japanese way will take much more time."

Cultural Values

Cultural values are long-standing judgments of what a culture considers good and bad, worthwhile and important. For instance, in U.S. culture, deeply held values include the importance of perseverance, hard work, optimism, future orientation, and individual self-worth. In traditional Asian culture, the focus is on hard work, perseverance, group orientation, and rule following; there is less emphasis on individuality. Some of these differences in cultural values emerged in the previous discussion of how differently Americans and Japanese view doing business. Clearly, workplace interactions involving American and Japanese individuals will probably be complex, based on these value differences.

In an effort to understand such differences in cultural values, it is useful to look for similarities in cultural values. Hofstede's (2003) classic research has identified four fundamental criteria against which specific cultural values can be considered:

1. *Individualism/collectivism.* Some cultures emphasize individuality, whereas others focus on group processes, or collectivism (see also Triandis, 1990).
2. *High/low power distance.* In some cultures, authority is centered in key individuals and not shared (a high power distance), and in other cultures, power is decentralized and even shared equally (a low power distance).
3. *High/low uncertainty avoidance.* Some cultures embrace uncertainty (low uncertainty avoidance), whereas others avoid uncertainty (high uncertainty avoidance).
4. *Masculine/feminine.* Highly assertive and less nurturing cultures are considered masculine, and less assertive and more nurturing cultures are considered feminine.
5. *Long-term orientation.* Some cultures have a long and others a short view of time, reflecting differences in past, present, and future time orientations.

In reviewing the values of a specific culture against these criteria, we should not think in terms of a culture being, say, either masculine or feminine but rather as occupying a position along a continuum that runs from masculine to feminine. Similarly, each of the other criteria can be thought of as identifying a range that spans two extremes or opposites.

Language

Every culture has a linguistic system, yet specific linguistic qualities may not transfer across cultures. Even if two people share the same language, the thought processes behind the words may not be the same, based on culture. For example, a Chinese man who spoke flawless English was conversing with an American coworker who kept using words such as *unique, individual,* and *self.* Despite his competence in English, the Chinese man was puzzled for most of the conversation. Finally, he asked, "What is this *individuality* you keep referring to?" The Chinese man, whose native culture focused on the group, not the individual, did not understand the concepts of individualism inherent in the American coworker's use of English.

Benjamin Whorf and Edward Sapir observed this linguistic phenomenon years ago. Their field studies, still relevant today, asserted that language filters people's perception of reality (see Rogers & Steinfatt, 2002). Today, we recognize *Whorf's hypothesis,* which asserts that an individual's language of origin creates a sifting and sorting of a message to match the best possible interpretation framed by language categories and experience.

The difficulty of inferring meaning through cultural differences compounds when jargon, slang, and special codes are used. This can be a special problem in the workplace, where such language is often prevalent. Imagine the confusion experienced when someone unfamiliar with North America sporting events tries to engage in a conversation with a coworker who is extremely familiar with the topic.

Interaction Rituals

Interaction rituals are those behaviors that people perform as regular aspects of associating with others—exchanging greetings, for example. For members of the same culture, these behaviors are performed automatically.

Some cultures have a variety of rituals for leave taking, or saying good-bye. Leave taking may be an elaborate process, involving implicit rules and a decided measure of time. Yet in other cultures, it is acceptable to stop a conversation abruptly and simply leave. For instance, an American might mark the end of a conversation with a minor apology, such as, "Well, I have an engagement and it's time for me to go" or "Sorry, but I've got to leave right now" followed by a friendly summary and a thanks for the conversation. Using this as an example, you can imagine the many cultures where such rituals have the same intent, but the form the ritual takes is difference.

Interaction rituals are also influenced by the role expectations associated with certain job positions. For example, as a corporate trainer or a teacher, what would participants from different cultures expect of you? Asian participants might expect a didactic approach, followed by hands-on training. By contrast, Americans might expect a PowerPoint presentation, followed by discussion, applied case studies, with humor and fun thrown in.

Gender Issues

Cultural differences in **gender** can influence expectations of communication and other behaviors. In fact, we could identify countless instances of male and female role diversity related simply to cultural expectations. For example, some cultures might expect males to speak with facts, while a culture like some from the Middle East might expect men to express themselves effusively, using touch and speaking passionately and articulately. As another example, a traditional Asian female may defer to her male counterpart during an important sales negotiation. These roles alter rapidly, however, so you should be aware of the changing experiences of men and women in various cultures.

Focusing on the workplace, researchers have attempted to improve understanding of gender as a culture itself. Woods's (2001) perceptive work on gender communication in organizations provides insight into gender-related problems and solutions in organizations. In particular, stereotypes of women and men explain why so much gender-based communication goes astray.

Many organizations have recognized how gender stereotypes have become ingrained in their culture and their policies and practices.

For instance, women in the various cultures may be stereotyped as *sex objects, mothers, children* (or associated with children), or *iron maidens.* Males may be contrasted stereotypically as *sturdy oaks, fighters,* and *breadwinners.* Such labeling bewilders employees, laboring under misperceptions of their real capabilities. In severe cases, holding onto these stereotypes leads to exclusion, sexual harassment, and the belief that men and women cannot work together.

Many organizations have recognized how gender stereotypes remain ingrained in cultural policies and practices. Even with laws to protect gender bias, you don't have to look too far to witness differences in promotion opportunities, pay, or allowances for family needs. In addition, an organizational climate that is hostile toward women can create suffering and a sense of being left behind, as exemplified by the lack of informal networking and mentoring relationships (say, through sports conversations or activities). These conditions define the *glass ceiling* and *glass wall* that some women experience.

IMPORTANCE OF MANAGING CULTURAL DIVERSITY

The variety and extent of cultural differences, as just outlined, should point to the need for increased understanding and awareness. The idea of managing cultural diversity is important in workplace communication for several reasons. In particular, when cultural differences are not acknowledged in the workplace, they pose potential barriers to communication. This situation results in losses such as low morale, low productivity, and potential litigation. Most experts who think about a global economy tell us the essentiality of leading with cultural diversity in mind.

Eliminating Potential Barriers

Cultural differences can pose barriers to workplace communication. One barrier occurs because coworkers respond to one another from perceptions of another person's group member or identity rather than a person's competence. This perception of differences is what initiates the process of intercultural communication. Recall from the model of intercultural communication, presented earlier in this chapter (Figure 7.1), that upon perceiving differences, we are driven to create harmony. In the best of cases, the result is functional such as good listening and team work.

Eliminating the Costs of Discrimination

Communication failure that results from cultural differences is costly, in several respects. Almost every day, stories appear in the news about cases of discrimination and harassment in the workplace. Consider these examples from the auto industry:

- Mitsubishi Motors paid out $34 million in 1998 to settle a sexual harassment lawsuit brought by the Equal Employment Opportunity Commission (EEOC) on behalf of about five hundred women at the company's Normal, Illinois, assembly plant.
- In early 1998, Ford agreed to a reported seven-figure out-of-court settlement to resolve a 1995 suit filed by nine workers alleging harassment at the stamping plant in Chicago Heights, Illinois.
- Linda Gilbert won a $21 million award from Chrysler in 1999 for sexual harassment at the Jefferson North Assembly plant in Detroit.

Also read Case 7.1, which relates a classic example of behavior that marginalizes various minorities and women in the workplace—this time at General Motors.

Case 7.1

Alleged Bias at General Motors

In recent years, workers at General Motors (GM) have alleged gender and racial bias. Thus far, the company's investigation has revealed nothing, but it will keep looking at its Pontiac East Assembly plant, from which numerous complaints of harassment have emerged. Workers have alleged being the victims of racial slurs, requests for sexual favors, and threatening phone calls. One complaint tells of a dead rat left in a personal locker.

Electrician Sandra Moore reported that on July 13, coworkers dropped buckets of water on her from the plant ceiling after she complained of sexual propositions and other harassment. Welder Pam Frazier, a Native American, claimed that supervisors refused to accommodate her shoulder injury by finding her another job, something they had done for male coworkers. And welder Deborah Torres said that coworkers made threatening phone calls while she was on the job because she dated a black colleague, who also filed a complaint. "It's been five years of harassment and threats," said Torres, a Hispanic woman who has worked at the Pontiac plant since 1977 (and whose father retired from that plant in 1994 after thirty-eight years with GM). "I'm sick of it. I just want to make a living."

The Michigan Department of Civil Rights is investigating all of these complaints. However, state officials turned Torres's allegations over to the Federal Bureau of Investigation's (FBI's) hate-crimes unit—the second such complaint received from GM's Pontiac plant that year. If you managed that plant, how would you address these issues?

Source: Historical reflection based on McCracken (2001).

Many companies provide training on racial discrimination and sexual harassment and monitor the workplace for violations and complaints—all of which is time consuming and costly. Regardless, many workplaces remain crudely insensitive to these general problems. More specific cultural differences—perhaps associated with an influx of immigrants or following some incident of terrorism—may need more direct and immediate attention, lest conflict escalate.

Accepting Cultural Diversity

As stated earlier, two contemporary developments indicate the need for understanding cultural diversity: the globalization of the world economy and the increasing diversity of the U.S. population. Individuals and organizations that wish to be successful in the twenty-first century must accept, even embrace, cultural diversity.

Scholars address the need for businesses not just to be aware of globalization, but to modify their behaviors and attitudes to adapt to a changing market (Abu-Febiri, 2006). For instance, performance standards or hiring practices often need to be adapted when overseas or dealing with big global differences. Most organizational cultures (Chapter 2) reflect a diverse range of traditions and cultures working in one organization. Each cultural person experiences that person's cultural traditions, values, rituals, and a sense of bellowing—called cultural identity. Many business and professional leaders today flex with this changing diversity and embrace the parts of the differences than can enrich an organization's sense of being part of a dynamic global community.

INTERCULTURAL COMMUNICATION STRATEGIES FOR PROMOTING UNITY

Implementing **strategies for intercultural communication** is an effective means of managing cultural diversity. Overall, these strategies focus on one fundamental axiom: Maximum communication time and effort produce the best outcomes.

Searching for Common Ground

As described earlier, our perceptions of others may lead us toward people who are like us and away from people who are unlike us. What we see as similar or dissimilar may refer to outward differences or to personal values and beliefs. Our uncertainty or anxiety over dissimilarity compels us to seek balance in this relationship. Without training, we perceive being different as being strange, as Gudykunst and Kim (2003) explain.

By contrast, we can think of our typical pattern of perception as offering an opportunity for intercultural communication. By emphasizing similarities, developing a common code, and expressing selfless respect, we can encourage positive communication among people from different cultural backgrounds. Thus, in searching for common ground, we can manage the perception of differences.

Adapting to Low- and High-Context Cultures

Many years ago, Hall (1976) identified a cultural principle that even today explains why so much misunderstanding occurs in organizations. He identified two kinds of cultures—**low-context and high-context cultures**—each of which has its own rules of how to process information. Hofstede (2003) has described a similar two-pronged cultural theme using the term *uncertainty avoidance.*

You may recall we introduced the idea in Chapter 2 of a *low-context culture* that relies on messages that use explicit information. These cultures thrive when everyone knows as much as possible relevant to his or her role. The goal is complete clarity. Individuals who identify with low-context cultures may communicate in ways that rely on having explicit and complete information, clearly defining their expectations, norms, and customs. Members of such cultures are generally informed of what they are to do and how they are to do it. They are not expected to gather information from the context, for the context holds little information.

For example, the service unit of a Fortune 500 company has established a clear set of expectations and timelines for customer service calls. For a typical call, if a customer has a computer breakdown, the service technician goes through a detailed checklist that everyone in service equally understands and can process with a customer. The goal is to solve the customer's problem in less than one hour, given routine matters. By educating its employees in detail to handle each other's calls, to follow precise procedures, and to follow through on service with a final callback and complete report to the manager, the company helps reduce the losses that result from lack of information.

A *high-context culture,* on the other hand, provides little overt information. Rather, members are expected to gather information from the context. Working in such a culture—which may also be called a *low-information environment* or an *implicit information culture*—is frustrating for some individuals, who feel that they spend a good amount of time floundering, unaware of expectations.

Samantha experienced some of this frustration in her first permanent job after college. She was hired by a well-known electronics firm to work in the scheduling department, but after several weeks, she felt she knew little about the requirements of her job and what was expected of her. Her supervisor answered her questions with vague responses that shared little information. Finally, Samantha talked with the company's director of human resources, who agreed that this department often experienced ambiguous communication. Samantha's supervisor, who had immigrated to the United States from Cambodia some fifteen years before, was simply acting in concert with her culture's norms, according to which an individual should be encouraged to discover his or her goals rather than be told them outright. To resolve the difficulty this created for new employees, vital information was provided to them outright by human resources, which maintained respect for the role and values of the supervisor.

Intercultural communication styles, which are rooted in high-context culture, employ ambiguity in strategic ways to facilitate solutions to difficult situations, which may themselves be ambiguous or have developed over time. Consequently, intercultural communication tends to employ more intuition and feelings to guide conversations and meetings.

Another college graduate, Lea, had an experience similar to Samantha's when she went to work at a small business operated by recent Middle Eastern immigrants in the midwestern United States. During the single hour of training she received, she was told, "Just do what you know best and help us move forward." Over the next two months, she realized that she had to do quite a bit of asking and experimenting on her own to find out what was expected in doing her job. Lea was unaccustomed to relying on nonverbal communication and unexplained expectations. However, this high-context, implicit style of communication was familiar to the owners of her company, and that set the tone for the organization's culture.

For any outsider, asking questions is important, as are making keen observations and paying attention to matters such as procedures, expectations, and rituals. One can learn what to do using the information embedded within the situation and ultimately function very well, once a person switches gears, and realize that is the means of communication that's available.

Adapting to Group and Individual Cultures

Hofstede (2003) has identified significant thematic differences among global cultures. For example, people in Latin America, Africa, Asia, and the Middle East generally identify with themes of group-centered communication and communal policies related to their collective culture. By contrast, people in Western cultures embrace themes of individuality. Thus, Americans might prefer to make a point quickly and get on with the decision making. By contrast, Asians might tend to be deliberate, taking long periods of time and using moments of silence to check with various levels within the organization before making a decision. Intercultural scholar Triandis (1990) also investigated the duality represented in the individualism/collectivism continuum.

Both Triandis and Hofstede suggest that when coworkers experience different cultural styles of communication, they experience frustration. Intercultural communication among people with such diverse perspectives calls for patience and understanding.

Adapting to Task and People Orientations

Another way of looking at cultural differences is to identify **task-oriented and people-oriented cultures**. In some cultures, people tend to spotlight their jobs and their respective responsibilities. People in such task-oriented cultures tend to be viewed as organized, initiative-oriented, decisive, and direct (Moran, Harris, & Moran, 2007). In other cultures, the focus is on people and

Strategies for intercultural communication help us cross cultural and social boundaries in order to heighten productivity and satisfaction in the workplace.

personal relationships. Individuals in people-oriented cultures may be considered highly empathetic, caring, considerate, and process oriented. Moreover, they tend to be more interested in facilitating interaction than in completing tasks.

In reality, a culture rarely fits either of these orientations exactly but tends toward one or the other. For example, American culture tends to be task oriented, whereas Mexican culture tends to be more people oriented.

Adapting to Cultural Hierarchy

Hofstede's (2003) research has described the degree of social distance that individuals maintain. This concept, called *power distance*, explores how cultures structure relationships around a social hierarchy. In a high-power distance culture, comfortable distances are maintained between individuals in different classes or groups. People occupy various positions in the cultural hierarchy and communicate according to the expectations of their positions. Such a culture may seem authoritarian and nonparticipatory, as indicated by a formal style of leadership, a high degree of control, and an assertive communication style. By contrast, a culture that has a low-power distance is characterized by participation, adaptability, flexibility, and the tactful pursuit of goals.

Adjusting Linearity

Cultural differences can also be found in *linear style*, or what is considered appropriate for changing topics in conversation and other communication. In some cultures, the time must seem right to discuss certain topics, and changing the subject or introducing a sensitive subject may be viewed as abrupt and rude. With regard to these differences, it is important to be flexible and nonjudgmental (NACE/Jobweb, 2002).

Understanding Nonverbal Interactions

As described in Chapter 4 on nonverbal communication, an array of behaviors communicates meanings without involving the exchange of spoken words. In addition, whereas certain gestures and facial expressions are considered universal, many more are not. In fact, most types of

SKILLS AT WORK 7.1
Cultural Differences in Nonverbal Communication

Consider these differences in what nonverbal behaviors mean to people in different cultures:

- **Eye contact and facial expressions.** In China, gazing directly at someone may be viewed as impolite, whereas in the United States, looking someone in the eye is a sign of integrity and trustworthiness. Facial expressions such as smiling and frowning are also interpreted differently in various cultures.
- **Gestures.** Gesturing profusely is typical of the people in many southern European cultures, such as the Italians and Greeks. However, in British culture, gesturing a lot may create the impression of being nervous or out of control.
- **Personal space.** Among Americans, the typical interaction distance is about 3 feet. However, Latin Americans tend to converse at around 2 feet; Africans, at 18 to 20 inches; and Middle Easterners, at 12 to 15 inches. People in Asian cultures typically maintain the greatest personal space in conversation. Of course, the amount of space considered appropriate can vary depending on the intimacy and formality of the relationship.

What do you know about cultural differences in nonverbal communication, perhaps based on your travels or educational experiences in other countries or in certain regions of the United States? If you were to take a job in another country or to travel extensively, say, to Asia or Latin America, in preparation what would you try to learn about communication?

nonverbal communication are culturally specific, which makes this area a huge potential source of misunderstanding. Consider the guidelines presented in Skills at Work 7.1 for understanding cultural differences in certain types of nonverbal language.

Avoiding Hasty Generalizations

A variety of processes explain why we tend to make *hasty generalizations* or to jump to conclusions about people who are different from us. One explanation is our need to reduce uncertainty and anxiety about perceived cultural differences, as discussed at several points earlier in this chapter (see also Figure 7.1). To satisfy this need, we may judge others unfairly, resorting to ethnocentrism and perhaps indulging in stereotypes and prejudice. Our tendency to make attributions (as noted in Chapter 3 on interpersonal communication) offers another explanation, in that we may attribute motives and attitudes to others without having an accurate basis for doing so. Again, we may generalize about others and perpetuate stereotypes.

As we engage in intercultural communication, we must be cautious about allowing cultural and group differences (such as physical qualities, values, attitudes, and customs) to have a negative influence. In the absence of knowledge and understanding, it is easy to resort to making hasty generalizations (see Case 7.2 on the next page).

Engaging in Cultural Adaptation

As you may have realized by now, many of the problems associated with cultural differences and intercultural communication can be traced to individuals' poor ability to adapt to new situations. Many people are comfortable knowing only what they already know and doing what they have

Case 7.2

Hasty Generalization in the Workplace

Hassan began working as a software programmer for a large corporation in North Carolina in August 2001, just weeks before the terrorist attacks of September 11. Since then, his coworkers have treated him with contempt. They view his dress with disdain, eschew his religious convictions, make fun of his Saudi Arabian ancestry, and have even gone so far as to place anonymous threatening messages on his desk. Hassan was educated in the United States and became an American citizen when he married an American woman nearly seven years ago. He considers himself a patriotic American, but his coworkers refuse to see him as such.

How would you address this problem? What strategies for intercultural communication might be useful? Why?

always done. They may resist or even fear change of any kind. Thus, people who enter a new social, ethnic, or national culture may initially experience **culture shock**. In moving to new surroundings, engaging in new roles, and experiencing major changes, people go through a process called **cultural adaptation**. Within the context of a new organization, this transitional progression is often referred to as *organizational socialization* or *acculturation*.

CULTURE SHOCK—WHAT HAPPENS DURING CULTURAL ADAPTATION   Entering a new culture brings with it many different kinds of stress, including lacking a supportive network, having low self-esteem, and being inadequately prepared for communication. In terms of communication, these behaviors are common:

- Expressions of aloneness
- Statements of feeling down or depressed
- Irritability or defensive communication
- Avoidance of communication and otherwise disengaging from others
- Statements of great fear and extreme frustration

In addition to recognizing these behaviors, it's useful to understand the stages that people typically go through in experiencing culture shock and then adapting to a new culture (see Figure 7.2):

1. *Stage 1: Feeling good.* Feelings of excitement and self-satisfaction mark the first stage, or the onset of culture shock. In this early stage, the individual may view things in an extremely positive light, sometimes appearing naïve.
2. *Stage 2: Disappointment.* Once the routines and realities have set in, the individual may begin to feel some of the stresses and anxieties indicated earlier. Various coping mechanisms may be applied, including these:
   - *Fight:* Irritability or outright hostility
   - *Flight:* Avoidance behaviors
   - *Filter:* Distorted perceptions that minimize or exaggerate reality
3. *Stage 3: Adjustment.* In the end, the individual adjusts to the new culture.

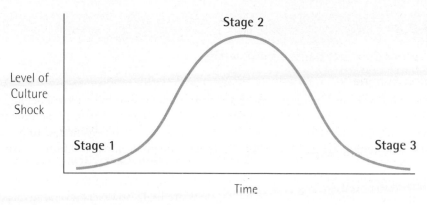

FIGURE 7.2 The Process of Cultural Adaptation

Managing Cultural Adaptation

Although most people experience these stages as temporary, the stresses associated with cultural adaptation can be enduring. As a manager or supervisor, knowing about these stages can be useful in encouraging employees who are going through adaptation (Hall, 2002). In fact, understanding employees' experiences and providing training may be part of your role as a future managerial communicator (Dodd, 1998).

Consider these guidelines for managing cultural adaptation:

1. Just knowing these stages can help you appreciate the temporary nature of transition stress. Business and professional communicators should attempt to normalize the negative feelings regarding adaptation.
2. Networking and building relationships in the new culture will make the adjustment proceed more quickly.
3. It helps to be innovative and a bit of a risk taker. For example, varying eating habits, clothing, and travel and being willing to explore can make the adjustment easier.
4. Find a mentor or someone who can coach you on the basics of the new culture.
5. Read about the new culture and the nature of change, and then write about your experiences in a journal.
6. Practice healthy stress reduction techniques.

Moving into a new culture and going to work in a new corporate culture have much in common. The culture shock stages one often experiences and related adjustment strategies of even a new job are surprisingly similar, since both types of change represent a life cycle of adaptation. It seems we usually just want to "survive" as we start.

This chapter ends with a case study that will give you the opportunity to apply what you have learned about cultural diversity and intercultural communication to problem analysis, negotiation, and collaborative problem solving. In Case 7.3 on the following pages, you will find a situation summary along with summaries of the employee role, the supervisor role, and the manager role. Use these summaries to develop several role-playing scenarios. For instance, the manager role and the employee role can be used in a negotiation role-play. Any of the roles can be used together for a mediation role-play or a collaborative problem-solving role-play. Each player should receive a situation summary as well as the summary of the role he or she will play.

Case 7.3

Negotiating Conflicts Caused by Diversity

Situation Summary

Ridgemont Incorporated has experienced a recent dramatic shift in employee demographics. The number of European American employees has decreased by 25 percent, and the number of African American and Hispanic employees has increased by 30 percent and 10 percent, respectively. The demographics of the supervisors, who are predominantly European American, have not changed.

The company is trying to diversify its workforce by increasing the number of supervisors from other racial and ethnic groups. Tensions are high, however. Several managers and employees have complained about the amount of resources being devoted to new employees. In addition, comments have been overheard about the need to "get our company back" and the importance of not letting "them" take over. Yesterday, in the employee cafeteria, an employee said, "Gee, this used to be such a nice place to work."

The company has always had its share of employee disputes, but there have definitely been more conflicts than usual in the last few months. Most have involved verbal exchanges between two or three employees of different ethnic/racial backgrounds. The most recent dispute, which was between European American and African American employees, involved nine employees. All of them were suspended, but the European American employees received one- or two-day suspensions while the African American employees received three- to five-day suspensions.

The company has a peer-mediation program, and all employee disputes that do not involve theft or serious physical injury are referred to it for resolution. If the employees cannot resolve their differences, then everyone is suspended pending a resolution from management.

Employee Role

You are an African American male and a six-year employee of Ridgemont. Over the past three years, you have noticed a steady increase in racial/ethnic tension, which you feel is in direct proportion to the increased hiring of employees of color. When you first started working at this company, you felt very much like an outsider. You still do, given the makeup of the supervisory staff. Even so, with the hiring of more people of color, you have been able to develop a feeling of belonging. Last year, you got involved in the mediation program because you felt that it would be a good way to deal with some of the things that were happening in the company.

You and some other employees met with a supervisor a couple of days ago to talk about the unfair treatment of employees of color who had gone to the mediation program. The supervisor has spoken to his manager, and the manager has requested a meeting with an employee representative to discuss the issue. The other employees have chosen you. You have not had much contact with this manager, but you know she is supportive of mediation and in fact founded the company's mediation program. You also know that she approves all work suspensions.

In sum, you feel very apprehensive about going into this meeting and don't really expect to get anywhere. You cannot imagine that the manager will admit that racism permeates this company. However, your fellow employees are counting on you, so you will do your best.

Case 7.3 *(Continued)*

Supervisor Role

You are an African American male. You have worked at Ridgemont Incorporated for eighteen years, the last five of them as a supervisor. You were the first African American promoted to the position of supervisor in Ridgemont's history. While you feel you earned the promotion through good work and loyalty to the company, you have heard gossip over the years about your promotion being a gesture of tokenism.

You have a reputation among both employees and other supervisors for being honest and fair. As a result, several employees have come to you to talk about what they perceive as unfair treatment in the selection of who is sent to mediation. They claim that every dispute that involves European American employees goes to mediation, but when the dispute is between African American or Hispanic employees, they are automatically suspended. The employees believe that the only reason the European American employees were suspended at all in the recent nine-person dispute was because one of the African American employees was seriously injured. Even so, the European American employees were suspended for fewer days than the African American employees.

You have spoken to your manager about these reports and have been asked to participate in an upcoming meeting with her and an employee representative—in fact, one of the employees who approached you. Although you will do what you can to resolve these racial tensions, you are somewhat nervous about being put in the middle between your manager and your workers.

Manager Role

You are a European American female and have been the manager of Ridgemont Incorporated for ten years. During that time, you have had to deal with a number of complex situations. You have always prided yourself on your ability to listen and communicate with staff, employees, and supervisors. Recently, a number of unsettling events have taken place at the company, most of them involving reports of insensitivity to racial, religious, and ethnic differences. You really want to resolve these matters, but the fact is, you are thinking about leaving the company. While you do not want to leave in a crisis, you have been quietly looking into other job offers.

One of your supervisors met with you yesterday to discuss employee reports that mediation is not being used fairly across the company population. Employees of color feel that they are more likely to be suspended after disputes than are European American employees, and they pointed to a recent example of such unfair treatment. You find this hard to believe. The company has never had a double standard of justice. When an employee is suspended, it's because his or her offense warrants it. In addition, the mediation program was your "baby" and thus reflects your flexibility and fairness in handling employee conflicts.

Nonetheless, you are concerned about employees' perception of unfairness and so have agreed to a meeting. You have asked the supervisor you met with to have his employees select someone to represent them. You will meet with this representative and the supervisor to discuss the concerns of African American and Hispanic employees and to assure them that everyone is treated the same in your company.

Analysis

What issues seem to underlie the racial/ethnic tensions at Ridgemont? What differences in perception are indicative of these issues? What should be done to investigate the issues thoroughly? What should be done to resolve these issues?

In Perspective

Cultural diversity can be defined as differences in group identity, ethnic or national origin, religious belief or practice, gender or sexual preference, and economics. When cultural differences emerge in the workplace, the response must be to manage them through improved understanding and communication. The specialized segment of communication studies that considers the relationship between culture and language is called *intercultural communication*.

A model of intercultural communication offers insight into how perceived differences affect communication in the workplace. When interacting participants perceive significant group or cultural differences, their comfort level will drive them to reduce their uncertainty or anxiety by creating harmony with others. That need ideally leads to positive results that represent functional outcomes. When people fail to understand or respect such differences, the result is dysfunctional outcomes, such as ethnocentrism, prejudice, and stereotyping.

A number of cultural elements must be considered in managing diversity: in-groups and out-groups, preferences for styles of conversation and conflict, linguistic differences, interaction rituals, and gender issues. In an effort to understand such differences, it is useful to look for similarities in cultural values. Specific cultural values can be considered against four fundamental criteria: (1) individualism/collectivism;

(2) high/low power distance; (3) high/low uncertainty avoidance; and (4) masculine/feminine.

Managing cultural diversity is important in workplace communication for several reasons. In particular, when cultural differences are not acknowledged in the workplace, they pose potential barriers to communication and thus productivity. This results in increased costs in a number of areas. Finally, in today's world, embracing cultural diversity is essential to participating in the global economy.

Implementing strategies for intercultural communication is an effective means of managing cultural diversity. Those strategies include searching for common ground; adapting to high- and low-context cultures; adapting to group and individual cultures; adapting to task and people orientations; adapting to cultural hierarchy; adjusting linearity; understanding nonverbal behaviors; and avoiding hasty generalizations.

People who enter a new social, ethnic, or national culture may initially experience culture shock. In moving to new surroundings, engaging in new roles, and experiencing major changes, people go through a process called *cultural adaptation*. Understanding employees' experiences and providing training in this area may be part of your role as a future managerial communicator.

Discussion Questions

1. In your view, what are the three most important issues related to intercultural communication and cultural diversity in the workplace? Why?
2. In your view, what are the three least important issues related to intercultural communication and cultural diversity in the workplace? Why?
3. What are some of the differences in communication styles and business practices between Asian and American workers? How could difficulty be avoided by addressing some of these differences in advance of doing business?
4. What are the reasons for cultural diversity? For instance, how do social and demographic factors such as gender, age, and education influence interpersonal relationships in organizations?
5. What strategies would you use to ensure quality intercultural communication in a culturally diverse organization? How could the training of new employees make use of these strategies?

Exercises

1. Use the headings and subheads in this chapter to create a list of intercultural communication issues and strategies that should be addressed by contemporary organizations.
2. Using the list created in Exercise 1, conduct an intercultural communication audit of a local organization to which you can gain access. (You may do this as a team or as an individual.) Observe operations and interview selected employees to learn about intercultural communication policies and practices. Present your findings in a written or oral report.
3. Interview two community leaders in your area who represent groups outside the cultural majority—for example, the African American community, the Hispanic community, the Native American community, the Asian American community, and so on. Identify each individual's major concerns and provide examples that explain why these are major concerns. Also describe each individual's approach to intercultural communication, identifying strategies he or she has tried and guidelines he or she follows for successful communication.
4. Create a training unit on a particular aspect of cultural diversity or a specific strategy for intercultural communication. What would you select and why? Conduct the training in class or at your place of work and measure the effects of your training with an attitude scale. Can attitudes be changed with education and training?

References

Adu-Febiri, F. (2006). The destiny of cultural diversity in a globalized world. *Review of Human Factor Studies*, *12*(1), 30–64. Retrieved from Academic Search Complete database.

Brislin, R. (1993). *Understanding culture's influence on behavior*. 2nd ed. Orlando, FL: Harcourt, Brace, Jovanovich.

Dodd, C. H. (1998). *The dynamics of intercultural communication*. 5th ed. New York: McGraw-Hill.

Gudykunst, W. B., & Kim, Y. Y. (2003). *Communicating with strangers*. 4th ed. New York: Random House.

Gudykunst, W. B., & Ting-Toomey, S. (1992). Toward a theory of conflict and culture. In *Readings on communicating with strangers*, ed. W. B. Gudykunst & Y. Y. Kim. New York: McGraw-Hill.

Hall, B. J. (2002). *Among cultures*. New York: Harcourt College.

Hall, E. T. (1976). *Beyond culture*. New York: Anchor.

Hofstede, G. (2003). *Culture's consequences, comparing values, behaviors, institutions, and organizations across nations*. 2nd ed. Thousand Oaks, CA: Sage.

Kume, T. (1985). Managerial attitudes toward decision-making: North America and Japan. In *Communication, culture, and organizational processes*, ed. W. B. Gudykunst, L. P. Stewart, & S. Ting-Toomey. Newbury Park, CA: Sage.

Landis, D., Bennett, J. M., & Bennett, M. J., Ed. (2004). *Handbook of intercultural training*. 3rd ed. Thousand Oaks, CA: Sage.

McCracken, J. (2001). GM's alleged bias. *Detroit Free Press*, August 23.

Moran, R. T., Harris, P. R., & Moran, S. V. (2007). *Managing cultural differences*. 7th ed. New York: Elsevier

NACE/Jobweb. (2002). How to communicate in a diverse workplace. Available online: www.collegejournal.com/successwork/onjob/20010403.

Rogers, E. M., & Steinfatt, T. M. (2002). *Intercultural communication*. Prospect Heights, IL: Waveland Press.

Triandis, H. (1990). Individualism-collectivism: Implications for intercultural communication. Paper presented to the Intercultural and International Communication Conference, Fullerton, CA.

Woods, J. T. (2001). *Gendered lives: Communication, gender, and culture*. Belmont, CA: Wadsworth.

Managing Group Communication and Workplace Teams

After reading this chapter, you will be able to do the following:

- Understand the nature of small-group communication and the types of outcomes that result.
- Understand the types and functions of communication networks.
- Apply leadership skills in managing small groups and teams.
- Conduct effective group discussions and problem-solving sessions.
- Apply rules of procedure and brainstorming techniques in the small-group context.

No man is wise enough by himself.

TITUS MACCIUS PLAUTUS

Today's focus on **group and team communication** represents a paradigm shift in the history of organizations. Many developments have led to this emphasis on small groups and teams, including recognition among organizational leaders of the power of human capital. By leveraging human resources, just as they would finances and facilities, organizations have responded to the call for group and team communication in leadership. Clearly, communication, which is vital to effective group relationships, constitutes a significant part of organizational life (Tubbs, 2001). From informal group gatherings to formal participation in decision making, establishing a plan for small-group communication is essential to human resource management in modern organizations.

DEFINING SMALL-GROUP COMMUNICATION

In this text, we will define a **small group or team** as consisting of three to fifteen members—but preferring an average of between six and eight. However, the number of people in the group is not nearly as important as other considerations. For example, the people standing at a corner, waiting for a bus, do not constitute a small group for our purposes.

Team researchers prefer to talk about what groups do and how members think about themselves as a part of a group (Ebrahim, Ahmed, & Taha, 2009). The following qualities help us picture what makes a small group:

1. *Purpose.* The members of a small group perceive they are a group because they have a purpose.
2. *Interdependence.* Team members must rely on each other for input and activity (Wilson, 2002).
3. *Interaction.* Small groups and teams communicate and interact among themselves.
4. *Outcomes.* Team members have an assigned task to produce or manage.
5. *Satisfaction.* The members of teams can define their satisfaction that comes from being a member of a group.
6. *Structure.* Groups have a structure—leadership or responsibility to each other and to the whole organization.

GROUP OUTCOMES

As just stated, most small groups and teams are working toward some sort of outcome—something they are to produce or manage. Two major outcomes are typical: (1) fulfilling a designated task or purpose and (2) creating morale or satisfaction among group members.

Task Outcomes

In general, research shows that teams and groups tend to outperform individuals particularly on complex task. In examining the differences between individual efforts and group efforts in producing **task outcomes**, researchers have found that groups produce a better quantity and quality of work. For example, West, Brodbeck, and Richter's (2004) literature review and critique offers substantial evidence for team effectiveness:

1. Of the three practices in hospitals that lowered patient mortality, in first place was staff working in teams.
2. Of 57 studies reporting productivity improvements in companies, 42 of the 57 demonstrated gains in productivity and in satisfaction as highly related to team working.
3. Using self-directed teams had the 4th strongest effect of 18 interventions on a company's financial performance (even stronger than financial rewards and training).

Similarly, Kauffeld (2006) reports that self-directed teams were more competent than traditional organizational groups on 7 of 12 competence measures. No wonder that group communication authors Harris and Sherblom (2002) boldly declare that "reliance on individual rewards is counterproductive to team building" and that the "vital component in effective organizational change is teamwork" (p. 148).

These impressive task outcomes can be linked with the high level of information sharing (such as giving feedback and offering criticism). Like workers on an assembly line, group members add value to one another's ideas, thus lending to the quality of the final product. Perhaps the only situation in which an individual could outperform a team is when someone alone has the ability to solve a simple problem more efficiently than is possible for a group.

Satisfaction outcomes involve creating morale, a sense of cohesion, and liking among group members.

Satisfaction Outcomes

When individuals participate in groups, they experience higher satisfaction and greater liking for the larger organization. Chapter 2 discussed the benefits derived from participatory management. Similarly, this chapter suggests that small-group leadership styles that encourage member interaction produce greater **satisfaction outcomes** among members, including greater liking for one another and more cohesiveness. For example, Whiteoak's study (2007) reveals that perception of the group influences satisfaction and cohesion among university faculty members. Furthermore, greater satisfaction results when teams experienced leaders provide continuous feedback and are sensitive to group members (Ebrahim, Ahmed, & Taha, 2009).

Less obvious though equally important are *informal groups*, in which individuals who are engaged in some common task meet on a more casual or unstructured basis. At times, their meeting may be highly purposeful—for example, a factory work group meeting after hours to discuss the operation of a new machine or a group of administrators working over lunch to review a new office procedure. Such groups are meaningful to employees for releasing tension, debriefing, maintaining member satisfaction, and so on. Whether informal groups meet over coffee or lunch, they provide arenas in which members are willing to express true feelings and deal with rumors.

COMMUNICATION NETWORKS IN SMALL GROUPS

The channels of communication available to small groups, called **communication networks**, are the means by which group members have access to one another. These networks comprise pathways or patterns of communication among group members.

In small groups, two basic types of networks have been identified—centralized and decentralized—and within each type, there are several subtypes (Wilson, 2002). As we discuss each type, we will examine its relationship to various group outcomes, particularly efficiency, morale, leadership, and information overload.

Before we move ahead, let's look at an organization that struggled with the functioning of small groups because of issues with communication channels. Case 8.1 introduces the NOFT organization and describes how group members blocked effective communication, leading to struggles over control.

Case 8.1

Communication and Control

The NOFT organization* experimented for four years with using teams in decision making and policy implementation. The appointment of various task groups got them off to a good start. But soon the groups ran into trouble. Cliques or coalitions developed among members, to the point that the complete groups met less and less frequently and finally not at all. A power struggle erupted, in which the smaller coalitions within teams began hoarding information, making most of the decisions, calling meetings when other members could not attend, controlling the input for meeting agendas, and controlling the output by holding their own meetings following whole team meetings. In essence, these coalitions controlled and maintained the channels of information. By violating the principles of information availability and member access, these small groups brought about their own demise.

What could have been done to avoid this result? In particular, how might the formation of cliques and coalitions among group members be prevented?

*This is a fictitious name of a real organization.

Centralized Networks

In **centralized networks**, communication among group members occurs through a central person or persons. That person's role is like that of a gatekeeper, through which information must pass before being distributed to the other group members. A centralized network may be created by organizational policy or hierarchy or may result as an artifact of informal leadership. Figure 8.1 illustrates the two types of centralized networks: the wheel and the chain.

WHEELS   In a *wheel* network, group members are restricted to communicating through a centrally located person. Again, what is central may be because of this person's official role or that this person has agreed to be the gatekeeper.

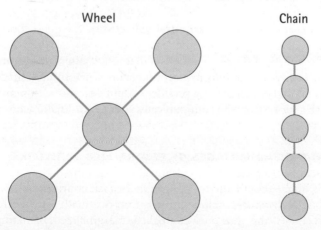

Wheel   Chain

FIGURE 8.1 Centralized Networks

Case 8.2

Communication and Low Morale

A small professional service organization, composed of twenty employees, continued to receive reports of isolation and feelings of inadequacy from its members. Several gifted employees resigned, and conflict seemed to be everywhere. To deal with this matter, a consultant was hired.

After some investigation, the consultant discovered two reasons for the employees' feelings of isolation. First, a communication network had developed (in line with the overall organizational culture) in which all ideas, innovations, and significant pieces of information had to be channeled through a central person—namely, the chief administrative officer (CAO). Unfortunately, the CAO was not good at communicating with employees, holding feedback meetings, and otherwise conducting business in a group format. This led to information overload, low productivity, and the feeling that the CAO was trying to control the highly professional employees and their work.

The second problem was an outdated phone system. Calls from outside had to be routed through a central system rather than directed to individual offices. There was no voice mail; instead, a receptionist took messages and left them in employees' mailboxes. Although the receptionist was generally competent, she was overworked and in many instances had caused delays and errors in receiving messages. The other issue was that the receptionist was housed in the outer office of the CAO. This wheel placement only increased employees' perception of the CAO's controlling nature.

Suppose you are the consultant hired to look into these problems of morale. Given what you've found out, what would you recommend in terms of solutions?

[handwritten note: · Centralized system leads to resentment]
[handwritten note: · Gatekeeper not skilled]

The limits of this type of network are obvious in terms of the potential for omitting, redirecting, or misinterpreting information as it is summarized or passed on (Hoover, 2002). Unfortunately, team members may feel frustrated and marginalized if a central leader continues to do this, contrasted with leaders who embrace and nurture team members (Ebrahim, Ahmed, & Taha, 2009). Case 8.2 illustrates problems linked with wheel networks.

CHAINS In a *chain* network, the second centralized network, members communicate with only two other people. Similar to the wheel, these centralized leaders may have assumed their role or been appointed. Regardless of the reason, the fact that information sifts through these intervening relationships creates potential information distortion if not an undesired hierarchy. For instance, a chain occurs when a senior vice president communicates with a middle manager who communicates with a supervisor who communicates with a coordinator who communicates with an employee.

ADVANTAGES AND DISADVANTAGES OF CENTRALIZED NETWORKS Researchers have identified a number of advantages and disadvantages of centralized networks. A centralized network *advantage* is efficiency—if the task is simple or task coordination is needed (Beebe & Masterson, 2000). *Disadvantages* include information overload, information distortion, and member dissatisfaction if they feel over-controlled, marginalized, or manipulated (Harris & Sherblom, 2002). Consider Gale's experience in Case 8.3.

Case 8.3

Central Network Overload

Charles, Jason, Susan, and Seranda—the four partners in a small company—had become so busy that they had dispensed with their weekly planning meetings and were now transmitting information to one another only through Gale, the company's administrative assistant. Understandably, Gale felt increasingly overloaded, to the point that she hated going to work some days. In addition, the lack of interpersonal contact among partners had created some misunderstanding and even conflict.

The tension erupted one day when Gale complained to Charles, "Seranda and Jason have been pushing me to move their projects along, and now today, you want me to drop everything and get this mailing out. I have a general idea of what's involved in each project, but I don't know enough to make the decisions that you all seem to expect of me. You guys really need to talk with each other. I can't take this anymore!"

The company doesn't want to lose Gale, whom they consider an invaluable employee. But they aren't in the position to hire more administrative help either. What can the four partners do to make their current centralized network function more effectively?

Decentralized Networks

In a **decentralized network**, information passes more randomly among group members, not exclusively through a centrally placed individual or gatekeeper. Figure 8.2 illustrates the two types of decentralized networks: open-channel, or circle, networks and all-channel networks.

OPEN-CHANNEL OR CIRCLE NETWORKS   A *circle*, or *open-channel, network* encourages almost complete interaction among team members. For reasons of personal leadership or appointment, interaction is excluded from all members. In face-to-face groups interaction occurs mostly to one side or the other, with limited or no contact among people directly across from one another.

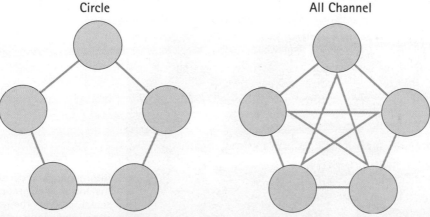

FIGURE 8.2   Decentralized Networks

ALL-CHANNEL NETWORKS   An *all-channel network* allows interaction among all group members. An example is an organization in which all employees can easily and freely access one another's offices and workstations or through e-mails and virtual teams to communicate to any other team members.

ADVANTAGES AND DISADVANTAGES OF DECENTRALIZED NETWORKS   Organizations that use decentralized networks experience both advantages and disadvantages. As *advantages*, decentralized networks work well for complex tasks (more knowledge capital available), they avoid information overload for a central leader, and the participatory nature of this structure facilitates member satisfaction. The main *disadvantage* is the increased time to complete tasks. Future managers who structure groups or teams should weigh these issues when structuring groups.

Virtual Teams and Groups

With today's ability to leverage computer technology, personal data devices, instant messaging, videoconferencing, cell phones, e-mail, and document sharing software, **virtual networks** emerge as part of new technology opportunities in the workplace. These structures present opportunities data analysis, document retrieval, technology-based training, and virtual meetings. For instance, this author frequently meets with a virtual team on a regular basis to make decisions and set policy for team members in Boston, Washington, Philadelphia, Texas, and Canada. The author conducts training online using Skype aligned with PowerPoint with clients from New Zealand, the Netherlands, and the United States. While face-to-face meetings are frequent in the workplace, it is not unusual for teams today to e-mail data and conduct business by attachments and text messages more than meeting traditionally.

 The research presented regarding virtual networks and teams is emerging and still incomplete. The data we have, however, point out significant advantages. These *advantages* include higher productivity and competence, clear responsibility, information richness such as colorful visuals, and obviously time/travel savings (Kauffeld, 2006; Ebrahim, Ahmed, & Taha, 2009). These considerable advantages have led some authors in recent literature to refer to the "romance of teams," as if to say that so many advantages might skew our understanding of disadvantages. The research indicates that despite the many advantages, virtual networks and teams experience *disadvantages* such as difficulty in determining whose role it is to clarify the group's purpose and ultimately make decisions. Second, they also experience a lack of low performance if members

Information and decision making in small groups should seek to identify the task and its solution along with promoting satisfaction among group members.

are not adequately selected and trained specifically for virtual networking. Third, they miss cohesion and social bonding, features almost always present in face-to-face teamwork.

LEADERSHIP IN TEAMS AND SMALL GROUPS

Group leadership is complex and multidimensional. Fundamentally, group leadership centers on quality information and interpersonal communication skills. Although a popular conception is that leadership resides in only one person, in fact, group members often rise up to handle leadership function according to situational needs.

Examining leadership styles in the context of the small group provides a rich area for understanding group behavior. As noted in Chapter 2, each organizational leadership style has its advantages. Similarly, the three **small-group leadership styles** discussed in the following sections are important foundations so that future managers can apply the advantages of each one, depending on the needs of the group (Brilhart, Galanes, & Adams, 2001).

Highly Directive Leadership

The *highly directive leadership* style leads with an authoritarian method of dealing with group members. The drive for task and productivity is extremely high, but the concern for people and satisfaction is low. Such a leader typically offers only one-way communication, usually in a downward manner.

The advantage of this leadership style lies in its efficiency to achieve task outcomes. In an emergency or when confronted with a simple task, this style is particularly effective; autocratic leadership saves time in such situations. If the task is complex or demands a number of solutions, however, the directive leader must be extraordinarily knowledgeable or efficiency could suffer.

The chief disadvantage of highly directive leadership concerns some group members' perception that they have not been heard or feeling that they have limited input. If communication is one way, decisions might seem to be simply handed down to them. Since praise and nurturing styles are not typical of this style, a directive leader can appear controlling, manipulative, and power hunger to ensure compliance. Key patterns of behavior are as follows: fairly rigid, critical of others' work, offering little feedback, leaning significantly on rules, and providing little encouragement.

Participatory Leadership

Under the *participatory leadership* style, a designated leader offers guidance, suggestions, listening, and concern for members while also showing concern for completing tasks. The net effect of this leadership style is to form a partnership involving two-way communication (Beebe & Masterson, 2000).

Participatory leadership in small groups typically produces moderate task efficiency but high satisfaction. Thus, members feel happy about their involvement, but the multiplicity of effort takes more time. One exception occurs when a task is complex or requires many solutions; then, a participatory, democratic style produces higher productivity and quality than does a directive style. In general, participatory leadership correlates with the following qualities: people-centered, encouraging, tolerating alternative views, using praise honestly, serving others ahead of self. Case 8.4 on the next page presents an example of the effective use of participatory leadership.

Negligent Leadership

A third style of team leadership is *negligent* (or *laissez-faire*) *leadership*. This type of leader offers such little guidance or direction that this style closely matches a nonleader situation. He or she offers complete freedom and movement in the group. If asked for information, the negligent

---

Case 8.4

The Right Kind of Leadership

Jack, a young and newly hired transportation manager with a large trucking firm, was confronted by Scott, an experienced dockworker, with the question of how he wanted a particular truck loaded and processed. Aware of Scott's longevity at the company (and his own relative inexperience), Jack responded by asking Scott his opinion: "You've been doing this for a long time, so you probably have a good idea of the best way to load this truck. How would you do it?"

By taking this approach, Jack made the transaction take a few minutes longer than if he would have just told Scott what to do. But in handling the question this way, he scored points among Scott and the rest of the dockworkers. Following this situation, morale was much improved. Jack's participatory approach also paid off in another way: Scott's question was intended as something of a test, instigated by the older employees to see how the new leader would handle things. The credibility of the young manager was never questioned again.

Suppose Jack had applied a highly directive leadership style to this situation. What different outcomes would likely have resulted?

---

leader will respond. Otherwise, the leader takes no part in decision making and offers little advice or direction. To use an analogy, this type of leadership is like a cold, limp handshake: neither has much life, and both are unsatisfactory. Unless you just need to get out of the way for a genius individual or team to work, this style offers little evidence for task productivity or satisfaction.

CONDUCTING RESULTS-ORIENTED GROUP COMMUNICATION

Knowing now which leadership style you can choose, you are ready to move into the actual process of leading a group or team toward a goal. It is important to remember that the designated leader of a small group or team has the overall responsibility for two main outcomes: ensuring continuity toward the group's goals and maintaining satisfaction. In other words, we can ask: (1) What needs to be communicated to accomplish the group task? and (2) What needs to be communicated to maintain member satisfaction? Thus, group talk can be categorized as *group task outcomes* or *group satisfaction outcomes*. With these two outcomes as foundations, we present in this section a practical, yet well-tested, set of phases through which the group leaders can take the group, beginning with initiating group discussion, going to the problem-solving phase, and emerging with the concluding phase.

The Initiating Phase of Group Discussions

Well-informed and well-intentioned group members, sometimes from the most sophisticated of groups, frequently walk away from discussions frustrated because a clear purpose was not set or an appropriate time was not allotted. Ironically, this frustration stems from a misunderstanding of how to initiate and structure a group discussion. The first step is to send out an early agenda to allow others to prepare for the upcoming discussion.

SEND OUT AN EARLY AGENDA   An agenda needs to be prepared and sent out as early as is reasonable so that team members can allocate time, adjust schedules, and prepare. The agenda should indicate starting and ending times, the place of the meeting, any resources needed, the attendees, the goal of the meeting, and the discussion items. A sample meeting planner is presented in Figure 8.3.

BEFORE THE MEETING

As the chairperson, ask these questions:

- Is this meeting necessary?
- Do I need a group?
- How else might I achieve this?
- Do others agree that a meeting is needed?
- Is this really my issue?

If a meeting is not necessary, consider these alternatives:

- One-on-one conversation
- Phone call
- Social gathering
- Memo
- Decide on your own

As a participant, ask these questions:

- What results are to be achieved?
- How will we know when they have been met?
- What process will be used to handle the matter?
- What role am I being asked to play?
- What can I do to prepare?
- What constraints might there be on the discussion?

Supplies Needed

Speaker

- Flipchart, paper, pens
- Overhead projector, sheets, pens
- Slide projector and control

Participants

- Pens, pencils, highlighters
- Paper
- Any premeeting materials distributed

Facility Considerations

Main room

- Seating/size
- Flexibility in setup
- Ventilation/acoustics
- Audiovisual capabilities

Additional rooms (if needed)

- Always available?
- Number and seating/size
- Equipment
- Proximity to main room

Ease of access

- Transportation to/from
- Access for people with disabilities
- Message system

DURING THE MEETING

Chairperson

- Start on time
- Follow agenda
- Keep to time limits
- Encourage ideas
- Close on note of achievement
- Thank participants

Participants

- Arrive on time
- Bring necessary materials
- Stay focused
- Don't talk too much
- Don't be afraid to speak up
- Note action items and follow-up

Notes:

FIGURE 8.3   Meeting Planner

EXPRESS THE PURPOSE OF THE MEETING   At the beginning of the meeting, it is a good idea to rearticulate the fact that the meeting has a stated purpose and goals. Doing so will reduce uncertainty.

EXPLAIN THE GOALS BY USING KEY QUESTIONS   A team can only move toward its goal when it understands the decision to be made. To reach that understanding, it's useful to frame the decision outcome as a question. Four of the most typical question types are as follows:

1. A *question of fact* asks about a situation's existence, under what conditions it exists, and how it may be defined. Key words include *what, why,* and *when.*

EXAMPLE

"Why are employees dissatisfied with the current evaluation form?"

2. A *question of conjecture* focuses on the future. Key words include *what if, future,* and *scenarios.*

EXAMPLE

"What if inflationary market pressures continue at the current rate during the next decade?"

3. A *question of value* argues the worth of something and thus goes a step beyond a question of fact. Key words include *should, value, ought,* and *worth.*

EXAMPLE

"Should employees be asked to evaluate their supervisors?"

4. A *question of policy* goes a step further and asks what recommendations or actions should be taken. Key words include *how, methods,* and *steps.*

EXAMPLE

"What method should employees use to evaluate their supervisors?"

As these examples demonstrate, a question provides more direction than a simple statement of the decision to be reached. How the question is worded is extremely important, however, so we recommend these techniques:

1. **Be specific.** Avoid vague questions like "What about the new marketing program?" This example is too general. A better alternative is a question of fact, such as "What is the new marketing plan?"
2. **Be simple.** Avoid questions that are long and rambling, such as "When and under what circumstances should market procedures be governed by personnel other than administrative experts, unless they are unavailable, in which case personnel options should be voted on by

regular staff and other management?" Again, formulate a question of fact: "Who will implement the market plan?" or "How will the marketing plan be communicated?"

3. ***Don't unnecessarily limit the alternatives.*** Questions that lend themselves to yes/no answers obviously limit the group to choosing between two alternatives. Open-ended questions, on the other hand, leave the group free to consider a full range of policies. For example, the question "Do you want to increase the distribution of our product or not?" may unnecessarily limit a group's alternatives. The question "How can changes in our product distribution process best meet our customers' needs?" allows the group to consider more of the possibilities.

4. ***Avoid biased wording.*** The question "Is it possible for regular staff members to make suggestions to marketing executives?" displays a bias that staff members are mere underlings and have nothing significant to contribute.

CLARIFY LEADERSHIP   Another part of initiating is to clarify the leadership expectations. Is there an appointed leader? Is the leadership to be selected from among the members? Is the leadership to be shared or emergent as time goes on? Finally, what is the needed group leadership style, which we documented above?

In any case, leadership should concentrate on achieving key functions, such as the following:

- Clarifying the group's purpose and presenting the key questions
- Clarifying meetings and times
- Staying on task and ensuring adequate data are presented
- Maintaining balanced interaction
- Concluding the group and presenting a final decision or plan

The Problem-Solving Phase of Group Discussions

Conducting a group discussion next turns to developing a problem-solving process. These four steps are commonly used among teams:

STEP 1: RECOGNIZE THE DIFFICULTY   At the start, identify the difficulty and its symptoms or observed effects. Unless participants realize that a problem exists, decision making will seem irrelevant.

STEP 2: VENTILATE FEELINGS   The group should spend time early in the process to share and iron out potentially damaging feelings and conflicts. Some problems may be personally agonizing for team members, and they will be able to cope more adequately if a cathartic opportunity is available. This step also helps expose hidden agendas that may limit interaction and increase hostility without dealing with these emotions as much as is reasonable.

STEP 3: DESCRIBE THE PROBLEM   Your goal in describing the problem is to be as specific and clear as possible. Follow these steps:

1. ***Word the problem or question and have available research.*** It is amazing how many group discussions proceed without members fully realizing the nature of the problem or having meaningful data at hand to begin evidenced-based discussions.

2. ***Analyze the problem.*** Using the research gathered, analyzing means the group sorts out the symptoms, causes, and effects of the problem.

3. *Providing information, clarification, and reanalysis.* Information is often communicated to provide members with important facts and observations. Sometimes, groups need to slightly modify or redefine the issue at this point.

EXAMPLE

"Seventy-five percent of our departmental expenses are being used by office management, and that leaves little extra for travel to develop the Jones account."

Clarifying ideas and information. Group members may take the responsibility for explaining data or concepts when clarification is needed.

EXAMPLE

"The line item indicated as 'fifteen percent expenses for the office' includes miscellaneous funds for account development. This funding is not development travel."

Asking for ideas and information. Group members may ask one another for information.

EXAMPLE

"Are you sure about those figures? And how do we access those funds?"

Critiquing information. Evaluating information in terms of its meaning or usefulness is another task of group communication.

EXAMPLE

"If we don't take more care to examine our budgetary forecasts for new accounts in the future, our department's ability to develop new business will be diminished. We must find new funding for account development."

Reanalyzing information. Once information has been offered to the group, members may weigh its advantages and disadvantages. This is particularly likely when the group arrives at the solution stage of decision making.

EXAMPLE

"Your idea of presenting our needs to the senior vice president seems feasible on the surface, but I see three disadvantages in trying to implement that idea."

STEP 4: DEVELOP SOLUTIONS   The final step is to develop solutions to the problem, which involves the following:

1. *Set up criteria.* Use these criteria for developing satisfactory solutions:
   - A solution(s) that best solves the problem
   - A solution that is workable and feasible
   - A solution that is not too costly

- A solution that does not create more problems or add disadvantages
- A solution that can be implemented in a reasonable amount of time

2. *List the solutions.* Generate as many solutions as possible, using brainstorming and similar techniques for encouraging the free exchange of ideas. Suspend judgment until all the solutions have been presented for consideration.

3. *Evaluate the solutions.* Go down the list of solutions and discuss the pros and cons of each one. Judge each against the criteria the group agreed on earlier. All evaluations should be challenged and supported.

4. *Choose one solution.* Rank the solutions as a group and then choose one.

5. *Implement the solution.* Develop a plan by which the solution can be implemented. Be sure to address issues of feasibility.

The NOFT organization, introduced earlier in this chapter, applied this process in making critical changes. See Case 8.5 for an example of how this process works in the real world.

Concluding Group Discussions

After the step of developing solutions, the job is not yet finished. The group's work must be brought to a close, typically deciding on an action or recommendation and communicating a plan. Here are some common methods.

CONSENSUS   In reaching a *consensus*, members continue discussion until they reach agreement. By continuing to explore all points of view, members work out their differences and arrive at what seems the best answer. This isn't to say that members don't have reservations; however,

---

Case 8.5

Overcoming Barriers to Quality Service

In early client surveys, the NOFT organization discovered that the services it offered were considered of high quality but that employees made it difficult for clients to access those services by erecting self-serving barriers and using operations-centered communication rather than client-centered communication (see Chapter 7). NOFT's chief administrative officer (CAO) called a series of meetings to challenge employees and their managers to address these issues. Over a period of several months, the group identified its major weaknesses and approved the division heads to move forward in presenting solutions to the group.

   At this point, the process was flawed. Although well intentioned, the CAO and the managers working alongside him continued to make autocratic decisions and use a downward style of leadership communication. Realizing this problem, the leadership went into the group decision-making process. They began by venting a lot of pent-up emotions. Then they encouraged the group to identify all the dimensions of the problem: its causes and effects, its signs and symptoms. Then, they customized the criteria against which to judge their list of solutions: (1) a solution must give authority to the trainers in the NOFT group, (2) a solution must be able to be adopted by all the trainer members of their staff, and (3) a solution must not cause disrespect for trainers. Currently, NOFT is on its way to energizing its staff and providing a new day for its list of clients.

   Think about how to apply this decision-making process with members of a group to which you belong.

• Great product, bad customer service

when they feel fairly close to the direction of a decision, they will be comfortable in agreeing. If an issue is especially troublesome to a member, then he or she may call for a vote or go with a minority report. Or, a person may accept the majority and simply agree to disagree.

SUSPEND DISCUSSION   When an impasse seems evident, the wisest course of action may be to hold off on making a final decision until another meeting. This may be necessary in cases in which members have strongly divided opinions.

MINORITY REPORT   When differences cannot be resolved but a decision must be made, the leadership may consider submitting a *majority report* and a *minority report*, reflecting unreconciled differences between members.

MEDIATION OR ARBITRATION   On some occasions, teams need to make decisions or plans through *mediation*, in which an objective person from outside the group is brought in to help members reconcile their differences and ultimately develop a consensus. When the group is being torn apart with conflict and continuing with the same approach appears useless, mediation can be helpful. *Arbitration* occurs when an outside objective person listens to both sides and hands down a decision. If the factions of a divided team agree to abide by the arbitrator's decision, it is called *binding arbitration*, to which there is no appeal.

MAJORITY VOTE   Many organizational cultures are accustomed to voting on important matters to decide their outcomes. With an extremely large group, this is one of the most practical means of decision making. However, in a small group, voting can create a feeling of disunity, as it forces a win-lose scenario. Some experts therefore recommend that voting be reserved for close situations or quasi-legal reasons. Clearly, a 7 to 0 vote conveys something quite different than a 4 to 3 vote, say, in electing a vice president.

Perhaps the best advice that can be offered about group decision making is the old adage about not attacking the person but attacking the idea—provided members are willing to share their ideas in a spirit of cooperation. In addition, members must set as goals task outcomes and satisfaction outcomes in order to be productive and enjoy healthy group relationships.

Achieving Group Satisfaction Outcomes

1. *Showing solidarity.* It is important for group members to express support for each other and for the group's efforts as a whole.

EXAMPLE

"I like that idea. It's changed my whole conception of the problem."

---

2. *Showing agreement.* When members concur with one another, they continue to show support and also move ahead in decision making.

EXAMPLE

"You've expressed exactly what I have been feeling about this problem. Let's move ahead with our analysis."

---

3. *Providing emotional support.* One of the most devastating effects (in terms of limiting the effectiveness of small groups) occurs when members feel excluded from participation. The social function of group interaction is essential in providing a comfortable emotional climate—one in which people are willing to express themselves.

EXAMPLE

"I think you may have some interesting insights about the cause of our dilemma. Do you feel like sharing some of that information right now?"

4. *Managing conflict.* Inevitably, conflict arises, and when it does, group members should share the leadership role of diffusing the situation.

EXAMPLE

"It's clear we don't all agree on a solution. Why not have each of us detail the reasons a particular solution is important to us. In doing so, maybe we can express some of our personal feelings and then proceed to finding a great solution."

5. *Providing tension release.* When tension seems to build in one individual, members should help him or her find a release. One way to do so is to use humor, such as joking and teasing, as long as it's appropriate and not intended as sarcasm.

EXAMPLE

"Maybe we just haven't been listening carefully enough to what you've said. Would you mind explaining again your feelings about what you consider to be the best solution?"

How many of these behaviors have you observed in small groups in which you have participated, whether at work or school? Complete the assessment of satisfaction outcomes in Skills at Work 8.1 on the next page to measure the satisfaction you derived from membership in a specific group.

Overcoming Group Communication Barriers

Inevitably, despite everyone's best effort, several forces are at work that rip groups apart or at least make the group experience tedious or dissatisfying. Here are some of the most common forms of barriers, or **blocking behaviors**.

HIDDEN AGENDAS   A *hidden agenda* is an ulterior motive or unstated purpose for doing something. In a small-group situation, one member may provide information that represents his or her own self-interest. For example, Joseph may invite group members to discuss the problems currently facing the company's personnel department for the stated purpose of information sharing. His ulterior motive, however, may be to take over the management of that department himself. Thus, his surface comments mask the hidden reasons for this discussion.

GROUPTHINK COMMUNICATION   Although supportive communication is helpful to the team, too much conformity actually obstructs the critical thinking that is needed to arrive at a good solution. The concept of *groupthink*, detailed in the original work of Irving Janis (1982),

SKILLS AT WORK 8.1
Assessment of Small-Group Satisfaction Outcomes

Think of a small group or team you have participated in—preferably one that you found effective in achieving its goal or task. With that group in mind, respond to each of the following statements by choosing one of these answers:

5 = Always   4 = Frequently
3 = Sometimes   2 = Seldom
1 = Never

Write each answer on the line in front of the statement. After you have responded to all the statements, add up your answers to produce a total score.

_____ **1.** After meeting with the group, I find that I'd like to continue meeting as much as possible.

_____ **2.** This group is open to everyone's ideas; rarely does anyone feel put down.

_____ **3.** The group's discussion is well organized and always moving toward a goal.

_____ **4.** Group members try to harmonize and understand one another's points of view, even when there is disagreement.

_____ **5.** This group is really attractive to me; I feel close to almost everyone in it.

_____ **Total Score**

Here's what your score says about your level of satisfaction with membership in the group: If your score is 15 or less, you seem to have had a dissatisfying group experience. If your score is 16 or above, your scores indicate satisfaction. Does this assessment seem accurate, based on your experiences with the group? Why or why not?

refers to the faulty decision making that results when not all viewpoints are heard and fully weighed for their value, good and bad. A well-known historical example of groupthink is summarized in Case 8.6.

What insight can we gain from cases like this? What stimulates groups to make uncritical, risky choices?

- *Avoiding confrontation.* Some group cultures discourage disagreement, while some members feel apprehensive communicating in a group—especially being critical or disagreeable. Silence is then interpreted as agreement and thus conformity.
- *Maintaining unity.* Unity is highly desirable, and cohesion is the quality that makes team members feel close to each other. So it's understandable when teams sacrifice a decision in favor of conformity (Wilson, 2002). Anything else may be viewed as disagreement or disloyalty. To avoid this, members simply agree even if they secretly disagree with a proposal.
- *Being in the presence high-status members.* Conformity increases in the presence of high-status leaders. Team members are reluctant to express their different points of view in the presence of power, for a variety of reasons.
- *Feeling invincible.* Some overconforming, groupthink behavior can be explained by a team's norms—for example, the belief that nothing can touch them. Consequently, plans and policies may be formed through reckless or uninformed decision making.

SPECIAL PLEADING   This form of communication occurs when a team member advocates a position on behalf of constituents outside the team. If other members go along with this special advocacy, the decision that results might not be made on the merits of the proposal or in the best interest of the team.

Case 8.6

The Bay of Pigs Incident

President John F. Kennedy learned a hard lesson about effective group decision making with the Bay of Pigs incident in 1961. That incident involved a failed attempt by fourteen hundred Cuban exiles to invade their homeland and overthrow Fidel Castro. Trained and equipped by the U.S. Central Intelligence Agency (CIA), most of the invaders were killed or taken prisoner.

At the cabinet meetings at which plans for the invasion were discussed, Kennedy had voiced his opinion and ultimately approved the plan for invasion. Sadly, however, some of his advisers had failed to speak their minds because, it was later learned, they did not want to disagree with the president. Their desire to show solidarity resulted in blocking the free flow of information, and the tragedy that resulted is generally considered the most vulnerable moment of the Kennedy administration.

Kennedy learned from that tragedy, however. The next year, during the Cuban missile crisis, he deliberately did not attend cabinet-level discussions. Instead, his brother, Attorney General Robert Kennedy, chaired the meetings. This time, criticism and free thought were freely exchanged, and most historians agree a better decision was reached in this crisis.

What other events can you think of in which groupthink was likely involved? For example, criticism has been leveled against the National Aeronautics and Space Administration (NASA) regarding the decision making that preceded the space shuttle disasters. And in another example, the leadership of Enron Corporation seemed mostly to go along with aggressive decisions that resulted in the company's collapse and a federal investigation into its accounting practices.

PULLING RANK   Using one's status or position to make a point or convince team members of some plan is manipulative and blocks communication. As noted earlier, individuals can be intimidated by the presence of leaders or others with power.

INTERRUPTING   Another way to block team performance is to interrupt others, say, during a meeting or presentation. This communication behavior in effect disorients members, allowing the dominant individual to exert undue influence.

DEFENSIVE COMMUNICATION   There are many defensive communication behaviors, including reacting angrily, withdrawing, and giving the so-called silent treatment. Group members should be careful not to allow such behaviors to control group interaction.

With a clear sense of task orientation and a high level of tolerance, group members can press toward their goals and overcome these and other negative blocking behaviors. Figure 8.4 on the next page provides a useful tool for assessing team communication.

STRATEGIES FOR CONDUCTING LARGE GROUP MEETINGS

Beyond the methods for effective group and team functioning, there are many times when leaders are faced with conducting a large group meeting. We thought it helpful to provide a basic outline of two tools to meet this condition. By following standard rules of procedures, one has methods especially useful when a group needs structure and must conduct a formal vote. The second tool in

| Team Name _____ | | Team Assignment _____ | | |
| Reviewer _____ | | Date of Review _____ | | |

	Quality of Performance			
	Excellent	**Good**	**Fair**	**Poor**
Developed key goal, purpose, and questions	☐	☐	☐	☐
Reviewed major symptoms of the problem	☐	☐	☐	☐
Analyzed the problem	☐	☐	☐	☐
Chose one solution after considering alternatives	☐	☐	☐	☐
Conducted research and presented evidence	☐	☐	☐	☐
Developed plan for implementation	☐	☐	☐	☐
Experienced participation by all members	☐	☐	☐	☐
Applied leadership style appropriate for situation	☐	☐	☐	☐

Comments:

FIGURE 8.4 Team Communication Assessment

the subsequent section is brainstorming, a method to encourage creative thinking in which members can exchange ideas and develop new ideas without critique.

Rules of Procedure

Formal meetings that involve large groups of people or that may be attended by individuals from outside the regular group membership often follow rules of procedure, sometimes called **parliamentary procedure**. For instance, city council meetings, department meetings, student board meetings, and the like may all follow such rules so as to implement structure and avoid chaos. Experience has shown that meetings can be streamlined and conflicts avoided through consistent application of procedural rules.

Another important reason for following rules of order is to conduct a formal majority vote. A vote may be needed to make a decision among a large group of members, to end discussion of a matter and proceed with implementing a plan, or to resolve close differences among members. A set of standards for formal voting procedures is detailed in such widely available guides as *Robert's Rules of Order* and *Sturgeon's Rules of Order* (Capps, Dodd, & Winn, 1981). The actual details for applying Robert's or Sturgeon's rules are complex, but here are some beginning points.

CONDUCTING A FORMAL MEETING The standard format for conducting a formal meeting is as follows:

1. Call to order
2. Minutes of previous meeting: correct or amend
3. Reports of officers, standing committees, or boards
4. Reports of special or ad hoc committees
5. Unfinished or old business
6. New business
7. Adjourn

MOTIONS TO MAKE DECISIONS   Formal decision-making models rely on the processes of making, discussing, objecting to, and voting on motions. A *motion* is a statement of a team member's position that the other members will ultimately decide by vote. The motion procedure involves these steps:

1. The presiding officer recognizes the member, and he or she makes the motion. The appropriate wording is "I move that . . ."
2. The presiding officer asks if there is a *second,* or an affirmation of the motion. If there is no second, then the motion dies.
3. If the motion receives a second, the presiding officer restates the motion and calls for discussion.
4. Members discuss the motion.
5. At some point, a member calls for the *question,* or the vote (or the presiding officer prompts a call for the question). This usually occurs when the discussion slows down, but if members still want to discuss, a call for the question is premature.
6. The motion is voted on, and the results are announced.

Most types of motions are passed with a simple majority—that is, approval by over half of the membership. However, some types of motions require a two-thirds majority to pass, such as: motion to limit or extend debate, call for the question, and motion to rescind an earlier vote.

Brainstorming Techniques

The **delphi technique** is an approach to brainstorming, but instead of involving face-to-face or direct interaction regarding a problem or issue, group members share ideas through e-mail or other communication without actually meeting. The leader assembles group members' responses to questions and issues and after a designated time or several rounds of give and take, a consensus is achieved. Here are some simple steps for this technique, adapted from Beebe and Masterson (2000):

1. The group leader presents a key question, problem, or issue and sets the process in motion, soliciting ideas for a solution.
2. The leader corresponds with each member to clarify his or her responses and then lists aspects of the problem and solution until a final summary occurs.
3. The leader continues to nurture the process of summarizing feedback and solutions until a consensus is reached.

For more information on the variety of topics covered in this chapter, go online to the sites listed in Web at Work 8.1.

WEB AT WORK 8.1
Small-Group Communication

These websites provide useful information about managing small-group communication:

- **www.uky.edu/~drlane/capstone/group** Honors Capstone Course workbook material on groups.
- **www.abacon.com/commstudies/groups/group.html** Allyn & Bacon's communication studies website.

- **http://jobfunctions.bnet.com/whitepaper.aspx?docid=71266** Looks for communication and interpersonal resources.
- **www.fripp.com** Consultant Patricia Fripp offers insightful articles on communication, including team development.
- **www.accel-team.com** Team-building resource.

STRATEGIES FOR TEAM BUILDING IN THE WORKPLACE

Peter Drucker predicted almost three decades ago the global workplace would comprise autonomous teams. Drucker's prediction has already become true as we've already indicated ways in which teams in the workplace have continued to capture the spotlight. A workplace characterized by cutting-edge technology, fast-paced research and development, and highly informed employees is replacing a traditional workplace in which individuals in the top levels merely channel information and orders to lower level employees who implement the requests.

The popularity of teams does not merely extend group communication, although there are similarities, but teams represent a radically new organizational design within organizational culture. Moran, Harris, and Moran (2007) refer to this new design as the "meta-industrial work culture" and identify these significant characteristics:

- Enhanced control over workspace
- Increased participation and involvement
- High levels of organizational communication and information sharing
- Emphasis on an entrepreneurial spirit within the organization
- High performance and improved productivity

The effectiveness of teams can be seen in a range of world class companies. For instance, Kodak, Motorola, and Procter & Gamble all use teams in a variety of ways. Your value as a future manager will be enhanced if you understand the significance of teams and how to use them in the workplace.

DEFINITION AND MODEL OF TEAMS

To provide a fundamental understanding of teams, we will begin by defining **teams** as structured entities within larger organizations, sharing a mission and goals, and we will explore a life-cycle model that explains how teams develop over time. Team usage has occurred in two waves. The first wave applied a consulting approach that extended principles of participatory management from such models as McGregor's (1967) theory X and Y and Herzberg's (1968) notion of motivating factors. During this wave, organizational theory moved toward reliance on employees as instruments of decisions. An illustration is provided by the early IBM approach to teams, an approach that Hardaker and Ward (1987) described as training key leaders to interact in teams with top management along with employees selected from various company departments all to work internally for a short time on a specific project.

The second and current wave recognizes teams as significant units within an organization, more in line with the foundations of systems theory. The approach emphasizes teams as self-directed, collaborative, and empowered (Kaplan-Leiserson, 2005; Kauffeld, 2006).

Like living organisms, teams move through various stages that influence their work. We might think of team development, therefore, as a **life-cycle model**, such as the model presented in Figure 8.5:

1. *Forming* involves a collection of individuals coming together, discussing their purpose, and getting started.
2. *Storming* involves the group's ventilation of past, current, and potential conflicts.
3. *Norming* involves team members identifying themselves as a group, organizing their mission, and actually beginning the task they are expected to complete.

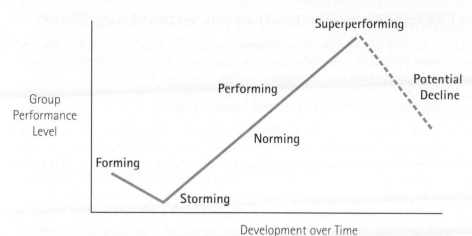

FIGURE 8.5 Model of Team Development

4. *Performing* involves the group developing a strong bond, acquiring knowledge and making decisions, and taking responsibility for those decisions.
5. *Superperforming* involves the team being highly productive and innovative and functioning at peak efficiency.

Each stage is measured against team benefits, as represented by the group's ability to add knowledge and innovation, to make responsible decisions, and to be self-directed as a leadership unit in the organization. In terms of performance, a decline actually occurs after the initial forming stage, while the group confronts its mission and its objectives. Following this storming period, performance increases. During the next two stages, norming and performing, the team is working on becoming a highly motivated, self-directed entity, ultimately blossoming in the superperforming stage. The performing and superperforming stages also illustrate the benefits to the organization of utilizing educated and creative employees to innovate and implement products and policies. During these last two stages, team members experience cohesion, motivation, satisfaction, and high productivity (Katzenbach & Smith, 1994).

As illustrated in Figure 8.5, the life-cycle model highlights an important reality: teams decline unless they redefine goals, reenergize the mission, or make similar efforts at rejuvenation. That is a reason why business and professional communicators need to be aware of such models and their role to align team success.

WEB AT WORK 8.2
Building and Managing Teams

Consult either of these sites for resources about how to build and manage teams in the workplace:

- **www.fripp.com/art.team.html**
  Provides working articles to improve team skills.

- **www.cvc-inc.com/freeresources.asp**
  Provides resources to improve team skills.

HOW TO FACILITATE HIGH-FUNCTIONING WORKPLACE TEAMS

Researchers have identified three **functions of teams** that satisfy organizational and personal needs. They include information/knowledge/innovation needs being met, the need for self-directed leadership; and the need for individual achievement and satisfaction.

Providing Information, Knowledge, and Innovation

As teams move toward high levels of performance, they provide the organization with a rich source of information and ideas, including innovations such as product development and policy changes. In serving this information function, teams are like **quality control circles (QCCs)**, a concept that emerged from the larger movement known as *total quality management (TQM).*

TQM strives to produce higher-quality products in order to fulfill a growing customer drive for better, yet less expensive, products. Organizations assume that their employees are part of the so-called social capital that will enable them to generate outcomes beyond what is possible through traditional management. QCCs, in particular, function by acquiring information and implementing meaningful changes in organizations through regular employee feedback (Beebe & Masterson, 2000).

Providing Self-Directed Management

The need for teams to be self-directed stems from the organizational guideline to "do more with less." Thus, teams need to do more than come up with good ideas; they must also work as self-governing units to implement those ideas. For example, in companies such as 3M, employee teams have the opportunity to create products in research and development programs (sometimes labeled as the "skunk works" as a name for such entrepreneurial efforts). If a product sells at a predetermined level, then the creation team is given status as a new department in the company.

In other situations, teams remain independent units that work autonomously to achieve their designated tasks within the larger mission and purpose of the organization. Figure 8.6 illustrates the various team responsibilities.

High-performance teams encourage innovation, self-direction, and communicating goals and expectations.

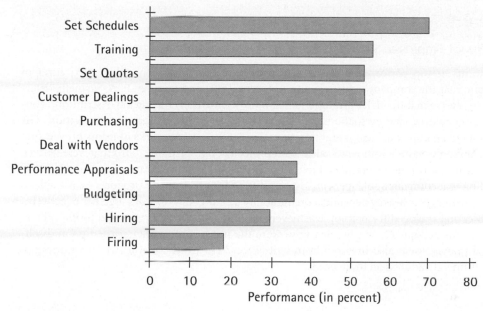

FIGURE 8.6   Responsibilities of Self-Managing Teams   *Source:* Based on Moran, Harris, and Moran (2007).

Providing Achievement and Satisfaction

Finally, teams benefit the individuals who comprise them by providing opportunities for achievement and thus satisfaction. For instance, teams encourage raw leadership to emerge and become polished. Teams can incubate innovation in ways that traditional roles may find threatening. Teams award achievement opportunities for go-getter type employees whose talents and ideas otherwise may go overlooked. However, teams can also experience burn-out or feel isolated from the rest of the organization. That is why it is important for future leaders to apply an understanding of these team dynamics being discussed and select and train team members appropriately. As illustrated by Case 8.7 on the next page, it behooves an organization to create teams that benefit their members.

WHAT MAKES A SUCCESSFUL TEAM?

Case studies in the literature and communication experience in building successful organizational teams point to a number of **qualities of successful teams**. Not surprisingly, each quality involves specific skill in communication.

Communicating Vision and Mission

According to an old adage, "Life without a purpose is like a ship without a rudder. Both wind up on the beach—a derelict." This saying provides a metaphor for the need to communicate a team's vision and mission:

- A *vision* is an inspiring but general statement of direction—a sense of the future and where the group wants to be, say, in one year.
- A *mission* is a short, specific statement of clearly stated outcomes—the plan for achieving the vision.

Case 8.7

Benefits of Employee Satisfaction

The exodus of top performers was so disruptive to Aquatec, a chemical manufacturer in Michigan, that the company's chief executive officer (CEO) and founder, E. A. Savinelli, determined to reverse that trend. He arranged for team involvement in creating job descriptions, conducting job analyses and evaluations, and determining levels of employee compensation. The development of individual teams and the increasing reliance on networks of teams proved successful. Not only was the company's talent pool protected, but the innovations that were derived from teamwork resulted in enriched job descriptions and improved creativity among staff. According to a company spokesperson, "The quality of the services and products we are able to provide customers is heavily dependent on the ability of our people to work together effectively."

Meeting the need for employee achievement and satisfaction is what led to the utilization of teams at Aquatec. But in what ways were the needs to provide information and self-directed management also involved in this situation,? How did the effective functioning of teams ultimately address all three needs?

Source: Based on Hopkinson (1991).

Successful teams identify their vision and mission early in their development.

Examples of mission statements abound. Unfortunately, many are vague and lack the specificity needed in a good mission statement. Consider the following examples:

EXAMPLES

"The company expects increased profits next year."

"The organization will broaden its membership base."

The questions raised but left unanswered by these mission statements are fairly obvious: How will the company know when its profits have increased, and how much of an increase is desired? How much does the organization want to broaden its membership base, and how will it go about doing that? These issues cannot be communicated if they are not stated in specific and understandable terms. As will be addressed in the following sections, it is important to state outcomes—exactly what will be accomplished and how it will be measured or documented.

The power of having a grand vision and a specific mission is illustrated by Case 8.8, which describes the success of multinational corporate giant IBM.

Communicating Strategic Goals and Activities

Essentially, a team's mission and goals work together to produce strategic planning: What do we want to do, and how can we do it? The mission is accomplished through setting and then achieving goals, which are specific inputs to achieving desired outcomes. As just mentioned, outcomes

Case 8.8

A Bigger and Better Vision and Mission

IBM's European operations were interested in developing a larger market share. They had the vision of serving a wider number of clients, and so they created a three-part mission for one of their units: (1) "Prepare IBM World Trade (Europe, Middle East, Africa Corporation) employees to establish their businesses," (2) "Organize high-level seminars for IBM customers," and (3) "Make a significant contribution to IBM's image in Europe." This statement of mission indicated who would be affected—that is, World Trade employees—and measures were developed to assess the outcomes in terms of business success, customer satisfaction, and company image.

By envisioning something bigger and better, IBM ultimately reinvented itself. Today, it sells more service and consulting products than actual hardware, and it competes successfully in a worldwide market. How might IBM and similar providers of technological services and products have to continue to adjust and fine-tune their vision and mission to stay competitive?

Source: Based on Hardaker and Ward (1987).

must be clearly stated. Furthermore, goals must be measurable, which means each goal must be devoted to a single issue. Here are some examples of teams' outcomes:

EXAMPLES

"Reduce safety risks by 50 percent by June 1."

"Increase the average customer sale from $24 to $28."

"Reduce customer complaints from 12 percent to 5 percent or less in two years."

"Increase customer service ratings from 78 percent to 90 percent in three years."

It is useful for teams to proceed from vision to mission to goals. As they do so, they should consider these questions:

1. What is the major outcome(s)? How will we know when that outcome has been achieved? How will the outcome(s) be measured?
2. What action steps will be necessary to plan and implement this goal? What primary tasks and secondary tasks must be accomplished?
3. What financial, facility, equipment, and personnel resources are necessary? Will people from outside the organization be needed in the project?
4. Which team member is responsible for each action step?
5. When will each action step be started and completed?

Communicating Expectations

Nothing is more demoralizing to teams than believing that they have been charged with accomplishing a goal or plan only to discover later that it was not taken seriously or was perhaps undermined by leadership (Abernathy, 2000). Whether a team will operate in the short or the long term, it needs to be given significant responsibility along with accountability for the outcome. Old structures of power leadership must be removed in order to empower teams. This shift in expectations involves a number of organizational changes, as identified by Katzenbach and Smith (1994):

From	To
Individual accountability	Mutual support
Dividing those who think from those who do	Everyone thinks and does
Managerial control	Self-directed management
"A day's pay for a day's work"	Productivity-inspired growth

An historical example of the different outcomes that can result from these changes in expectations occurred at the Motorola Company in the early 1990s. Existing business units were re-formed as teams to produce new concepts and products; the teams succeeded because they worked within a set of boundaries, had a mission, and were held accountable for their progress. As a result, the Iridium project was launched with numerous business partners who continued to utilize self-managing teams. The financial results were staggering: multibillions of dollars in projected revenues over future years (Kinni, 1994).

Communicating Commitment and Norms

Successful teams leverage the enthusiasm of their members. Once a team accepts their responsibility, they are often willing to work long hours because of their commitment to their mission and goals.

Since teams form, disband, and form again around new projects, it is important to develop **team norms** of personal commitment and rules for operation (DeWine, 1994). Although norms and rules cannot be handed down, neither can team members do as they please. Having clear expectations from team members is crucial to success. The norming stage of team development, discussed earlier, occurs when teams successfully bond and share enthusiasm.

To get an idea of which norms are most fundamental to successful teams, let's review research based on consultation with the Pfeiffer & Company (Hoffman, 1995) which identifies *comfort zones*, or norms which need to be developed and communicated.

1. *Goals and objectives.* Need to set up the goals for the group
2. *Mutual support.* Members work well with openness, nurturing/renewal, and a sense the group values them
3. *Encouraging creativity/experimentation.* Use tried-and-true approaches versus try new and different approaches
4. *Individual recognition.* Public and visible versus private and quiet

To address these topics and more by completing the assessment scale in Skills at Work 8.2.

Communicating with Senior Leadership

In a successful high-performance team, the group needs to link the team with the larger organization's leadership. A person for that role may serve as a contact person or may actually perform as a team leader. In either case, that person's role of keeping senior leadership informed is vital to team performance.

SKILLS AT WORK 8.2
Assessment of Team Norms

Think about a small group you have worked with on the job or at school, and evaluate it using the following scale. For each item, circle the number (1, 2, 3, 4, or 5) that best represents how the group functioned or how members operated.

1. *Goals and objectives*
    Determined from above   1 2 3 4 5   Determined by team
2. *Openness*
    Focus solely on business   1 2 3 4 5   Discuss personal issues
3. *Conflict resolution*
    Avoid all conflict   1 2 3 4 5   Confront every conflict
4. *Orientation to hierarchy*
    Go through leadership first   1 2 3 4 5   Do it; then tell leadership
5. *Mutual support*
    Members work best on own   1 2 3 4 5   Work best with one another
6. *Reporting*
    Report significant events   1 2 3 4 5   Report specific details
7. *Decision making*
    All decisions by leadership   1 2 3 4 5   All decisions by team
8. *Leadership*
    One person leads   1 2 3 4 5   Leadership roles shared
9. *Creativity/experimentation*
    Use tried-and-true approaches 1 2 3 4 5   Try new approaches
10. *Control/procedures*
    Follow established procedures   1 2 3 4 5   Bypass procedures
11. *Self-evaluation*
    Evaluation from outside   1 2 3 4 5   Team evaluates itself
12. *Working overtime*
    Work regular hours   1 2 3 4 5   Overtime shows dedication
13. *Member does not perform as desired*
    Transferred or fired   1 2 3 4 5   Retained and coached
14. *Nurturing/renewal*
    Wastes productive time   1 2 3 4 5   Needed for rejuvenation
15. *Individual recognition*
    Public and visible   1 2 3 4 5   Private and quiet

Take a minute to look back over your responses. Are most of your answers in a certain range—say, 1s and 2s? 4s and 5s? Or are they fairly scattered? What do you think these numbers say about the functioning of your team?

For instance, at Motorola, strategic business units communicate with team members from cross-functional teams and various units around the company. These highly motivated professionals have formed teams around norms of self-management and empowerment. Team sponsors play crucial roles in maintaining communication (Kinni, 1994).

At companies such as Kodak and IBM, this same concept is applied by designating an *owner* for every program and every business process. This person must accept responsibility for moving the group process along to its intended completion. Furthermore, no owner is to have more than three or four business processes to manage. Finally, each owner must keep senior leadership informed in order to stay viable (Hardaker & Ward, 1987).

Communicating Significant Amounts of Information

To move from the forming and storming stages of the life-cycle model into the more productive stages of norming and performing, a team must develop its mission, purpose, accountability, and rules. These things happen when a team engages in free-flowing discussion not impeded by formal leadership. For instance, Moran, Harris, and Moran (2007) have suggested the following guidelines for communication and information sharing by team management:

- Recognize that diversity is healthy.
- Meet frequently at first until members are accustomed to the team's norms and one another.
- Develop rules and norms, particularly those that focus on commitment and performance outcomes. In IBM teams, no one is allowed to be a "hitchhiker." Everyone is expected to buy into the program and not miss any meetings.
- Tolerate uncertainty and ambiguity.
- Reward each member's achievement.
- Be open to change and innovation.
- Maintain communication that is goal relevant and achieves the assignments.
- Share leadership functions.

OUTCOMES OF SUCCESSFUL TEAMS

Across the literature about training and development, there has been a call to identify the **outcomes** of the training and educational services provided both in-house and by outside trainers. Moreover, measurable outcomes appear to link with high performance (Kirkpatrick, 1994). The following list spells out the performance measures often expected of high-performance teams (Dodd, 2000; Moran, Harris, & Moran, 2007).

1. Revenues and profits to increase
2. Expenses and waste to decrease
3. Customer satisfaction to increase and complaints to decrease
4. Quality (actual and perceived) of products and services to increase
5. Inventory to be reduced
6. Cycle time or time for a process from beginning to end to be reduced
7. On-time delivery to increase
8. Image and impression management to increase
9. Vision casting, mission statements, and goal setting to increase
10. Conflicts within the organization to be reduced; harmony to increase
11. Strategic planning and successful implementation to increase
12. Technology for meetings, research, and analysis to increase
13. Interpersonal communication effectiveness to increase

Thus, a range of outcomes can be expected within an organization because of teamwork.

Case 8.9

Documenting Successful Team Performance

As you read the following examples of exceptional team performance, think about what outcome or outcomes are involved in each. That is, what measurable change or changes were brought about by the successful work of teams?

- Aquatec, a chemical manufacturer, experienced less turnover of top performers (Hopkinson, 1991).
- Motorola's Iridium, Inc., subsidiary managed to obtain a $6 billion investment by demonstrating the success of self-managed teams, resulting in revenues of $2 million per employee for one major part of the organization (Kinni, 1994).
- At one time, the Tallahassee Democrat was unresponsive to its readers' needs, experienced poor print quality, and lost revenues of $10,000 per month. The implementation of teams led to improvements in customer service and printing and zero revenue loss (Katzenbach & Smith, 1994).
- Motorola shifted to special production teams and experienced a reject rate drop from 3.5 percent to 1 percent, an approximate 20 percent reduction in cycle time, and the elimination of late product deliveries.
- A small Texas retail company with six locations experienced major changes when it utilized team-building concepts. To begin, it expanded its number of goals from a traditional 10 to an innovative 85. Furthermore, it enjoyed an increase in revenues of 16 percent in one year. Finally, the value of the average customer purchase increased by 37 percent, and the customer service satisfaction rate increased by 15 percent (Dodd, 2000).

   In closing this chapter, turn to Case 8.9, which presents several more notable examples of how the work of teams yielded exceptional performance outcomes. These examples provide solid evidence of the advantages of implementing a high-performance team culture. As a future manager, your work in effective team building will make a difference for your organization's employees, leaders, customers, and investors.

Successful teams focus on results that facilitate increased organizational productivity, reduced expenses, and high employee morale.

In Perspective

A small group or team can be defined as consisting of three to fifteen members—or an average of between six and eight. It can be characterized using these criteria: purpose, interdependence, interaction, outcomes, satisfaction, and structure. Two major outcomes typify team outcomes: (1) fulfilling a task and (2) creating member satisfaction.

Small groups usually involve three basic types of communication networks. In centralized networks, communication among group members occurs through a central person or persons. In decentralized networks, information passes more randomly among group members, not exclusively through a centrally placed individual or gatekeeper. A third network is virtual groups, where teams utilized increasing technology for meetings, saving time and generally increasing efficiency.

There are three small-group leadership styles, each of which has various advantages, depending on the needs of the group. The highly directive leadership style is an authoritarian method. Under the participatory leadership style, a designated leader offers guidance, suggestions, listening, and concern for members while also showing concern for completing tasks. A third style of negligent (or laissez-faire) leadership offers little guidance or direction.

The communication that occurs within groups can be categorized as serving group task outcomes and group satisfaction outcomes. Such outcomes will not be achieved, however, when barriers are erected to group communication. The most common forms of barriers, or blocking behaviors, are hidden agendas, groupthink or communication, special pleading, pulling rank, interrupting, and defensive communication.

Being able to conduct group discussions is an essential leadership skill. Conducting a group discussion can be broken down into three parts or steps: (1) initiating the discussion, (2) developing problem-solving strategies, and (3) initiating a conclusion. Two strategies of large group meetings can be useful tools: following rules of order and brainstorming in which members exchange ideas without immediate critique.

While the communication process among groups and teams involves these skills outline, team building involves an additional set of leadership skills. *Teams* are structured entities within larger organizations, sharing a mission and goals. A life-cycle model explains how teams develop over time in these five stages: (1) forming, (2) storming, (3) norming, (4) performing, and (5) superperforming. Each stage is measured against team benefits, as represented by the group's ability to add knowledge and innovation, to make responsible decisions, and to be self-directed as a leadership unit in the organization.

Researchers have identified three functions of teams that satisfy organizational as well as personal needs: (1) the need for information, knowledge, and innovation; (2) the need for self-directed leadership; and (3) the need for individual achievement and satisfaction. Achieving a balance between fulfilling organizational and personal needs is critical to the team's success. Case studies in the literature on organizational teams, as well as experience in communicating with and developing teams, point to a number of qualities of successful teams. Those qualities involve specific skill in communicating vision and mission, strategic goals and activities, expectations, commitment and norms, and information and in communicating with senior leadership.

Those who empower teams expect outcomes that affect the entire organization. Among the performance measures often expected of high-performance teams are increases in revenues and profits and decreases in customer complaints and processing times. Outcomes are realized when an organization experiences change in one these areas.

Discussion Questions

1. For what reasons is small-group communication important in today's organizations? Based on your own experiences, what supports the role of teams or groups? What denies it?

2. What are the best measures of task outcomes? of satisfaction outcomes?

3. What types of network design do you think are used in most organizations? Why?

4. Identify the advantages and disadvantages of each of the three different leadership styles. When would you use each of these leadership styles? Why?

5. In concluding a group discussion, when would you try to reach a consensus, when would you call for majority and minority reports, and when would you ask for a vote? What risks does a leader take in using these methods?

6. Describe the virtual office of the future. What will be the advantages and disadvantages of working this way? How would you as a manager feel about your employees working in a virtual office structure? Why?

7. If you were interviewing for a job, how would you respond to a question about the benefits of teams in organizations? Why are teams important? What makes them successful? What examples could you give to support your position?

8. What is the relationship among an organization's vision, mission, and goals? Use some hypothetical or real examples to illustrate what you mean.

9. Imagine that you are preparing to speak at your organization's division meeting. Your purpose is to charge a new set of teams with their individual responsibilities. Outline at least three major points you will make in your speech about the qualities of successful team performance.

10. Companies such as 3M and IBM use the term *ownership* to describe employees' responsibility for their work. How does this concept coincide with the principles behind effective teams?

11. Review the list of outcomes near the end of the chapter. Which five outcomes do you consider most important? Why?

Exercises

1. Review the discussion of task roles in group communication, and then survey several people to ask their perspectives on the significance of these roles. What types of task communication are they comfortable performing? What types do they expect leaders to manage? Report your findings to the class.

2. Conduct the same survey regarding satisfaction roles in group communication. In order for individuals to find satisfaction from group membership, what seems necessary? For instance, how does morale building take place in groups?

3. Interview someone who regularly conducts meetings. What guidelines can he or she offer for creating a good agenda? What rules of procedure does he or she use? What problem-solving sequence does he or she follow? How does he or she usually conclude a discussion?

4. Write your own scenario—perhaps your personal story or that of someone you know—of how a group improved its decision-making process through consensus building or applying rules of order or brainstorming techniques.

5. With a team of classmates, interview the leader of a company about the use of teams. What does the leader view as the pros and the cons? What experiences have led him or her to this viewpoint? Present your findings.

6. Interview four or five people you know about their experience with teams at work. (They don't have to work at the same place.) Do they like working in teams? Why or why not? Also use the assessment from Skills at Work 8.1 to measure their responses to the items about team norms. What are the results? How do the results of the assessment fit with what the individual reports about experiences with teams?

7. With a team of classmates, construct your own model of team development. What happens to teams over time? Why? Display the results on a graph and explain your model to the class.

8. With a team of classmates, make your own list of expected team outcomes. What changes can you identify? What measures can you use to verify these changes? Why are these outcomes relevant to most teams?

References

Abernathy, D. J. (2000). Thinking outside the evaluation box. *Training and Development*, July, pp. 225–228.

Beebe, S. A., & Masterson, J. T. (2000). *Communicating in small groups: Principles and practices.* 6th ed. Boston: Longman.

Brilhart, J. K., Galanes, G. J., & Adams, K. (2001). *Effective group discussion: Theory and practice.* 10th ed. New York: McGraw-Hill.

Capps, R., Dodd, C. H., & Winn, L. J. (1981). *Communication for the business and professional speaker.* New York: Macmillan.

DeWine, S. (1994). *The consultant's craft.* New York: St. Martin's Press.

Dodd, C. H. (2000). Communication intervention in organizational development and level IV outcomes. Paper presented to Training and Development Division, National Communication Association.

Ebrahim, N., Ahmed, S., & Taha, Z. (2009). Virtual teams: A literature review. *Australian Journal of Basic & Applied Sciences, 3*(3), 2653–2669. Retrieved from Academic Search Complete database.

Hardaker, M., & Ward, B. K. (1987). Getting things done: How to make a team work. *Harvard Business Review*, November–December, pp. 112–116.

Harris, T. E., & Sherblom, J. C. (2002). *Small group and team communication.* 2nd ed. Boston: Allyn & Bacon.

Herzberg, F. I. (1968). One more time: How do you motivate employees? *Harvard Business Review, 46*, 53–62.

Hoffman, C. C. (1995). *The 1995 annual: Volume 2, Consulting* (pp. 29–39). San Diego: Pfeiffer & Company.

Hoover, J. D. (2002). *Effective small group and team communication.* New York: Harcourt College.

Hopkinson, M. (1991). After the merger: Paying for keeps. *Personnel Journal*, August, pp. 29–31.

Janis, I. (1982). *Groupthink.* 2nd ed. Boston: Houghton Mifflin.

Kaplan-Leiserson, E. (2005). Virtual work: It's not just for members of the Jedi Council. *T+D, 59*(8), 12–13. Retrieved from Academic Search Complete database.

Katzenbach, J. R., & Smith, D. F. (1994). *High performance teams.* New York: Anchor.

Kauffeld, S. (2006). Self-directed work groups and team competence. *Journal of Occupational & Organizational Psychology, 79*(1), 1–21. Retrieved from Academic Search Complete database.

Kirkpatrick, D. J. (1994). *Evaluating training programs: The four levels.* New York: Berrett-Koehler.

Kinni, T. B. (1994). Boundary-busting teamwork. *Industry Week*, March 21, pp. 72–74.

Moran, R. T., Harris, P. R., & Moran, S. V. (2007). *Managing cultural differences.* 7th ed. New York: Elsevier.

Tubbs, S. L. (2001). *A systems approach to small group interaction.* 7th ed. New York: McGraw-Hill.

West, M., Brodbeck, F., & Richter, A. (2004). Does the 'romance of teams' exist? The effectiveness of teams in experimental and field settings. *Journal of Occupational & Organizational Psychology, 77*(4), 467–473. Retrieved from Academic Search Complete database.

Whiteoak, J. (2007). The relationship among group process perceptions, goal commitment and turnover intention in small committee groups. *Journal of Business & Psychology, 22*(1), 11–20. doi:10.1007/s10869-007-9047-8.

Wilson, G. L. (2002). *Groups in context: Leadership and participation in small groups.* 6th ed. New York: McGraw-Hill.

CHAPTER 9

Managing Interviews in the Workplace

After reading this chapter, you will be able to do the following:

- Understand the purposes of different types of interviews.
- Know the structure of an interview and what happens during each phase.
- Distinguish among the various types of interview questions.
- Apply the communication skills vital to being an effective interviewee.
- Apply the communication skills vital to being an effective interviewer.
- Create an effective résumé and cover letter in seeking employment.

Know how to listen, and you will profit even from those who talk badly.

PLUTARCH

KEY TERMS

interview *(p. 182)*
employment selection interview *(p. 182)*
information-gathering interview *(p. 186)*
performance appraisal interviews *(p. 187)*
complaint or grievance interviews *(p. 188)*
disciplinary interview *(p. 188)*
group interview *(p. 189)*
exit interview *(p. 189)*
telephone interview *(p. 191)*
videoconference interview *(p. 191)*
media interview *(p. 192)*
interview structure *(p. 192)*
types of questions *(p. 195)*
question-sequencing patterns *(p. 199)*
cover letter *(p. 182)*

When a coworker suggested that Phil should consider seeking a more advanced position at the hospital where they worked, he responded that he would "just stay put." Sure, a better position would bring new challenges and other benefits, but the very thought of doing something new was daunting. He would have to think about it.

Well, it took some coaching and education, but Phil eventually applied for that more advanced position at the hospital. The result was that he was offered *two jobs*, both of which involved moving up the professional ladder and receiving all the benefits that went with that, including increased salary. Phil actually found himself in the position of having to pick from two great alternatives.

Like Phil, you can overcome whatever might be holding you back from pursuing goals and making strategic career moves. You can remove part of the mystery (and even fear) by achieving a better understanding of interviewing and being more successful in the interviewing process. For instance, knowing the structure of a typical interview demystifies the process for many interviewees. In the same way, knowing the options for question types and how to structure an interview can help ease interviewer anxiety. Finally, knowing how to create a good résumé and **cover letter** will help ensure prospective employees that they have a good chance of being recognized and offered an interview.

IMPORTANCE OF INTERVIEWING

A special form of group communication is the **interview**, in which groups of two or more gather for a specific exchange of information. As a highly focused communication event, an interview is more than a visit or chat with an employer. Often, formal interviews serve to gather information about personnel decisions or to exchange ideas for specific innovations. Less formal interviews may be held to brainstorm ideas or clear the air about problems or conflicts. Regardless, the impressions made in interviews can last a lifetime and shape outcomes ranging from getting a job to settling a dispute.

Unless you have a thorough background in workplace communication, you have probably had little if any training on how to interview effectively. Research has found that the biggest detriment to the interviewing process is an interviewee with poor communication skills. One study compared common behaviors of interviewees in unsuccessful interviews with those of interviewees in successful interviews (Ayres, Keereetaweep, Chen, & Edwards, 1998). In the unsuccessful interviews, individuals shared these common problems:

- Concern over being evaluated
- Fear of saying the wrong thing
- Lack of attention to proper interview attire
- Negative self-talk
- Distance from the interview process; not appearing engrossed or engaged

By contrast, successful interviewees displayed these behaviors:

- Less anxiety and more confidence
- Thorough preparation, including company research
- High motivation; knowing why he or she wanted the job
- Appropriate attire for an interview
- Good communication skills; visualization of success
- Positive self-talk; ability to block out distractions

TYPES OF INTERVIEWS

By knowing the usual types of interviews you are likely to encounter, you can often reduce your concerns about the interview process. Interviews are conducted for many more purposes, ranging from information gathering and performance appraisal to telephone and videoconferencing interviews. As you consider each type of interview, look for ways to apply specific communication skills where real-world cases and other examples are presented.

Employment Selection Interviews

An **employment selection interview** obviously involves a prospective employee and an organizational representative. This type of interview can be thought of as a two-staged screening process: does the organization want this person as an employee, and does he or she want to be their employee? A second stage of selection interviewing involves identifying where to place a candidate.

The selection process not only builds on initial screening and potential department placement, but the process may also include skills testing and a group interview.

GOALS AND PURPOSE   From the point of view of the interviewee, the most important goals of the employment selection interview are as follows:

- To apply for the job
- To determine his or her organizational fit
- To learn about salary and benefits
- To present a good image

The interviewer's primary goals in this type of interview are essentially these:

- To learn about the candidate's qualifications for the position
- To determine what would motivate the candidate to take the job, if offered

Candidates who are clearly qualified and those who are clearly not qualified are easy for interviewers to spot. It's the candidates in the middle that interviewers have the most difficulty evaluating. Without a doubt, you can increase your chances of being hired by engaging the interview skills presented in this chapter. To help you in the process of seeking employment, review Skills at Work 9.1 on the next page, which provides useful sources of job opportunities.

COMMUNICATION SKILLS FOR INTERVIEWEES   You should do as much as you can to raise the likelihood of hiring success. Becoming a competent interviewee is an important step in that direction. To improve your skills in this area, follow these guidelines:

1. **Prepare.** Having a good résumé may get you in for an interview, but once there, you must be prepared to perform. The level of preparation needed to participate in a successful interview is as much or more than that needed to deliver a public speech. That preparation should focus on these two areas:
   - **Trends in the field.** Find out what is happening in the field in which you would like to work—say, political journalism. Learn about current trends and issues, basic jargon and terminology, and key figures and organizations. Also look into what might be considered typical jobs and assignments in this field. Is this work you would like to do? Is this work you are qualified to do?
   - **Details about the company.** In preparing for a specific interview, learn about the company's history, locations, management structure, products and services, stock values, and organizational culture and values. Why do you want to work here? Why should they want to hire you?

Information about both of these topics can be obtained from Internet searches, visits with current or former employees of the company or profession, evaluations from corporate newsletters and other publications in the field, and evaluations from independent sources. The research librarian at your university or college also will be an excellent resource. Stock values and corporate economic information are available through most online investment tools (such as www.Ameritrade.com and www.MSN.com).

Finally, consider that what you learn about your prospective field or employer will help you anticipate interview questions, such as "What do you know about our company?" and "Why do you want this particular job?" Being prepared to answer these questions will demonstrate your competence and credibility.

SKILLS AT WORK 9.1
Finding Job Opportunities

Where do people find leads on jobs? These resources, listed in order of usefulness for general work situations, have been found worthwhile:

1. **Networking.** Research indicates that most job leads are found through networking. So talk to your friends, family, members of your congregation, alumni of your university or college, professionals you meet, and neighbors. Let them know you are looking for a job and what types of jobs you are interested in. Also keep in mind that the people you don't necessarily know well or see often may be the best sources of information, as they belong to a network that you probably do not.

2. **College placement service.** Many companies come to college campuses and set up interviews through the college placement service. Find out how to get information about who is coming to campus and when, and arrange for interviews with prospective employers.

3. **Career agencies.** Career agencies and other types of job placement services are informed of job openings by companies and then attempt to match their clients (that is, people who come to them looking for jobs) with those openings. Often, however, the biggest advantage that comes from using such a service is "getting your foot in the door," so to speak. In other words, a service may find you a job that is not your ideal job but that may lead to networking and thus eventually getting a better position, perhaps even within the same company.

4. **Newspaper ads.** Occasionally, an individual finds a great position by answering a classified ad, but this isn't something to count on. Looking at ads can, however, help you see the kinds of positions available in your area and the requirements generally associated with them. Similarly, reviewing ads might help you identify companies that seem to be hiring.

5. **Internet sources.** Many job recruitment sites have developed over the years, which provide searching and matching services and have postings from companies all over the world. These sites have specific requirements for how to post a résumé, which will be addressed later in this chapter (see the section "Electronic Résumés").

How many of these resources have you used in previous job searches? Which ones do you need to learn more about and perhaps try in the future? What other sources have you found worthwhile?

2. **Practice.** Familiarize yourself with the interview process and become more comfortable with answering interview questions by practicing with a friend or classmate. While you don't want to appear to have memorized answers to even basic questions, you do want to appear confident and know what you will say.

3. **Stick to the point.** As much as possible, answer the interviewer's questions directly and stay on the topic. However, don't be afraid to offer examples, cases, or personal experiences to help illuminate an answer, to illustrate how you would handle a problem, or to demonstrate your background and knowledge. A good rule of thumb is to answer open questions with brief narratives of one minute or less and to answer closed questions with simple of answers of around twenty seconds. (We will discuss open and closed questions later in this chapter.)

4. *Know your mission and objectives.* Develop a sense of personal mission that you can state as your objective for seeking a position. This idea of mission is life changing, as indicated by best-selling author Stephen Covey (1995) in his book *First Things First*. Once someone has a sense of mission, he or she often develops a perspective that lends passion to his or her pursuits.

Having a sense of mission also contributes to having confidence. For example, a candidate for a high-status position was practicing in preparation for an interview. When the mock interviewer asked, "Why do you want to come here? Specifically, how does this company fit into your overall plans?" the interviewee could offer no reasonably credible explanation. The question had surprised him. Upon self-reflection, he prepared an excellent statement of mission that he was able to present in the actual employment interview. In fact, his statement won him the position. It set him apart from many other candidates, who lacked this vital information.

5. *Know your strengths and weaknesses.* The so-called killer question in many interviews is the one that asks the interviewee to describe his or her strengths and weaknesses. Do not be afraid to tell about your competencies, but don't overstate them either. (Be sure you can actually perform the way you say you can.) In describing your areas of weakness, perhaps present them as areas where you "want to grow." For instance, instead of saying "I never did learn how to do that very well" or "I have trouble with things like that," it might be better to say "I have yet to learn that skill" or "I am looking forward to an opportunity to learn and develop." Tell the truth but frame it using language that indicates your readiness to move, learn, grow, and develop. Case 9.1, which tells the story of a confident and experienced professional, illustrates how he handled a "killer" question.

Case 9.1

Answering "Killer" Questions

Here's a bit of dialogue from the interview of a successful professional who was looking to advance his career. In particular, here's what happened when he was asked to describe his strengths and weaknesses:

INTERVIEWER: Describe your strengths for this position.

CANDIDATE: In general, my work for the last ten years in budgeting, forecasting, problem solving, conflict managing, and innovating new programs has led to a 37 percent increase in my unit's productivity, with a relatively flat expense trail.

After this response, the candidate was asked to elaborate, and he explained details of this summary. Then the interview moved on:

INTERVIEWER: How would you describe your greatest weaknesses for this position?

CANDIDATE: Well, I guess I'd have to say I can't think of any weaknesses. I've worked so hard, I think the outcomes speak for themselves.

How well did this interviewer do? How would you rate his response to the "strengths" question? How about to the "weaknesses" question? What might he have done differently?

By the way, he did not get the position.

COMMUNICATION SKILLS FOR INTERVIEWERS   What if you find yourself not as an intervie-wee, but in the role as an interviewer? Being a good interviewer also requires certain skills:

1. Know the material on file about the candidate so you are not searching through paperwork while you try to talk with him or her. Perhaps highlight points on his or her résumé or application that you find significant or that you want to mention or ask about. Moreover, prepare by being familiar with these other important materials: job title, job requirements, job pay/benefits, and company guidelines.
2. Do what you can to put the candidate at ease and facilitate his or her interview. Maintain eye contact, provide affirmations, and use other nonverbal behaviors to show that you are interested and friendly.
3. Explain the interview's purpose and outcomes.
4. Follow a standard interview form and protocol.
   • Organize the interview and plan the questions in a comfortable or logical order.
   • Ask a variety of question types (see later in this chapter).
   • Ask about the candidate's strengths and weaknesses.
   • Ask for a situational analysis (for instance, "In the situation you just described, how did you handle the next step?").
5. Prepare a good follow-up statement that you can make at the end of the interview. Be sure to explain where the process goes next.

Information-Gathering Interviews

A second interview type seeks as its purpose to gather information. These fact-finding meetings assess situations, events, and persons.

If you are conducting an **information-gathering interview**, preparation and staying on target are the keys to success. General rules for the interviewer are as follows:

1. Clearly identify the purpose of the interview. Some people are nervous about these types of meetings, not understanding that gathering information is a normal part of communication in the workplace. Instead, they may think that the information they provide will be used later in a performance evaluation or disciplinary review.
2. Have a complete outcomes list. What is it you need from this meeting? What do you hope to gain from holding this interview?
3. Organize questions as content, process, and relationship types of questions. (We will discuss types of questions later in the chapter.)
4. Stay with observable facts, descriptions, or behaviors.
5. Avoid asking questions of character or attributing motives to others.
6. Review any legal issues that might be raised by the questions you ask.

If you are being interviewed for information, keep these points in mind:

1. Clarify what you understand to be the purpose and expected outcomes.
2. Answer questions directly and base your answers on what you know. Do not attempt to answer questions beyond your scope of knowledge.
3. Use measurable or observable data and descriptions.
4. Avoid innuendo, rumor, gossip, or guessing about others' motives.

Performance Appraisal Interviews ③

Performance appraisal interviews, which review past work performance, usually follow a formal, standard procedure that is rooted in the organizational culture. They can no doubt be nerve racking for the interviewee and the interviewer as well, but following some simple rules can reduce the level of anxiety and make the interview successful for both parties:

1. *Set the time and place.* The interviewer should send out an agenda and advance materials as needed. Many people have a high need for information and must have the opportunity to prepare for meetings and interviews. The interviewee demonstrates credibility with this kind of preparation and forethought.

2. *Clarify the purpose.* The interviewer should point out how the performance appraisal fits with normal or routine company procedures, how everyone is a part of the process, and so on (unless, of course, this appraisal is somehow not normal or routine). Interviewees should not feel that they have been singled out when, in fact, each employee goes through this type of interview.

3. *Identify criteria for evaluation.* If the purpose of the interview is evaluation, not only the interviewer but also the interviewee should receive advance notice of the performance criteria that will be used. No one should be blindsided by newly stated standards or criteria in a performance interview. The same holds for any type of interview in which some criteria will be used in the discussion.

4. *Restate the criteria early in the interview.* Restating the criteria gives both parties an opportunity to ask for or give feedback regarding their understanding.

5. *Communicate nontask criteria.* Many organizations informally apply criteria or standards that are not clearly expressed and perhaps not clearly linked with job performance—for example, manner of dress, level of cooperating with other employees, experiences together as a department or team, communication expectations, and various mannerisms. These subtle, often hidden expectations can emerge during an interview and surprise the interviewee who expected his or her performance evaluation to be based solely on the achievement of tasks. When the situation seems appropriate, the interviewer should bring these issues to the surface. He or she will need to decide if these issues are relevant to a performance review and, if so, determine how to evaluate their significance. The problem with using these informal expectations as criteria is that they are difficult, if not impossible, to measure. How does someone know when he or she is meeting corporate cultural expectations? How is an employee supposed to know what they are and how important they are? To remain informed, employees should keep an open dialogue with their supervisors and others who can help them understand these expectations.

6. *Steer clear of personal issues.* Some performance appraisals delve into the interviewee's personal life, habits, beliefs, and so on. Interviewers should avoid these issues unless they have been articulated as criteria for doing the job and understood in advance to be relevant to the interview. However, one important exception is being identified more and more often in employees' contracts: namely, when an employee's personal life interferes with his or her job performance, disapproval and even sanctions can result. Examples include receiving an inordinate number of personal phone calls at work, having a personal situation or routine affect on-the-job safety or productivity, and using the Internet at work for personal reasons.

7. ***Ask for or offer data.*** In most performance appraisals, the interviewer often uses vague questions to document performance, such as "Did you meet your goals?" "How did your boss or coworkers respond?" or "Are you satisfied with your performance?" However, critics have suggested that this approach used in organizations today is highly subjective, asks for little real documentation, and remains vulnerable to interviewee personal likes or dislikes. A better approach involves an ongoing system to document performance-related events, recording dates, activities, and degrees of success. Common sources of data include client/customer evaluations, self-evaluations, peer evaluations, supervisory evaluations, and performance measures. This *portfolio approach* makes it possible to produce an accurate report of an employee's work.

8. ***Close with plans for the future.*** In closing, the interviewer can offer coaching or assistance to boost performance where needed, and the interviewee can describe how he or she plans to work differently in the future. Both parties may decide (or the organization may require) a follow-up meeting to set goals for the next period of review.

Although information about past performance can help shape the future, it is recommended that the performance appraisal interview be separated from the goal-setting and planning interview. Doing so allows managers and workers to place the evaluation information in perspective. Sometimes, both managers and employees want to move forward immediately and launch new goals, but without providing some time between conducting the evaluation and setting future goals, the two processes become convoluted.

Complaint or Grievance Interviews

The airing of complaints or grievances in the workplace is the norm, so interviews for the purpose of addressing these concerns should be viewed as opportunities for communication and growth. Unfortunately, **complaint or grievance interviews** are often difficult and painful for both parties. To make these types of interviews more positive, follow these guidelines:

1. Make the complaint specific, identifying the time and date, what happened, who was involved, how frequently this has occurred, and so on. Also, provide evidence to back up your claim, if possible.

2. Determine the procedure to be followed in filing a complaint or grievance. Unions have procedures by which grievances are filed and processed with the company. However, nonunion and nonprofit organizations may not have formal rules on how to act on these matters.

3. In difficult situations, conflict management and resolution may be insufficient. In these cases, formal mediation and alternative dispute resolution approaches may be needed (see Chapter 5 on conflict communication).

4. Once the complaint has been addressed, all of the parties need to let it go. Moving forward may not be easy, but forgiving and welcoming behavior is needed.

5. The details of the complaint and its resolution must be kept confidential.

Disciplinary Interviews

A more intense type of complaint hearing is the **disciplinary interview**, for which the major outcome is a reprimand. Understandably, these situations can be emotional, involving tears and embarrassment, anger and frustration, and sometimes relief and joy. The tone set in disciplinary situations must balance feelings of confrontation and hope. To achieve this balance, the primary interviewer in a disciplinary review should do the following:

1. Carefully explain the situation. Sometimes reading a letter is an effective way to begin the interview.
2. Outline what has led up to the current situation, being as objective as possible.
3. Try to be understanding. Ask the interviewee for information and allow him or her to ask you for information as well. Interviewers who talk but do not listen open themselves up to potential litigation. Listening does not necessarily mean that you agree, only that you want to understand.
4. Seek common ground in reaching an agreement. At the very least, ensure that both parties understand why this situation is unacceptable and must therefore be resolved.
5. Take extensive notes during the interview.
6. Follow through with the appropriate actions. In the case of an official reprimand, most organizations require an outline of the information and procedures to document the meeting and its outcomes. If the result is involuntary termination, then compliance with human resources policies is also in order.
7. Communicate only about the offending behavior. Do not stray into other issues.
8. Offer help. Try to provide coaching, mentoring, training, or other services to help this employee improve at his or current job or do well in another organization. Be sure to do what you promise you will do.
9. If the meeting has the potential to be volatile, have at least one other person attend it with you.
10. Maintain absolute confidentiality. Share information only with those who have an official "need to know." Otherwise, you may commit a breach of ethics or expose yourself to litigation.

Group Interviews

Sometimes, an interview is conducted in a group format. A group of interviewers may talk with a single interviewee, or a single interviewer may talk with a group of interviewees. The following principles have helped individuals being interviewed in **group interview** situations:

1. Show appreciation to the panel of interviewers for the perspectives they have shared and the questions they have asked.
2. Maintain positive facial expressions and eye contact with panel members. In particular, make eye contact with the individual asking you a question.
3. Stay confident.
4. Anticipate more disruptions and noise than you might expect in a one-on-one interview situation.
5. Avoid criticizing the other interviewees in your group, whether through a direct comment or some form of nonverbal behavior. Being supportive of others and their views will make you stand out.

While some individuals find group interviews a bit intimidating, others do quite well in them. As illustrated in Case 9.2 on the next page, having good communication skills is a definite plus in a group interview situation.

Exit Interviews

An **exit interview** occurs when an employee is preparing to leave an organization, and its purpose is to gather informative feedback that will help the organization improve. Many organizations follow a standard protocol for exit interviews, asking for pertinent information about the

Case 9.2

Standing Out in a Group Interview

Robert was completing a master's degree in communication while also participating in the premed program. When it came time to apply to medical schools, he wondered how he would do. He had good grades but only average admissions scores. Nonetheless, he received offers from *seven* prestigious medical schools—something that's virtually unheard of. When asked to explain his extraordinary success, Robert shared the following insights:

> My communication education played a significant role in my interviewing. During group interviews, we were matched with five or six interviewees at a time in different phases. When the other candidates were asked questions, they often hesitated or turned out to be overly competitive toward others in the group, such as arguing or denying previous answers of their fellow candidates. In contrast, I communicated with a lot of eye contact, confidently affirming and appreciating any previous responses from my cohort of candidates, and then building on other answers to express any additional views. Never once did I criticize others or fail to affirm. When I later learned of my success in being admitted to these schools, my reflections led me to believe that my response pattern set me apart from all the other candidates.

Have you ever participated in a group interview? If so, how did you do? If not, do you think you would be comfortable being interviewed this way? What communication skills might you have to work on to prepare for a group interview?

Note that Robert currently practices medicine in the southern United States and makes regular mission trips to poverty-stricken countries to provide free medical services.

In a group interview, maintain eye contact with all interviewees, listen to each member, and avoid criticism unless asked specifically.

individual's employment experience. Employees should understand, however, that they do not necessarily have to consent to an exit interview.

Depending on the reason the employee is leaving, the exit interview can take any of several routes. Someone who is leaving on good terms will likely provide positive suggestions for making the organization better. However, someone who has had a negative experience and is perhaps resentful or bitter may offer a skewed perspective. In that case, it is best for the interviewer to listen and not argue. Sometimes, the exit interview serves a cathartic role, bringing to the surface emotions such as grief and regret upon leaving the organization. There may be other benefits associated with exit interviewing, such as wanting to fulfill the final task of the current position and reaching a sense of closure before moving on.

The interviewee, who is normally the exiting employee, has the right to say whatever he or she needs to in this interview. However, before saying anything, he or she should ask what will happen with the information he or she provides. Will it make a difference? Will it come up at some later point, maybe even in another position at another company? Good judgment should be exercised, regardless.

As always, the information shared should be kept confidential, except on a "need to know" basis. Depending on the comments of the interviewee, follow-up actions might be appropriate, such as counseling, further visits, and reconciliation. The exit interview provides a critical opportunity to shape the organization's image. Consequently, probing yet compassionate interviewing is recommended.

Telephone Interviews

Most interviews are conducted face-to-face, but sometimes conducting a **telephone interview** is an economical way to achieve the given purpose. In addition to the principles already stated in this chapter, these guidelines apply to conducting such interviews:

1. Speak clearly.
2. Adjust the volume, as needed, after asking the interviewee if you are too loud or too soft.
3. Avoid using a cell phone when discussing confidential information.
4. If you aren't sure, ask if anyone else is on the line or can hear on a speakerphone.
5. Ask permission of the interviewee if you want to use a speakerphone or have someone else on the line.

Videoconference Interviews

Videoconference interviews are conducted via Skype or other Internet technology. Again, the previously stated principles of interviewing apply, along with these suggestions:

1. Videoconferencing technology can be uneven. Depending on the modem and line capabilities, movements may appear jerky and cause motion sickness. It's therefore best to keep random movements to a minimum.
2. Look directly at the camera, as if making eye contact with a live person.
3. Identify visual aids or objects with additional technology where possible. If the needed equipment or materials are not available, move the visuals very close to the camera and ask whether they can be viewed. Alternatively, send electronic or FAX copies, as needed.

Media Interviews 10

Suppose that your job puts you in the position of having an unexpected TV or radio reporter shoving a microphone at your face. Or maybe you will be expected to be interviewed on talk shows or to give prepared statements to the public. In order to both look and sound good, you must understand the nature of **media interviews**. To move toward that goal, consider the straightforward guidelines presented in this section, which are based on the experiences of skilled communication consultants and on suggestions from a TV anchor and communication professor, Dr. Larry Bradshaw (2007):

1. Be aware of the time allotted for your remarks, which is likely only seconds. Usually, an edited "sound bite" is 10 seconds, more or less; being allowed 30 seconds would be remarkable. Chances are you will be shown in a background setting, in the foreground with video and only the reporter's voice, or in a brief clip.

2. Speak clearly and present your message in short, easy-to-understand sections or chunks. Think of how your message could be stated in three or four bullet points. Presenting it in this way might encourage a reporter to create a graphic of those very bullet points, further enhancing your message.

3. Avoid providing examples and telling stories that cannot be related succinctly and have the desired effect. Again, time is a critical factor.

4. Come up with a standard phrase that you can incorporate in answering questions. For instance, if a reporter asks "What will your company do to reach agreement with the striking workers?" you might respond, "Our company is redoubling efforts to work with employees through these difficult times." If the reporter persists, asking "How far apart are the two sides on the issue of pay?" you might say something like "We are concerned with this and other issues and have redoubled efforts to work with our employees in resolving them." In other words, repeat your main theme in responding to successive questions.

5. Most reporters will want to use your response to a question without making their asking of the question audible. To ensure listeners will understand the context of your response, begin with a restatement of the question. For example, if asked "When will the new company CEO come on board?" respond with something like "Our new company CEO will come on board early next year."

6. When asked more than one question at a time, sort them out in your answer by saying something such as "Let me respond to one issue at a time. First, . . ."

7. Look at and speak to the interviewer, not the camera. Remember that the audience is looking in on your conversation with the reporter. In a group interview situation, however, look occasionally at the camera and at the other panel members.

8. Dress appropriately in terms of the background and lighting of the situation.

9. Be cordial to media representatives. It's their job is to get the story. Moreover, being kind and helpful may earn you better coverage—now or in the future.

10. Acknowledge the reporter and his or her technical staff—those behind-the-scenes people who often receive little attention and credit.

STRUCTURING EFFECTIVE INTERVIEWS

Like any other type of presentation, interviews have a unique structure. When both participants understand that structure, the interview will be organized and thus predictable. The **interview structure** commonly followed involves four phases: (1) the introduction, (2) the questions,

(3) the closing, and (4) the follow-up. The purpose and content of each will be described in the following sections.

Introduction Phase

The *introduction* is brief and sets the stage for communication between the participants. The interviewer should have all needed materials ready and have the meeting place and time scheduled and organized. The interviewee should come prepared and dressed for the occasion. The introductory phase has two general purposes:

1. ***Establishing the relationship.*** Having the ability to establish rapport and form short-term and focused relationships is a valuable skill in the workplace. Interviewing success correlates with this quick ability to connect with others. Interviewers generally try to set a tone of friendliness and helpfulness by presenting a number of nonverbal and verbal messages that make people feel welcome and comfortable. Interviewees need to be relaxed and respond freely to the interviewer, as if he or she is someone they might like to know more in the future.

2. ***Orienting participants to the interview.*** In order to ensure that both the interviewer and the interviewee understand the reason they are meeting and what the meeting will likely involve, the interviewer should go over the following topics:
   - The purpose
   - Procedures that will be followed
   - The time limit
   - The "big picture" of the company or job
   - The need for the interviewee to be accurate

Question Phase

The second phase of an interview, the *question phase*, comprises the questions asked by the interviewer and the answers given by the interviewee. This is essentially a conversation and should involve the same type of give-and-take. Thus, good interviewers are not judgmental or threatening; rather, they try to evoke useful information from the people they are interviewing. For instance, if an interviewee seems a bit stuck here and there, a good interviewer will provide some nudging to move things along. Sometimes, reapproaching the topic with a less threatening question will relax everyone enough to get back on track.

In the question phase, interviewees should follow these suggestions:

1. ***Give honest and relevant answers.*** Talking around the point, faking an answer, and switching topics are all transparent strategies that any good interviewer will see through. Answer the question that's asked of you as accurately as you can. Consider the following responses to this interviewer's question:

EXAMPLES

Interviewer question: "Describe your experience in developing customer service responses for Internet inquiries."

Interviewee limited response: "I've been working for six months with all kinds of people. One reason I majored in communication is because I love people and they love me. Like my grandpa always said, 'People are the most important part of your life.' When I first came down to the department, it was in disarray and disagreement. We've made a lot of progress and most of the people who link through the Internet to our department go away happy customers. I guess you'd say we are doing something right. Mostly because we decide what each person wants and try to provide it on the spot."

Interviewee better response: "Our Internet customer service department currently deals with customer inquiries without a prompted response set. While the results have been helpful, with a 90 percent efficiency rating, we could improve with more exact answers and communication training for all who answer these inquiries."

To be fair, the first answer contains some good ideas regarding intuitive helpfulness to customers and motivation for serving customers, but it rambles and gets to the point only indirectly. The second answer is not only more direct and forthright, but it also indicates the individual's desire to make continuous improvements in the workplace.

2. *Maintain a positive attitude.* By keeping a positive mental outlook, you will do better in the interview and may even enjoy it. Think of trying to help the interviewer by responding to his or her need to give and receive information.

3. *Use narratives and examples.* In general, you want your answers to be brief and to the point, but there are also times for elaboration. Even yes/no questions can benefit from an example or narrative. The goal is to be vivid but brief. Here are some examples:

EXAMPLES

Interviewer question: "Did you like your training for your nursing career?"

Interviewee limited response: "Yes, I liked it."

Interviewee better responses: "Yes, I did. One reason I found it helpful was . . ."

"Yes, the training program I completed prepared me clinically beyond the normal limits of this kind of training. For example, I assisted with hematology analyses of blood gases in the ICU. Such experiences prepared me to handle a number of crises."

It seems logical that if the interviewer received a simple "Yes" response to the question, he or she would then have to follow up with the question "Why?" By anticipating that and responding accordingly, the interviewee appears insightful, confident, and helpful.

We will discuss specific types of questions in the next section of this chapter.

Closing Phase

In the *closing phase* of the interview, the interviewer normally presents a summary or outline of future steps, if necessary. This is also when the interviewer asks the interviewee if he or she has any questions. If the interviewer does not offer time for questions, the interviewee should respectfully request time for this purpose—for example, "Before we go, I wonder if we have time for me to ask you a couple of questions." Few interviewees are ever turned down with such a genuine inquiry.

Interviewees who ask good questions have done their pre-interview homework. In an employment selection interview, for instance, good questions ask about things like corporate vision, descriptions of departments, qualities of ideal employees, and so on. Questions that focus on compensation and benefits, that call for an immediate decision, that seem irrelevant or imprecise, that misuse humor, or that come across as arrogant will do more harm than good in terms of making an impression.

Follow-Up Phase

The interview itself is usually not the end of the interviewing process. Rather, many interviews are followed by some degree of activity, which is the purpose of the *follow-up phase*. For instance, after an information-sharing interview, notes and data are processed, and after a complaint or disciplinary interview, a report will be issued and some resolution will probably be implemented. In the case of an employment selection interview, these important follow-up behaviors enhance an interviewee's probability of being hired:

1. Sending a short thank-you note to the interviewer.
2. Calling or writing back to indicate your continued interest, if you have not heard in the time expected.
3. Providing new information. Sometimes, an interview fails to tap information that the interviewee feels is important. In these situations, it is appropriate to send a note or e-mail with this additional information to the interviewer. Be sure to indicate, once again, your interest in the position and then add a brief statement about the new information, such as this:

EXAMPLE

"After our interview, it occurred to me that you might be interested in the relative advantages of the new customer service protocols you asked me about during the interview. The protocols have raised customer service by 15 percent. I'd be happy to share them with you or your management team sometime."

The interviewer's role in the follow-up phase also involves setting a timeframe for communicating the hiring decision and promptly letting candidates know when it's been made or when more information might be needed.

INTERVIEW QUESTIONS

Communicating effectively by answering questions well is rooted in the ability to anticipate the types of questions asked in most interviews. As is true of understanding the general four-part structure of an interview, having this foundation of knowledge about question types will also help reduce uncertainty and anxiety.

Types of Questions

The **types of questions** asked during the question phase of an interview can be categorized as follows: (1) closed questions; (2) open-ended questions; (3) hypothetical open-ended questions; (4) probing questions; (5) third-party questions; and (6) leading, loaded; and illegal questions.

CLOSED QUESTIONS   The types of questions that ask for direct and relatively closed answers are collectively known as *closed questions*. There are three basic types of closed questions.

Yes/No Questions. A question of this type is straightforward and calls for a direct answer of *yes* or *no*.

EXAMPLES

"Are you from this state?"

"Do you enjoy budgeting analysis?"

"Have you worked in this kind of nonprofit organization before?"

Unless the interviewer states otherwise, it is often a good idea for the interviewee to elaborate slightly in responding to a yes/no question. Otherwise, the interview becomes awkward and filled with unwanted pauses. As noted earlier, your amplification conveys additional information and sends an important message about your confidence and expressiveness.

Fill-in-the-Blank Questions. This type of question also requires a short answer—usually, a single word or a short phrase.

EXAMPLES

"What spreadsheet program do you use most?"

"When did you first begin to use PowerPoint presentations?"

"What other websites have you found useful in learning about training?"

"Whom would you recommend to provide customer service for our new office?"

Multiple-Choice Questions. The interviewee is invited to select an answer from a slate of alternatives in responding to this type of question. Multiple-choice questions usually ask *who-*, *what-*, and *when*-type questions.

EXAMPLES

"In selecting a new department leader, would you prefer Alexis, Kayla, or Will?"

"Among the clients that we could expand our business plan with, would you start with Jones, Smith, or Andrews?"

"Which vendor has provided the best service in your experience: X, Y, or Z?"

OPEN-ENDED QUESTIONS   *Open-ended questions* ask respondents to answer in unstructured ways, allowing them great freedom in setting the tone and pace of the interview. Like essay questions, open-ended interview questions usually involve *how-*, *where-*, and *why*-type questions.

EXAMPLES

"Where would you locate the new expanded display in the store?"

"How would you conduct a communication audit in the organization?"

"Describe a recent situation that gave you a lot of satisfaction in dealing with a client."

"Why would you include leadership analysis as part of a communication audit?"

HYPOTHETICAL OPEN-ENDED QUESTIONS   When the interviewer sets up a hypothetical scenario and asks for a solution to or analysis of it, he or she is asking a *hypothetical open-ended question.* Like any open-ended question, the response to a hypothetical question need not follow a prescribed format.

EXAMPLES

"Suppose that an irate customer asks to speak with the customer service coordinator. You have been hired for that role. What would you do with this angry person?"

"A client company seeks to upgrade its network capabilities. As our manager of network services, what would you do with that request if the company had little budget for the project?"

"Imagine that one of the employees in your department of twenty people comes in ten minutes late every few days. Company policy requires promptness. As this individual's supervisor, how would you deal with her?"

PROBING QUESTIONS   A *probing question* follows the response to a previous question and asks for more information.

EXAMPLES

"I see. Tell me more."

"After that, what happened the next day?"

"I see what you're saying, but what else does this mean to you?"

"I understand your point, but why do it that way?"

THIRD-PARTY QUESTIONS   A less threatening way of eliciting information about sensitive topics is to ask for the views of a general third party and not the individual's own personal views. By posing third-party questions, the interview can avoid putting the interviewee on the spot or otherwise intimidating him or her.

EXAMPLES

Threatening questions: "Do you believe morale is low in the organization?" "How would you evaluate the senior manager's performance in the company?"

Less threatening questions: "What seems to be the morale level of most departmental members?" "What's the general impression of the senior manager's performance among the people in your unit?"

LEADING QUESTIONS   A *leading question* asks the respondent for a specific, predetermined response—in effect, leading the respondent to a desired answer. Such questions can be manipulative and disallow disagreeing with the slant of the question.

EXAMPLES

"Our plan should be up and running in a week, don't you think, Sean?"

"Our sales team's potential has not lived up to expectations. What do you think, Robert?"

LOADED QUESTIONS   A *loaded question* implies guilt or fault, no matter how someone answers it. It's a double-bind question in that each answer makes some unflattering or unintended indictment, usually a personal one.

EXAMPLES

"Kim, has your department ever improved their faulty expense account methods?"

"Have you stopped coming in late?"

Clearly, questions of this nature pose a win-lose proposition, with the interviewer winning and the interviewee losing. Later in this chapter, we will look at some ways to answer these kinds of interview questions.

ILLEGAL QUESTIONS   As mentioned earlier in this chapter, delving into certain personal topics means asking *illegal questions*. Interviewers as well as interviewees should be aware of the following commonly mentioned illegal (and largely irrelevant) topics:

Age, Gender, and Appearance. It is illegal not only to ask questions about an individual's age, gender, or appearance, but also to ask him or her for a photograph.

EXAMPLES

"As a male in your forties, how would you compare yourself to the twenty-something college graduates who will apply for this job?"

"As a pretty young woman working among all these macho men, how do you think you will get along?"

Marital Status and Family

EXAMPLES

"Are you getting married anytime soon?"

"Do you think you will ever have to leave early for your children's activities?"

Physical Disabilities. A question such as the first one in the following example may be appropriate if the question ties specific, documented job performance to a person's physical abilities to a perform that task. However, a question such as the second one is illegal because what it asks is unrelated to a task.

EXAMPLES

"Since the job description includes physical criteria for lifting, do you have any physical or health limits or need accommodation in this area?"

"Do you have any physical disabilities?"

Both interviewers and interviewees should be aware of topics that cannot legally be addressed, including race/ethnicity and national origin.

Race/Ethnicity or National Origin

EXAMPLES

"Where are your ancestors from?"

"How long have you lived in this country?"

Religious and Political Beliefs

EXAMPLES

"Who did you vote for in the last presidential election?"

"What church do you go to?"

Organizing Questions

As an interviewer, what are your options for asking which question when? In addition, as an interviewee, in what sequence might questions be asked? There are four basic **question-sequencing patterns**: (1) the funnel, (2) the inverted funnel, (3) the hourglass, and (4) the diamond.

The Funnel Sequence. The funnel sequence is a deductive pattern in that the questions move from general to specific (see Figure 9.1 on the next page). That is, the sequence begins with broader, open-type questions and then moves to narrower, closed-type questions.

EXAMPLES

Broad/open: "Describe your views of the marketing division's five-year plan."

Broad/open: "How would you resolve the inconsistencies in the plan?"

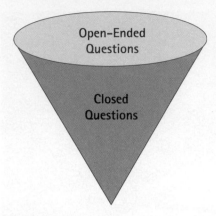

FIGURE 9.1 The Funnel Sequence

> *Narrow/closed:* "Do you think either Sloan or Kettering would be an effective leader?"
>
> *Narrow/closed:* "Is Sloan the person for the new leadership role?"

The Inverted Funnel Sequence. The *inverted funnel sequence* is just the opposite of the funnel sequence (see Figure 9.2). The initial questions are narrower and more closed, and the pattern moves toward increasingly broader and more open questions.

EXAMPLES

> *Narrow/closed:* "Is Sloan the person for the new leadership role?"
>
> *Narrow/closed:* "Do you think either Sloan or Kettering would be an effective leader?"
>
> *Broad/open:* "How would you resolve the inconsistencies in the plan?"
>
> *Broad/open:* "Describe your views of the marketing division's five-year plan."

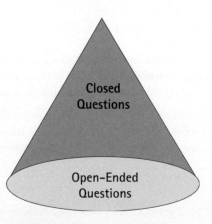

FIGURE 9.2 The Inverted Funnel Sequence

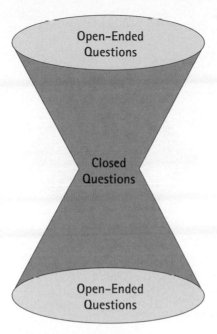

FIGURE 9.3 The Hourglass Sequence

The Hourglass Sequence. In the *hourglass sequence*, the questioning starts by following the funnel sequence—that is, beginning with broad, open questions and moving toward narrower, more closed questions. However, when a point needs further elaboration or new information becomes known, the questioning goes back to more open-type questions. Thus, the opening and final parts of the sequence parallel one another—hence, the term *hourglass* (see Figure 9.3).

EXAMPLES

Broad/open: "Describe your views of the marketing division's five-year plan."

Narrow/closed: "Do you think either Sloan or Kettering would be an effective leader?"

Narrow/closed: "Is Sloan the person for the new leadership role?"

Broad/open: "How would you resolve the inconsistencies in the plan?"

The Diamond Sequence. In the *diamond sequence*, the questioning begins by following the inverted funnel sequence, moving from narrow, direct questions to broad, open questions. Again, to provide clarification or to elicit new information, the questioning goes back to narrow, closed types of questions again (see Figure 9.4 on the next page).

EXAMPLES

Narrow/closed: "Do you think either Sloan or Kettering will be an effective leader?"

Broad/open: "Describe your views of the marketing division's five-year plan."

Broad/open: "How would you resolve the inconsistencies in the plan?"

Narrow/closed: "Is Sloan the person for the new leadership role?"

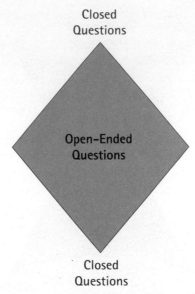

FIGURE 9.4   The Diamond Sequence

Communication Skills in Answering Interview Questions

A number of communication skills for answering interview questions successfully have already been described in this chapter. The overriding principle behind them is to provide the information that's been requested while managing your image in a positive manner.

WHAT CAN I DO ABOUT BEING SO NERVOUS?   Most people are anxious about things they don't understand. I hope that by now, you have a better understanding of the basics of interviewing: the structure followed, the types of questions asked, and so forth. That understanding alone should take care of some of the uncertainty. You can expand your knowledge even more, thus further reducing your anxiety, by researching the organization you are interviewing with to learn about its culture, mission, products/services, and so on. Finally, by practicing and requesting honest feedback from friends and classmates, you can sharpen your skills and feel more confident about going into the interview.

WHAT IF THEY ASK ME SOMETHING I DON'T KNOW?   Never lie or make up an answer. The best thing is to say, "I don't know." In addition, help manage your image on this point in two ways. First, indicate how you have not yet explored this area but are interested in learning as you develop your career. Consider this exchange:

EXAMPLE

Interviewer: "Describe your experience with inventory control systems."

Interviewee: "I have not worked previously with inventory control. However, I understand the principles of process analysis, which might be helpful in designing inventory control modifications."

A response like this indicates your receptivity to new ideas, your interest in continuing education, and so on.

Second, consider how the question may be related to a similar product or topic that you have experience with and then link your answer to the related product or topic. (Make sure, however, that the two are related and that your answer will be relevant.) For instance, in responding to a question about using a particular type of software, you could say, "I have not used Lotus Notes, but I know Excel Spreadsheet and have solved similar problems using it."

WHAT IF I'M ASKED AN EMBARRASSING OR POTENTIALLY ILLEGAL QUESTION?   You have several choices in this situation. First, you can state "I prefer not to answer that question," while indicating your puzzlement as to the question's job relevance. Using a second approach, you meet the question head-on by asking your own follow-up question. Here is an example:

EXAMPLE

Interviewer: "Do you plan to have a family anytime soon?"

Interviewee: "I'm not quite sure, Mr. Smith, how my family decisions affect my suitability for this position. Whether I am married or not or have a family or not, my goal is to perform well for the company. I take great pride in my work. Why are you asking? Is the company taking a survey or something about families of employees?"

If you can defuse the question by minimizing it or using humor, you will usually fare better than if you try to take on the interviewer.

HOW CAN I HANDLE "KILLER" QUESTIONS?   As explained earlier in the chapter, "killer" questions can overwhelm you if you have not given serious thought to how to answer them and then practiced doing so. Here are suggestions for facing several common killer-type questions in interviews:

"What are your strengths and weaknesses?" Be honest in describing both. Don't exaggerate your strengths or be arrogant in talking about them. Also, make sure you will be able to back up anything you say in this regard. In describing your weaknesses, try to put a positive spin on them by presenting them as "areas in need of improvement" or "challenges for the future." Avoid using negative language such as this:

EXAMPLES

"I've never been very good at handling conflict."

"I wish I knew more about current developments in printing technology."

Instead, reframe your shortcomings in positive, optimistic terms:

EXAMPLES

"Like most people, I am always trying to be better at managing conflict."

"To supplement what I know about current developments in printing technology, I've attended several seminars and am taking a class next month."

"How would you . . .?" In asking for explanations of procedures or solutions to problems, interviewers are looking for signs of problem solving, creativity, and confidence, not just content. Here's an example from someone who did not have much experience but provided a good answer and made a positive impression:

EXAMPLE

"You are asking about how to create a communication grievance procedure. I have never worked with grievance policies, but I believe strongly in following three basic communication principles: listen, offer feedback to the person registering the complaint, and recommend options for solutions."

"Tell me about your most difficult . . . (case or client or problem)." The best answer to this type of question involves providing a good narrative that shows how you analyzed the situation and then resolved it.

"Why are you seeking this position?" Of course, the answer to this question will depend somewhat on your personal situation. Regardless, avoid giving a trivial answer or one that comes across as needy or complaining. Instead, try to state a sense of mission and express an optimistic outlook.

EXAMPLE

"My life goals and consequent training in communication have centered on the joy I experience when problems are solved or managed. This commitment extends to the very nature of this position, as I understand the proposal."

HOW CAN I PRESENT THE BEST POSSIBLE PROFESSIONAL IMAGE?   During the interview, maintain control over both your verbal and nonverbal communication. In terms of verbal communication, listen and focus. Make sure you understand each question before you attempt to answer it. If you don't comprehend the wording or jargon used, calmly rephrase the question to clarify—for instance, "When you ask . . ., do you mean . . .?" Try not to appear flustered or confused. Keep your answers to the point, but add examples and specific instances whenever relevant.

In focusing on your nonverbal behaviors, avoid anything that will make you seem nervous, such as fidgeting. Maintain eye contact and a pleasant facial expression. Also, speak using a normal conversational tone and volume. Many people find that when they are nervous the pitch of their voice goes up, the volume goes down, or their voice cracks. Also avoid extremely long pauses (unless you explain your delay) and filling in with *umms* and *wells*. Take the time you need; do not be in a hurry.

To get a final bit of insight into the interviewing process, consider Figure 9.5, which presents a typical summary form used by an interviewer to document the results of an interview. Note the qualities that the interviewee is rated on to assess performance.

Finally, see Appendix D on Written Communication for vital information on writing résumés and cover letters. You will find those principles and examples helpful.

Applicant: _____

Position: _____

Date of Interview: _____

Date Available for Hire: _____

Salary Requested: _____

Quality	Excellent	Fair	Poor	Comments
Attitude	☐	☐	☐	
Confidence	☐	☐	☐	
Education	☐	☐	☐	
Enthusiasm	☐	☐	☐	
Experience	☐	☐	☐	
Skills	☐	☐	☐	
Overall	☐	☐	☐	
Other:				

FIGURE 9.5   Interview Summary

In Perspective

An interview is a special form of communication in which groups of two or more gather for a specific exchange of information. The type of interview we hear about most often is the employment selection interview, or job interview. However, interviews are conducted for many more purposes—including gathering information, evaluating performance, handling complaints and grievances, addressing issues of discipline, working with groups, and obtaining exit information—and via formats such as the telephone, videoconferencing, and other media.

Like any other type of presentation, an interview has a unique structure. The introduction is brief and sets the stage for communication between the participants. The second phase of an interview, the question phase, comprises the questions asked by the interviewer and the answers given by the interviewee. In the closing phase, the interviewer normally presents a summary or an outline of future steps and asks the interviewee if he or she has any questions. Finally, the follow-up phase involves such activities as requesting further information and informing job applicants of the decision.

The types of questions asked during the question phase of an interview can be categorized as follows: (1) closed questions, (2) open-ended questions, (3) hypothetical open-ended questions, (4) probing questions, (5) third-party questions, and (6) leading, loaded, and illegal questions. Questions are organized according to four basic question-sequencing patterns: (1) the funnel, (2) the inverted funnel, (3) the hourglass, and (4) the diamond.

Discussion Questions

1. What was your last interview experience like? Was it what you expected? Were you prepared for the questions that were asked? How did you feel about the responses you gave? What was the outcome of the interview?

2. How would you respond to a "killer" question about your strengths and weaknesses? What would you state as your strengths? What would you state as your weaknesses? How could you present them in the best possible light?

3. If you were leaving a job, would you like to participate in an exit interview? In what ways would doing so be helpful to the organization? to you? In what circumstances might participating in an exit interview be uncomfortable? Would you still do it?

4. Compare and contrast the four different types of question sequences. How might familiarity with these sequences help you as an interviewer? as an interviewee?

5. What types of activities might be involved in the follow-up phase of an interview? What is expected of the interviewer in this phase? What is expected of the interviewee?

Exercises

1. With several classmates, role-play employment selection interviews for the following positions. Discuss personal mission statements, and try to portray the sense of vision and purpose that would be communicated by each applicant. Use the Interview Summary presented in Figure 9.5 to evaluate each interviewee.
   • Personal exercise trainer
   • Construction site manager
   • CEO of a large toy company
   • Head of marketing for the largest grocery store chain in the city
   • Graphic designer

2. With several classmates, assemble the equipment needed to role-play a videoconference interview or a media interview. Create a scenario—such as a political talk show—and write a script that includes the roles of interviewer and interviewee. Practice the presentation and then videotape it. Present the video to the entire class.

3. Choose a company or an organization that you would consider working for, and do some research to gather background information for use in preparing for an employee selection interview. Determine what specific information would be useful in preparing for the interview. Examine a range of sources in finding this information.

4. Choose a company or an organization that you would consider working for, and find out how to submit an electronic résumé to it. Does the company or organization have its own online bank? Do they have a form that you are expected to follow or complete? What directions do they provide?

References

Ayres, J., Keereetaweep, T., Chen, P. E., & Edwards, P. A. (1998). Communication apprehension and employment interviews. *Communication Education, 47,* 1–17.

Bradshaw, L. (2007). Interviewing with the media. Personal communication.

Covey, S. (1995). *First things first.* Los Angeles: Merrill.

Hamilton C., & Parker, C. (2001). *Communicating for results.* 6th ed. Belmont, CA: Wadsworth.

Hutchinson, K. L., & Brefka, D. S. (1997). Personnel administrators' preferences for resume content: Ten years after. *Business Communication Quarterly, 60*(2), 67–75.

McKay, D. R. (2010). Career planning and communication. http://careerplanning.about.com/od/communication/a/email_etiquette.htm.

Managing Public Presentations in the Workplace

After reading this chapter, you will be able to do the following:

- Realize the importance of making public presentations in business and the professions.
- Identify the qualities that serve as the foundations of effective speaking.
- Understand the need to build speaker credibility by demonstrating competence, character, charisma, and co-orientation.
- Address the need to build confidence as a speaker and assess your own confidence level.
- Understand the relevance of audience demographics and be able to conduct an audience profile.

KEY TERMS

foundations of speaking *(p. 207)*
public presentations *(p. 208)*
credibility *(p. 209)*
competence *(p. 209)*
character *(p. 210)*
charisma *(p. 211)*
co-orientation *(p. 211)*
confidence *(p. 213)*
communication apprehension *(p. 213)*
audience analysis *(p. 217)*
demographics *(p. 220)*
audience profile *(p. 222)*

Always bear in mind that your own resolution to succeed is more important than any one thing.

ABRAHAM LINCOLN

When you receive a call, asking you to make a presentation, you will want to deliver the right message and make a great delivery. You will want to be successful in informing or influencing your audience. Yet like many people, you may experience some apprehension about speaking. What skills do you need to make an effective presentation?

This chapter, the first in the unit on making public presentations, identifies three **foundations of speaking** that will establish the basic skills and knowledge you need as a business and professional communicator. Those foundations, which will be referred to in this book as the "three Cs," are credibility, confidence, and consultation about the audience. By focusing on these foundations, you can lay the groundwork for excellence as a public presenter—and further develop your ability as a speaker.

IMPORTANCE OF MAKING PUBLIC PRESENTATIONS

Public presentations can take a variety of forms, such as informative speeches, briefings, formal reports, technical reports, spontaneous reports, inspirational messages, and persuasive speeches. Most professionals agree that being able to present publically significantly heightens your value to an organization and to your personal life (Case 10.1).

In a national study of one thousand human resource managers (selected at random), these individuals rated speaking skills as having a 90 percent importance among factors for first-job skills and job success and an 80 percent importance among factors expected for managerial expertise (Winsor, Curtis, & Stephen, 1997). Similarly, other studies have identified the belief that

---

Case 10.1

The Power of Effective Presentations

The chief executive officer (CEO) for a large company was experiencing a lot of anxiety about making an upcoming speech to his employees, to the point that it was affecting his ability to prepare. The situation he had to address in his speech was critical: sales were flat and a sense of doom hovered over the employees. Without obtaining additional contracts, the company would have to reduce staff, a potential event that fueled everyone's sense of foreboding. Furthermore, the CEO knew that he wasn't a good speaker. After his speeches, employees usually felt worse, it seemed. His halting delivery, inability to connect ideas, and lack of enthusiasm left much to be desired.

Taking charge of the situation, the CEO consulted a professional speech coach and set to work on improving his skills. During their work together, the speech coach learned that the CEO had overcome major obstacles in life and in fact had been the leader of a U.S. Olympic team some years ago. Other stories from his life also came out, revealing this man to have led an interesting life and to have a strong character. The speech coach encouraged him to make use of these stories in speaking and to take confidence from what he had achieved in life.

The CEO took that advice and worked some of the stories into the speech that he was preparing for his employees. First, he tried out the stories on friends and family during dinner conversations, and then he practiced his speech in front of a number of audiences, asking for their feedback and fine-tuning his content and delivery.

The day of the speech arrived. The CEO felt excited and confident as he stepped up to the podium. Then, without even using notes, he gave the most inspiring speech his employees had ever heard from him. When he finished, the room was momentarily quiet, and then the audience erupted into applause that soon turned into a standing ovation. Later, everyone complimented him on what an outstanding job he had done in explaining the situation and motivating the audience. The company made a dramatic turnaround after this event, proving that his message had had the desired impact. The CEO himself commented, "I've never felt such confidence in my life. I prepared what I knew. I practiced like never before. I changed my delivery to be consistent with what I believed about our company's future and myself. I guess it showed."

What has your experience been as a speechmaker? Have you made presentations in the classroom? Have you ever spoken to an audience outside the classroom?

Source: Based on Fripp (2002).

communication ability results in positive impressions about organization and its leaders' effectiveness (Aprix, 2003). One of the foundations involved in forming such impressions is credibility.

BUILDING CREDIBILITY

It has been said that people do not "buy" the company as much as the person that represents the company. Thus, one of the most important aspects of preparing yourself as a speaker is to consider your **credibility**. Specifically, how will people perceive you based on how believable you are? If you lack credibility, your message has little chance of being believed, let alone embraced.

Breslau (2001) confirms the need for managers to increase their credibility in a modern business world that has seen dot-com companies disappear overnight. In terms of inspiring future managers to be innovative and lead the way to change, she suggests that mastering the elements of credibility helps leaders gain confidence and purpose. These elements come into view in the hypothetical challenge presented in Case 10.2.

Research in communication has demonstrated that when the speaker's credibility is perceived, his or her message has a significant impact on the audience (Dodd & Lewis, 1992). In addition, research has identified four factors that determine a presenter's credibility: (1) competence, (2) character, (3) charisma, and (4) co-orientation.

Competence

Competence is the audience's perception of the speaker's expertise. They will assess whether you have done enough preparation and are knowledgeable enough to be believed. Even if you are not an expert on the topic you plan to speak about, you can develop your competence by doing solid research and preparation. Here are some suggestions:

1. Read background information as well as topic specific research. In general, revealing a broad knowledge base and experience with a subject helps an audience perceive your competence.

Case 10.2

Creating Credibility

Suppose that you have been hired as new director of a new company program. To launch the program, you are planning to make a presentation to your local branch of the company. However, in preparing for that presentation, you have identified several serious challenges:

- Your marketing team demands that you follow a different client-processing procedure than you have used successfully in the past.
- The company's home office dictates a policy that does not fit the local organizational culture and operation.
- You are new to the organization and wonder how receptive existing employees will be to your ideas.
- You are not sure how to prove that your innovations will benefit the company in terms of increasing time, profits, and morale.

How can you build credibility in the eyes of your boss, your clients, and your coworkers? How will their image of you affect their willingness to receive and act on your message?

SKILLS AT WORK 10.1
Assessing Your Competence

Answer these questions to check your competence as a speaker:

- Are you committed to learning and developing your knowledge and skills in your profession?

- Do you present yourself as a learner?
- Do you convey the sense of wanting to share information?
- Do you know your subject (or how to conduct research in this area)?

---

2. Cite expert testimony to heighten your own competence. This shows you are prepared and can be trusted.
3. Use a variety of evidence types to support your message: statistics, examples, illustrations, testimony, and so on and avoid reliance on just one source of evidence.
4. Know your content and the order in which you plan to present it. That is, have your information and outline ready. Nothing makes you look more incompetent than losing your place or hitting miscues with visual aids.
5. Present yourself with poise and confidence.

How competent do you perceive yourself as a public presenter? To answer, complete Skills at Work 10.1.

Character

The second element of speaker credibility is **character**. The audience's perception of the speaker's character is, in fact, their sense of the speaker's trustworthiness based on their experiences before, during, and after the speech. Ancient orator Quintilian identified character as the main ingredient in *rhetoric* when he defined it as "a good man speaking well." As with competence, you must create a perception of trust. What qualities will demonstrate your trustworthiness? In direct terms, here is what is important. First, show fairness. Indicate your impartiality to the audience by being truthful and accurate. Make clear that conclusions are based on solid information and reliable sources. Show respect. If your audience finds you arrogant, they will immediately question or deny your trustworthiness. Sometimes audiences mistrust speakers who are too innovative or who overlook basic traditions and values—especially those held dear by the given audience. Check character with Skills at Work 10.2.

SKILLS AT WORK 10.2
Assessing Your Character

Character is about trust. Your audience will perceive you as being trustworthy when you are honest and open with them. Answer these questions:

- Have you researched the topic so as to present information that is truthful and fair?

- Do you have the audience's best interests in mind?
- Do you understand the audience's values and traditions?

Charisma

Charisma, the third element of speaker credibility, involves the speaker's enthusiasm for the audience, the occasion, and the message itself. The speaker has a great deal of power at his or her disposal to use language and nonverbal behavior to get the audience interested and then hold their attention.

We tend to believe speakers who are dynamic, enthusiastic, lively, and genuinely interested in their topics. This is not to suggest that you adopt a phony or otherwise inappropriate sense of enthusiasm. (That would distract your audience and probably destroy your trustworthiness and competence.) Rather, friendliness and assertiveness are at the heart of charisma. Guidelines for developing charisma include:

1. *Vocal enthusiasm.* Speakers who use a monotone voice or lack animation can appear boring. For instance, examples that experts believe represent good enthusiasm include U.S. figures such as John F. Kennedy, Billy Graham, Ronald Reagan, Bill Clinton, Sarah Palin, and Barack Obama—who were believable not only because of what they said but how they said it. An unfortunate example of the intoxicating power of charisma is found in the story of former Enron executives, which is told in Case 10.3.
2. *Delivery emphasis.* Rather than make every point in your presentation using the same tone of voice, volume, and so on, try to emphasize memorable points. That is, make changes and use pauses in your vocal delivery.
3. *Assertiveness.* Show that you are an independent thinker and willing to stand up against the odds. If you seem to follow the bandwagon or are hesitant to commit to a position, why should an audience believe you? By demonstrating assertiveness in resisting the tide of opposition, you will enhance your perceived charisma.

Co-Orientation

The final element of speaker credibility is called **co-orientation**, and it refers to the speaker's compatibility with the audience. As mentioned earlier, audience members want to know that a speaker understands and perhaps even agrees with their values, interests, and beliefs. The speaker who establishes this common ground conveys a form of *relational credibility*. Strategies center on

Case 10.3

The Power of Charisma

The executive team of the CEO, CFO, and others collectively had an incredible ability to leverage charisma and data to convince employees and other investors to continue the purchase of stock and investment in corporate resources (even when these leaders were doing the opposite), they complied. The reports excluded significant financial details in making the case, but sadly for the employees and investors, they overlooked the missing information because of the enthusiasm for Enron's future. These leaders ultimately were subjected to federal investigation for these questionable accounting and trading practices and convicted.

Think of someone you know who has considerable charisma or who offers the facts. How do others typically respond to that person? What sort of influence seems to come from being charismatic, even when data indicate a different direction? As Skills at Work 10.3 indicates, assessing and improving enthusiasm is a valuable asset, but only in the context of ethics and accuracy.

SKILLS AT WORK 10.3
Assessing Your Charisma

Determine your level of charisma by responding to these questions:

- Do you show genuine enthusiasm for your topic?
- Do you convey its importance?
- Do you show personal motivation and reasons for interest in your topic?

- Do you speak in a flat and monotone voice?
- Do you look directly at the person or audience when you are speaking?
- Do you use gestures while you speak?

---

two things: (1) identifying similarity (beliefs, values, attitudes) and (2) identifying common experiences (telling a story others relate to, making them feel connected to you). See Case 10.4.

Lovas (1999) cites the significance of co-orientation in these remarks to sales managers: "You'll see your sales force turn into a unit of industry and community leaders. When new prospects see them care about people, rather than quick profit, their production will increase and their clients will remain loyal" (p. 2). Lovas also points to companies that have implemented training in this area and enjoyed these results: very low turnover rates, very high morale, loyalty increases, and profits that rise from 25 to 100 percent.

Recap on Credibility

The combination of competence, character, charisma, and co-orientation all adds up to credibility. When these qualities are genuine and define the person that you are, they will serve you well in a variety of situations. Thus, we think of credibility as something a person develops because he or she is a person of substance.

Case 10.4

Connecting with the Queen

Some years past, Queen Elizabeth was visiting the United States to attend the Kentucky Derby and was expected to speak to the audience gathered at the event. What could the queen of England possibly have in common with these individuals?

She began her speech by telling about how every year in England, there is also a championship horse race and that she always attends it because of her great love for the sport. This statement brought immediate applause from the audience. Later reports indicated that people felt a sense of connection with the queen, as if she were really one of them. In just moments, with a few carefully chosen words, Queen Elizabeth won over what could have been a hard-to-reach audience.

Suppose that you have to speak to an audience with whom you seem to have nothing in common. What topics might be useful in establishing common ground with virtually any audience?

SKILLS AT WORK 10.4
Assessing Your Co-Orientation

Respond to these questions with your audience in mind:

- What values, interests, and beliefs do you share with your audience?
- What experiences do you have in common with your audience?

- Do you have your listeners' best interests in mind?
- How can you establish common ground with this group?

Timm (2001) wraps this idea with the following ingredients for a success "recipe" in making presentations to business and professional audiences: be reliable, show empathy, make it simple, practice, and be enthusiastic.

BUILDING CONFIDENCE

The second foundation of speaking—that is, the second "C"—is **confidence**. Communication practitioners agree on the significance of confidence in effective public speaking. And, don't feel alone if you feel low on this ingredient.

Underlying many speakers' struggle with confidence is something called **communication apprehension**. A multifaceted concept, it can be thought of as an individual's fear of real or anticipated communication in a one-to-one setting, small group, meeting, or public presentation. The bad news is that everybody faces some degree of apprehension before giving a speech. The good news is that this apprehension can be alleviated (McCroskey, 2001).

Symptoms of Communication Apprehension

Some of the common symptoms of communication apprehension include sweaty palms, shaky knees, a dry mouth, a shaky or strained voice, and a feeling of stomach butterflies. Rest assured that good speakers report similar feelings.

What explains these responses? When you face an important event, extra doses of adrenaline and other hormones are released into your bloodstream. Your body is trying to provide you with extra energy. This physiological response can be considered a natural "shot in the arm" that provides you with the resources needed to accomplish the special task. Consequently, the nervousness you feel can actually boost your effectiveness.

Overcoming Communication Apprehension

From the outset, be aware that in extreme cases of communication apprehension, treatment techniques may be required beyond those addressed in this book. However, reducing communication apprehension comes down to some things you can control and what areas you can work on. Applying the following five strategies can help you achieve this control: (1) being prepared, (2) practicing, (3) using positive self-talk, (4) identifying positive audience members, and (5) doing physical activity (DeVito, 2000; Dodd & Lewis, 1992; O'Hair, Friedrich, Wiemann, & Wiemann, 1995).

BEING PREPARED   Of all the steps you can take to overcome your apprehension, being prepared is probably the most important. To be fully prepared means being thorough at all of the stages involved in presenting a speech. For instance, take the time to do good research and then give yourself enough time right before delivering the speech to check and review your sources. If you are unsure of your information or your sources, you will likely feel anxiety when you have to get up before an audience. Also spend sufficient time organizing your information into a message that people can follow. One good idea is to finish organizing a day or two before giving the speech and then going back to it; this will give your ideas time to mature. This "incubation period" also allows more practice time, a point we'll make repeatedly.

PRACTICING   The amount of time a person spends practicing a speech is linked directly with his or her effectiveness and ease in delivering that message. So give yourself enough practice time. For a ten-minute speech, you should go over it four or five times. For a longer speech or one that involves visual aids, give yourself more time.

When you have practiced enough, you will find that the words come out smoothly, almost automatically. You will sound and appear more polished speaking naturally than you will sound if reading from a script.

Practice with a friend, in front of a mirror, or with a recording device to gain helpful feedback. A run-through with an audience of one or two can also boost your confidence when you have to speak to a larger group.

USING POSITIVE SELF-TALK   Communication apprehension is sometimes a mind game. Without minimizing the real fear involved, it is important to point out that you can control certain aspects of your emotions. An effective technique for doing so, called *rational emotive therapy (RET)*, comes from noted therapist Albert Ellis. He identified how irrational beliefs can be overcome by subjecting them to rational analysis.

The RET technique was applied to communication apprehension and tested in a classic, yet unique, research study (Watson & Dodd, 1984). Various individuals with communication apprehension were presented with training to help alleviate this problem. To replace the negative self-talk that is common in such situations—for example, "I'll fail," "I never should have accepted this role," and "I'd rather die than get up there"—the individuals were helped to develop skills in creating more positive self-talk, or "mental tapes"—for example, "I can do this," "Nothing bad will really happen," and "People will like my message."

To apply this strategy of positive self-talk, it's important to understand that most people play two kinds of tapes. Ellis referred to our negative self-talk, which brings up all of the things that could possibly go wrong, as *irrational statements* or *fears*. These negative statements become increasingly broad, ultimately resulting in our being overwhelmed by dark, pessimistic, and exaggerated views of our self-worth, the audience, the occasion, and the speech. Consider the following:

EXAMPLES

"I really wish I had prepared more."

"My mother told me I should never take a speech class."

"My roommate tried to discourage me from taking this class as a freshman. I know now that I should have waited until I was a senior."

When you practice your speech sufficiently, you will experience confidence and better audience attention.

To circumvent the playing of these negative tapes, feed your mind with positive tapes just before you speak. Tell yourself things like this:

EXAMPLES

"This is an exciting topic."

"I'm really glad I have this opportunity to share these ideas with these fellow students."

"This audience is going to love the kinds of things I have to say."

"I may not have every point prepared exactly perfectly, but I have a very clear idea of what I want to do in this speech and where I am going."

"I'm really thankful to have the opportunity to be here today."

Recap on Confidence

Overall, confidence grows with experience. Although you may always have some feelings of apprehension, the more public speaking you do, the less apprehension you will feel. One way to gain this experience is to give speeches every chance you get—for instance, doing a short talk to a group of students or presenting a report to a committee.

In their book *Great Speakers Aren't Born*, Kops and Worth (2000) offer these suggestions for improving communicator confidence:

- Make sure that your message is relevant to your audience.
- Grab your audience's attention right from the start.
- Use anecdotes, examples, and other vivid illustrations to hold your audience's attention.
- Use visual aids to enhance your message, when appropriate.
- Perform nonverbal behaviors (gesturing and making eye contact) that demonstrate confidence and enthusiasm.
- Close your speech with a sense of finality and reflection.

SKILLS AT WORK 10.5
Assessment of Communication Apprehension

This instrument is composed of twenty-four statements from the Personal Report of Communication Apprehension or PRCA (McCroskey, 2001) that describe feelings about communication with other people. For each statement, indicate in the space provided one of these responses:

1 = Strongly agree   2 = Agree
3 = Undecided   4 = Disagree
5 = Strongly disagree

Don't be concerned with the fact that many of the statements are similar. Also keep in mind that there are no right or wrong answers. Work quickly so as to record your first impressions. When you have finished responding to the statements, add up your total score and then proceed to the other scoring information that follows.

_____ 1. I dislike participating in group discussions.

_____ 2. Generally, I am comfortable while participating in group discussions.

_____ 3. I am tense and nervous while participating in group discussions.

_____ 4. I like to get involved in group discussions.

_____ 5. Engaging in group discussion with new people makes me tense and nervous.

_____ 6. I am calm and relaxed while participating in group discussions.

_____ 7. Generally, I am nervous when I have to participate in a meeting.

_____ 8. Usually, I am calm and relaxed while participating in a meeting.

_____ 9. I am very calm and relaxed when I am called upon to express an opinion at a meeting.

_____ 10. I am afraid to express myself at meetings.

_____ 11. Communicating at meetings usually makes me uncomfortable.

_____ 12. I am very relaxed when answering questions at a meeting.

_____ 13. While participating in a conversation with a new acquaintance, I feel very nervous.

_____ 14. I have no fear of speaking up in conversations.

_____ 15. Ordinarily, I am very tense and nervous in conversations.

_____ 16. Ordinarily, I am very calm and relaxed in conversations.

_____ 17. While conversing with a new acquaintance, I feel very relaxed.

_____ 18. I am afraid to speak up in conversations.

_____ 19. I have no fear of giving a speech.

_____ 20. Certain parts of my body feel very tense and rigid while giving a speech.

_____ 21. I feel relaxed while giving a speech.

_____ 22. My thoughts become confused and jumbled when I am giving a speech.

_____ 23. I face the prospect of giving a speech with confidence.

_____ 24. While giving a speech, I get so nervous that I forget facts I really know.

_____ **Total Score**

Scoring

You will compute one total score (which you should have just entered on the preceding page) and four subscores relating to the various communication contexts: group discussions, meetings, interpersonal conversations, and public speaking situations. To compute your four subscores, add and subtract the scores for individual items as follows:

SKILLS AT WORK 10.5 *(Continued)*
Assessment of Communication Apprehension

Communication Context	Scoring Formulas
Group discussions Subscore _____	Begin with a score of 18 and then add the scores for items 2, 4, and 6. Then subtract the scores for items 1, 3, and 5.
Meetings Subscore _____	Begin with a score of 18 and then add the scores for items 8, 9, and 12. Then subtract the scores for items 7, 10, and 11.
Interpersonal conversations Subscore _____	Begin with a score of 18 and then add the scores for items 14, 16, and 17. Then subtract the scores for items 13, 15, and 18.
Public speaking situations Subscore _____	Begin with a score of 18 and then add the score for items 19, 21, and 23. Then subtract the scores for items 20, 22, and 24.

A total score of 84 or above indicates a generally high level of communication apprehension. What is your total score? What is your highest subscore? Do these assessments surprise you in any way? Why or why not?

Source: From J. C. McCroskey, *An Introduction to Rhetorical Communication*, 8th ed. (Boston: Allyn & Bacon, 2001). Copyright © 2001 Allyn & Bacon, a division of Pearson Education, Inc. Used with permission of the publisher.

With each occasion, your experience will accumulate, your uncertainty will fade, and you will feel more confident.

CONFIRMING AUDIENCE ANALYSIS

The final speaking foundation is to engage in **audience analysis,** or to examine the traits that characterize the individuals to whom you will be speaking. The significance of audience analysis has been recognized since the days of Aristotle, who saw knowledge of the audience as a major tool for crafting effective presentations. We would do well to remember his timeless advice: "Know the audience."

Knowing about your audience has a number of benefits. First, it can help you select and then narrow an appropriate topic. Once you link your audience with a relevant topic, you can narrow and develop the topic accordingly. In addition, tailoring your message to your audience will help gain and hold their attention. Of course, all these things will help improve your feelings of credibility and confidence —and add impact to your speech.

In recent years, the terms *marketing profile* and *target marketing* have been used to describe approaches to audience analysis. Counseling, interviews, sales meetings, briefings, persuasive presentations, and negotiations all represent situations in which conducting an audience profile will yield useful knowledge to enhance your message.

Audience Experience and Topic Knowledge

Each person in the audience brings to the speaking occasion knowledge and experience about the topic. These individuals' collective history should bear on your choice and organization of support materials. Various practitioners would have you ask these questions (Epson Corporation, 2000; Walsh, 2002):

- What experience do audience members have with this topic?
- Why are they interested in this topic?

- Do they like it or dislike it? Are they skeptical about it? angry about it? pleased about it?
- Is the audience a potential sales market, or will the audience members become clients?
- Are they looking for a competitive advantage because of learning about this topic?
- How does their experience compare with their knowledge of this topic? Have they heard other presentations about it?

Clearly, these questions form the foundation for evaluating your audience's level of knowledge about your topic. Having determined that, you must achieve a balance between providing too much information in your speech, thus overwhelming the audience, and providing too little, thus boring them. You don't want to talk over their heads or insult their intelligence. Your goal is to forge a link between their current knowledge and the speech's outcome.

Audience Knowledge of the Presenter

Also ask yourself what the audience will know about you as the presenter:

- What will audience members understand about your background? Will they trust you? Will they be concerned about your role as a speaker and whether it will affect them (such as a supervisor speaking to employees)?
- What will audience members assume about your intentions toward them as a speaker? Will they think you are trying to persuade them? inform them? sell them something?

Audience Motivation and Values

Much of your audience's motivation is rooted in why they are attending your presentation. Maybe they want to, or maybe they have to. Either way, you should anticipate what the audience expects. Fulfilling their need for information will be vital to your success. Ask yourself these questions about expectations:

- Will the topic be relevant to the audience for only a limited time (such as the topic is a product or timely event)?
- Is the audience looking for service, convenience, cost, or quality?
- Will you interact with this audience again or just this once (for example, if they meet regularly)?

Values are enduring beliefs about what is worthy and truthful. There are personal values—such as believing in the power of optimism and the worth of perseverance—and there are group and organization values—such as believing in the effectiveness of teamwork and showing loyalty toward leadership.

To see how identifying the audience's attitudes and values can help you tailor your message, look at Figures 10.1 and 10.2, which present data from an audience survey. Figure 10.1 indicates that 50 percent of the audience is neutral about the topic at hand, 30 percent are for it, and 20 percent are against it. Obviously, these figures show that the audience members' experience and knowledge of this topic have influenced how they feel about it. The data in Figure 10.2 illustrate audience members' values in terms of their general outlook on life: 80 percent are optimistic, 60 percent are innovative, 70 percent are fatalistic (believing that they do not have control over life), and 60 percent feel people are a mixture of good and bad qualities. Again, this information will be valuable in determining the audience's receptivity to your topic and what adaptations are needed to address their values.

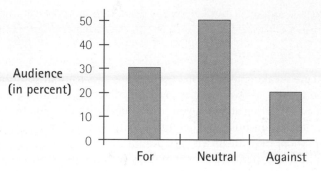

FIGURE 10.1   Audience Attitudes

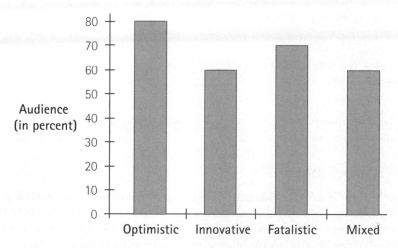

FIGURE 10.2   Audience Values

Occasion for the Presentation

Knowing the *occasion* for the audience being at your presentation is another key piece of information. Some typical occasions include meetings to inform, enlighten, motivate, challenge, criticize, entertain, inspire, praise, and control or manipulate. These questions help understand the dynamics of occasions between the speaker and the audience:

- Time: How often does the audience meet? Is this an annual event? a one-time event? a weekly meeting?
- Membership: Do audience members comprise a defined group, such as a team or a department? Is that membership the reason for the occasion?
- Topic: Did the audience come strictly because you are the speaker, or did they come because of the topic?

Your challenge is to meet the audience's expectations of the occasion. Unlike other contexts for speaking, business and professional communicators need to consider these organizational occasions for and genuinely some of these typical expectations (Customer-focused selling, 2001; Timm, 2001):

- To expand existing customers' or clients' use of products or services
- To broaden the base of services or products and customer traffic

Case 10.5

Speaking to the Sales Team

Suppose that you are speaking to the worst performing sales team in your division. They have held this position for the last two quarters, and they have shown no signs of improvement. You have scheduled a meeting at which you plan to deal with this situation. But what should you say? What information might be helpful? What information might be harmful? How might you inspire those individuals who are pessimistic about turning things around? What can you draw on in your experience to help in this situation?

Source: Based on Epson Corporation (2000).

- To motivate or inspire employees
- To increase revenues
- To reduce expenses
- To discuss benefits

Case 10.5 gives you an opportunity to apply what you have learned about analyzing the audience. Consider how you can meet their needs and yet achieve your purpose in speaking.

Audience Demographics

In addition to the issues considered so far, it is important to consider the audience's **demographics**: that is, their makeup in terms of factors such as age, gender, education, income, occupation, family and marital status, residence, and culture. The value of this information is based on the assumption that people often identify with others who share these qualities. For instance, a member of the millennial generation will likely have different values and attitudes than a baby boomer. By knowing which members are in your audience, you can adapt your presentation.

GENDER   Research has demonstrated that understanding gender differences can enhance the presentation of a message. Information on gender should influence your selection of examples, illustrations, case studies, and statistics and the amount of intense language you use. For example, using football stories to illustrate key points to a mostly female audience may be ineffective, if not offensive.

AGE   The significance of age differences is obvious: Audience members of different ages have lived through different experiences and thus have different perceptions. For example, the best-selling books *Generations* (Howe & Strauss, 1992) and *Millennials Rising* (Howe, Strauss, & Matson, 2000) identify these demographic age groups:

- The *civic generation* were teens or children during the Depression and World War II (that is, during the 1930s and 1940s).
- The *silent generation* were children born just after World War II, when individuals were coming home from the war. These individuals feel left out; they were neither heroes nor victims.

- The baby boomers, born between 1945 and 1964, grew up with more affluence and safety than their parents did and so have a different set of values.
- The members of *generation X* (born between 1965 through 1985), *generation Y* (born after 1986), and the *millennial generation* (born after 1993) hold unique sets of experiences.

By choosing support material that matches audience members' age-related knowledge and experience, you can target your message more effectively. Age is often a significant factor in achieving meaningful outcomes.

EMPLOYMENT   It is reasonable to assume that a bank president will have different knowledge and experience than a rancher and that a retired person may view information differently than someone who is working full-time. It follows that sensible guidelines should be used for adapting a presentation to the audience based on the nature of their employment.

Epson's Presenters Online guidelines (2000) identify types of workplace audiences and provide tips on how to interact effectively with them:

Audience Type	Communication Suggestions
Executives	Use a tone of suggestion; be formal but don't lecture.
Peers	Use a tone of mutual respect and sharing; ask for opinions, experiences, and feedback.
Team members	Speak in terms of *we*; acknowledge group success and accept group blame.
Special-interest	Relate to their primary issues or needs; show your group's understanding.

To illustrate, here is an instance of the benefits of addressing the needs of a special-interest group, an online training program. An executive from a health-care corporation was preparing to speak to a luncheon meeting of a women's health group. In her introduction, the executive focused on how her company had developed a free health clinic for inner-city women. By using this example to start her presentation, she identified with an issue that was important to her audience. She did not come across as a highly paid executive in health care, but as a concerned peer to the health needs of this target audience. As you can imagine, her speech was a huge success (Epson, 2000).

INCOME   A related demographic is the income of the audience, which is often called *socioeconomic status*. Again, it seems reasonable that individuals with a higher income level will have different attributes than individuals with a lower income level. By knowing how your audience values money, for instance, you can select relevant examples and data.

EDUCATION   Preparing your speech with the audience's education level in mind makes sense in terms of deciding the amount and type of support material to use, the length of the speech, the complexity of the discussion, and the use of language. In particular, are audience members high school graduates or college graduates? Do any hold advanced degrees? What continuing education have they undertaken? What vocational training have they had?

RESIDENCE   Another demographic category to consider in audience analysis is residence. For example, what percentage of the audience are renters or homeowners? Do they live a large city, a suburb, a small town, or a rural area? If they are city dwellers, do issues such as crime, political and community development, transportation differences, and neighborhood factors influence their perceptions?

CULTURE Culture involves such elements as region of the nation, racial/ethnic background, urban/rural background, and family system. Each person has a cumulative set of experiences based on his or her background within a cultural group. As a speaker, be sensitive to these differences and tailor your topic material and delivery appropriately. Be careful, however, not to engage in negative stereotyping, which can result in appearing arrogant or patronizing.

MARITAL AND FAMILY SITUATION An individual's concerns and perceptions are shaped by his or her marital and family situation. Being single, married, or having children are variables to remember when selecting cases, illustrations, and narratives. Choose materials that will link your topic with your audience's lives, if appropriate.

RELIGIOUS AFFILIATION Do audience members have a single religious outlook or a variety of outlooks? What is your religious outlook? How relevant is religious affiliation to discussion of your topic? Whereas a quotation from the Bible may be powerful in speaking to a Christian audience, such a message could offend people of other faiths.

GROUP MEMBERSHIP Do audience members belong to special groups—say, a labor union or a political party? Citing data from large business interests will not have the impact of quoting labor studies or referring to labor law. Similarly, in addressing a group of nursing educators, discussing ethics for physicians will be less effective than citing ethics research from the *Journal of Nursing*. Quoting a well-known Democrat to a mostly Republican audience may not make your point.

HOBBIES AND INTERESTS Do your listeners have common interests or hobbies? An audience composed mostly of people with a passion for computer programming will find examples from computer research sources not only relevant but perhaps compelling.

Conducting an Audience Profile

By using the demographic categories just described, you can develop an **audience profile** for use in preparing your speech. Not only can you research and identify the key traits, but you can also graph them, as illustrated later in this section.

To get the information needed to conduct an audience profile, do any of the following:

- Ask the individuals who are planning the meeting for information on who is expected to attend.
- Interview a sample of expected audience members.
- Review company newsletters and other literature that describes or is aimed at your audience.
- Review industry news and trends by going online and by reading professional journals.
- Research benchmark organizations and competitors.

Let's consider an extended example of how to profile an audience using the audience whose attitudes and values were reported in Figures 10.1 and 10.2. Now look at Figure 10.3, which reports these five types of demographic information about the audience:

A. *Age.* Ten percent are in the 18- to 25-year-old group, 40 percent are in the 26- to 35-year-old group, and 50 percent in the 36-plus group.

Use the information you gather in conducting an audience profile to identify those traits that will most influence the audience's receptiveness to your message.

B. *Education.* Ten percent completed high school, 70 percent completed college, and 20 percent have graduate degrees.

C. *Marital status.* Sixty percent are single, and 40 percent are married. Of those who are married, 45 percent have children.

D. *Religious attendance.* Eighty percent are active in some religion, and 20 percent are inactive.

E. *Employment position.* Seventy percent are managers; 30 percent are support staff.

When we put all these data together, an audience profile emerges. Namely, the audience is composed primarily of women who are 36-plus years old, single, college educated, active in a religion, and working in a professional management role. Furthermore, their attitudes and values are essentially neutral toward the topic, they have stronger-than-average values of optimism, innovation, and fatalism, and they view others as a mixture of good and bad qualities.

To help you conduct other audience profiles, consult the online resources in Web at Work 10.1 on p. 225, which provide demographic and other data.

ENVIRONMENTAL CONDITIONS   Four environmental conditions should influence your topic selection and speech development. The first condition, *audience size*, should be considered in determining your presentation style. For instance, when speaking to a small, informal group, you can be more conversational and perhaps even remain seated. A larger, more formal situation will mean a more structured approach and may demand attention to standing before a podium, working with a microphone, and using multimedia equipment.

The *physical setting*, or where you are going to speak, is another important consideration, involving these issues:

1. *Seating.* How close or distant will you be from the audience? How are the chairs arranged? Are there obstructions that block members' view? Obviously, these issues will affect your ability to connect with the audience.

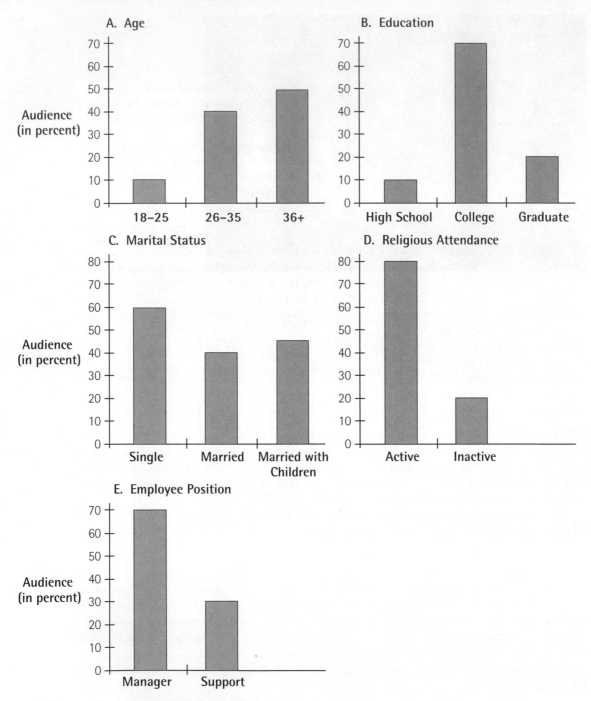

FIGURE 10.3 Audience Demographics

WEB AT WORK 10.1
Audience Analysis

Consult these online sources of audience information:

- **www.presentersonline.com** Epson Corporation's online training site.
- **www.totalcommunicator.com/ vol2-4/knowaudience.html** Provides delivery profiles for audience analysis.

- **www.mindtools.com/CommSkll/ SpeakingToAnAudience.htm** Indicates how to choose topics in relation to an audience.
- **www.ljlseminars.com/audience.htm** Professional speaker and skills expert Lenny Laskowski talks about audience analysis.

2. ***Temperature and equipment.*** If the room is too hot or too cold, both you and your audience will be distracted and uncomfortable. When the microphone doesn't work and the lighting is bad illustrate other distractions. Ask the facilitator to address this matter before you speak. Distractions can be frustrating, as illustrated in Case 10.6.

The *time of day* when the speech is given creates different expectations for speeches. For example, noon presentations are typically short and may be prone to distractions. For an after-dinner speech, the audience may settle in and expect to be entertained more than at other times. The use of visual aids may also be different, depending on time of day and other physical conditions.

ADAPTING TO THE AUDIENCE   Whatever the source of the information you use in conducting an audience profile, you must be able to put it to good use by adapting your presentation appropriately: the introduction, the body, and the conclusion. To do so means making a number of inferences or educated guesses about what traits will most influence the audience's receptivity to

Case 10.6

Conditions beyond Control

A sales account representative reported an unfortunate experience in presenting her speech on revenue projections. She knew the audience would be highly interested in what she had to say because of the careful analysis she had conducted. Using this and other information, she had prepared and rehearsed thoroughly, created an excellent PowerPoint presentation, and made sure the room would be perfect. When she got up to speak, she felt confident and enthusiastic. Only one thing was wrong: in the room next door was a loud group of people, whose singing and laughing intruded upon the presentation again and again. The audience became increasingly distracted as the speaker went on. Unfortunately, her primary reaction was one of frustration.

What could she have done to deal with this distraction? How did becoming frustrated likely affect the communication of her message?

SKILLS AT WORK 10.6
Understanding Your Audience

Suppose that you are preparing a presentation on the need for financial planning. How will you adapt that presentation for each of the following audiences?

> **Audience 1:** 60 participants, 50 to 62 years old, males and females, 80 percent married, high socioeconomic status, assembled at 7:00 PM for the monthly meeting of their local travel club.

> **Audience 2:** 35 participants, 26 to 40 years old, homemakers in one-income households, 75 percent married with children, mostly college graduates, gathered for their weekly luncheon and volunteer service project with the Junior League.

> **Audience 3:** 15 participants, all law students, 22 to 34 years old, 82 percent single, 70 percent have student loans, mostly from politically conservative families in the Midwest, gathered in the student union at 6:00 PM as part of an ongoing personal development seminar.

your message. Consider your main points and support materials, your language, and your delivery by asking these key questions (Audience analysis, 2000; Zubrick, 1994):

1. *Main points and support materials.* What main points will be effective in communicating your message to this audience? What supporting materials will they find credible? What information might be confusing? What can you do to enhance their understanding?
2. *Language.* What level of formality will this audience be comfortable with? Will they understand the vocabulary and terminology associated with this topic? What can you do to ensure that understanding? What type of humor, if any, will be appropriate?
3. *Delivery.* How much will the audience know about this topic? How interested will they be? How can you capture their attention right from the start with a good introduction? How can you maintain their interest throughout the rest of your presentation? Again, what level of formality is appropriate? What sorts of gestures and other nonverbal behaviors should you use?

To apply what you have learned, complete Skills at Work 10.6, which asks you to tailor a presentation about financial planning to three different audiences.

In Perspective

Public presentations can take a variety of forms, such as informative speeches, formal reports, inspirational messages, and persuasive speeches. Three foundations of speaking establish the basic skills and knowledge needed to make effective presentations: credibility, confidence, and consultation about the audience.

Credibility, which comprises the audience's perception of the speaker's believability, is determined by four factors: (1) competence is the audience's

perception of the speaker's expertise; (2) character is their perception of the speaker's trustworthiness; (3) charisma is the audience's perception of the speaker's enthusiasm for them, the occasion, and the message; (4) and co-orientation is their perception of the speaker's similarity with them.

The second foundation of speaking is confidence. Researchers and communication practitioners agree on the significance of confidence to effective public speaking. Unfortunately, many speakers experience communication apprehension: the fear of real or anticipated communication in a one-to-one setting, small group, meeting, or public presentation. While everybody faces some degree of apprehension, it can largely be alleviated through training and insight. Five strategies have proven useful in reducing apprehension: (1) being prepared, (2) practicing, (3) using positive self-talk, and (4) identifying positive audience members.

The final speaking foundation is consulting to engage in audience analysis. Considerations should include the audience's experience with the topic, knowledge of the topic, knowledge of the presenter, motivation and values, and occasion for attending. In addition, it is important to consider demographics: that is, the audience's makeup in terms of age, gender, occupation, family and marital status, and so on. These data can help to make an audience profile, determine what factors influence an audience's receptivity to your message, and tailor your presentation accordingly.

Discussion Questions

1. Why is establishing credibility so essential to a speaker's success? How can a speaker best accomplish this credibility? How can the person introducing the speaker affect his or her credibility? Provide examples.
2. How does practicing build confidence? What methods have you used to practice? How well have they worked?
3. In delivering a presentation to a classroom audience, what should you consider in terms of the occasion? That is, why is the audience there, and what do they expect? How should you tailor your presentation accordingly?
4. Do you think demographics provide an accurate basis for judging a given audience's receptivity to a message?
5. Where can you find the information needed to conduct an audience profile? What types of sources or methods of information gathering seem the most reliable and accurate? Why?

Exercises

1. Conduct a brief survey of twenty or more people to ask their views about what makes a credible speaker. What qualities seem common among the responses? Do they fit the elements of credibility described in this chapter?
2. With a team of classmates, create a hypothetical audience by defining their attitudes, beliefs, and values along with a range of demographic qualities. Then discuss how you would approach tailoring presentations about several different topics—say, animal testing, campaign financing, and kayaking—to this audience.
3. Choose one of the audiences from Skills at Work 10.6 and prepare a brief presentation on a topic of your choice. Focus on the main points and support materials you would use, the language choices you would make, and the delivery you would provide to best communicate your message to this group.
4. Survey a total of twenty or more people from three or more demographic age groups: for instance, from the millennial generation, generation X, and the baby boomers. Ask about their preferences for delivery style and language use. Also ask about their perceptions of speaker credibility. After gathering the information, assess the responses by generation type and then compare them across generations. What similarities and differences do you find?
5. Individually or with a team of classmates, gather examples of the power of charisma from newspapers and magazines. What do these examples reveal about charisma? In particular, what types of influence do charismatic individuals seem to have?

References

Audience analysis. (2002). Available online: www.ask.com/main/metaanswer.asp.

Breslau, K. (2001). Dot-com demise. *Newsweek: Special Report*, April 30.

Customer-focused selling. (2001). Available online: www.businesstown.com/sales/face-customers.asp.

D'Aprix, R. (2003). The big challenge is engaging leaders. *Strategic Communication Management, 7*(5), 14.

Devito, J. A. (2000). *The elements of public speaking.* 7th ed. New York: Longman.

Dodd, C. H., & Lewis, M. L. (1992). *Human communication: Developing positive life experiences.* 2nd ed. Dubuque, IA: Kendall/Hunt.

Epson Corporation. (2000). Presenters Online. How to present to different types of audiences. Available online: www.presentersonline.com.

Fripp, P. (2002). Using the magic of words. Presentation to the National CCCU Technology Conference, Abilene, TX. Available online: www.fripp.com/articleslist.html.

Howe, N., & Strauss, W. (1992). *Generations: The history of America's future, 1584 to 2069.* New York: Perennia.

Howe, N., Strauss, W., & Matson, R. J. (2000). *Millennials rising.* New York: Vintage.

Kops, G., & Worth, R. (2000). Excerpt from *Great speakers aren't born.* Available online: www.communicatebetter.com/resources book.

Lovas, M. (1999). *Beyond wave marketing.* Dallas: About People Press. Available online: www.aboutpeople.com/credibilitymarketing.

McCroskey, J. C. (2001). *An introduction to rhetorical communication.* 8th ed. Boston: Allyn & Bacon.

O'Hair, D., Friedrich, G. W., Wiemann, J. M., & Wiemann, M. O. (1995). *Competent communication.* New York: St. Martin's Press.

Timm, P. R. (2001). Eight key ingredients build customer loyalty. Available online: www.businessknowhow.com/manage/eightkeyingredients.

Walsh, S. (2002). Available online: www.personal.psu.edu/users/s/b/sbw3/workbook.

Watson, A. K., & Dodd, C. H. (1984). Alleviating communication apprehension through rational emotive therapy: A comparative evaluation. *Communication Education, 33,* 257–266.

Winsor, J. L., Curtis, D. B., & Stephens, R. D. (1997). National preference in business and communication education: A survey update. *Journal of the Association for Communication Administration, 3,* 170–179.

Zubrick, A. H. (1994). Available online: www.ask.com/main/metaanswer.asp.

CHAPTER 11

Managing Presentational Skills in the Workplace

After reading this chapter, you will be able to do the following:

- Understand the importance of language in presenting your message.
- Recognize the effects of vocal delivery and bodily delivery.
- Identify and apply the four methods of delivery.
- Develop and use visual aids effectively in making presentations.

Make sure you have finished speaking before your audience has finished listening.

DOROTHY SARNOFF

Explaining the importance of **presentational skills** in speaking is a bit like explaining the importance of presenting food attractively on the plate. In each case, paying attention to matters of style and delivery will make the content entirely more palatable, even pleasing.

Many organizations today have made a strategic commitment to improving the quality of presentations. These organizations are not content with tired, worn-out speeches and all-too-familiar jokes. Rather, they expect their members to be experienced and dynamic speakers, capable of communicating in a range of situations. Your challenge, therefore, is to master the skills that will allow you to be one of those speakers.

ELEMENTS OF LANGUAGE STYLE

Language is the chief means by which ideas are communicated. Thus, learning about **language style**—that is, choices of words and structures—will enhance your ability to communicate ideas more effectively. One essential element of language style is vividness.

Vividness

Your language needs to be alive, brilliant, and colorful. It needs to be compelling. It needs to move people and shake them up. You can create **vividness** by choosing words that give the feeling of movement and excitement.

BEING COLORFUL   Through the use of colorful language, you can paint pictures for your audiences that evoke mental and emotional images. For example, in describing a car *going* down the street, saying that it is *careening* down the street or *creeping* down the street lends important detail and makes the message more dynamic as well. Moreover, using the word *careening* or *creeping* also adds *alliteration*—that is, repeating consonant sounds in successive words. Similarly, using colorful words creates more dynamic descriptions. Saying that people were *madly dashing through the pelting rain* sounds more alive and exciting than saying they were *walking through the rain.*

Of course, in business and professional communication, you need to strike a balance between facts and descriptions of those facts. In some situations, you have to use specific words to make an informative or technical point. Yet in other situations, providing vivid descriptions of data and procedures will help you encourage understanding and motivate change. Case 11.1

Case 11.1

Improving upon "Dry" Language

Read this excerpt from an actual technical report:

> Inventory control analysis reveals excessive flow-through processing time. From purchase to point of sale, the inventory holding time is eight weeks. The warehousing costs along with this slow turnover rate cost an estimated $200,000 per year in unnecessary delays and expenses. Change of the process is in order.

When this report came across the desk of the company's chief executive officer (CEO), he was concerned. While it stated important facts about the company's inventory control issues, it was overly technical for a speech he needed to make. Given the broad audience of community members and line employees to which the speech would be presented, this was not acceptable.

The CEO took out his pen and revised the report, still providing the factual information but adding this message:

> I know we have great intentions. All the same, we are holding our products too long before we sell them in the stores. Without realizing it, we are hoarding precious produce, stealing opportunities from hungry customers who beg to see our latest designs. Unless we change, we inadvertently risk gobbling up slices of our future bonus pie.

Thus, the CEO livened up the original report by discussing the issue in terms of *we* and by using a metaphor that likened the company's products to produce, or food. Both strategies helped make the report more accessible to its broad audience, especially the less technically oriented members. This motivated employees to make a rapid turnaround in procedures.

What likely would have resulted if the report had been distributed in its original form? Would most audience members have understood the facts of the situation? Would most have understood the need for change? Why or why not?

presents a situation in which some overly "dry" technical language was made more vivid and led to these very results.

USING METAPHORS   As illustrated in Case 11.1, the use of a metaphor is another way to make language more vivid. Put simply, a *metaphor* describes one thing by comparing it to another. For example, you could describe a problem by using the metaphor of *troubled waters*, and you could describe continued difficulty as being in a *black hole*. Obviously, your intended meaning is not literal in either case; rather, you are suggesting an image or a likeness. Metaphors are therefore considered *figures of speech* or *figurative uses of language*.

Metaphors can be found throughout business and professional communication. Consider the numerous sports comparisons—such as *step up to the plate* and *hit a home run*—that are used to refer to taking responsibility and achieving successful outcomes. Water metaphors also are popular—*the dam has broken, the tide has turned,* and *we're up a creek without a paddle.* You can heighten your skills in this area with practice by turning ordinary objects and events into colorful metaphors.

USING NARRATIVES   Telling *narratives*, or stories, is also an outstanding approach to today's speaking. While stories not only make a vivid point, stories convey much more. They tell cases, they illustrate, they connect feelings not just facts. Case 11.2 shows how one company president used a familiar story about a starfish to encourage her employees.

Clarity

Another element of language style is **clarity**, or making sure that your audience comprehends what you are saying. Sometimes, clarity is best achieved by being direct. Other times, it is best achieved by scaling down your language and using simple rather than complex words. Consider how to be direct, use simple words, and use concrete words.

BEING DIRECT   Avoid using a lot of words when a few words will do. Look at these three ways of saying the same thing:

EXAMPLES

Indirect: "In clinical trials and in-depth laboratory research, organic compounds, such as the highly saturated hydrogen/carbon mixture based in the gelatinous context derived in the bottled samples here, aerobic substances are known to cause bacterial decay, especially when confronted with an oxygenated environment in post threshold heated conditions, lead to ultimate product demise."

More direct: "Because of the oil content in mayonnaise, it should be refrigerated after opening the container."

Even more direct: "Refrigerate after opening."

USING SIMPLE WORDS   An unwieldy application of opulent language sows adulterated seeds of confusion by not eschewing obfuscation. Ouch! Put more simply, using unfamiliar language is confusing. This doesn't mean you should never use esoteric words. Just use them wisely. For example, the judicious use of words such as *loquacious* and *obtuse* may convey precision and stimulate your audience. But too much rich language can be confusing and even seem arrogant, depending on the situation. For the most part, clarity is achieved through simple, direct language.

Case 11.2

Creating Effective Narratives

The president of a midsized company planned to introduce a new volunteer program to her employees at the company's annual awards dinner. Here's the message she started with:

> Here at and Company, we have a commitment to helping not only each other but others in our community. The company's record is one of corporate community reaching out to the large community. I know you will all become involved in the upcoming community events.

The president realized her message was dull and dry and that it would hardly inspire anyone to get involved. After thinking about several ways of making her message more vivid, she decided to add a narrative. Here's the revised message:

> We at Clark and Company have always believed in reaching out to our community. We may find that frustrating, at times, when we work hard and don't see the results. But let us remember the old story of a lone man walking on a beach that's covered with tens of thousands of starfish. Washed ashore by the tide, the fish were stranded and dying by the minute. The man picked up one starfish and tossed it back into the sea, and then he tossed another and another as he made his way down the beach. A passerby expressed puzzlement and asked, "How can you possibly do any good by throwing only a few starfish back, when you can see the beach is covered with them for miles? How can it make a difference?" Tossing back yet another starfish, the man replied, "It makes a difference to this one."

The company president's speech was so compelling that her employees eagerly signed up for the new volunteer program. They also came away from the event with a renewed sense of satisfaction in their company and its president.

Can you think of a narrative that relates a similar message about getting involved or making a difference? You might want to be on the lookout for such stories in the newspaper, on television, and in religious and inspirational materials for use in some future presentation of your own.

USING CONCRETE WORDS   A third way to achieve clarity is to use *concrete words* (which evoke a sense of touch, sound, smell, sight, or taste) instead of *abstract words* (which are more theoretical and conceptual). To illustrate concrete language, think of different ways to say the word "automobile":

EXAMPLES

Somewhat concrete: "car"

More concrete: "Ford"

Very concrete: "1967 red vintage Ford Mustang with a white interior and a 289 engine with a three-speed transmission on the floor"

Thus, the more concrete your language, the more vivid the mental image you create.

BALANCING THE USE OF TECHNICAL LANGUAGE   As mentioned earlier, the use of technical language, such as jargon and terminology, is necessary in some instances. If you are knowledgeable in a technical area, you may be tempted to assume that your listeners are knowledgeable as well. Making that assumption may often be justified, but it's not necessarily safe. Many audiences, even from within the same organization, are clueless when it comes to the meaning of certain technical language.

This poses a dilemma for many professionals. On one hand, if they avoid using technical words, they might seem to be talking down to the audience and thus appear condescending and childish. On the other hand, if they give the audience too much credit for technical expertise, they might overestimate the audience's understanding and fail to communicate the message.

The way out of this dilemma is to know your audience and then match your content and language to their understanding and expectations (see Chapter 10 on audience analysis). In a mixed audience—say, one comprised of technical-type employees and their managers (who may not have the same degree of technical expertise)—you should err on the less technical side in making word choices. Keep in mind that by using language that only you and a handful of audience members understand, you will likely defeat the purpose of your presentation (see Case 11.3).

Relational Language

Compared to written communication, spoken communication uses more **relational language**: words that link the speaker with the audience, such as *we* and *us* as opposed to *you*, *I*, and *them*. In applying relational language, you create common ground with your audience and heighten their perception of your credibility.

Look again at Case 11.1, the story of the CEO who livened up an otherwise dull report and motivated his employees to change. In addition to fine-tuning the language, he also avoided blaming anyone for the situation and made a remarkable use of relational language: nine relational words in a speech that lasted only twenty-five seconds!

Words Have Feeling in Their Meaning

Words can have two kinds of meanings: **connotation** refers to the meanings that words suggest, and **denotation** refers to the meanings of words in the dictionary. To illustrate, what's the difference between the words *house* and *home*? Most of us think of a *house* as a physical structure (a denotation) and a *home* as a place where loved ones live together (a connotation).

Case 11.3

Talking in Code

In a budget meeting of the deans and vice presidents of a university, the chief financial officer (CFO) and the dean of the business school became engaged in a high-level conversation about budget forecasting and its long-term implications for the university. Unfortunately, the language they used was accounting code—full of jargon and abbreviations—and thus made no sense to the rest of the attendees. They needed to hear these concepts discussed in common terms in order to understand them.

Have you ever participated in a meeting like this or perhaps attended a class or lecture in which the language used was way over your head? What can you do in such a situation? How can you recognize that this is happening in making your own presentations?

Connotative words are wrapped in an emotion, which means their use can trigger certain responses. For example, words like *freak*, *pothead*, *motorcycle jockey*, and *nerd* all have emotionally charged meanings. Before you use words like these, consider what they will mean to your audience as well as to your topic. Will they create the impression you intend to create? You can avoid slipups in using connotative words by jotting down the preferred words on your speaking outline.

Words and phrases can also have connotations unique to an organization or company. Every organization has a vocabulary that conveys so-called shorthand concepts. Such a telegraphic system of communication certainly is efficient, if everyone understands it. Many managers are surprised, however, to learn how often this shorthand evokes emotional responses among young employees, those with limited experience in the organization, and those who have been marginalized to some extent by the organization. In these cases, certain words and phrases can enflame, not clarify. For example, one organization (not the real name) stated its mission in the slogan "XYZ in the world, making the XYZ difference." Unknown to the leadership, employees sarcastically interpreted the slogan as "The XYZ difference: No holidays, low pay, and downsize the organization at all cost."

ELEMENTS OF DELIVERY

After you have carefully crafted your language style, your next step is to craft your delivery. **Delivery** is "the use of vocal qualities and bodily qualities to create meaning in a message." Vocal qualities refer to things like pitch, rate, and volume. Bodily qualities refer to things like eye contact, facial expression, gesturing, and stance. Upon fitting these qualities to your message and the occasion, you will command attention and improve understanding.

Vocal Delivery

What makes **vocal delivery** effective? In general, success can be stated in a single principle: vary your use of vocal qualities throughout your presentation. More specifically, apply this principle to your use of pitch, rate, and volume:

1. *Pitch.* Vocal pitch refers to how high or low your voice is in terms of tone. It is the up-and-down modulation of the voice. To vary your pitch while speaking, think of gradually working back and forth between high points and low points. You can also vary pitch more dramatically to provide emphasis on certain words and phrases. The worst thing you can do is to maintain a monotone pitch throughout your speech. Doing so suggests that your topic is not very important, and it may put your audience to sleep.
2. *Rate.* You can also vary your rate, or how quickly or slowly you speak. Try not to speak slowly all the time or quickly all the time. Rather, vary the rate to fit what you are saying. If you are making a point that does not demand great thought, you might speed through it. But if you want to give a point greater clarity, emphasis, or accent, slow down.
3. *Strategic pauses.* A strategic short pause can emphasize a point for emphasis. A caution is in order here: beginning speakers often pause too long and too often (usually at the end of each sentence). After awhile, the presentation is too predictably rising and falling followed by a long pause. Like any pattern in speaking, variation is needed to prevent boredom and to maintain attention.
4. *Volume.* How loudly or softly you speak should also be controlled for effectiveness. Again, don't do one or the other all the time. This will be tedious for the audience, and they will

lose interest. Create strategic changes, such as louder on some points and softer on others. A common mistake among professionals new to public speaking is to speak too softly too much of the time.

Bodily Delivery

As noted earlier, **bodily delivery** includes behaviors such as eye contact, facial expressions, and posture or stance. In the context of making presentations, the concern is with how these behaviors affect your audience's understanding of your message.

Discussions about what makes effective bodily delivery often center on the word *natural*. Unfortunately, what comes as *natural* may result in a negative effect, perhaps because it's too stilted or slow or lacks the vocal delivery variation discussed earlier. Think of *natural* as meaning "genuine" and "engaging." Even if you discover some bad habits, there is always room for improvement.

HARMONIZE BODILY DELIVERY WITH THE MESSAGE   Business and professional communicators have learned that effective speakers use a combination of body stance, gestures, facial expression, and eye contact. When these nonverbal features align with the points of the speech, the resulting synchronization enhances interest in the verbal message.

Of course, gestures that are out of place or ill timed seem ludicrous. We have all seen comedians portray characters whose gestures are uncoordinated with their messages. In the same way, making artificial attempts to throw in gestures (because you thought that speakers are supposed to make gestures) will not serve a good purpose.

The importance of engaging in nonverbal behaviors goes far beyond our discussion here. The points you should take away from this discussion are that effective bodily delivery creates clarity, boosts rapport, builds trust, and conveys interest. Undeniably, the audience can perceive the speaker's attitude from the stance he or she takes and read the speaker's feelings of friendliness or apprehension from his or her facial expressions.

MATCHING BODILY DELIVERY TO THE TOPIC AND OCCASION   Judging appropriateness is probably one of the most difficult aspects of delivering a presentation. There are no universal principles addressing this concept. Instead, you must rely on your own common sense and artistic ability to recognize what is expected by the audience, the occasion, and the purpose and what you need to do to perform effectively given these expectations.

If you have real questions about what is appropriate in a certain situation, then do some audience research. What do they typically expect? What has worked in the past, or better yet, find out what didn't work very well. You don't need to feel encumbered by tradition or occasion. At the same time, show respect and exercise good taste.

To check your own delivery style, including vocal and bodily elements, review the list of common mistakes in Skills at Work 11.1 on the next page. Review the suggestions, with an eye toward improving your own vocal and bodily delivery.

METHODS OF DELIVERY

The literature on speech communication identifies four primary methods of delivery: manuscript delivery, memorized delivery, impromptu delivery, and extemporaneous delivery.

SKILLS AT WORK 11.1
Common Delivery Mistakes

Review this list of common delivery mistakes. Which aspects of delivery do you need to work on?

1. *Relying on one kind of gesture.* Use a variety of gestures throughout your presentation. Become aware of movements you make repeatedly, perhaps out of nervousness.

2. *Using the same vocal characteristics.* Again, practice variety in your rate, volume, pitch, and pauses. Force change, if needed.

3. *Appearing unnatural or uncomfortable.* If your voice is strained, your gestures are forced, or you otherwise step beyond the bounds of your personality, your audience will sense it and your credibility will be diminished.

4. *Making random body movements.* Moving around too much or in erratic ways will distract your audience. Make your movements deliberate by focusing on some point of your message.

5. *Making random hand movements.* Again, making random movements will be distracting to the audience. In addition, speakers who pick at their ears, brush back their hair, put their hands in their pockets, and so on will be seen as nervous. Even worse, sophisticated audiences will find these habits annoying and judge the speaker as being poorly prepared and lacking in credibility.

6. *Looking at only one side of the audience.* Many successful speakers divide their audience into six or eight segments and maintain eye contact for one or two seconds with the segment that seems to have the friendliest, most involved members at that moment.

7. *Looking above the heads of the audience.* Looking at the walls, the floor, or the ceiling are obviously not desirable either. Again, keep direct eye contact with your audience members.

8. *Overusing pauses and making vocalized utterances.* Whereas pausing deliberately is an effective strategy, pausing too much or for too long with no legitimate purpose is a mistake. Filling these pauses with vocalized utterances—for instance, *uhh; umm; uh, you know, like cool; OK; all right; whatever*—only makes matters worse.

9. *Appearing stiff and stilted.* Don't cling to the podium and stand so straight as to appear stiff. Relax and reveal your energy and enthusiasm for your topic, your audience, and your occasion.

10. *Overgesturing to the point of distraction.* Don't let your gesturing get out of control. Practice gesturing and other elements of bodily delivery to make sure every movement connects with some point of your speech.

11. *Overrelying on notes or manuscript.* If you practice enough, these aids will become less necessary. And with experience, you will learn to glance at your notes or manuscript but not read from them.

Manuscript Delivery

In the **manuscript delivery** method, the speech is written out in its entirety and read aloud to the audience. The chief advantage of this method is that it ensures precise language use, which will be important if you must use specific vocabulary or want to avoid using certain connotative words. However, this advantage is overcome by these disadvantages:

1. This method can lessen spontaneous insights, which can at times be more effective than what you prepared.

2. It is difficult to take in and respond to feedback when you are reading from a manuscript.
3. You may come across as being wooden and stiff in terms of your bodily delivery, and you may sound unnatural and mechanical in terms of your vocal delivery. Many audience members perceive a lack of confidence and enthusiasm when they hear someone read a speech. Of course, alternatively, you can read with dynamism.
4. Delivering a manuscript speech may inhibit your movements and gestures, lessening the effectiveness of the speech.

For the most part, the manuscript method limits the delivery. If you need a manuscript, then be sure to practice with significant delivery enhancements like eye contact, vocal variety, or enthusiasm. Obviously, at times you need this method in which a word-for-word, exactly worded message is demanded. Such a situation might include delivering a technical report or giving a legal opinion, in which a miscommunication could have severe consequences. In cases like this, you may want to have a reviewer for your speech in order to recommend the best possible wording.

Memorized Delivery

A **memorized delivery** is similar to a manuscript delivery in that the speech is written out, but the speaker commits the entire speech to memory. Again, being able to ensure exact language use is a clear advantage. More important, because the speech has been memorized, this method allows the opportunity for movement and thus full use of bodily delivery options. With memorization, the speaker can concentrate more on delivery and less on content.

The disadvantages to the memorized method are as follows:

1. Again, there can be a lack of flexibility and spontaneity in terms of content and delivery.
2. If you recognize audience feedback, you may not respond as effectively because essentially you are reciting.
3. If you lose your place in your speech, you will be embarrassed and probably find it difficult to get back on track without missing a cue or eliminating information.

Impromptu Delivery

The **impromptu delivery** method involves speaking without any specific preparation. In short, someone calls you to stand up to speak without preparation. Some occasions necessitate speaking in this way—for example, the boss calls on you in a meeting, or you have an opportunity to present an idea in an elevator speech. The primary advantage of this method is its spontaneity, and that is the primary disadvantage as well. Most impromptu speakers ramble, using too many words and providing too few details to make the presentation worthwhile.

The more speaking you do, the better you will likely become at impromptu delivery. With time and experience, it can become a useful art. However, for most presentations the benefits of preparation are with question.

Extemporaneous Delivery

Extemporaneous delivery refers to speaking from notes or an outline that contains key words, phrases, and ideas. Without a doubt, this type of speech is well prepared. A great deal of research occurs; the material is tailored to the audience; elements of language use and delivery have been considered. While the order in which you intend to make your points has been set, the exact wording has not. Much of the final wording will be practiced in advance but will be delivered spontaneously.

Using extemporaneous delivery allows the speaker to practice and use few notes. This approach allows greater eye contact, opportunity for improved gestures, and an audience response to your confidence and sincerity.

Extemporaneous speaking has several advantages. For instance, you can evaluate and respond to audience feedback as you go. In addition, you can look and sound more natural. You can be less inhibited in using nonverbal behaviors, and your language can be more creative and vivid at the moment of utterance.

Together, these advantages underscore speaker credibility. In contrast, lacking these qualities can undermine credibility. As Dr. Larry Winn (2006) has stated, "A speech is not an essay with legs." For example, during the 2000 presidential campaign, candidate Al Gore was frequently criticized for his stiff, synthetic-sounding delivery, despite his clear grasp of content. While former president George W. Bush's made many speaking mistakes, one occasion stands out as a classic speech moment, in which he demonstrated the advantages of an extemporaneous delivery. During his prepared comments addressing the emergency rescue workers two days after the September 11 attack on the World Trade Center in New York, amidst a tangled web of debris, he rose on a makeshift platform to encourage rescue workers. His beginning was an awkward manuscript-type moment, but within a few minutes into the speech, members of the large audience yelled, "We can't hear you." Without hesitation, Bush grabbed a nearby bullhorn and with his hand on a shoulder of a rescue worker retorted, "Well, I can hear you." He used this feedback opportunity to realign his presentation into a memorable extemporaneous delivery and an effective speech of hope.

Extemporaneous speaking is not without disadvantages. One is that you may not utter the exact word or phrase you had planned to in making a special point. In addition, your speech may lack verbal economy. With careful planning—such as making notes of keywords and plans for verbal vigor—you can overcome these disadvantages. In general, the advantages that come from being spontaneous and yet prepared win out.

Check your skills as an extemporaneous speaker by reviewing the guidelines in Skills at Work 11.2.

KEYWORD SPEAKING OUTLINE   In planning your extemporaneous speech, create a **keyword speaking outline**, and then use it to guide your delivery. Figure 11.1 is an example of such an outline, which guided the speaker through a presentation on workplace safety. So that you can experience what the speaker said while speaking extemporaneously from this outline, here is the text of the introduction:

When Hoover Dam was built so many decades ago, some fifty men were killed. Unsafe cliff-scaling equipment, lack of safety procedures during cement mixing, and

SKILLS AT WORK 11.2
Guidelines for Extemporaneous Delivery

Experienced and novice speakers alike will find this list of guidelines useful. Use it to evaluate your skills in extemporaneous speaking.

1. Memorize the first two or three lines of your introduction so as not to forget what you were going to say and start out badly.
2. Write on your notes or outline key words and phrases that will lend vividness and clarity to specific points in your speech.
3. While you can be flexible in your choice of words and presentation of details, keep the main points of your speech in order so that you do not become lost or confused.
4. Write out your conclusion or at least some of the significant words and

phrases you would like to use. Doing so will help you acknowledge when you arrive at this point of your presentation, preventing you from making a weak finish or just stopping.

5. Keep your notes to a minimum, using key words and phrases but not writing out a detailed text. Practice to the point that you can glance down at your outline or notes but not depend on them to know where you are.
6. Relax! Consider extemporaneous speaking is a kind of heightened conversation with your audience. Think of them as your friends. Think of them as happy and excited about your message. Be glad that you are there, and approach this occasion with confidence and enthusiasm.

an overzealous schedule led to death during those Depression years. Our sophisticated safety techniques today far outdistance the flirtations with disaster of the 1930s construction. Or are we so removed?

Just two weeks ago, the horrible news that Will Roper lost two fingers in the unit 2's press made those yesteryear stories come alive again. The report that followed showed how we have neglected the primary directive of safety for our employees.

Thus, we stand today, ready to turn around unsafe practices, outdated equipment, and policies that all too swiftly push us to act without hesitation for each person's protection. To better understand our company's safety problems, let's first review our industry's most common safety problems, and then our company's safety issues. Finally, let's turn to solutions and actions that will make us competitive yet the safest organization in the business.

In reading through Figure 11.1, the keyword outline on the next page, you'll see that the entire speech contains some jargon (that is, "AMA and CDC of 2004") that refers to reports by industry sources. You'll notice, too, that the key points in the body of the speech are connected by transitions, internal reviews, and previews, which will be discussed in the next chapter. Finally, in the conclusion, the speech calls for solutions, personal motivation, and action and comes to a strong close with a quote that links new ways with a better future.

PRESENTATION TECHNOLOGY AND COMMUNICATION

A vital part of making public presentations, especially those that present informative and technical material, is to incorporate visually appealing support materials. Today, leaders in business and the professions expect quality **visual communication tools** as an expectation of presentations.

Introduction

Story about Hoover Dam

Link story with company's last safety problem

Transition and preview of key points

I. Most common safety problems

II. Problems unique to our company

III. Remedies over the years

["Let's start . . ."]

Body

I. Most common safety problems

    A. Causes: stress, budget, ignorance of issues

        1. Examples: 98 William's CD Ency.-100

        2. Case study: Michigan's Pontiac Plant

[Transition]

    B. Symptoms are familiar

        1. Employee avoidance

        2. Managers ignore: Mang. Comm. Qrtly. 2002

        3. Budgets reduced: U.S. News, October, 2003

        4. Problems persist anyway

[Internal summary and preview]

II. Problems unique to our company

    A. Contagious

    B. Problem: McNiece report of 2001

    C. Instances: Omar Hendley, Virginia, 6 yrs.

    D. Examples: Equipment

[Internal summary]

[Transition and preview]

III. Remedies over the years

    A. Olden times: Online journal Business

    B. Current approaches best: AMA and CDC (2004)

        1. Analysis

        2. Action plan

        3. Implementation

        4. Follow-up

["In short . . ."]

Conclusion

Summary: Problems are many but solutions are available now

Motivation: How can we count on you? It is in your best interest [Explain]

Strong close: As Von Goethe once said, "Nothing is more damaging to a new truth than an old error." We urge you to act now with new truths.

FIGURE 11.1 Keyword Speaking Outline

Many technologies can help us achieve the goals of competent knowledge transfer, while we still preserve dynamic personal delivery.

Integrating Presentational Skills with Presentation Technology

To illustrate what this involves, consider the following scenario, which opens an incisive article by Diane Porter (2001), associate editor of *Presentations* (a journal devoted to improving speech and technology presentational efforts):

> You are called into your boss's office late one Friday afternoon. He clears his throat, looks you straight in the eye and says, "I need you to present our quarterly sales figures to the board of directors on Monday morning." What do you do? Turn white? Pass out? Smile confidently and start thinking about what you want inscribed on your gravestone?

Chances are, how you react to this scenario will depend on your experience and training as a speaker. In fact, many students and even experienced professionals have never learned good public-speaking skills and have rarely stood before an audience. Furthermore, many of these individuals have not experienced the benefits that come from the intelligent use of presentation technology.

The lack of communication training is known among experts in education and business. Porter echoes this sentiment:

> Companies hire people who can do the jobs they need done. Today, it is almost a necessity to have excellent public speaking skills and training to presentation technology. That's because the corporate world has learned that communication—with customers, clients, and business partners—is one of the most important things executives and employees should know how to do well. Most companies would prefer that their neophytes make their most fundamental mistakes in a classroom setting rather than in the field, where money and sales are on the line.

Porter also argues, however, that college graduates today are expected to have strong business skills in addition to strong communication skills.

> In response, colleges and universities have refocused their efforts on offering communication courses that prepare students for careers in business and the professions. The communication skills deemed important also include the presentational technology tools available to us today. Basically, we want to be able to integrate technology tools such as social media, mobile learning, distance conferencing, PowerPoint, and instant texting or surveys with a mix of speaking skills using powerful language and delivery.
>
> From a theory standpoint, we can identify two types of media (Timmerman, 2002):

- *Rich media* are able to transmit multiple messages, have a degree of personal focus, and use natural language; voice mail is a good example of this medium. Mobile learning that offers instant feedback and text dialogue opportunities illustrates, too.
- *Lean media* do not provide immediate feedback and do not explicitly indicate the recipient of the message; Web sources illustrate these media.

Basically, media selection correlates with the nature of the task: simple tasks can use lean media whereas complex tasks demand rich media.

The point is that we integrate lean and rich media, technology communication, and face-to-face speaking in ways to capture all advantages. Essentially, when we combine effective speech with good visualization techniques, we are in fact using a rich medium. The advantages, as Timmerman states, include a personal focus of hearing with the benefits of learning by seeing.

Communicating When Using Technology

One low-tech type of presentation—meeting and presenting interpersonally—is a very important one. In the absence of technology and visual materials, the speaker's delivery becomes the vehicle for transmitting ideas and supporting them with solid data and logic. However, this part of the book identifies how to use some of the tools. Sometimes, the simple ideas, like flipcharts, sticky posters on the wall, are very effective for trainers and professional consultants along with higher technology instruments. So, you might balance all these strategies and you read further (Munter, 1998; Charney & Conway, 1998; Porter, 2001).

USING FLIPCHARTS, POSTERS, AND NONELECTRONIC BOARDS   Flipcharts, posters, chalkboards, and whiteboards can be effective low-tech visual aids in some situations because of their nonthreatening, nonintimidating appearance. They are especially useful for recording key terms and central ideas. Moreover, they are inexpensive, and they can be easily moved to other locations or used in later sessions, such as brainstorming activities. When brainstorming, ideas can be recorded on posters or whiteboards to facilitate reinforcement and recall of the ideas generated.

While the use of presentation technology has its advantages, the power of having good presentational skills cannot be underestimated.

These visual aids have several disadvantages. It is difficult to illustrate complex images using these media, particularly at a size large enough for many audiences to see. In addition, posters and the like can be messy and thus unintelligible. As such, they may seem unprofessional and too low tech in certain settings.

To use these media well, follow these basic guidelines:

1. Ensure that the sizes of letters and figures are large enough for the audience to see and recognize without straining.
2. Make the lettering and figures neat and plain.
3. Avoid putting too much on a single poster or chart; as stated earlier, key terms and central ideas are appropriate.

To understand the significance of following these guidelines, compare Figures 11.2 and 11.3, which show the same information presented in a disorganized and an organized fashion, respectively.

USING HANDOUTS, OBJECTS, SOUNDS, AND MODELS   Providing a handout can be a useful means of presenting a large amount of data and can also serve as a good memory aid to follow up a detailed report. Objects, too, can serve an important visual function by providing tangible

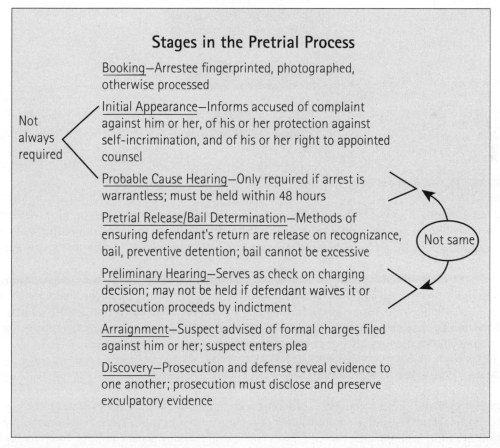

FIGURE 11.2   Disorganized Chart or Poster

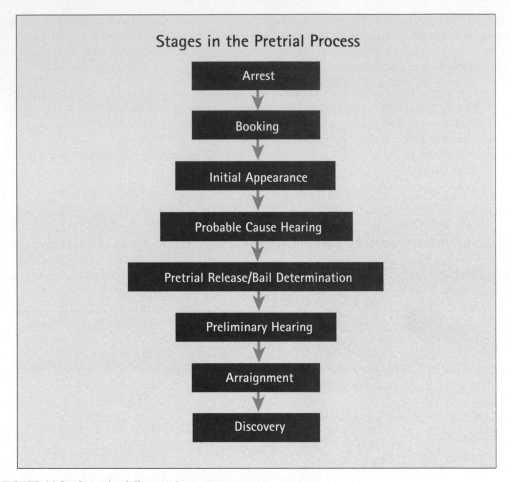

FIGURE 11.3   Organized Chart or Poster

representations of things the audience may never have seen (or at least not in person). Without hearing them, an audience would have difficulty appreciating the nuances of a Bach sonata or a bird's call. Finally, a model is very important in describing, say, a technique of structural bridge engineering.

As with posters and charts, it is important that the materials you show the audience are big enough for them to see and understand from where you are showing them (or loud enough, in the case of sounds). Passing objects and models around the audience is not usually a suitable alternative because audience members will not be looking at these items at the same time you are describing them and may become distracted. Handouts also can be distracting.

USING OVERHEAD TRANSPARENCIES, ELECTRONIC OVERHEADS, AND PHOTOGRAPHS
Presenting images such as graphs and photographs as transparencies by using an overhead projector or document imager is common in training and education. The advantages of this more high-tech approach are low cost, ready availability of equipment, working in a lighted environment, and some flexibility with the use of acetate sheets and special marking pens. The chief disadvantage is that depending on how well they are prepared, these visuals may appear unprofessional. This is an

increasing concern, given the prevalence and graphic capability of PowerPoint presentations, which we will turn to next.

However, to use overhead technology successfully, follow these suggestions:

1. Check all equipment ahead of time to ensure that it's working, that the lightbulbs are good, the screen is clean, power is available, and so on. Also give yourself some time to practice with the equipment just before your presentation.
2. In presenting text, use the 4 × 4 rule: No more than four lines per transparency and only four words per line. Furthermore, use a plain typeface in a size large enough for the audience to see, given the size and arrangement of the room.
3. In presenting graphics, ensure that the image is of suitable quality, whether it's been drawn or scanned. Once more, consider the room. As with text, don't put too much on a single transparency. One photo or graph per transparency is appropriate (see Figure 11.4).
4. During your presentation, avoid pointing to images and information using your finger; use a pointer or pencil.

USING POWERPOINT PRESENTATIONS   The visual tool used most frequently in training and increasingly in education is the **PowerPoint presentation**. Applied in classrooms, training centers, and within Web-based interactive programs and or educational programs (such as Blackboard or Moodle), this software is part of today's quality presentations and is expected.

The chief benefit of a PowerPoint presentation is that it provides excellent visual quality while allowing interaction. That is, the speaker and the audience can interact while the image is being shown. In addition, a PowerPoint presentation allows all the advantages of face-to-face speaking while facilitating the explanation of complex material. The audience will find it easy to follow the organization of the speech with a PowerPoint presentation, which will encourage memory. Finally, developing a PowerPoint presentation is creative and fun, especially with the use of good color and pictures.

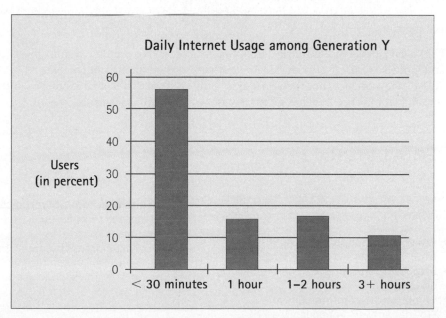

FIGURE 11.4   Slide Presenting a Graphic   *Source:* Based on Pulley (2000).

The problems from the past, such as expensive equipment and projectors, have virtually been eliminated. Most trainers, for instance, pack their laptops and a lightweight projector on the airplane. About every classroom or training center has the necessary computers and tools. However, even with its popularity, it is surprising how many people make simple, correctable mistakes when using PowerPoint.

Practitioners suggest these basic rules for developing and presenting PowerPoint slides:

1. Use 40- to 44-point type for titles and 30- to 36-point type for headings. Avoid using type smaller than 32 point for anything.
2. Use less than eight lines of type per slide, unless there is a significant reason to include more. We still see extreme amounts of text in presentations—not only does that violate the idea behind using this tool, it leaves confusion for many audiences.
3. Choose background colors carefully. For instance, bright colors tend to wash out words and pictures.
4. Use appealing art and photos but avoid clutter or being too "busy" or "artsy" for business audiences.
5. Do not rely on your visual aids, no matter how wonderful they are. You are still the speaker.

For additional information about creating PowerPoint presentations, go online to the sources listed in Web at Work 11.1 as well as to Microsoft's website or other providers for ideas on templates to make your preparation easier.

Figure 11.5 illustrates a PowerPoint graphic depicting a speech on adolescents, pointing out themes such as teens' technology emphasis, values of optimism, appreciation of diversity, and personal uniqueness and savvy.

Communication Tips When Using Any Visual Aid

Despite the advantages of using visual technology, they can be less effective if they are prepared or used badly. The following strategies for the professional use of visual aids apply to both low- and high-tech media:

1. Use visual aids when a technical description is in order. For example, maps, objects, graphs, and models are all effective in explaining when words alone are not enough.
2. Talk to the audience, not the visual aid. Many speakers fail to maintain eye contact and respond to audience feedback when they are working with visual aids.

WEB AT WORK 11.1
PowerPoint Presentations

Go to these sources to learn more about creative PowerPoint presentations:

- **www.science.iupui.edu/SAC98/ppt.html** A robust view of visual strategy.
- **http://actden.com/pp** A basic tutorial on using PowerPoint.
- **www.pptfaq.com/index.html** Provides answers to frequently asked questions (FAQs) about PowerPoint.

- **www.bitbetter.com/powertips.htm** Offers tips and tricks for using PowerPoint.
- **www.office.microsoft.com** Possible assistance available with further searching.

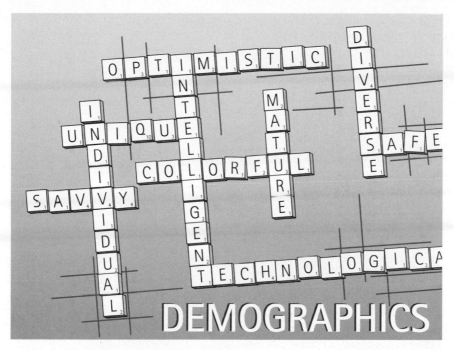

FIGURE 11.5   PowerPoint Graphic   *Source:* Pulley (2000).

3. Stay in charge of the presentation. Do not let the visual aids control the speech; rather, the speech should control the visual aids.
4. Reveal each visual aid only at the point in the presentation when it is mentioned. Otherwise, cover it so as not to distract the audience from what you are saying.
5. Make sure the visual aid and its elements (such as type and graphics) are large enough for audience members to see from all corners of the room.
6. Use only professional-looking visual aids. Get help, if you need it. Check out the many great online templates.
7. Keep the room as light as possible while maintaining adequate visual aid appearance. In using PowerPoint, some speakers dim the lights, rather than turn them off completely, so they can interact with the audience.
8. Stand in front or to the side of the visual aid, not behind it. Similarly, don't stand in way of a visual.

A final suggestion for using visual aids is to introduce them using *transitions*. As you recall Figure 11.6 (shown on the next page) from the sample speaking outline, the speaker's notes show where to provide transitions in moving from point to point. You can do the same thing to indicate where to show and explain visual aids.

Here's a four-step model of how to work transitions and descriptions into your presentation:

1. Transition to visual aid
2. Description of key elements
3. Explanation of main point
4. Transition to next point

First Slide

Global Change: Overview

Drucker
- connected economies
- leaner companies
- more specialized
- more volunteerism; growth of nonprofits

Christopher
- identity is the key
- U.S. afraid to cope with diversity; no global identity

Second Slide

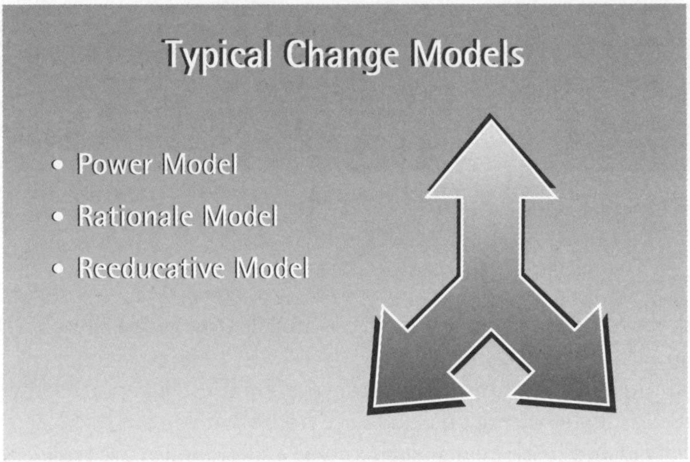

Typical Change Models

- Power Model
- Rationale Model
- Reeducative Model

Third Slide

Work Cultures: Synergy and New vs. Old Cultures

High-Synergy Society
- win/win cooperation
- benevolent, helpful
- power used for service

Low-Synergy Society
- self-centered
- win/lose
- individualistic, noncooperative
- power for personal profit, not group good

FIGURE 11.6 Examples of PowerPoint Slides

Now let's apply this model to an actual speech, identifying the transition, description, main point, and next transition used for each PowerPoint slide in a series of three:

First Slide

1. *Transition to visual aid:* "Drucker believed in global economies, as this slide reveals."
2. *Description of key elements:* "Drucker's vision would lead to more connected economies, lean companies with lowered expenses, more specialization tracks for workers, and a rapid growth of nonprofits with many volunteers."
3. *Explanation of main point:* "Noted corporate expert Christopher agrees, adding that the United States has been afraid to launch its identity as 'global'. Thus, the U.S. economy is lagging behind."
4. *Transition to next point:* "How can we change this outlook toward a more global view of our economy?"

Second Slide

1. *Transition to visual aid:* "Three models are typically applied to create change, as this next slide reveals."
2. *Description of key elements:* "Note that the power model calls for a top-down mandate of change. A rationale model expects evidence, and a reeducative model introduces seminars and training to gradually convince the company of the need for change."
3. *Explanation of main point:* "Specifically, ways to create change already exist."
4. *Transition to next point:* "What are the immediate benefits of change?"

Third Slide

1. *Transition to visual aid:* "This final slide shows how we can energize growth and cooperation among coworkers with a new outlook."
2. *Description of key elements:* "A high-synergy corporate culture offers a win-win situation, including less competition and more cooperative opportunities for everyone. These can be used for benevolent and service reasons, not just personal gain. In contrast, a low-synergy corporate culture offers self-centered, win/lose activities. Power, not sharing, becomes the name of the corporate game."
3. *Explanation of main point:* "Specifically, we can change the future of the work culture."
4. *Transition to next point:* "Where do we go from here to make these changes?"

ETHICS AND PRESENTATIONS

With our communication environment exploding freely with communication messages from books and movies to speeches and Internet sources, a presenter's temptation is to assume the prevalence means I can pull it up and use it at will. In fact, there are free use laws and communication ethics to observe for business and professional communicators. This section cannot cover every circumstance, but several key highlights illustrate the importance of applying ethical communication. It helps to put yourself in the shoes of an artist, a speaker, a writer, a Web developer, or a friend who has created a message, an event, or a production only to have someone take it and use it for their own purposes. You can imagine how this might feel if you were the creator of the product.

Fair use laws indicate that we can quote materials and paraphrase ideas within certain boundaries as long as we acknowledge the source. Those boundaries include short usage, educational usage, and usage for critique or review. In other cases, we must seek permission. For instance, when you write a paper for a class, you can quote or paraphrase from a journal or book and then indicate the source material. However, to use an entire article as your presentation would demand permission. Even then, you must indicate it is not your source.

Similarly in a speech, we encourage quotations and the use of ideas. Central to the dialogue and debate of new ideas is deconstruction and construction. However, what we experience as professional teachers and trainers is that all too often, there is a major failure to cite the source of the idea. In other cases, such as in conducting training, the presenter has overused or borrowed a model without permission. In these cases of professional production or artistic development, one must not use a product wholesale without permission. It is usually acceptable to present an alternative model or artistic piece, again if there is an acknowledging of the original genesis of the idea or concept that led to your adaptation or modification.

Concerning the use of movie clips from YouTube or Google Video, the issue is to acknowledge the source. And in those cases, one should not present significant lengths of a commercial artistic production without purchasing or renting, such as in showing a movies to a class or in a training program. Most music and movies can be purchased or rented very inexpensively. This ethical use encourages the future of great productions and artistic designs, otherwise eroded by lack of compensation for one's hard work.

We don't like to admit this, but some speakers think that wholesale borrowing of a speech from a friend or from an Internet or other published source gives them the right to present that speech or message as their own. This is an ethical violation. Again, fair use and source acknowledgement is a norm, but not extensive or rampant application.

With so many Internet sources at your fingertips, it is permissible to look and use, but the principle is to acknowledge and apply fair use. If the material or production states copyright sanctions, you are only allowed to paraphrase and not use their quoted materials except as fair use laws. And, do not use copyrighted visuals, artistic productions, music, or models with copyright statements from a Web site without permission.

It seems that templates and designs from software providers with programs you or your company have purchased are presented as meant to be used, so those are obvious exceptions.

Finally, ethical communicators avoid making up facts or stories to make their point. The goal in communication is truth and clarity. Obviously, fabrication violates the noble goals of truth and credibility.

In Perspective

Organizations today expect their members to be experienced and dynamic speakers, capable of communicating in a range of situations. In developing presentational skills, there are two primary areas of focus: language style and delivery.

Since language is the chief means by which ideas are communicated, learning about language style—that is, choices of words and structures—will enhance your ability to communicate ideas more effectively. Language style can be improved by creating vividness and clarity, by using relational language, and by understanding the applications of connotation and denotation.

Delivery is defined here as "the use of vocal qualities and bodily qualities to create meaning in a message." Vocal qualities comprise pitch, rate, volume, and strategic pausing. Bodily qualities encompass eye contact, facial expression, gesturing, and stance. By fitting these elements of delivery to your message, you will command the audience's attention and improve their understanding.

The literature on speech communication identifies four primary methods of delivery. In the manuscript delivery method, the speech is written out in its entirety and read aloud to the audience. The memorized delivery method is similar in that the speech is written out, word for word, but the speaker commits the entire speech to memory. The impromptu delivery method involves speaking without any specific preparation. Extemporaneous delivery refers to speaking from notes or an outline that contains key words, phrases, and ideas.

Making public presentations involves the integrating the advantages of various visual technologies with sound public speaking principles. Especially when presenting informative and technical material it is important to use the appropriate tool appropriately. The chapter identifies numerous rules for good visual presentations.

Finally, the chapter warns the reader to apply a quest for truth. That means applying communication ethics to your research and use of materials in a presentation.

Discussion Questions

1. If you were to make a case for communication training in an organization, why would you recommend the inclusion of presentational skills? What is the significance of being a good speaker in today's business and professional world?
2. Outline the main points of a training seminar that would focus on language style. What should be included? Why?
3. What qualities of vocal delivery are typically distracting to an audience? What types of bodily delivery are typically distracting to an audience? Why?

4. Compare and contrast the appropriate uses of the four methods of delivery: manuscript, memorized, impromptu, and extemporaneous. When is each most effective versus least effective?
5. What are the advantages and disadvantages of using PowerPoint presentations? Does your own experience with PowerPoint fit these observations? Why or why not?

Exercises

1. Survey ten or more class members about what they feel are the most common bad habits in speechmaking. What behaviors do they find distracting or annoying? What behaviors lessen the speaker's credibility? Compile the results of the survey and present them to the class.
2. Videotape five or more television commercials that illustrate different vocal rates—that is, some fast and some slow. Play the recording before a focus group, your classmates, or some friends. Which rate do they like best and why? Which rate do they like least and why?
3. With some classmates, give impromptu speaking a try. Begin by writing some topics on slips of paper (one topic per slip), and then put them in a cup or box. Have each person draw a slip of paper and get up and speak on that topic; set a time of limit of, say, two or three minutes per speaker. After everyone has had a turn, discuss the experience. What are the challenges of impromptu speaking? What would it take to improve impromptu goals?

4. Experiment with two types of PowerPoint background and lettering combinations: (a) a dark background with dark lettering and (b) a light-dark combination (that is, a light background with dark lettering or a dark background with light lettering). Show the slides to an audience and ask which combination they prefer. What reasons do they give for liking one or the other? Which combination do you prefer and why?
5. Record your voice. Using a marker and a piece of paper, chart your *rate* using dots and dashes and your *pitch* using up-and-down lines. Review this chart to see if you tend to fall into the same patterns, sentence after sentence. If you do that, practice altering these qualities and modify your vocal delivery.
6. Observe some good speakers and try to model your vocal delivery after theirs. Don't think of this as copying others but as identifying what they do well and learning from it. In the end, your delivery should integrate your personality.

References

Capps, R., Dodd, C. H., & Winn, L. J. (1981). *Communication for the business and professional speaker*. New York: Macmillan.

Charney, C., & Conway, K. (1998). *The trainer's tool kit*. New York: American Management Association.

Munter, M. (1998). Meeting technology: From low-tech to high-tech. *Business Communication Quarterly, 61*, 80–87.

Porter, D. (2001). College presentation training. *Presentations*, January, 40–46.

Pulley, J. (2000). Generation-Y demographics. Presentation at the National Youth and Family Conference, Abilene Christian University, Abilene, TX.

Timmerman, C. E. (2002). The moderating effect of mindlessness/mindfulness upon media richness and social influence explanations of organizational media use. *Communication Monographs, 69*, 111–131.

Winn, L. J. (2006). The effects of style. Personal/Interview, Bowling Green, Kentucky, July.

CHAPTER 12

Managing Informative Presentations in the Workplace

After reading this chapter, you will be able to do the following:

- Select a topic that meets the needs of your audience.
- Write a clear purpose statement and thesis statement.
- Develop the main points and provide support to make them credible and understandable.
- Plan an organizational design for the body of the speech.
- Write a purposeful introduction and conclusion.
- Deliver special types of informative presentations.

Underpromise; overdeliver.

TOM PETERS

The outcomes desired of an **informative presentation** are (1) to provide new information, (2) to reinforce previously known information, and/or (3) to clarify understanding and reduce uncertainty. Thus, the primary test of success in delivering an informative message is to ask if the audience has come away with one or more of these outcomes satisfied.

Many people underestimate the planning and design needed to achieve these outcomes. When they think about giving a briefing, a report, a proposal, or long speech, they think it is less about preparing and more about talking. Alternatively, we hope this chapter helps you understand the link between great research, preparation, and organizational design along with good speaking skills to success. To put it bluntly, those who fail to present information clearly and support it accurately run the ethical risk of causing misunderstanding or providing poor or misleading information to message recipients, such as your own or other departments in the organization.

KEY TERMS

informative presentation *(p. 253)*
topic selection *(p. 254)*
purpose statement *(p. 256)*
thesis statement *(p. 259)*
main points *(p. 260)*
body *(p. 260)*
support *(p. 260)*
organizational design *(p. 264)*
outline *(p. 264)*
organizational patterns *(p. 267)*
introduction *(p. 269)*
conclusion *(p. 274)*
connections and transitions *(p. 277)*
oral reports *(p. 278)*
news release or briefing *(p. 278)*
elevator speech *(p. 280)*
speech of introduction *(p. 280)*

DEVELOPING INFORMATIVE PRESENTATIONS

Being able to prepare and present an effective informative message is a valuable leadership skill. To help you acquire that skill, the process of developing an informative presentation is discussed in this chapter as comprising ten steps. Some of this material may sound familiar, as we have touched on it elsewhere in the book. You may have come across similar material in courses on writing and rhetoric as well. Nevertheless, take the time and make the effort to understand this ten-step process as it is presented here.

Step 1: Analyze the Audience

As discussed at length in Chapter 10, audience analysis should guide you in developing your presentation. After all, you are speaking to address the audience's needs and concerns. Knowing your listeners in planning an informative presentation will inform many decisions along the way, from formulating your thesis statement to choosing support materials to organizing your main points.

Step 2: Select the Topic

Many presenters spend a lot of time on **topic selection**, such that it becomes an all-consuming task. This doesn't have to happen if you keep in mind some basic principles about topic selection.

PRINCIPLES FOR TOPIC SELECTION

First, consider your personal knowledge and interests. It is easier to plan and deliver a good speech when you know the material and are interested in it. The list that follows provides some suggestions for topics. As you go through it, jot down the potential topics that come to you in the first column in the Topic Selection Worksheet, Skills at Work 12.1:

- Jobs you have had or your parents have had
- Hobbies and recreational interests
- Courses you have taken and seminars you have participated in
- Places you have visited or things you have done
- Interesting people you have met
- Subjects you have read a great deal about
- Issues of local, state, or national interest that you feel strongly about
- Issues specific to your company or organization

Next, consider your audience. Experience has shown the wisdom of picking a topic that is clearly relevant to their needs. Doing so will make your presentation more interesting to them and will make you feel as though you are contributing to their welfare. For each potential topic you have identified, consider its application to the audience by asking yourself these questions:

- Will the audience be interested in this topic?
- Does this topic somehow relate to the audience's well-being?
- How do the audience's general characteristics (for instance, occupation, age, education, marital status) fit this topic area?
- Will this topic evoke some emotion in the audience, perhaps satisfying a curiosity, calming a fear, or stirring up enthusiasm?

SKILLS AT WORK 12.1
Topic Selection Worksheet

Use this worksheet to help you record and evaluate potential topics. Follow the directions presented in the text.

1. Topics of Interest to You	2. Topics Relevant to Your Audience	3. Topics That Fit the Occasion
_____	☐	☐
_____	☐	☐
_____	☐	☐
_____	☐	☐
_____	☐	☐
_____	☐	☐
_____	☐	☐
_____	☐	☐
_____	☐	☐
_____	☐	☐

POTENTIAL TOPICS

1. _____

2. _____

3. _____

4. _____

Source: Based on Dodd and Lakey (2006).

Based on your answers, review the potential topics you have identified. For each one that will also be relevant to your audience, put a checkmark across from it in column 2 of the Topic Selection Worksheet.

Finally, consider the occasion of your presentation:

- Does the occasion suggest certain topics? Does it rule out any topics?
- Will the setting make it difficult or impossible to speak on certain topics (the size and shape of the room, the availability of equipment, and so on)?
- What is the time limit for your presentation? Will this timeframe make it difficult or impossible to speak on certain topics (whether too much or too little time)?

Again, based on your answers, determine how many of the potential topics you identified in column 1 are still viable (that is, have not been ruled out). If the occasion suggests certain topics and you find them interesting, add them to column 1. Then repeat the review of audience relevance and occasion for those new topics.

WEB AT WORK 12.1
Topic Selection

These sources may be useful in helping you sort through topics:

- **www.totalnews.com** A search engine and directory of news designed to increase access to information.
- **www.ipl.org** The Internet Public Library provides "Subject Collections"

of a range of topics plus source materials.

- **www.cnn.com** The Cable News Network provides current news items that are organized by topic area.

At this point, you should be able to identify several topics from the worksheet that meet all three criteria. Write them down at the bottom of the worksheet and then choose one to use in working through this chapter. Circle it on the worksheet.

NARROWING THE TOPIC The next task is to narrow your topic. Good speakers agree on the importance of doing so. To plow a small plot of ground is better than plowing an entire field.

One way of narrowing your topic is to determine whether it can be divided into parts or stages or reasons and then choose one or more to discuss. In your speech, you will simply acknowledge that you are focusing on, say, the three major parts or the most important reason. That way, you don't have to develop the complete topic.

Consult the Web sites listed in Web At Work 12.1 for more information on how to select a topic.

Step 3: Select the Purpose

What is a **purpose statement**? It is a complete sentence that describes what you want to accomplish with your presentation. You will use it to develop your speech and may or may not state it to your audience.

Do you really need a purpose statement? Yes. Having one will help you stay focused and on target when researching and writing your speech. If you know what you want to achieve, you will be able to determine what kind of information is needed and how to present it. Thus, stating the purpose of your speech is significant.

Communication research has identified four basic purposes of presentations:

1. *To inform.* The informative speech aims to create understanding, enlightenment, or clarification by presenting information. This might include a demonstration, an explanation of how something functions, or an oral briefing, report, a proposal, an elevator speech of your ideas, or longer speech or lecture.
2. *To persuade.* In this case, the aim is to bring about a change of feelings, opinions, beliefs, attitudes, or behaviors within the audience. Persuasion may also include trying to reinforce the audience's current beliefs or behaviors, to discontinue their current beliefs or behaviors, or to prevent future beliefs or behaviors. To persuade an audience demands proof, often through applying logic, building arguments, and making motivational appeals.

3. *To entertain.* Making people feel good—perhaps by using humor or by examining some point of unusual interest or fascination—is the purpose of many presentations. For instance, many after-dinner speeches are designed to achieve this outcome.

4. *To inspire.* Many speeches that are called *persuasive* can also be described as *inspirational* in that they stimulate lofty goals and motivate demonstrations of values. In the workplace, this can mean appealing to achievement, self-direction, strategic planning, and so on.

Each purpose not only defines a different outcome but also invites a different approach. For example, since a speech to inform involves clarification, it will require materials that amplify, describe, or explain. Since a speech to persuade encourages change, the supporting materials must provide evidence and motivation. In order to make the audience feel good or to help them laugh or be amused, a speech to entertain will use materials that have irony, sudden switches, and short-story elements. Finally, a speech to inspire will involve rhetorical devices that describe future possibilities so as to motivate audience members toward a new vision.

In writing your purpose statement, follow these guidelines:

1. *Describe the results that you are seeking.* State what you want the audience to be able to do or know as a result of hearing your speech.

2. *Be specific.* State your purpose in such a way that you can measure whether you have accomplished it.

3. *Be realistic.* Make sure that your purpose can be accomplished in the time allotted and that the audience is capable of fulfilling it.

In many cases, narrowing your purpose will also sharpen its focus. The process of narrowing that begins with selecting and focusing on a topic continues in stating your purpose and, as we'll see later in this chapter, throughout stating a thesis and indeed throughout the entire speech-preparation process. It is a fairly natural process that unfolds as you learn more about your topic and consider how best to present that information to others.

For instance, suppose your informative purpose is to explain how a nonprofit service organization provides food to its clients. You might begin with a purpose statement like the first one in the following examples and then, upon realizing that it needs to be more specific, write the second purpose statement:

EXAMPLES

Original purpose statement: "Food goes through the system to needy clients, and this is how it works."

Revised purpose statement: "To explain the complexities of how food is procured, stored, and provided to needy clients in the community is the goal of today's presentation."

Note that one of the changes that made the second purpose statement more specific was the use of the word *explain.* Choose from among these key words and phrases for developing a specific statement of purpose:

amplify	shed light on	show
explain	give details about	signify
illuminate	make plain	point out
generate knowledge of	indicate	disclose
clarify	explore	reveal

The question of whether to state your purpose to the audience is an intriguing one. Some communication scholars believe that you should develop your purpose solely as a guiding principle to use in planning. Others argue for disclosing your purpose to the audience. Perhaps the best advice is to develop your purpose statement in planning your speech and present it to the audience only when doing so would benefit them. In general, stating your purpose to the audience early on is beneficial in an *informative* presentation because it will inform them of your intended outcome. However, in a *persuasive* speech, it may be more effective to state your purpose later in the speech, when you reveal your goal of changing an attitude or behavior.

We'll look at additional examples of purpose statements for informative presentations later, in the discussion of organizational patterns. But before moving on, evaluate the purpose statements in Skills at Work 12.2.

SKILLS AT WORK 12.2
Evaluating a Purpose Statement

To get some practice in evaluating your own purpose statements, work through this detailed review of the following statement of purpose:

"To inform the staff about sales opportunities in California."

What is wrong with this purpose statement?

- It does not state the speaker's intended outcomes in any measurable way. What does it mean *to inform*? And how would you know if the staff became informed?
- It is not specific. What staff? What sales opportunities? All of California?
- It is not realistic. This is too much to cover in one speech, particularly a short one.

How will these problems affect the audience's information?

- The speech will not be oriented toward a specific audience, and the speaker will be unable to measure what the audience has learned.
- The speech will provide a lot of surface information and will seem disjointed and unorganized.
- The audience will not be able to take in all this information in one sitting.

Now consider this revised purpose statement:

"After hearing my speech, the marketing staff will be able to identify and briefly describe two sales locations in San Diego, California."

Why is this purpose statement better than the original one?

- It explains what the audience will be able to do as specific outcomes: *to identify and briefly describe.* Given how the purpose has been narrowed, these outcomes will be measurable.
- The speaker has limited the purpose to discussing two sales locations in a specific part of California. In addition, the speaker has identified the staff to which this speech is addressed.
- The speaker can accomplish this purpose in the allotted amount of time, and the audience will be able to accomplish the stated outcomes.

How will these improvements affect the audience being informed?

- The speech will be more audience oriented, focusing on the needs of the marketing staff. In addition, the speaker will be able to determine if these individuals came away knowing about two sales locations. This purpose is measurable.
- The speaker will know exactly what to cover in order to accomplish the purpose. Therefore, the speech will be focused and organized.
- The audience will be able to take in the information in one sitting.

Source: Adapted from Dodd and Lakey (2006).

Step 4: Formulate a Thesis Statement

The **thesis statement** is the main assertion that you will make in your speech—a summary statement, essentially. It is a statement of your topic that is worded as a claim to be proved or a theme to be developed. Thus, you must be able to distill the topic of your speech into a single sentence.

How is this different from a purpose statement? A *purpose statement* defines the speech's outcome, such as to inform or to persuade. However, a *thesis statement* summarizes the central idea, something like a headline. It states the main idea that you want the audience to come away with. As such, it is usually first stated in the introduction of your speech. A *preview* then follows, which provides a snapshot of the major points you plan to develop.

You need to write a thesis statement for several reasons. First, it will give you focus and provide a means of weighing information. You will be able to ask yourself if certain information fits this main idea of your speech. In addition, your thesis will help you make the transition from what you want to do (as stated in your purpose) to actually doing it. It identifies two things: your topic and what you are saying about it.

Consider some examples of informative thesis statements followed by previews:

EXAMPLES

Original thesis statement: "New construction methods are being used."

Revised thesis statement: "With building costs out of control, engineers are developing innovative low-cost methods to build new homes."

Preview: "In the next few minutes, I'll explain the two best methods of building that will save you time and money."

Original thesis statement: "Communication helps marriages."

Revised thesis statement: "Good marriages rely on lots of talking and listening."

Preview: "Today, you'll see just how listening, affirming your spouse, and being open minded are the best communication tools for marriage."

Skills at Work 12.3 presents another evaluation activity—this time, looking at thesis statements.

SKILLS AT WORK 12.3
Evaluating a Thesis Statement

As before, work through this review and determine what can be done for improvement. Here's the thesis statement:

"My speech is on management theory."

What is wrong with this thesis statement?

- It is identifying the speaker as the subject.
- It is not focused on a specific topic; that is, *management theory* is an immense topic.
- It does not summarize the main idea. What about management theory will be discussed? What point does the speaker intend to make?

Now consider this revised thesis statement:

"The origin and history of management theory continue to influence modern-day approaches to leadership."

Why is this a better thesis statement?

- It defines exactly what the speaker will talk about and removes the speaker as the focus.
- It makes a claim, something the speaker can set out to demonstrate or prove. He or she will provide evidence that shows this claim to be true.

Step 5: Develop the Main Points

The fifth step in developing a presentation is to develop the **main points**, or the key ideas, that will amplify or prove the thesis statement. These main points will comprise the **body** of your presentation.

In an informative presentation, you want to answer questions about how something works or what something is. Each main point in the body should answer a question or need: Why should I accept this? What are the reasons for this? How can I be sure of the accuracy of this information? Accuracy and ultimately your credibility are at stake in answering these questions. Careful research, providing sufficiently detailed support, and using a variety of credible sources are crucial to preparing effective informative presentations.

Some topics suggest the main points that should be developed. For instance, an informative speech on how to reduce home-building costs could involve three efficient strategies (which would be identified in the thesis statement). In the speech body, these three strategies would be presented as the three main ideas:

EXAMPLE

"(1) Create a modified pier and beam foundation with the new Sims-Barney balance machine. (2) Utilize recommended after-market plumbing, wiring, and air conditioning units. (3) Purchase prefabricated walls and roofing approved by national wall construction codes."

Similarly, a presentation on the value of interpersonal communication to maintaining a strong marriage could be developed in three parts that describe the three most helpful communication principles:

EXAMPLE

"(1) Listening opens partners to hearing facts as well as feelings. (2) Affirmation provides acceptance. (3) Openness makes us look at our weaknesses to improve the marriage."

Step 6: Support the Main Points

In each of the presentations just described, the speaker would provide sufficient **support** material for the main points and note the sources of that information. That's the sixth step in developing an informative presentation. Understanding the different types of support materials available is valuable in terms of knowing how and where to begin (Beebe, Beebe, & Ivy, 2001; Seiler & Beal, 2008).

TYPES OF SUPPORT As you review the different types of support, keep in mind that some will be more or less appropriate for certain kinds of topics. Your purpose statement and thesis statement should guide you in selecting the right types of support for your presentation.

Examples. Examples are real cases and situations. In presenting an example, provide enough details for people to understand what happened. Also be sure to tie the example to the point that you are making, as done here:

EXAMPLE

"Creating excellence in customer service is not that hard. The first step is listening. Selina does that very well when she looks customers in the eye, smiles, and nods her head, indicating she understands the problem."

Illustrations. Longer and usually more in depth than examples, illustrations are stories and anecdotes that are hypothetical or true. They should be chosen because they provide a poignant message and have a clear relationship to the topic at hand. One speaker described Roger Bannister, whose experience in a tragic fire as a child all but ended any hopes of physical achievement. Yet despite his apparent disability, Bannister achieved greatness as one of the first runners in history to break the four-minute mile. The speaker's point in using this story was that nothing should deter individuals from trying to achieve their goals.

Narrative. A narrative gives a visual account or description in the form of a story. A long and detailed illustration would likely qualify as a narrative.

Testimonial. The speaker who can say, "I was there, I saw it happen," establishes enormous credibility because audiences tend to believe eyewitness accounts, or testimonials (provided the accounts are not overdone and that they sound accurate). As with other types of stories, a testimonial should make some illuminating point and be relevant to the topic of the presentation.

Statistics. Statistics, or facts, provide specific, objective information about the intensity or frequency with which something occurred. Compare these two statements in terms of audience understanding and speaker credibility:

EXAMPLES

"Most of the employees I've talked with in our company believe the competition is soft and will go out of business."

"According to an employee survey conducted just last week, 84 percent believe the competition is losing sales and will fall below national averages in six months, allowing a 6 percent margin of error."

Clearly, the second statement is much more authoritative and thus believable.

Expert Authority. To quote a source that the audience will find credible can be effective in providing support. In reading about your topic, you will come across names of experts and authorities in the field. Using evidence of this type will not only back up your point but also increase your credibility (McCroskey, 2001).

Historic and literary figures provide another rich source of quotations, and while they may not always reflect authority, they will generate interest and spur motivation. For example, President John F. Kennedy's classic motivational quote illustrates: "Ask not what your country can do for you; ask what you can do for your country." The words of Shakespeare also exemplify. For instance, the quote "Our doubts are traitors and cause us to lose the good we oft might win by fearing to attempt" reflects the notion of paralyzing uncertainty.

Case 12.1

Using Analogies

The chief financial officer (CFO) of a large company was preparing a presentation in which he intended to introduce a series of new procedures to the accounting staff. He searched for an effective way of describing the pitfalls of corporate resistance to new ideas and ultimately came up with this analogy:

> In 1888, a group of pioneers traveling in wagons was crossing the Pecos River from New Mexico to Texas. At the crossing, an enterprising young man waited with a team of mules to help people across. He explained, "The bottom of the river has soft sand and you'll likely get stuck. For one dollar, I'll pull you across." The family in the first wagon paid the dollar and was helped successfully across. When the second wagon approached, the family scoffed at the young man and declared confidently that their horses could cross the river unassisted. To their chagrin, they got stuck. The young man, still nearby, got them free and pulled them the rest of the way across. But the charge was five dollars.
> And so, let's recognize that in the short run, we may save a dollar, but in the long run, our failure to accept innovation may cost us the company!

> What are the two things being compared in this analogy? How effectively does it make the point about resisting change?

Definition.   Several types of definitions can be used to provide support. One type of definition is objective or literal; it is the denotation (that is, dictionary meaning) of a concept. A second type of definition is operational; it goes beyond an objective explanation and indicates how a concept works or what it means. A third type of definition explains origins and process; the etiology of a disease, for instance, defines by describing the process of how the disease emerges and spreads. A fourth type is to define by negation: telling what something is not.

Analogy.   An analogy describes how two things are alike: one thing that is known and one thing that is not. For instance, in his first campaign for president, Ronald Reagan compared the U.S. presidency (the position he wanted) to the California governorship (a position he had already held) in outlining some of his platform proposals. This strategy rested on an analogy: If it worked in California, it will work for the nation. See Case 12.1 for an analogy that was used to explain the idea of corporate resistance to new ideas.

FINDING SUPPORT MATERIALS   Research to find speech support materials is amazingly easy today. The library catalogues and physical browsing through periodicals and books is always interesting. Of course, when in doubt, librarians are professional researchers who can provide significant guidance.

In the context of any search, there are many indices for about every topic. These can be found in library catalogues. However, it is practical to use online search engines. Some of these are linked through a university or college sources, such as EBSO databases and search systems such as Infotrac and Lexis-Nexis. We may need to try out different search engines to find out what's available on your topic. See Web At Work 12.2 for a list of search engines.

The issue we might raise in support research is to identify quality sources. Use those that are clearly unbiased, have credibility, and sizable collections. Typically, personal Web sites, blogs, or sources dedicated to or known as biased information sources do not offer the search for truth we expect in a well supported presentation.

WEB AT WORK 12.2
Search Engines

Here are some of the most common and useful tools for searching online:

	www.google.com
	www.ask.com
www.yahoo.com	**www.excite.com**
www.lycos.com	**www.hotbot.com**
www.bing.com	**www.webcrawler.com**

Reference-type materials, such as dictionaries and encyclopedias, often provide good background information. Also reputable news sources, the *New York Times* and the *Wall Street Journal*, supply credible support material for many topics. It is helpful to read the newspaper on a daily basis to look for articles that relate to your topic. Indices are available for major newspapers, such as the *New York Times Index*.

If your topic is of local or regional interest, consult the Chamber of Commerce or state-level organizations. The U.S. government publishes materials on an endless variety of subjects; you can find them in print or online. For business-related topics, see what's available from professional organizations and trade associations.

Do not overlook personal interviews with, say, experts in your organization, community, or university, and locate taped speeches of nationally recognized politicians and spokespersons. You may even want to conduct your own survey via telephone or mail or distribute a questionnaire or attitude inventory to classmates or coworkers.

Of course, the Internet will provide access to these resources and more.

ETHICS AND CITING SOURCES   Regardless of what sources you use in gathering support materials, it is imperative that you cite those sources orally in presenting your speech. Specifically, you need to cite sources when you use any of the following:

- Ideas and suggestions that are not your own
- Other people's stories, anecdotes, and examples
- Arguments and proofs that others have developed
- Descriptions made by others
- Statistics and data
- Quotations

The primary purpose for citing sources is to avoid *plagiarizing* someone else's work. In addition, citing sources adds to the impact of your support materials and enhances your credibility as a speaker. Note that the failure to cite sources can have both ethical and legal implications, depending on the situation.

Step 7: Develop an Organizational Design

The best presentations, informative and otherwise, begin with a strong introduction, move on to a body that contains a series of strong main points and relevant support material, and close with a strong conclusion (see Figure 12.1 on the next page). We will talk about introductions

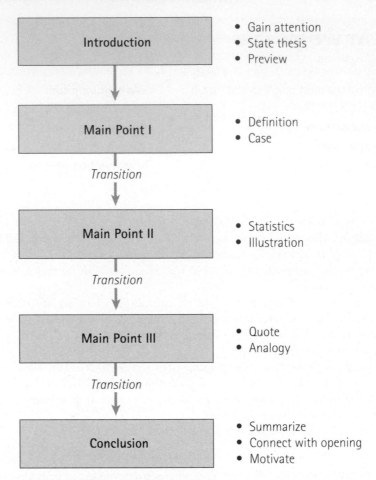

FIGURE 12.1 Structure of an Informative Presentation

and conclusions later in this chapter. In this section, we will discuss what goes into the body of a speech, or the **organizational design**. Planning that design involves two basic tasks: (1) creating an outline and (2) choosing an organizational pattern.

CREATING AN OUTLINE   Sometimes presenters resist speaking from an **outline** or even preparing one, feeling that doing so will stifle their creativity or in other ways be more of a burden than a help. That is occasionally true, particularly for very experienced and charismatic speakers. But for most speakers, especially inexperienced speakers, it is useful to have an outline. The very process of outlining will help you shape your message, making it clear and focused. You will plan how to take your audience through your information to create understanding and psychological effectiveness (DeVito, 2000a, 2000b; Dodd & Lewis, 1992).

Some individuals deny the benefits of outlining because they are not sure of how to create a good outline. The mechanics of outlining especially get in the way for some presenters. Let's review the mechanics and also address the basic issues people wonder about when trying to organize a speech.

Use Consistent Symbols. The standard outline creates a hierarchy of main points, subpoints, subsubpoints, and so on. A designated set of symbols identifies the elements at these various levels. For instance, main points are designated by Roman numerals, subpoints by capital or uppercase letters, subsubpoints by Arabic numbers, and so forth. In addition, elements of the same level are aligned on the same indent from the side of the page, as illustrated here:

I. Main point

   A. Subpoint

   B. Subpoint

      1. Subsubpoint

      2. Subsubpoint

Provide One Idea or Key Word per Point. The hierarchical structure of an outline is more than just a mechanical convention; that is, the hierarchy should organize the content as well. Under main point I, for instance, subpoints A and B should provide support. Thus, the information at each new level of the outline should support what was stated in the previous level. The level of detail goes from general to specific—from I to A to 1 and so on.

Write a complete sentence or question for each main idea (that is, I). However, key words or phrases will suffice for all of the levels of subpoints (that is, A, 1, a, etc.). In any case, write the key phrases exactly as you intend to say them; that way, you can strive for excellence in your language style. Following this practice can also help you reduce anxiety, since you will know how you are going to begin each next point. Avoid overlapping and repeating information, and avoid having too many levels of subpoints. If your outline is disorganized and confusing, it may contribute to a poor performance.

Another rule of outlining is that when you break one point into related subpoints, you must create at least two subpoints. (Theoretically, this makes sense, since you can't divide something into less than two pieces.) That means you can't have an A without a B, a 1 without a 2, and so on. If you can't divide, say, a main point into two or more subpoints, then leave it as a single main point.

Include All the Elements. Although our stated goal in this section was to discuss developing the body of the speech, be aware that your outline will include the introduction and conclusion, too. And in outlining the introduction, you will include your purpose statement and thesis statement. Other information will also be included in your outline. Here's what is typically included, in order of appearance:

1. *Identification information.* Provide your name along with whatever additional information your instructor requires. (Find out!)
2. *Title, purpose, and thesis.* Provide the title of your speech followed by your purpose statement and thesis statement.
3. *Introduction.* Your introduction may be written out as a single block paragraph or sentence by sentence (that is, each new sentence would be a subpoint—A, B, C, and so on). Either way, it's a good idea to write out the entire thing. At the start of your introduction, you want to gain the audience's attention, and at the end, you will actually state your thesis and preview. (See Step 8, later in this chapter, for more on writing your introduction.)
4. *Body.* This is the core of the speech and contains your main points and subpoints. Express your main points as complete sentences and the different levels of subpoints as key phrases or words. In most presentations, you will have three to five main points. Follow the structure

and symbols described earlier in this section, and add transitions between main points to connect your ideas and lead the audience from one to another. (See later in this chapter, Step 10, for suggestions on adding transitions and connections within your presentation.)

5. *Conclusion.* Like your introduction, your conclusion may be written in paragraph format or full-sentence format. Bring your speech to a close by providing a brief summary of your main points and ending with a sense of finality, maybe using a clincher statement or punchline. Don't end with something like "Well, that's all I have to say. Thank you." (See Step 9 about writing conclusions.)

6. *Bibliography.* Provide a complete bibliography or references list to identify the sources you used. Check with your instructor for requirements as to what academic style to use (for instance, Modern Language Association [MLA], American Psychological Association [APA], and so on).

Figure 12.2 is an example of an outline that was prepared according to these guidelines. Note, too, from this example that your outline should be typewritten and double-spaced. Use a

---

Catherine Logan
Dr. Rydell
COMS 111
March 9, 2008

(Informative Speech #1)

Title: The Common Cold: Menace to the Workplace

Purpose: After hearing my speech, the audience will be able to identify the characteristics of the common cold and effective methods for treating the common cold.

Thesis: The common cold is a highly contagious virus that is best treated by the traditional remedy of rest, aspirin, and plenty of fluids.

Introductions:

If you were asked, "What is the most common human ailment in the world?" would you be able to respond with "the common cold"? According to U.S. Public Health report (Sabharwal, Mahajan, & Gupta, 2009), most adults average two to three colds each year. Today, I would like to answer two questions: (1) What exactly is a cold? and (2) What is the best thing to do when you get one?

[*Transition:* Let's start with the first question: What exactly is a cold?]

Body:

I. The common cold is an infection of the upper respiratory system.
   A. Viral infection
      1. Caused by over 100 different viruses (MacKenzie, 2009).
      2. Not caused by chill and dampness
   B. Symptoms
      1. Dry, scratchy, or tingling sensation in nose or throat
      2. Body temperature may trop, cause chills
      3. Stuffy nose, sinuses
      4. Headache

FIGURE 12.2 Sample Outline for an Informative Speech

C. Highly contagious
   1. Sneezing and coughing
   2. Contact with skin
      a. Can survive for 6 hours (Lipman, 2010)
      b. Examples: Touching doorknobs, facets, etc.

[*Transition:* So, you are bound to catch a cold sooner or later. What is the best treatment to follow when you do catch one?]

I. Over the years, people have tried many remedies to combat the common cold.
   A. Previous centuries: bizarre, something dangerous (Browning, 1998, AMA online journal)
      1. Bleeding to remove the infection
      2. Foul-smelling salve, rag around neck
   B. Traditional modern therapy best (AMA and CDC from Browning, 1998)
      1. Rest—to fight virus
      2. Aspirin—to reduce fever, aches
      3. Fluids—to loosen chest, prevent shock

[*Internal summary/transition:* In short, there is no magic cure for the common cold. The best remedy is still to get plenty of rest, take aspirin, and drink plenty of fluids.]

Conclusion:

People have been putting up with colds ever since Adam and Eve were thrown out of their virus-free paradise. I hope you now have a better idea of just what a cold is and what you should do when you get one. When you are stricken with this most common human ailment in the world, remember that the best remedy is rest, aspirin, and plenty of fluids—so bring on the Gatorade!

Bibliography:

Browning, Nancy. "A historical sketch of treatments for the common cold." *Online Journal of the American Medical Society.* 1998. Available online: www.ams.org. Accessed October 8, 1998.

Lipman, M. (2010). Is it a cold or the flu? *Consumer Reports, 75*(2), 14. Retrieved from Academic Search Complete database.

MacKenzie, D. (2009). Common cold may hold off swine flu. *New Scientist, 204*(2734), 12. Retrieved from Academic Search Complete database.

Sabharwal, S., Mahajan, A., & Gupta, S. (2009). Swine Influenza A (H1NI Virus) flu or common cold. *JK Science, 11*(4), 170–171. Retrieved from Academic Search Complete database.

FIGURE 12.2 Sample Outline for an Informative Speech *(continued)*

professional-looking, readable typeface (perhaps Times or Palatino) in 12-point type. Print it on standard-sized white paper (that is, 8½" × 11); allow 1" margins at the top and bottom and 1½" margins at both sides. If your instructor has other formatting requirements, follow them instead.

CHOOSING AN ORGANIZATIONAL PATTERN   Now that you have created your outline, you have developed an overall plan for your presentation. Next, you want to "package" your message in the way that will best produce effective understanding. To do so, you will choose an **organizational pattern,** or one of several logical structures. In the sections to come, we will look at six organizational patterns that are appropriate for longer informative speeches and lectures, short oral reports, and briefings in business and the professions. It should become clear in reading these sections that certain topics lend themselves to certain patterns more readily than others.

Topical Pattern. The topical pattern is perhaps the most common of the six. It involves breaking the presentation down into major components, with no attempt to organize them according to function or order. In other words, you simply cover the components in whatever order seems most logical. For example, a speech dealing with the importance of corporate fitness programs might be organized into these three topical components:

EXAMPLE

   I. Corporate fitness programs ultimately save money.
   II. Corporate fitness programs involve little employee time.
   III. Corporate fitness programs stimulate employees' productivity.

Spatial Pattern. The spatial pattern organizes a presentation on the basis of space. For instance, suppose you were planning a presentation on how to build a home. Using the spatial pattern, you could describe the process literally from the ground up: the foundation, the walls, and the roof. In a speech on relaxation techniques, you could use the human body to provide the spatial organizer, moving from the head to the toes: how to relax the scalp muscles, the facial muscles, the shoulder and arm muscles, the stomach muscles, the legs, calves, feet, and even the tips of the toes. Finally, in a speech on statewide agricultural crops, you could organize your information by regions: north, south, east, and west, for instance.

Chronological Pattern. Time is the organizational factor in the chronological pattern, which is appropriate for topics that involve movement or development. For instance, the topic of flood control could be presented following a chronological pattern: flood control before 1930, between 1930 and 1999, and from 2000 to the present. As another example, a presentation on marital satisfaction could organize the following stages of development:

EXAMPLE

Purpose: "To have the audience understand and be able to remember the critical life cycle stages in a marriage."
Thesis: "Marital satisfaction changes across the stages of early marriage, through the childrearing years, and on to the launching of children and empty-nest years."
   I. Marital satisfaction is normally high during the first two years of marriage.
   II. Marital satisfaction tends to decrease during years 3 through 15, the childrearing years, without improved marital communication.
   III. Marital satisfaction tends to increase in years 15 to 25, as children eventually leave home and the couple learns to reinvest in communication time.

Cause-to-Effect and Effect-to-Cause Pattern. Another logical way of organizing information is to show *causality*: how a cause resulted in certain effects or how an effect was produced by certain causes. Let's review an example from the health field, beginning with an effect and then identifying its causes:

EXAMPLE

Purpose: "To have the team members identify and remember the common causes of heart attacks."
Thesis: "Heart attacks are caused by five major risk factors."

I. The causes of heart attacks include these risk factors.
   A. Lack of exercise
   B. Lack of proper diet
   C. Heredity
   D. Smoking
   E. Alcohol usage
II. Without intervention, the effects of heart attacks show up in two major ways.
   A. Personality change
   B. Diminished mental and physical responsiveness

In establishing causality, be careful not to make logical errors or to oversimplify things. For example, any single effect might have multiple causes and vice versa.

Known-to-Unknown Pattern. This pattern of organization makes use of the principle of familiarity. The general rule is to present familiar or known information before moving on to unfamiliar or unknown information. For example, if you, as a manager, wanted to speak to a nontechnical audience of employees about new evaluation techniques, you might start by reviewing the evaluation techniques already being used and then move on to changes. Obviously, to implement this pattern, you will need to understand your audience's level of knowledge.

Simple-to-Complex Pattern. This pattern organizes information from simple to complex, again trying to establish some foundation of knowledge at the start and then building on it. If, as the same manager, you were to present the new evaluation techniques to a group of technical leaders, you might begin with simple methods and proceed to the more complex methods.

Step 8: Develop the Introduction

So, you have developed an organizational design, which means you have created an outline and decided on an organizational pattern for the body of your speech. The next step is to create an **introduction**.

You may think it strange to develop the body of the speech before writing the introduction, but there is a good reason for doing so: you need to know what you are going to say in the body in order to write a good introduction. That is, you need to have the content of the speech well planned out and supported; that is what you will preview in your introduction.

Functions of Introductions

Evidence suggests that having a strong opening will grab the audience and focus them on the thesis. Bringing them to that point of focus is one of the primary goals of an introduction (McCroskey, 2001). Other goals are as follows:

1. *Gain attention.* This first part of the introduction is "the hook." You want to seize the audience's attention and focus them on one thing: your presentation. Keep in mind that audience members will be coming from a world of relationships, a world of academics, or a world of work. They will begin with a very different mindset than the one you intend to create for them. You must program them to your purpose and thesis.
2. *Build rapport.* The introduction should link the speaker with the audience, not only gaining the audience's attention but also building the speaker's credibility. By constructing a

social relationship, or developing co-orientation, you will build rapport with the audience and close any psychological distance that might exist. Address common interests and values and show the audience that you are going to talk about something that you and they are both interested in.

3. ***Orient the audience to your purposes and thesis.*** Another function of the introduction is to connect the audience with the purpose and thesis of your speech. If your purpose is to inform, that can be subtly conveyed. If your purpose is to persuade, you may not want to declare that at the outset, but at least make it clear that you have some concerns you hope they also share. After stating your thesis, then delineate the main points of your speech, alerting the audience to what is coming up. This is called the *preview* and usually comes at the end of the introduction.

4. ***Identify unusual words.*** Depending on the level of vocabulary, it sometimes is advisable to define certain words in the introduction, such as technical terms, acronyms, and jargon. This establishes common ground. Whether you need to identify words really depends on the audience. Be careful not to talk over their heads, using language they don't understand; yet don't condescend to them either, explaining terms they clearly know.

METHODS FOR GAINING AUDIENCE ATTENTION   Getting off to a good start is critical for both you and your audience. To ensure that you grasp their attention immediately, use any of the following methods.

Startling Statement. A startling statement is a bold, declarative remark that gets attention and makes a point. The point must be clearly related to the thesis of the speech, of course. Carl Hall, in a national contest, began his speech as follows:

EXAMPLE

"What I'm going to say to you is a bunch of garbage! That's right, a bunch of garbage! Because you see, ever since Adam and Eve ate the apple, humankind has not been sure what to do with the apple core. And we're living in a world where garbage and refuse is accumulating by the tons per day. And so what I am going to say to you is a bunch of garbage. But there are three ways that we can attack the problem of excess garbage and refuse in America today."

Quotation. A particularly interesting or poignant quotation will make the audience sensitive to your topic. If you cite, for instance, a well-known person or expert, the audience will likely feel your topic is worthwhile. Citing experts also heightens your own credibility. Consider this example:

EXAMPLE

"Shakespeare once said, 'Our doubts are traitors and cause us to lose the good we oft might win by fearing to attempt.' You know, things haven't changed a lot since Shakespeare's day, because there are many people in the world—perhaps in this audience before me today— who, in fact, are fearing to attempt and thus losing the positive good they otherwise might gain. This morning, let's focus on two ways we can prevent anxiety from crushing positive mental thinking."

Statistics. Like making a startling statement, citing statistics can be an immediate attention getter. This approach also helps you to build rapport, move through your orienting material, and share your thesis. Statistics can certainly be overused, but in most cases, they are effective, as this example reveals:

EXAMPLE

"In the next few decades, one out of four of you sitting in this room will suffer from cancer. And in the next fifteen years, as many as 70 percent of you will be somehow affected by cancer—either directly or indirectly by some member of your family or by a close friend. What can we do about the rising rate of cancer in our country? Are there some means by which we can prevent its ascendancy? Are there some things we can do to take better care of our bodies? These questions have been asked in recent years in medical journals, in classrooms, and in almost everybody's kitchen over a cup of coffee. And therein lies one problem, for studies have shown that dietary intake is linked with the rise of cancer. This morning, I would like us to explore three ways we can change our lifestyle and thus prevent cancer. Those ways include changing our diet, altering our exercise habits, and reducing our stress."

Real or Hypothetical Illustration. Another technique for developing an introduction is to develop a real or hypothetical illustration—a "What if?" scenario. Consider this one by communication professor Dr. Larry Winn:

EXAMPLE

"Nothing makes us feel more confident than to be at home in our beds, tucked away quietly after a long day. As you're sleeping peacefully, removed from the frustrations of our world, locked securely behind closed doors, at two o'clock in the morning it becomes rather hot. You push the covers off, thinking that you need more air in the room. By 2:10 you've noticed intense heat throughout and by 2:13 smoke fills the room; by 2:18 you lie asphyxiated on the floor, one of thousands of victims of smoke inhalation and fire every year in America. And those thousands of lives could have been saved by the simple installation of smoke detectors."

From this point, you would simply state your thesis and preview the main point of the speech:

EXAMPLE

"Today, I want you to understand three advantages of installing smoke detectors."

Case Example. A case example is an extended illustration or narrative that's explained in enough detail that people can learn from it, good or bad. For instance, one company's turn-around in productivity and customer satisfaction might be shared as a case example in the introduction of a presentation on the successful application of total quality management (TQM). A presentation about the importance of family communication might also begin with a revealing case example.

Questions.   Another attention-getting way to begin an introduction is to ask one or more questions. By simply probing, you will raise the interest level of the audience, particularly if the questions are meaningful and relevant to these individuals. For instance, asking an audience of parents about their concerns over finding suitable childcare would likely be effective. Here is a more extended example:

EXAMPLE

"How can you live ten more years, feel better, look great, and have more friends? Sound like a panacea? Hardly! Because the answer to that question really lies in adopting an exercise program as a part of your lifestyle. How does that happen? What are the dimensions of such a program, and what are the effects of an exercise program on one's lifestyle?"

Rhetorical Questions.   Still another way to begin an introduction is to use what is frequently called a rhetorical question. A rhetorical question is not really designed to elicit a response. Rather, it is intended to be thought provoking and usually has embedded within it an obvious answer. For instance, "What would you do with a million dollars?" is a rhetorical question. Obviously, you would find some quick use for the money. The question "You intend to graduate, right?" is obviously leading but also rhetorical in the sense that the answer is obvious. Such questions have the benefit of riveting audience attention to key issues.

GUIDELINES FOR WRITING THE INTRODUCTION   To write an effective introduction to your presentation, follow these suggestions (Adler & Rodman, 2001; Sprague & Stuart, 2003):

1. Gain your audience's attention right away with some type of "hook." Just be sure this attention-getting device is relevant to your audience and clearly connected to your topic. Otherwise, the audience may question your credibility.
2. Build rapport by establishing common ground with the audience—for instance, common beliefs or values, similar experiences or lifestyles, or shared concerns. When appropriate, use humor to connect with the audience and flatter them (as long as you are genuine). If you are an invited speaker, referring to the person who invited you may help audience members relate to you.
3. Focus audience members on your topic and thesis. Demonstrate your topic's relevance to them and thus why it's important that they listen to you. State your thesis using a declarative tone and identifying the key idea you want the audience to remember.
4. Near the end of your introduction, preview the main points you will offer to support your thesis. You need not go into a lot of detail here; just touch on the topics in the order in which you will discuss them.
5. It's a good idea to write out your introduction in its entirety, but make sure you don't just read it in your delivery. Practice to the point that you can pretty much recite it without looking constantly at your notes or outline. But have it available for safety's sake.

THINGS TO AVOID IN WRITING THE INTRODUCTION   If you get off to a bad start in your introduction, it can be difficult to recover. Try to begin well by avoiding these common mistakes:

1. *Taking too long.* Far too many speakers take forever to get to the point and state their thesis. Instead, they share a long narrative, an extended quotation, or more than one example,

story, or statistic. After getting the audience's attention, state your idea and move them into the body of the speech. If too long, you will lose them.

2. *Apologizing.* Don't get up and talk about why you are not prepared, why you are not the right person to be making this presentation, and so on. Apologizing will usually undermine the audience's motivation and your credibility, too. In addition, starting out on such a negative tone may undermine your confidence. By taking a more positive approach, you will show the audience your excitement and encourage them to listen.

As we did in the sections on purpose statements and thesis statements, we'll close this section with an evaluation activity. Skills at Work 12.4 asks you to evaluate an introduction using the information from this section.

SKILLS AT WORK 12.4
Evaluating an Introduction

Here's the original introduction to a speech on the topic of immigration:

> What opinion do you have about immigration? Immigration is often misunderstood. This has led many Americans to become less hospitable and less eager to share their homeland with immigrants. This is unfortunate because legal immigration, in fact, is a positive force that continues to benefit our country today, just as it has for the past several hundred years.

What is wrong with this introduction?

- The question intended as an attention-getter is weak.
- There is no attempt to relate the topic directly to the audience.
- There is no preview of the main points the speaker will cover.

Here's the revised introduction:

> "Give me your tired, your poor, your huddled masses yearning to breathe free, the wretched refuse of your teeming shore. Send these, the homeless, the tempest-tossed to me, I lift my lamp beside the golden door." Hopefully, most of us recognize this verse as the one inscribed on the tablet held by the Statue of Liberty. It speaks of the American ideology of a country founded as a safe haven for those less fortunate, whether for political, economic, or religious reasons.

However, as the influx of illegal immigrants has increased over the past several years, the hospitality of the general American public has worn thin. This is especially an issue in Texas. Most of us living here have been exposed to some commonly expressed sentiments regarding immigration in this area. Such sentiments have the capacity of tainting our overall view of immigration. Today, I would like to clarify the distinction between legal and illegal immigration and help make you more aware of several myths that are circulating in the United States about immigration. Legal immigration is, in fact, a positive force that continues to benefit our country.

Why is this introduction better?

- The opening quote will strike a chord with many individuals, gaining their attention as well as establishing common ground.
- Bringing the focus of the issue to Texas builds rapport with the audience and makes the topic relevant to them.
- The plan for the speech is previewed: to distinguish between legal and illegal immigration and to bring awareness to common myths.
- The statement of thesis at the end has a declarative effect.

Source: Adapted from Dodd and Lakey (2006).

Step 9: Construct the Conclusion

One of the last things to consider in developing your speech is, of course, to write the **conclusion**. By this point, you will have planned the body of your speech and written your introduction. Writing a good conclusion should follow naturally.

FUNCTIONS OF THE CONCLUSION   A good conclusion does several things:

1. *Summarizes main ideas.* Most conclusions first offer a summary statement at the end. Such a summary can take the form of simply enumerating the main ideas. It is usually considered better style, however, if those ideas are presented using different language. That way, the key ideas will be branded gently into the memories of audience members. Avoid beginning your summary, however, with "In conclusion" or "Let me summarize by saying . . ." Work on a more effective transition to move into your conclusion.

2. *Brings things to a close.* A conclusion needs to wrap things up for the audience and, as such, leave them feeling good about your presentation. It addition to enhancing the audience's recall of your message, the conclusion should make the audience feel fulfilled, as if they have completed a learning process. We'll discuss several methods of doing so in the next section. In short, find a way to end with punch and style. Pay special attention to developing and then delivering your last sentence.

3. *Motivates the audience.* Depending on which organizational pattern you use, your conclusion might also stir your audience to some action. In the case of an informative presentation, the audience should walk away feeling that what they heard is compelling and engaging. It should take them to a new level of awareness, discovery, knowledge, or clarity. In the case of a persuasive presentation, that new awareness might lead to action or change.

METHODS FOR WRITING THE CONCLUSION

Illustrations, Stories, and Case Studies. One method of developing the conclusion is to use a brief illustration or story that summarizes the main ideas and perhaps creates motivation at the same time. Case studies work well, too, perhaps describing people who adopted the measures that you have talked about. Short references to organizations, groups, and cultures are effective in establishing common ground with the audience.

If you used an illustration or story in your introduction, try to bring it into the conclusion. Doing so provides closure by showing the audience that you have come full circle. Recall from the previous section the hypothetical story used in the introduction to a speech about the importance of smoke detectors. Here's how that speech might conclude by extending the hypothetical story:

EXAMPLE

"As we finish today, let's revise the scene with which we began this presentation. Now, at two o'clock, you are awakened by the smoke detector that's in the hallway of your home or apartment or dorm. By 2:05, you're out in the hallway and arousing the other residents to exit using the fire escapes and escape hatches, as you have all rehearsed. By 2:10, you're all standing safely outside as the firefighters arrive. Now, instead of being a victim of asphyxiation, you are one of thousands of Americans who was saved because he or she installed a smoke detector."

Quotations and Pithy Statements. Reciting a poignant quotation or making your own clever remark is another good way to end. As with an illustration or story, try to extend something from

An informative speech conclusion should review the main points and offer a final statement or quote to remember the speech.

the introduction, such as a quote made there or even another relevant quote from the same individual. To reiterate, think about the words you will leave your audience with. For instance:

EXAMPLE

Well, as we said at the beginning, Shakespeare indicated that our doubts make us traitors. We can lose the good that would otherwise be ours because we fail even to try. Somehow, I have the feeling that after today's presentation, you are going to be applying two ways to reduce anxiety. Because of this information, instead of strangers becoming a difficulty for you, you will take your relation with strangers and acquaintances and see them in a more positive light. Second, I think the information today may have inspired some new ways to relax. Instead of our doubts making us traitors, as the Shakespeare introductory quote revealed, our doubts will make us curious enough to build bridges of new friendships and positive input. So, I look forward to implementing Shakespeare's advice and winning by not fearing to attempt.

THINGS TO AVOID IN WRITING THE CONCLUSION　　Just because the conclusion comes at the end of the speech (and you will therefore develop it near the end of the speech-preparation process), don't give it short shrift. Take the time to think through what you want to do and how you can best deliver your final remarks. Also avoid these common mistakes:

1. *Apologizing.* Apologizing in your conclusion will have the same effect as apologizing in your introduction, as discussed earlier: It will harm your credibility and make the audience feel as though they have wasted their time. Avoid saying things like "I don't know if I have made this clear." Apologizing or otherwise raising doubts about you and your presentation will serve no good purpose at this point.
2. *Adding new material.* This is not the time to flesh out points that you either forgot to make or didn't develop adequately in the body of your speech. Don't be tempted to work in

this material at the end, while you still have your audience. Summarize what you have said without adding anything new.

3. *Contradicting what's already been said.* You may have heard a speaker who makes bold statements throughout his or her presentation but then backs off or contradicts himself or herself in the conclusion. It's as if he or she is worried about having come on too strong, perhaps even being overbearing. Trying to smooth over pointed remarks or dilute them with further comments will confuse your audience and maybe even irritate them. Simply summarize, motivate, and offer a strong closing statement.

4. *Rambling.* Too many speakers wander in delivering their conclusions to the extent that their audiences become restless, bored, and even hostile. There is a point at which the audience has absorbed all that they will, and when you have arrived at that point, it is better to stop than to drone on. Again, the audience wants closure. Speakers who go beyond their time or fail to provide a real conclusion will destroy their future credibility.

5. *Being meek.* Finish deliberately. Don't let your voice trail off or your body language suggest that you're not sure whether you're done. Again, fine-tune your last statement and deliver it with confidence and authority. When you have finished, sit down. There is no need to say "thank you." Let your message sink into the audience's minds.

Use the information presented in this section to evaluate the conclusion presented in Skills at Work 12.5.

SKILLS AT WORK 12.5
Evaluating a Conclusion

Here's the conclusion to a speech on immigration:

> In conclusion, I have pointed out the distinction between legal and illegal immigration and have made you aware of several myths that are circulating in the U.S. about immigration. Hopefully, you now realize that, contrary to common public opinion, immigration is not a menace to our society. Perhaps even more so in states like Texas, we need to be careful about not allowing information about illegal aliens to cause us to form misguided perceptions about immigration as a whole. Canada has a much different policy toward immigration than the United States does. Legal immigration is, in fact, a positive force that continues to benefit our country. Let us continue to "lift the lamp beside the golden door." Thank you for your attention today.

What is wrong with this conclusion?

- Beginning with "In conclusion" is clunky. The words "I have pointed out"
would sufficiently signal to listeners that the speaker is moving into the conclusion.
- Ending with "Thank you" ruins an otherwise inspirational ending.
- Bringing up Canada's immigration policy introduces a new subject, as this presentation has focused on immigration in the United States.

What is good about this conclusion?

- The first several sentences do a good job of reviewing and summarizing the main points of the speech.
- By addressing the people living in Texas, the speaker makes the message personal, motivating audience members to consider their own beliefs and actions.
- Closing with the quote provides an eloquent finish. Also recall from Skills at Work 12.4, in which you evaluated the introduction to this speech, that doing so extends the quote used there.

Source: Based on Dodd and Lakey (2006).

Step 10: Providing Connections and Transitions

Don't be tempted to quit now. One important step remains: that of pulling together the various sections of your speech. In particular, it's important to connect the introduction with the body and the body with the conclusion. It's also important to lead your audience from idea to idea within the body of your speech. Remind them of where you have been, and show them where you are going.

Several techniques can be used to make these **connections and transitions**: using enumeration, providing transitions, asking questions, and previewing and reviewing.

USING ENUMERATION   *Enumeration* is the practice of verbal marking, for instance, by numbering major concepts or idea. Words such as "First," "Second," and "Third" achieve this purpose, as do phrases such as "The next point" and "Another idea." Why is enumeration effective? Audiences tend to remember major ideas when they are numbered. There is something about corporate culture (perhaps a linear mode of thought or problem solving) that makes enumeration especially effective in workplace presentations.

PROVIDING TRANSITIONS   Providing transitions between the major parts of a speech helps convey a sense of movement or progress. Doing so also creates *coherence*, or a sense of logical connection between ideas. When used effectively, transitions show the relationship between ideas: old and new, previous and upcoming, general and specific. Simple transitions include *and, but, also, yet,* and *or.* Also consider these more dramatic words and phrases and what each signals:

EXAMPLES

On the one hand	Finally	Furthermore
On the other hand	In addition	In other words
In contrast	For example	Moreover
Therefore	In general	Although

Moving from one point to another without some kind of transition is too abrupt. Use transitions to make the connections for your audience.

ASKING QUESTIONS   Another type of connection/transition strategy is to use a question. Instead of stating a key idea or point, introduce it with a question:

EXAMPLE

"Now that we have considered the advantages and disadvantages of this proposal, we may still wonder why we should be concerned with it. In other words, what is its significance? Let's turn to three significant issues that haven't yet been raised."

The question in this passage serves as a transition, leading from a previously discussed topic to a new one.

PREVIEWING AND REVIEWING   A *preview* tells the audience what is coming up next, whereas a *review* offers a brief summary of what was just covered. Using the two together provides a useful transition strategy:

EXAMPLE

"We have just examined the advantages of proposal X. Conversely, let us also note the disadvantages of this proposal."

As you can see, the first sentence provides a review of the advantages just discussed, and the second sentence makes the shift to discussing the disadvantages.

TYPES OF INFORMATIVE PRESENTATIONS

Thus far, we have discussed the process of developing an informative presentation. And from the examples used to illustrate various concepts, you have probably formed an idea of some of the situations in which informative speaking is done.

Informative speaking is done across a wide range of situations (Beebe, Beebe, & Ivy, 2001). Some of those situations are highly scheduled, involving a lot of preparation time and a large audience. Such a formal presentation, which may be called a *speech* or *lecture,* usually lasts over twenty minutes. However, other situations provide less notice and thus little time to prepare. While the presentation time may be short and the audience small, the speaker will be expected to deliver details in an organized way.

We will close this chapter on informative presentations by indicating several shorter versions of informative speaking: (1) oral reports and briefings, (2) elevator speech, and (4) introductions of speakers.

Oral Reports and Briefings

An **oral report** is usually shorter than a typical informative speech, lasting five to ten minutes. Like typical informative speaking, an oral report presents data, details, and may involve the use of visual aids. Oral reports and briefings are often presented to a small, specialty groups in an organization and may provide for a question-and-answer session following. Usually, the introduction is in the form of a framework: here is the situation or our history on this matter. Often, there is a problem or some issue indicated. Then, the speaker gives the present solution or state of affairs.

An oral report can take the form of a news release or briefing when the purpose of the communication is to announce problems, crises, innovations, or future plans. The audience of a **news release or briefing** is typically the public, but depending on the topic, the message may only be relevant to others in the organization or perhaps the industry.

At times, a briefing is preplanned and involves delivery of a short memorized speech to announce the desired news. At other times, the speaker is caught off guard and is expected to speak on the spot, without advance notice or preparation. In general, follow these suggestions for making effective news releases and briefings:

1. Identify your position or role.
2. Present the facts.
3. Offer solutions to problems, where appropriate.
4. Provide reassurance, where appropriate.
5. Be to the point.

Speakers are sometimes expected to deliver news releases and briefings on the spot, without advance notice or time to prepare.

Presenting a newsworthy message to an internal organizational audience can be challenging, but speaking to an external audience raises even more issues. Speaking to the press, in particular, can make the speaker feel as though he or she is in a pressure cooker.

Whether you are planning a news release or you simply have the questions asked by representatives of the media, here are some important guidelines you may recall from Chapter 9 (Bradshaw, 2007):

1. Be aware of the time allotted for your remarks. Usually, an edited "sound bite" is ten seconds, more or less.
2. Speak clearly and present your message in short, easy-to-understand sections or chunks.
3. Avoid providing examples and telling stories that cannot be related succinctly and have the desired effect.
4. Come up with a standard phrase that you can incorporate in answering questions—a mantra, so to speak.
5. To ensure listeners will understand the context of your response, begin with a restatement of the question.
6. When asked more than one question at a time, sort them out in your answer by saying something such as "Let me respond to one issue at a time. First, . . ."
7. Look at and speak to the interviewer, not the camera.
8. Dress appropriately in terms of the background and lighting of the situation.
9. Be cordial to media representatives.
10. Acknowledge the reporter and his or her technical staff.

Elevator Speech

There are times when you have a proposal or an idea which normally demands a written document and/or an oral informative proposal to present. However, you may find yourself in a totally unplanned, abbreviated time situation when someone asks you about your idea or proposal. You have only seconds to respond. What do you do?

The answer is affectionately called the **elevator speech**, because that one-minute going from one floor to another in an elevator may be the only time you have to tell the boss or some investor about your idea. How does this speech form work? There are two basic ingredients: (1) you must tell the problem and (2) show a value proposition to show how this venture solves the problem. Moreover, it will be successful when

> you are succinct;
>
> it is so easy to understand that your grandma can understand it;
>
> it is profitable and solves a problem; and
>
> it is irrefutable—that is, you can't leave them with more questions than answers.

Quite honestly, I would like you to see a YouTube illustration (some of my source for this advice) and inform your views of this powerful message genre ("The Elevator Pitch" at http://www.youtube.com/watch?v=Tq0tan49rmc).

Introductions of Speakers

Making a **speech of introduction** is not only a common task but also poses a unique speaking opportunity. To make the occasion memorable and enjoyable for you and the person you introduce, do these things:

1. Mention the speaker's name.
2. Introduce the occasion.
3. Explain the speaker's credentials and relevant experience.
4. Tell a brief story that will enhance the audience's feeling of trust in or closeness to the speaker.
5. Share why you are excited about hearing the speaker.

Above all, be brief. Your introductory remarks should usually be under a minute (unless the situation dictates an extended introduction). Often, you should memorize your introduction, to use just the right language and nonverbal actions and set up the speaker for maximum credibility. Here is a good example of an introductory speech:

EXAMPLE

"Shara Jacobs is a talented merchandizing specialist and is here today to introduce the upcoming spring fashions. Her talent is rooted in her educational background: she earned a bachelor's degree at Texas Tech and a master's degree at Texas A&M. That talent has blossomed over ten years with our company, during which she's led the women's fashions department into huge sales increases. On a recent trip to New York, two of her counterparts from competitive companies remarked, 'Shara is the best in the business.' To help us foresee our customers' needs and increase our profits again, I'm delighted to introduce Shara Jacobs."

In Perspective

The process of developing an informative presentation comprises 10 steps. Step 1 is to analyze the audience, which was covered in detail in Chapter 10.

Step 2 is to select the topic. The primary considerations in doing so should be your personal knowledge and interests; your audience's needs and interests; and the occasion of your presentation. Narrow your topic by looking for overlap among these three concerns.

Step 3 is to create a purpose statement: a complete sentence that describes what you want to accomplish with your presentation. You will use it to develop your speech and may or may not state it to your audience. Four general purposes can be identified: (1) to inform; (2) to persuade; (3) to entertain; and (4) to inspire. Each purpose not only defines a different outcome but also invites a different approach.

The next step is to create a thesis statement: a statement of your topic that is worded as a claim to be proved or a theme to be developed. It is usually first stated in the introduction of your speech. A preview then follows, providing a snapshot of the major points you plan to develop.

The fifth step is to develop the main points of the presentation, or the key ideas that will amplify or prove the thesis statement. These main points will comprise the body of the presentation.

The sixth step is to provide sufficient support material for the main points and to note the sources of that information. Your purpose statement and thesis statement should guide you in selecting the right types of support for your presentation. Types of support include examples, illustrations, narratives, testimonials, statistics, expert authorities, definitions, and analogies. Excellent sources for support materials can be found in any number of places and in both print and online versions. Regardless of what sources you use, it's imperative that you cite them orally in presenting your speech.

Step 7 is to develop an organizational design. For most speakers, it is useful to have an outline. The very process of outlining will help you shape your message, making it clear and focused. In addition, you want to "package" your message in the way that will best produce understanding. To do so, you will choose one of these organizational patterns: (1) topical pattern; (2) spatial pattern; (3) chronological pattern; (4) cause-and-effect pattern; (5) known-to-unknown pattern; or (6) simple-to-complex pattern.

Developing the introduction is step 8. A good introduction seizes the audience's attention, builds rapport with them, orients them to your purpose and thesis, and identifies for them unusual words (if necessary).

Constructing the conclusion is step 9. A good conclusion summarizes the main ideas, ends the presentation, and motivates the audience. In short, find a way to end with punch and style. Pay special attention to developing and then delivering your last sentence.

The final step is to pull together the various sections of your speech. In particular, it is important to connect the introduction with the body and the body with the conclusion. It is also important to lead your audience from idea to idea within the body of your speech. You can make these connections and transitions by using enumeration, providing transitions, asking questions, and previewing and reviewing.

Informative speaking is done across a wide range of situations—some formal and involving a lot of preparation and some not. An oral report or briefly is usually based on research and is typically presented to a small group within an organization. It may announce problems, crises, innovations, or plans. At times, briefing is preplanned and involves delivery of a short memorized speech. At other times, the speaker is caught off guard and is expected to speak on the spot, perhaps in front of the media. Suggestions for dealing with mediated communication are provided. Making a speech of introduction is not only a common task but also poses a unique speaking opportunity. Above all, be brief.

The chapter also includes important reminders of being ethical as an informative communication by using honest, unbiased sources, and doing diligence in your preparation so as to separate your assimilation and conclusion from research sources, so as to give credit and not misrepresent yourself when there are experts you've used.

Discussion Questions

1. Compare and contrast a purpose statement and a thesis statement. How are they alike? How are they different?
2. What makes a powerful introduction? Which of the functions identified is most important? Why?
3. How will the audience likely respond to a speaker who does not provide sufficient support for the main points of his or her presentation? Similarly, how will the audience likely respond to a speaker who doesn't cite the sources of his or her support?
4. What makes an ineffective conclusion? What mistakes are commonly made, and what effect does each have on the audience and the overall success of the presentation?
5. How can introducing a speaker ultimately affect the success of his or her speech? Give some examples to support your explanation.

Exercises

1. Choose a simple topic and plan a simple message that could be shared in, say, a five-minute presentation. In planning that presentation, first take a random approach (perhaps making some notes but nothing too specific) and then prepare an outline. How does each approach to planning affect your mindset, your work process, and your actual presentation?
2. Using the same simple topic and message, plan separate presentations using three of the six different organizational patterns (such as topical, spatial, and chronological). For this topic and message, which pattern seems best? How does the topic dictate the pattern chosen?
3. Using the same topic and message, write an introduction and a conclusion. Find a way to use the same story or quotation in both. What effect will this have on the audience?
4. Survey recent newspaper and magazine articles that are about the same subject—for instance, schools' accountability for student test scores and other outcomes. What organizational patterns are used in these articles? How does the choice of pattern seem related to the purpose of the article? Do some patterns put a different slant or spin on the topic? Provide examples to support your explanation.

References

Adler, R. B., & Rodman, G. (2001). *Understanding human communication.* 7th ed. Fort Worth, TX: Harcourt Brace.

Beebe, S. A., Beebe, S. J., & Ivy, D. K. (2001). *Communication: Principles for a lifetime.* Boston: Allyn & Bacon.

Bradshaw, L. (2007). Interviewing with the media. Personal Communication, Abilene, Taxes, April.

DeVito, J. A. (2000a). *The elements of public speaking.* 7th ed. Boston: Longman.

DeVito, J. A. (2000b). *Human communication.* 8th ed. Boston: Longman.

Dodd, C. H., & Lakey, P. N. (2006). *Communication resources.* Abilene, TX: Consulting Instructional Systems.

Dodd, C. H., & Lewis, M. L. (1992). *Human communication: Developing positive life experiences.* Dubuque, IA: Kendall/Hunt.

McCroskey, J. C. (2001). *An introduction to rhetorical communication.* 8th ed. Boston: Allyn & Bacon.

Seiler, W. J., & Beal, M. L. (2008). *Communication: Making connections.* 7th ed. Boston: Allyn & Bacon.

Sprague, J., & Stuart, D. (2003). *The speaker's handbook.* 6th ed. Belmont, CA: Wadsworth.

CHAPTER 13

Managing Persuasive Presentations in the Workplace

After reading this chapter, you will be able to do the following:

- Explain the outcomes related to changes in attitudes, values, beliefs, and behaviors.
- Identify the elements involved in persuading an audience.
- Recognize different organizational patterns for developing a presentation.
- Understand the need to provide relevant and credible support material.
- Formulate an argument based on sound logic and reasoning.
- Recognize common fallacies in reasoning.

One's first step in wisdom is to question everything—and one's last is to come to terms with everything.

GEORG CHRISTOPH LICHTENBERG

Recall from Chapter 12 that one of the four primary purposes of making presentations is *to persuade:* to bring about a change of feelings, opinions, beliefs, attitudes, or behaviors within the audience. Persuasion may also involve trying to reinforce audience members' current beliefs or behaviors, to discontinue their current beliefs or behaviors, or to prevent future beliefs or behaviors. To persuade an audience demands proof or evidence that the thesis or claim argued stems from sound reasoning. These are the basic elements of **persuasive presentations**.

In reading this chapter, keep in mind that most of the material in Chapter 12 on developing an informative presentation also holds true for developing a persuasive presentation. Accordingly, this chapter will not provide a similarly detailed review of the process. Instead, the unique features of persuasive speaking will be discussed, beginning with the purpose of bringing about change.

PERSUASION CHANGES OR REINFORCES ATTITUDES, VALUES, BELIEFS, AND BEHAVIORS

In order to prompt change, you must be aware of what people think, what they find valuable, what they believe, and how they act. In other words, you must understand their attitudes, values, beliefs, and behaviors.

Attitudes

An **attitude** is an evaluation of something—a feeling about whether it's good or bad, useful or not useful, and so on (Cialdini, 2001). Many social scientists believe that attitudes predispose people to respond in positive and negative ways to certain events, situations, people, and places, or to engage in *approach and avoidance tendencies.* In this sense, attitudes motivate actions. For instance, if you hate being around large crowds of people, you will probably not go to a state fair, a ballgame, or a rock concert. Similarly, if you think that big cities are centers of crime, poverty, traffic, and isolation, you probably won't visit New York on vacation or decide to move to Los Angeles.

Values

Values are enduring standards or ideals of what is worthwhile and not worthwhile. They may be specific to an individual or shared by the members of an entire culture. For instance, an educator's positive attitude toward joining a collective bargaining organization may stem in part from his or her values about security. On a larger level, the importance of achievement is a generally accepted American value. Other traditional American values are as follows:

- Individualism
- Proof and scientific backing
- Hard work and perseverance
- Neatness and cleanliness
- Energy and enthusiasm
- Loyalty and commitment
- Friendliness and cooperation
- Fairness and equality

Beliefs

Beliefs represent perceived truths—for instance, in a system of government, in an individual's integrity, or even in fate or destiny. The topic of corporate fraud could conjure up evaluative feelings about fraud (an attitude of aversion), values related to fraud (such as morality and ethics disavowing theft or stealing), and the belief that corporate fraud causes inflated prices and erodes societal morality.

Behaviors

Behaviors are actions. To continue with the example of corporate fraud, corresponding behaviors would include objecting to leaders, whistle-blowing on questionable individuals, and resigning in protest. Two kinds of behavioral change often result from persuasion in the workplace (Larson, 2007):

1. *Behavior as adoption* involves adoption of a practice, idea, or technology—for instance, using a new instrument for employee evaluation.
2. *Behavior as avoidance* involves rejecting a particular action or policy—for example, refusing to use a new type of employee evaluation.

Case 13.1

Bringing about Change

When Daniel became president of a prominent nonprofit organization dedicated to caring for children with special needs, one of his primary goals was to expand the organization's budget and thus its client capacity. In analyzing the situation, he realized that two things had to change first: (1) the values of the organization, as set by the board of trustees, had to become more aggressive and growth oriented in terms of fundraising and grant writing, and (2) the employees' behaviors had to change accordingly.

With several key staff, Daniel developed and implemented an internal campaign aimed at accomplishing these two changes with these two groups. And in just under two years, the results were phenomenal. The board shifted its values from being complacent to embracing outreach, which led to corresponding increases in receiving grants and raising monies. The staff was encouraged by this shift in values and participated wholeheartedly in the fundraising efforts. In addition, staff members increased their efficiency, allowing twice as many children to be cared for than had been possible before. Daniel's ongoing enthusiasm became infectious.

Trace what led to what in this scenario. Could the ultimate outcomes have been achieved in another way—say, with simply training the staff in fundraising techniques? Why or why not?

When the purpose of communication is to persuade, it is significant to know which of the four outcomes—attitudes, values, beliefs, or behaviors—is being targeted. Your selection of support materials should match the desired outcome. In most situations, it will be best to focus on one outcome at a time. In others, it will be logical to focus on changing an attitude, then a value, and so on. In still others, you might just initiate a dialogue and work toward specific outcomes later. Case 13.1 presents an example of focusing on one type of outcome and eventually seeing change in another.

BEGINNING THEORIES UNDERLYING PERSUASION

Cognitive Dissonance

People's need to rationalize decisions and reduce anticipated conflict about those decisions has been a keen area of study in persuasion. When our beliefs, perceptions of behaviors, or attitudes do not align, we feel off balance or troubled. This collision of beliefs, feelings, or behaviors and the inner conflict that results is known as **cognitive dissonance**.

For instance, when most of us buy something expensive, we begin to experience some degree of internal conflict. We weigh the advantages of the purchase against the disadvantages, considering the price, the quality, the usefulness, and so forth. When we do so, we are engaging in a process of *rationalization*. If we can justify our purchase, we will resolve the conflict and achieve *consonance*. However, if we cannot, we will continue to experience *dissonance* (see Figure 13.1 on the next page). Case 13.2 (also on the next page) presents a hypothetical workplace scenario of Sally, a manager stuck in dissonance after making what she thought was a good decision.

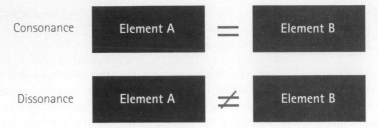

FIGURE 13.1 Consonance versus Dissonance

In the context of persuasive communication, the goal is to reduce cognitive dissonance by providing justification. Five techniques commonly achieve this goal:

1. *Discredit the source.* By "attacking the messenger," you can rationalize that his or her information should not be considered valid. Discrediting the source might involve attacking the person's credibility or assuming that he or she was just duped or misinformed on this topic. You might also question his or her source rather than the individual himself or herself. In Sally's situation, she would have to seriously consider the merits of discrediting the source, given that it's her boss.

2. *Point out advantages.* A second dissonance-reducing strategy is to recognize only the evidence that bolsters your decision. In doing so, however, make sure you can provide evidence to support the advantages you have pointed out: statistics, testimonials, case studies, and so on. For instance, in her next presentation to the managers' forum, Sally could justify her computer purchase with data that indicate its advantages in terms of quality service, immediate delivery, availability of training, and so on. She could say, "I may have paid more, but I got what I wanted."

3. *Point out disadvantages.* This alternative takes the opposite approach by pointing out only the disadvantages. To make this rationalization, you must identify all of the disadvantages. You might also look for others who agree with you and will confirm your reasons. To rationalize using this technique, Sally could show the disadvantages of purchasing the less expensive computer, such as getting bad service from that vendor, having to wait to get the machine, and so on. She could say, "Based on the needs of my department, this other vendor would not have worked out."

Case 13.2

Overcoming Cognitive Dissonance

Sally, a midlevel manager, purchased a $2,000 computer for one of the administrative assistants on her staff. Sally had looked at many computers and talked to countless salespeople, and this was the best deal she could find. The price was within her equipment budget.

The same day that the new computer arrived, Sally's boss dutifully stopped by to admire the purchase but then informed her that she could have purchased the same computer for only $1,200. "How could that be?" she wondered. "Why didn't I check around more? Now I've wasted some of my budget, and my boss thinks I screwed up."

What can Sally do to rationalize the situation and reduce her feelings of cognitive dissonance?

4. *Ignore the issue.* Dissonance reduction can occur by changing the issue or ignoring it entirely. This is essentially a method of diversion or denial. In justifying her computer purchase, for example, Sally could change the issue by arguing that purchasing new equipment helps reduce problems with employee morale. She could also act as if she did not know her decision was in question or avoid people who do not like her decision.

5. *Change attitude.* Cognitive dissonance can generate enough internal conflict that people change their attitudes to fit the dissonance-arousing information—going to the other side, more or less. Sally could send back the $2,000 computer and purchase the $1,200 one, changing her attitude, or she could attempt to change the other managers' collective attitude by making them understand that she made the right decision. (Clearly, this latter option is the one most people would prefer in reducing their own cognitive dissonance.)

In planning a persuasive presentation, consider how to reason with your audience in a way that anticipates their cognitive dissonance and provides them with a means of rationalization (McCroskey, 2001; Petty & Cacioppo, 1995).

Social Judgment Theory

How people come to evaluate information, form a position, and can then be moved to form a new position is explained by **social judgment theory** (Larson, 2007; McCroskey, 2001). This theory rests on the understanding that people evaluate information from a fundamental attitude or position, called an *anchor point.* For instance, on an attitude scale in which 1 means "strongly against" and 10 means "strongly for," level 4 represents the anchor point.

Most attitude theories stop here. However, social judgment theory recognizes that most people also embrace other positions on the continuum, to greater and lesser degrees. For example, a person may accept positions 1 through 5, even though 4 is still most preferred. This acceptable range, called the *latitude of acceptance,* represents a person's tolerable positions on an issue. Conversely, the range of positions that are not tolerable comprises the *latitude of rejection.* Finally, everything in between is called the *latitude of noncommitment.*

Upon hearing information, we evaluate it through the lens of our anchor point and align it with one of these latitudes. For instance, upon hearing a message that aligns with our latitude of rejection, we will more than likely discard it with disbelief. It just doesn't fit. Nevertheless, what if we could increase our level of tolerance and make it fit?

We engage in that change gradually and cautiously through what is called *incremental strategy,* which is another tenet of social judgment theory. We amend our tolerance level by inching toward a desired direction, becoming increasingly more comfortable with the message after repeated exposure to it.

A skillful communicator may present a series of messages to initiate the incremental strategy and try to change the audience's position. But before doing so, he or she should understand that three results, or *effects,* are possible:

1. *Assimilation effect.* When a message seems near our latitude of acceptance, we will likely accept it. Say, for instance, that our latitude of acceptance is 1 through 5. We would likely feel that a message rated 5.5 or 6 was close enough and map it into our latitude of acceptance. Doing so would result in enlarging our latitude of acceptance—in this case, ranging from 1 through 6. (Obviously, the latitudes of resistance and noncommitment would shrink correspondingly.) Suppose that a successive message averages at 6.5 or 7. If we followed the same process, we would expand our latitude of acceptance once more—this time from 1 through 7

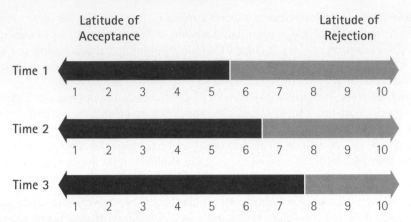

FIGURE 13.2   The Assimilation Effect

(and shrink our latitudes of resistance and noncommitment). By targeting messages in this way successively to expand an audience's latitude boundaries, a speaker can ultimately persuade that audience to reach a desired position (see Figure 13.2).

2. *Contrast effect.* The opposite of the assimilation effect is the contrast effect. When we judge a message harshly, finding it too far beyond our tolerable range, we routinely discard it. In our example, a message that is in reality a 7 could be judged as too extreme and rejected as if it were an 8 or a 9. A series of messages having this effect would ultimately result in making an audience more resistant to persuasion (that is, expanding the latitude of resistance and shrinking the latitudes of acceptance and noncommitment).

3. *Boomerang effect.* This result extends the contrast effect but results in the audience cementing the boundaries of their latitude of acceptance. Specifically, the audience does not give an almost-tolerable message the benefit of the doubt but instead rallies around a deeply held anchor point. Thus, if a speaker pushes too hard or too fast, the audience might simply hunker down. If they are feeling any cognitive dissonance, they may find ways to rationalize it and further resist modification from their position (as discussed earlier).

To manage this process effectively requires definite skill. You should generate a series of messages that run successively closer to the outside boundary of the audience's latitude of acceptance. Your audience analysis should provide you with an idea of the audience's anchor position. You must be careful, however, not to alienate the audience by producing premature contrast effects or encouraging the boomerang effect. This simultaneous balancing of objectives should rely on good preparation and audience research.

Regardless, your plan may not always work out. Sometimes people avoid extremes and stay in the middle; other times audiences avoid the discomfort of change. You should also consider the ethical issues involved in this approach to persuasion, since the temptation to deceive your audience might be high.

Audience Commitment

Research has shown that when audience members engage in small behaviors or make small changes in their attitude toward a topic, they are likely to embrace that attitude wholeheartedly. Similar to the notion of rationalizing to reduce dissonance, the principle of **audience commitment** states that modifying behavior, even slightly, predicts an attitude alignment consistent with the initial modification.

The principle of audience commitment underlies several techniques for spurring motivation and creating change in business and professional communication.

A number of techniques successfully motivate and create change in business and professional communication. Examples include having people stand up, raise their hands, sign cards, make testimonials, and give announcements. These techniques refer to methods of *self-persuasion* (Cialdini, 2001). Consider an example from the medical profession, in which the speaker at a meeting of professional staff warned against making poor diagnoses. The speaker asked each staff person to write down at least three incidents of bad diagnoses he or she had witnessed. When the staff became engaged in this way, their interest peaked and their involvement widened dramatically.

Again, an ethical warning is in order. This principle is easily manipulative without regard to content or free will. The audience has rights and needs to have accurate information in order to make decisions.

When applied within the boundaries of acceptable ethics, the audience commitment principle is most effective when the audience experiences free will. If people feel coerced into making certain kinds of behavioral commitments, the technique will backfire. In addition, for the technique to work, people must believe that their small commitments will have a larger audience or become highly significant other than satisfying the speaker. Finally, when making a commitment links with a form of reward, the commitment is deemed pleasant and the effect is thus more successful.

Inoculation

The principle of **inoculation** refers to building up the audience's resistance to other messages (which will likely be heard later) by convincing them of the value of your own message. This procedure refers to *counterpositional resistance*. For example, the salesperson who wants to sell a group of customers on an innovative solution to better quality service would want to inoculate those customers against other solutions that other salespeople might offer later.

Three techniques are relatively successful in inoculation:

1. *Supportive treatment.* Using this technique, the audience is given rational reasons for supporting the position, presumably giving them a foundation of knowledge by which they can deny an opposite position (O'Keefe, 2002).

2. *Refutation treatment.* This method encourages audience resistance by identifying and then refuting a sample of counterarguments that they will likely hear later. In essence, this method generates a cognitive defense system. If nothing else, the audience will not be surprised by the counterarguments when they do hear them.

3. *Generalized forewarning.* In this technique, the speaker warns the audience that some form of influence will attempt to affect them later. They are urged not to be surprised by the opposing messages (but the messages themselves are not spelled out).

Using the earlier example of the salesperson "pitching" a service innovation, here are three possible statements using the techniques just explained:

EXAMPLES

Supportive treatment: The salesperson would offer the customer group a number of reasons as to why his or her innovative approach is superior.

Refutation treatment: The salesperson would list the problems associated with previous and future service approaches, thus alerting customers to them.

Generalized forewarning: The salesperson would caution the customer group against others who may try to erode their belief in his or her plan and urge the customers to stand firm.

Research has shown that the refutation technique works best, followed by the supportive technique and then the generalized forewarning (Petty & Cacioppo, 1995). A combination of the supportive and refutation approaches is the most effective in establishing resistance (see Figure 13.3). Keep in mind, too, that not only is inoculation effective in persuading an audience to your message, but it can also help preserve your message once you have convinced an audience of its merits.

Message Order

Research has also shown that the arrangement of points in a message affects its persuasive impact. Two types of **message order** will be considered in this section: (1) one-sided versus two-sided messages and (2) strongest versus weakest argument first. After the discussions of these topics, we'll consider how the order of the messages can affect how they are received. This applies

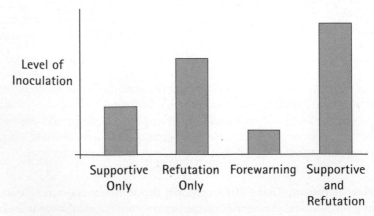

FIGURE 13.3   Inoculation Effects

to the two parts of a two-sided message and to two speakers presenting opposing messages in a single situation.

ONE-SIDED VERSUS TWO-SIDED MESSAGES   Sometimes the persuasive speaker must choose between presenting only one or both sides of a message. From a practical standpoint, a one-sided message works best under these audience conditions:

- The audience favors the advocated position.
- The speaker's credibility is high.
- The audience is not equipped to consider one or more other arguments.
- The speaker is expected to present only one side of a case.
- The audience is unlikely to hear the opposing arguments.

Conversely, a two-sided message works best under these audience conditions:

- The audience does not favor the advocated position.
- The speaker's credibility is moderate or low.
- Audience members are knowledgeable and likely to know about the topic.
- The speaker is not expected to be one sided.
- The audience is likely to hear the opposing arguments.

From an ethical standpoint, it's wise to present two sides (or at least to acknowledge that there are two sides) in terms of building trust and maintaining credibility.

STRONGEST VERSUS WEAKEST ARGUMENT FIRST   When presenting a persuasive message involves making a series of arguments, the speaker must weigh the relative merits of the arguments and decide in what order to present them for the greatest effect. Obviously, there are two possibilities:

1. *Strongest argument first/weakest argument last.* This method puts your best foot forward, so to speak. By making a good first impression, you may set the tone for the rest of the speech. Beginning with your strongest argument is especially effective when your audience is unmotivated and/or your credibility is low. Thus, you want to start out strong and maintain momentum.
2. *Weakest argument first/strongest argument last.* This method involves building momentum and finishing in a triumphant climax. It is most effective when the audience is highly motivated and/or your credibility is high. If this doesn't seem to make sense, think about what would happen in this audience/speaker situation if you presented your *strongest* argument first. You would create such an unreal expectation after making such a strong first point that your following points would seem weak by comparison. Finishing strong leaves an audience feeling good.

Of course, the ideal would be to have all strong arguments so that order would not be an issue. That's not often the case, however, so you should be able to recognize strengths and weaknesses and arrange them accordingly.

GOING FIRST VERSUS LAST   Which message or which speaker has the greatest impact in terms of persuasive ability: the first one or the last one? It depends on the situation. Before explaining how and why, let's define some terms. When the first message or speaker has the greatest impact, the result is the *primacy effect.* When the last message or speaker has the greatest impact, the result is the *recency effect.*

All things being equal (that is, in terms of the circumstances of the situation), the message or speaker that is heard first has the greatest impact, producing a primacy effect. The first message/speaker sets the stage and thus the mental agenda of audience members. However, if there is a time lapse between the first message or speaker and the second, a recency effect will occur. When the audience is interrupted in this way, they tend to remember the argument or speaker they heard last.

Thus, when asked to be one of two speakers in a discussion of opposing arguments, find out how the speakers will be scheduled and choose your position accordingly, if possible. If the speakers are to present their arguments back to back, try to go first. If there is to be a break or other time lapse between speakers, try to go last.

Fear Appeal

A message that links some inherent danger, threat, or harm with a course of action, attitude, or belief is a **fear appeal**. Usually, speakers make claims of harm or threat in the belief that it will alter an audience's attitudes, beliefs, values, or behaviors. Although fear appeals work, several other effects may offset the benefits.

Evoking fear sometimes erects a communication barrier known as *defense avoidance.* Thus, when an audience hears an intensely threatening message (one that confronts their social norms or suggests extreme difficulty), its members may choose to tune out and hear little or nothing else (Petty & Cacioppo, 1995). This effect is not absolute but rather seems to depend on a person's initial anxiety level or experience with the topic (Borchers, 2005). If you suspect that your audience could react with defense avoidance, you can perhaps lower the fear level of the threat.

A second factor to consider in making a persuasive fear appeal is the amount of reassurance provided in your message (Seiter & Gass, 2004). In general, when you offer reassurance in delivering your conclusion, your audience will be able to handle the fear. Conversely, if you provide little or no reassurance, you may simply overwhelm some audience members and prompt them to tune out (see Case 13.3).

Case 13.3

Alienating the Audience with Fear

Evan had been asked to give a presentation about several serious problems in the company to its board of directors. In planning the presentation, he decided to use the metaphor of "Rome is burning" to capture the sense of ongoing destruction. His main points amplified this idea. For instance, he quoted negative statements from several respected department heads and presented statistics that documented the company's declining performance.

The speech clearly conveyed a sense of doom and motivated the board to take corrective action. However, Evan's failure to provide any sense of reassurance served to impede plans for change. Several board members had tuned out his message and had to be informed about the issues. Even the board members who had listened intently wanted more information without charging ahead, given the bleak picture Evan had painted.

What could Evan have done to provide reassurance to board members? At what point does using a fear appeal go too far?

WEB AT WORK 13.1
Persuasive Speaking

To learn more about persuasive speaking, consult any of the following Web sites:

- **www.speechgems.com** A subscription site that provides persuasive techniques and content; for a range of occasions and presenters.
- **www.acjournal.org** The Web site of the *American Communication Journal*, the leading online scholarly refereed journal on communication.

- **www.roch.edu/dept/spchcom/ persuasive_organization.htm** How to organize a persuasive speech.
- **www.stresscure.com/jobstress/ speak.html** How to overcome speaking fear.
- **www.roch.edu/dept/spchcom/ anxiety_getting_started.htm** A helpful starter site to begin overcoming communication anxiety.

DEVELOPING PERSUASIVE PRESENTATIONS

Recall from Chapter 12 that **organizational design** involves two major tasks: preparing an outline of main ideas and selecting an organizational pattern for the body of the presentation. We will consider outlining within the following discussion of organizational patterns. Web at Work 13.1 provides sites to develop effective persuasive speeches.

Selecting an Organizational Pattern

Three particular organizational patterns are especially useful in planning persuasive presentations: (1) the problem/solution pattern; (2) the proposition/proof pattern; and (3) the motivational sequence pattern.

PROBLEM/SOLUTION PATTERN The problem/solution pattern begins with a problem and then offers a solution to that problem. In most persuasive presentations, audiences expect a plan to describe how the solution will be achieved.

The Problem. The first part of the speech discusses the problem. The use of problem analysis techniques is important in developing this part of the message. Asking questions such as these will aid in preparation:

- What is the felt difficulty? What are the symptoms of the problem? How do we know these symptoms exist? What manifestations have occurred?
- What are the causes of the problem? Is there a single cause, or are there multiple causes? How do we know whether these causes are real or imaginary?
- What are the effects of the problem? Are the outcomes measurable? Do they occur consistently?

The Solution. The second part of the speech discusses the possible solutions to the problem. Once more, ask yourself a series of related questions. Your goal now is to develop a set of criteria by which you can evaluate possible solutions and ultimately choose one:

- Has the solution been tried before? by whom? with what results?
- Will the solution actually solve the problem?

- What is the cost of implementing the solution?
- Is the solution feasible and capable of implementation? Will it cause additional and perhaps unexpected problems? If so, what?

In choosing criteria for solutions, consider the many implications for risk management and strategic planning. If you carefully consider these factors in recommending the best solution in your presentation, it will more likely be accepted and implemented.

The Plan. The problem/solution approach may include developing a plan for implementing the chosen solution. The plan must meet the criteria of a good solution and be open for evaluation later to see if it is working. By developing a plan around the best solution, the speaker can motivate the audience to get implement the plan.

Creating an Outline. In creating an outline for a problem/solution speech, follow this format:

1. *Introduction.* Open with an example or case that demonstrates the symptoms of the problem. Then state your thesis, define any unusual terms, and preview the forthcoming discussion of the problem and its possible solutions.
2. *Body.* The first major point in the body should be the problem; the first major subpoint should be the causes of the problem, and the second should be the effects. The second major point in the body should be the solutions; subpoints should address, in this order, all possible alternatives, alternatives that don't work, the best solution, and how the best solution will work. (See Chapter 12 for providing transitions between main points of the body.)
3. *Conclusion.* As stated earlier, the conclusion should present a plan for implementing the chosen solution. In addition, the conclusion should summarize the main points and restate the thesis. Finally, it should offer a strong closing statement—something that will motivate the audience to want to participate in the plan.

Figure 13.4 shows the outline of a problem/solution presentation on overseas health care. As a reminder, you should check with your instructor regarding his or her requirements for formatting an outline (see also the recommendations in Chapter 12).

Another illustration of a problem/solution speech occurs later in this chapter in the section on cause-and-effect reasoning. In speaking about the topic of crime prevention, you could begin by describing the nature of the problem, defining what the terms *crime* and *residents* mean, and identifying typical causes of crime. Then you could present solutions to the problem and review the advantages and disadvantages of each. Your plan could incorporate all of the solutions or recommend the best one.

Using the Problem/Solution Pattern. This pattern is easy to understand and clearly identifies areas of need as well as the solutions that will meet those needs (McCroskey, 2001). Even so, the success of this approach relies on intense analysis during the solution stage. By weighing the advantages and disadvantages of each proposed solution and narrowing down the list to a final best solution, the speaker encourages the audience. Thus, this organizational pattern is especially effective with reluctant or hostile audiences. Also, the refutation of the unchosen solutions can have the benefit of refuting later counterpersuasion, as discussed earlier in this chapter. Finally, the pattern is efficient and the approach it takes matches many decision-making models, which require the analysis of risk management.

PROPOSITION/PROOF PATTERN   The proposition/proof pattern of organization begins with a single contention (which becomes the thesis statement) and then offers proof in logical support of that contention (which serves as the main point of the body). For example, the thesis

Introduction:

Attention-getting statistics

Thesis

Preview problems/solutions

Body:

I. The problem of overseas health care has three primary symptoms.

   A. Insufficient funding

   B. Insufficient training

   C. Insufficient psychological support

[Internal summary and transition]

II. The solutions to this problem are clear.

   A. Increase funding

   B. Increase training strategies

   C. Increase psychological support

   D. Best solution: combine all three

[Internal summary and transition]

Conclusion:

Present plan

Summarize

Close with projected statistics

FIGURE 13.4 Sample Outline for a Problem/Solution Presentation

"Mental health professionals will benefit from attending a seminar on marital communication" could be supported by these three main points, each identifying a benefit of such seminar attendance:

EXAMPLE

   I. Enhanced counseling communication skills

   II. More effective counseling practices

   III. Increased satisfaction among mental health professionals

In another example, the introduction begins with this attention-getting question:

EXAMPLE

"What siphons the life of an institution, denies the credibility of managers, and ultimately cheats employees and customers? This creeping plague, known to us all as cost overage, is a corporate platelet clogging the arteries of most small companies today. After you see why this practice is hurting us all, I'm sure you will agree that the practice must stop."

Next, the speech would preview the three main points, and those three points would be supported in the body through analysis, reasoning, logic, examples, testimony, statistics, and the like. Finally, the conclusion would provide a summary, a motivation to action, and a final statement.

Creating an Outline. In developing your speech using the proposition/proof pattern, follow this general format:

1. *Introduction.* Seize the audience's attention, state the thesis (that is, the main contention), and preview the main points of the body (the proofs of the main contention).
2. *Body.* The first main point should present the first proof, and the subpoints should present the support material—say, an example. The second and third main points should present the second and third proofs, respectively, and be supported similarly—say, using statistics or case studies.
3. *Conclusion.* Provide a summary, a motivating statement, and a strong final remark.

Using the Proposition/Proof Pattern. This approach to organizational design works especially well for audiences who already agree with the basic points of the proposal and who are unlikely to hear or be able to process opposing views. In sum, this method is well suited for reinforcement of existing attitudes, beliefs, behaviors, and values.

MOTIVATIONAL SEQUENCE PATTERN   The motivational sequence pattern moves from general interest to specific action. Developed by Alan Monroe and various coauthors over the years (Ehninger, Gronbeck, McKerrow, & Monroe, 1986), it was designed to inspire an audience, transforming them from mild neutrality to excited motivation on behalf of a topic.

The motivated sequence comprises these five steps:

1. *Attention.* The purposes of the first step are to build audience rapport, gain audience attention, and focus audience interest on the topic. Thus, this step provides something of an introduction, given these purposes.
2. *Need.* Demonstrating a need involves describing an issue or a problem. It should be stated simply and directly; analysis is not the most important aspect here. Instead, the need should be related using some emotional appeal to heighten its significance. The audience must understand why the issue or problem is relevant.
3. *Satisfaction.* In this step, the speaker demonstrates how a policy, attitude, or behavior will solve the problem or issue (that is, the need) just described. In advocating this solution, there is no need to analyze all the different options; the speaker can simply propose a solution that will satisfy the need.
4. *Visualization.* This step involves intensifying the audience's feelings about the problem or issue. Visualization involves painting a mental picture of the solution and the particular part the audience might play in it. Examples of visualization abound, but one of the most well known is from the famous "I Have a Dream" speech of Dr. Martin Luther King, Jr., which was delivered in the 1960s, an era of racial riots and civil disturbances. In this speech, King used vivid imagery—for instance, describing red clay hills, black and white, the feeling of hand in hand, the imagery of food and tables and supper—to help audience members visualize their part in making a better world (Minnick, 1968). For another example of effective visualization, see Case 13.4.
5. *Action.* The fifth step in the motivational sequence asks the audience to take direct action. They already have a mental picture of themselves doing some kind of activity, but at this point, they must take concrete action or make a certain kind of commitment.

Case 13.4

Creating an Effective Visualization

One speaker motivated a group of organizational volunteers to join a YMCA tutoring program for young children with the following:

> I invite you not to think of your college education as only an experience to walk across the stage and receive a piece of parchment scrolling achievement. Rather, I would invite your academic achievements to have one more accent. Imagine yourself with a child's eyes fixed on you as you walk across the stage. Imagine that child you tutored sitting in the audience with more excitement than you feel, remembering, "She came for two years and now I can read and do math problems."

What picture does this speaker paint? How might this prompt individuals to become involved with the tutoring program?

The tutoring example presented in Case 13.4 is presented in more detail in Figure 13.5 on the next page, which is the outline for the presentation.

Using the Motivational Sequence. The motivational sequence is a deliberate strategy to create and then release emotions among audience members. In that sense, it is cathartic. But unless the sequence is developed successfully, resulting in action, audience members may actually become frustrated and feel somewhat helpless. The presenter should be aware of this possibility in developing his or her persuasive outcome.

The motivational sequence works especially well with audiences who are neutral or somewhat dissatisfied and thus in need of inspiration or motivation. This strategy moves them toward predetermined goals.

Providing Support Material

As indicated in Chapter 10, conducting an audience analysis is crucial to developing a presentation. If the speaker omits this analysis, then providing support material may be inappropriate or irrelevant. Support material must fit the audience as well as the topic and the occasion. This is particularly true for persuasive presentations.

In this discussion of support material, keep in mind the guidelines about finding and citing sources from Chapter 12 on informative presentations. Your persuasive speech should build on the principles and techniques introduced in that chapter. For instance, in persuasion, cases, analogies, examples, illustration, statistics, and quotations from authorities are all still valuable support materials.

BENEFITS OF EVIDENCE   In the vocabulary of persuasive presentations, support material is **evidence**. It is what is provided to prove the thesis, which is sometimes called the *claim*. In terms of effective persuasion, evidence has four positive effects:

1. *Evidence is what makes effective persuasion* (**Seiter & Gass, 2004**). Studies have found that good evidence can influence people's attitudes even if the speaker's delivery is not as

Introduction:

Attention: "By this time next year, there will be significantly more illiterate children."

Purpose: "To cause at least half of the employees to sign up for the YMCA tutoring program in order to solve the school dropout problems in the community."

Thesis: "The high dropout rate in our community can be solved by company employees volunteering two hours a week tutoring at-risk children in reading and math."

Preview: "Let's focus on why this issue is vital to our community and what we can do."

Transition: "Turn your thoughts to a need beyond your wildest nightmare."

Body:

I. Need: "One in five Americans under the age of 50 can't read or write adequately and is thus considered functionally illiterate."

Develop the concept that the level of illiteracy among American children living in poverty is getting out of control and must be corrected. Amplify with statistics, case examples, and the like.

II. Satisfaction: "Leading experts (cite them) indicate that if we could only reach children between the ages of 6 and 10 and increase their interest in reading through love, concern, and special programs of care, we could stop this rising tide of functional illiteracy."

Demonstrate how becoming involved for two hours a week through a YMCA program can change the rising tide of illiteracy among poor children. Explain how. Develop stories, cases, illustration, testimony, and so on.

III. Visualization: "Imagine yourself sitting at the kitchen table with a child who has been crying because she just can't understand a math problem. Then imagine that same child with a glowing smile (describe with details and vividness). Because of your help, she now understands math that was previously confusing" (other quotes, stories; paint a verbal picture).

Help the audience imagine sitting with a child and observing his or her natural curiosities emerge as he or she begins to read and understand how their involvement can begin to turn around the growing problem of functional illiteracy.

Conclusions:

Actualization: "The cards that we're passing out in the audience today will allow you to provide your name, address, and telephone number and make a minor commitment of only two hours a week to tutor some disadvantaged children. By your signing these cards, you can help solve a tremendous national need as well as experience a personal feeling of achievement. This is easy to do—the cards are available right now. This small commitment from you will mean a large step in the future of American children" (show how; testimony).

Brief summary

Strong close

FIGURE 13.5 Sample Outline for a Motivational Sequence Presentation

good as it should be. Of course, the opposite could be said, too: in the short run, particularly, an effective delivery can make evidence appear better. Nevertheless, evidence can help balance out elements of lesser quality.

2. *Relatively new and exciting evidence can cause audience stimulation and attention.* The reason is that making an unknown argument creates an element of surprise. This novelty creates high credibility for the presenter and increases the audience's acceptance of the topic.

3. *Evidence creates interest in the topic.* Unsupported assertions lack the compelling interest that evidence brings to the situation. As one listener said, "I did not know how important this issue was until I heard expert testimony, statistics, and case studies that I identify with. These really got my attention. I learned a lot of people are concerned about his topic."

4. *Evidence heightens speaker credibility.* It fosters the impression that the speaker is prepared, an expert, and knowledgeable on the topic.

Formulating an Argument

As mentioned earlier, persuasion relies on the application of logic. In order to influence an audience's thinking or behavior, you must present them with a logical reason to change and then provide the evidence to back up that reason. An understanding of the **types of reasoning** and each one's appropriateness will help you develop such an argument.

TYPES OF REASONING   Types of reasoning are similar to organizational patterns in terms of providing a structure with which to organize information. The difference is that we are now focusing on how to organize the elements of an argument. The types of reasoning discussed in this section are (1) cause-and-effect reasoning, (2) reasoning from sign, (3) reasoning from analogy, (4) specific-to-general reasoning, and (5) reasoning from classification.

Cause-and-Effect Reasoning.   Cause-and-effect reasoning involves identifying a cause and discussing the effects it has produced, or vice versa: discussing a set of effects and identifying what caused them. Such relationships are easy to find and provide convincing evidence in a speech.

Support material must fit the audience as well as the topic and the occasion.

However, to be effective, causal reasoning must use sufficient examples of similar situations, sufficient data to show change over time, and significant quotes from authority. In other words, a lot of evidence crafts a successful cause-and-effect argument.

For instance, suppose the city government hires you to lead a program for neighborhood crime reduction. In a persuasive presentation to a group of city leaders, you argue that placing streetlights in a strategic neighborhood will reduce crime in the entire community. Using cause-and-effect reasoning, you claim, "Adding streetlights will reduce crime." Of course, you must be able to prove that claim for your audience. Perhaps you can offer an example of another community in which streetlights were installed and crime went down. But how do you know that providing more lighting was what reduced crime? How do you know, for example, that city residents putting more lights around their homes didn't cause the reduction? Alternatively, perhaps when the streetlights were installed, a neighborhood watch program was enacted at the same time. Perhaps police protection was increased.

The obvious point is to be sure of your evidence. Discuss multiple causes and multiple effects when appropriate.

Reasoning from Sign. Reasoning from sign refers to observing one thing and using it to prove the existence of something that cannot be seen. In other words, you interpret your observation as a *sign* of something else. For example, if you see smoke coming from a window, it is a sign that there is a fire inside.

Once again, you must be able to prove that relationship. Thus, to be effective, sign reasoning must use sufficient examples regarding the link between a sign and what it is believed to represent. That is, smoke and fire must be connected. Without sufficient evidence, the argument will not hold.

Here is another example: "John has a great deal of peace in his life." Since people often conclude that peace is a sign of some inner quality, then the surface conclusion is: "John must believe or do something that brings about this condition." To prove this claim, we must establish an association between the sign—namely, John's behavior—and what that behavior represents—namely, some important source in his life.

Reasoning from Analogy. Another form of reasoning relies on analogy, or a comparison of two things—usually, one known and one unknown—to show how they are alike. In persuasive communication, reasoning from analogy shows that what worked in one place should work in another place. For example, the crime control argument made earlier using cause-and-effect reasoning also applies with an analogy: "Adding streetlights helped reduce crime in Community A, so doing so should reduce crime in Community B, as well."

As comparisons between two or more things, analogies are useful in *benchmarking*, which is a form of research and analysis in which one organization compares with one or more others. Increasingly, benchmark findings provide exciting ways to develop new policies and make corporate decisions.

Remember, too, that a good analogy can make an abstract concept more concrete. For instance, in introducing a new procedure, a speaker might say, "Adopting this new approach will involve making changes similar to those we made two years ago when we adopted the new building use policy." The speaker would then attempt to make a direct comparison between the two.

Analogies can be highly motivating, too. Your company president might hope to create a "can do" spirit among employees by saying, "We were successful with Product A in the past, so we will likely be successful with Product B now."

Unfortunately, most analogies are imperfect. At issue is whether the two things being compared are very similar. For example, suppose a speaker argues, "If a tax reform law has been

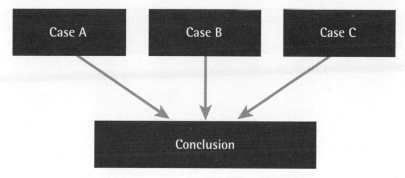

FIGURE 13.6 Specific-to-General Reasoning

successful in the state of California, it should also work in Oklahoma, Kansas, and Nebraska." This evidence overlooks the differences among these states. Is California like the other three states? A better analogy might make the same case about two obviously similar states.

Specific-to-General Reasoning. Another form of reasoning examines specific cases and then draws a general conclusion. This approach, often labeled *inductive reasoning,* functions like this: You begin with observations of specific cases—call them Cases A, B, and C. Next, you look for commonalities among the cases. Finally, you draw a conclusion (see Figure 13.6). Here's a simplified example:

EXAMPLE

The cows in field A eat grass.

The cows in field B eat grass.

The cows in fields A, B, and C all eat grass.

Therefore, all cows eat grass.

The same type of reasoning could be applied to any number of workplace topics. For instance, suppose three highly successful organizations all have corporate fitness programs. The conclusion could be drawn that providing a corporate fitness program contributes to an organization's success.

This kind of reasoning frequently appears in persuasive presentations. The strength of this approach is that it allows you to draw general principles. This kind of reasoning will not hold up, however, (1) if insufficient numbers of observations are used (have you observed enough cows eating?), (2) if the sampling is biased (how do we know these cases are typical?), and (3) if legitimate differences are overlooked (half the organizations without fitness programs were also productive).

Reasoning from Classification. Reasoning from classification is the opposite of specific-to-general reasoning. That is, in reasoning from classification, the speaker begins with a generalization or accepted principle and moves to specific cases (see Figure 13.7 on the next page). This is *deductive reasoning.* In other words, you argue that what is true of a given class of elements is true of any one element in that class.

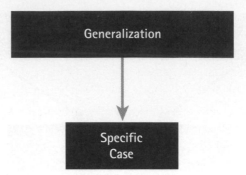

FIGURE 13.7 Reasoning from Classification

If the people in Group A are smart and Kim is a member of Group A, then Kim must be smart.

If all ducks fly south for the winter and Gertrude is a duck, then Gertrude must fly south for the winter.

If all people are mortal and Joe is a person, then Joe must be mortal.

Such reasoning can be effective in making an argument. Indeed, it is sometimes hard to know how to refute such an argument. Complete the exercise in Skills at Work 13.1 to check the reasoning behind such arguments.

IDENTIFYING FALLACIES IN REASONING By applying evidence and logic to the argument presented in Skills at Work 13.1, we were able to identify some potential weaknesses in reasoning. As a speaker, you should anticipate how your audience will examine your argument, looking for weaknesses in your reasoning. In order to help you avoid being vulnerable in this way, this section

---

SKILLS AT WORK 13.1
Evaluating an Argument

In completing this activity, let's use this argument based on reasoning from classification:

> "If all ducks fly south for the winter and Gertrude is a duck, then Gertrude must fly south for the winter."

The first thing to evaluate in such an argument is whether you accept the initial generalization—that is, the statement of classification. In our example, is it true that all ducks fly south for the winter? If you can find an example of a duck that does not, you will have disproved this generalization and thus the entire argument.

Next, you must verify that the second statement is true: that Gertrude is indeed a duck. If you can prove that she is, say, a loon instead, you will have disproved this statement and again, the entire argument.

Suppose that you have found both of the statements true. Does this necessarily mean that you have to accept the conclusion that's been drawn? You don't if you can find exceptions to the conclusion. For instance, ducks that are pets and ducks that have their wings clipped don't fly south for the winter. If Gertrude fits either of these descriptions, you can prove the conclusion false.

of the chapter explores common **fallacies in reasoning.** You would do well to look for these fallacies in your experience as a consumer of persuasive appeals, too.

Quotations from Nonauthorities. To support a claim with a quotation from someone who is not an authority in that field is clearly a fallacy. Learn to recognize these six kinds of authorities, or witnesses, and to evaluate the legitimacy of their evidence:

1. An *unbiased witness* is perceived as the most objective. He or she has nothing to gain or sell and should be a reliable source of evidence.
2. A *reluctant witness* has something to lose by giving his or her testimony but has come forward anyway. Audiences usually trust this type of source.
3. A *biased witness* is perceived to have something to gain by testifying in favor of the issue. Even if he or she is a reliable authority, this type of authority lacks believability and is difficult to trust.
4. A *misplaced authority* is someone who is cited as an expert in a different, sometimes unrelated field, regardless of whether he or she is an authority in this area.
5. *Applying popularity as authority* involves using as a source of support someone who is well known or popular but not considered a credible authority on the topic at hand.
6. An *unspecified authority* involves citing a group of experts but not a specific expert—for example, "Psychologists say," "Scientists reveal," "Authorities write." A more specific authority is a more credible one.

Insufficient Use of Cases, Observations, or Signs. It is easy to reach a conclusion from reasoning by sign without having sufficient cases, observations, or signs to support that conclusion. For example, the feeling of pain in the chest could be a sign of a heart attack, but it could also be a sign of indigestion or of sore muscles. A good diagnosis would involve doing a number of tests and narrowing down the potential sources of chest pain. A sufficient amount of evidence must establish the relationship suggested in reasoning from sign.

Faulty Reasoning from Analogy or Causation. It is also easy to suggest causation or similarity without having sufficient evidence. Common errors in cause-and-effect reasoning are (1) assuming a single cause when there are multiple causes, (2) assuming a single effect when there are multiple effects, (3) overlooking multiple causes and multiple effects, and (4) overlooking unknown or unanticipated causes or effects. In addition, in reasoning from analogy, a common error is to suggest similarity between items that are not very similar. It is important to consider whether there is a sufficient basis for comparison, and even when similarities exist, it is important to determine whether they justify the conclusion being drawn.

Hasty Generalization. A generalization concluded without sufficient evidence—whether too little evidence or too random evidence—is called a *hasty generalization*. This fallacy is similar to the problems associated with reasoning from specific to general.

False Dilemma. Another reasoning fallacy is to categorize things as either/or—for example, "You are either a liberal or a conservative." Such reasoning fails to consider alternatives or any middle ground between two extremes. In most situations, this is not realistic—hence, the term *false dilemma*.

Attacking the Person. Unfortunately, some speakers attack the person instead of the issue, hoping to discredit the person and by extension his or her idea or cause. This tactic is sometimes referred to as the *ad hominem attack*. There are several variations of this fallacy:

1. A *simple accusation* of a person illustrates an attack—for instance, "I can't accept your idea because you weren't there when we opened the store." Clearly, the attacker is accusing

or blaming the other individual for something that may have had no bearing on the issue at hand.

2. *Name-calling* occurs when a person is labeled, thereby conjuring up certain behaviors attributed to him or her—for instance, "You nurses are money-grubbers, which explains why you are going on strike."

3. *Labeling*, which is less intense than name-calling, occurs when a person is classified as a member of a group (perhaps incorrectly) and something negative is said about the group—for example, "Your accounting background comes through in meetings like this. We don't need bean counters; what we need is vision and insight."

Bandwagon Technique. This approach assumes that a popular position is the correct position because everybody else seems to believe it or accept it. A perusal of advertisements finds any number of illustrations of the bandwagon technique, including this one: "Come on down to the fall sale, where everyone is buying their favorite jewelry at closeout prices." The fallacies are obvious. How do we know everyone is buying? Is this really a closeout? Are these sale prices just like the sale prices two months ago?

"Two Wrongs Do Not Make a Right." Another fallacy is to justify a current behavior as right or ethical because of someone else's wrong or unethical behavior. For instance, "My boss plays golf almost every afternoon, so I should be able to take off when I want." The logical question is how the two behaviors are linked. And if they are linked, does one justify the other? Here is another example: "Candidate A got away with his abuse of power when he was in office; therefore, Candidate B should not be blamed for her abuse of power." Trying to justify Candidate B's behavior because of Candidate A's obscures the basic issue: that both of them were wrong.

Appeal to Tradition. Another fallacy in reasoning is claiming something to be true or right just because it has stood the test of time. For example, "Shakespeare is truly an outstanding author. He has been acclaimed for centuries." Is the passage of time the only reason for Shakespeare's greatness? Here's another example: "The MBA at our university is a great graduate degree. Just look at the successful people who have come through the program in the past forty years." Again, more reasons than time likely lie behind the program's success.

Faulty Correlation. Many people reason incorrectly that when two things happen at the same time, one must have caused the other. The fact that the rise of cancer in the United States has coincided with the rise of television viewing does not provide sufficient evidence that television viewing causes cancer. To examine the validity of an argument based on correlation, ask these questions:

1. Why are these two things tied together? In the TV-and-cancer correlation, what are the organic and cellular processes that could even make this happen?

2. Has this correlation been seen before? If the correlation is repeated over time, the evidence is stronger.

3. Is the correlation statistically significant? Again, a correlation cannot be considered sound without additional corroborating evidence.

Ethics in Persuasion

As mentioned in other chapters, ethical communicators conduct research and present the message in a way that avoids falsehood and seeks truth. Many experts agree that persuasion is an areas where it is all too easy to fall prey to unethical communication (Larson, 2007; Pham, & Avnet, 2004). Thus, remember several ethical principles:

1. Avoid coercive forms of communication. Excessive threat, inappropriate fear arousal, or unresolved dissonance arousal can present situations which could spiral out of control from ethical view.
2. Indicate and acknowledge alternative views when they exist—importantly, an individual's *choice.*
3. Seek to use data and critical reasoning, not purely emotion.
4. Avoid recommending unsafe practices or unhealthy habits (Cooper, & Kelleher, 2001).

In Perspective

In order to bring about change, you must be aware of what people think, what they find valuable, what they believe, and how they act. In other words, you must understand their attitudes, values, beliefs, and behaviors. When the purpose of communication is to persuade, it's significant to know which of these four outcomes is being targeted. Your selection of support materials should be matched to the desired outcome.

Research has identified a number of principles of persuasion. The principle of cognitive dissonance describes the conflict people feel when their beliefs, perceptions of behaviors, or attitudes do not align. Social judgment theory explains how people come to evaluate information, form a position, and then move to form a new position. According to the principle of audience commitment, when audience members engage in small behaviors or make small changes in their attitude toward a topic, they are likely to embrace that attitude wholeheartedly. The principle of inoculation refers to building up the audience's resistance to other messages by convincing them of the value of your own message. The arrangement of points in a message affects its persuasive impact; this is the principle of message order. A message that links some inherent danger, threat, or harm with a course of action, attitude, or belief is a fear appeal.

Organizational design involves two major tasks: preparing an outline of main ideas and selecting an organizational pattern for the body of the presentation.

Three particular organizational patterns are especially useful in planning persuasive presentations: (1) the problem/solution pattern; (2) the proposition/proof pattern; and (3) the motivational sequence pattern.

In the vocabulary of persuasive presentations, support material is *evidence.* It is what is provided to prove the thesis, which is sometimes called the *claim.* In order to influence an audience's thinking or behavior, you must present them with a logical reason to change and then provide the evidence to back up that reason. An understanding of these types of reasoning and when each is appropriate will help you develop such an argument: (1) cause-and-effect reasoning; (2) reasoning from sign; (3) reasoning from analogy; (4) specific-to-general reasoning; and (5) reasoning from classification.

As a speaker, you should anticipate how your audience will examine your argument, looking for weaknesses in your reasoning. In order to help you avoid being vulnerable in this way, you should be able to identify common fallacies in reasoning, such as quotations from nonauthorities; insufficient use of cases, observations, or signs; faulty reasoning from analogy or causation; hasty generalization; false dilemma; attacking the person; bandwagon technique; "two wrongs do not make a right"; appeal to tradition; and faulty correlation. Finally, use good ethical practices as outlined in the chapter's last section.

Discussion Questions

1. Why is providing sufficient and credible support, or evidence, particularly critical in persuasive communication?

2. If you could use only one kind of evidence to provide support for the claim in your persuasive speech, what kind would it be? Why?

3. Which of the principles of persuasion do you find most interesting in terms of predicting people's behavior? Why?

4. Suppose you are preparing to deliver a persuasive presentation to a very unmotivated and likely disinterested audience. How should this factor into your decision on what type of organizational pattern to use?

5. Give examples of topics that might be developed effectively using these types of reasoning (that is, one example per each type of reasoning): (a) cause-and-effect reasoning, (b) reasoning from sign, (c) reasoning from analogy, (d) specific-to-general reasoning, and (e) reasoning from classification.

Exercises

1. Before a focus group, a class group, or a group of friends, deliver a two-minute persuasive speech on a topic of your choice (1) without evidence and then (2) with evidence to support your main points. Ask your audience to compare the two speeches in terms of their persuasive ability. What differences did they observe? What difference did having or not having evidence seem to make?

2. Look through the editorial pages of several magazines and newspapers. Can you identify uses of the problem/solution pattern, the proposition/proof pattern, and the motivational sequence pattern in these arguments? Choose two or three editorials that you feel present strong arguments and discuss the organizational pattern used in each. What makes this argument successful?

3. Working by yourself, find five or six examples in the media of the use of fear appeals. For each, evaluate the level of the threat made and whether this strategy had its intended effect or resulted in audience avoidance. Then meet with several classmates and compare findings. Overall, how frequently are fear appeals made, and how successful are they?

4. Look through the editorial pages of several magazines and newspapers again, but this time, identify fallacies in reasoning. What types of fallacies do you find? Are some more common than others? If so, which ones?

References

Borchers, T. A. (2005). *Persuasion in the media age.* 2nd ed. New York: McGraw-Hill.

Cialdini, R. B. (2001). *Influence: Science and practice.* 4th ed. Boston: Allyn & Bacon.

Cooper, T., & Kelleher, T. (2001). Better Mousetrap? Of Emerson, ethics, and postmillennium persuasion. *Journal of Mass Media Ethics, 16*(2/3), 176–192. Retrieved from Academic Search Complete database.

Ehninger, D., Gronbeck, B. F., McKerrow, R. E., & Monroe, A. H. (1986). *Principles and types of speech communication.* 10th ed. Glenview, IL: Scott, Foresman.

Larson, C. U. (2007). *Persuasion: Reception and responsibility.* 11th ed. Belmont, CA: Thomson Learning.

McCroskey, J. C. (2001). *An introduction to rhetorical communication.* 8th ed. Boston: Allyn & Bacon.

Minnick, W. C. (1968). *The art of persuasion.* 2nd ed. Boston: Houghton Mifflin.

O'Keefe, D. J. (2002). *Persuasion theory and research.* 2nd ed. Thousand Oaks, CA: Sage.

Petty, R. E., & Cacioppo, J. T. (1995). *Attitudes and persuasion: Classic and contemporary approaches.* Dubuque, IA: Wm. C. Brown.

Pham, M., & Avnet, T. (2004). Ideals and oughts and the reliance on affect versus substance in persuasion. *Journal of Consumer Research, 30*(4), 503–518. Retrieved from Academic Search Complete database.

Seiter, J. S. & Gass, R. H. (2004). *Perspectives on persuasion, social influence, and compliance gaining.* Boston: Allyn & Bacon.

CHAPTER 14

Managing Customers and Client Communication and Sales

After reading this chapter, you will be able to do the following:

- Understand the meaning of customer service.
- Describe strategies and models for improving customer service through enhanced communication.
- Discover customer needs and develop customer-centered messages.
- Apply customer service methods and skills to improved telephone communication.
- Deal effectively with angry customers.
- Initiate organizational change to improve customer service.
- Identify the principles of sales presentations.
- Discuss various strategies for finding potential customers and clients.
- Describe the steps involved in conducting a sales interview.

A good listener is not only popular everywhere, but after a while he gets to know something.

WILSON MIZNER

Success in business requires training and discipline and hard work. But if you're not frightened by these things, the opportunities are just as great today as they ever were.

DAVID ROCKEFELLER

In his best-selling book *Why We Buy: The Science of Shopping*, Underhill (1999) describes the results of thousands of hours of research linking sales to **customer service** and merchandising. Based on this research, he concludes that effective customer contact and good customer service result in increased outcomes. To realize how much, consider these examples:

- IBM's growth in recent years has been based on improved service, not products.

- Southwest Air, virtually unknown twenty years ago, is now ranked the number-four airline in the United States. By thinking small, Southwest has empowered each facility to operate flexibly and ensure a quick turnaround (for instance, twenty minutes for cleaning a plane and unloading the baggage). The result has been lower fares and more business (NPR, 2000).

- A Florida-based drug store was selling suntan lotion in Minnesota in October.

- Harley-Davidson increased sales by serving customer needs for apparel and parts in addition to motorcycles.

- Drug stores have encouraged one-stop shopping by selling food and drink products in addition to medical supplies.

- After observing women trying to shop while handling their coats and purses, thus leaving only one hand to buy, Old Navy offered tote bags to carry purchases while in the store.

- Family restaurants have alienated customers by having too many tables for two, which won't accommodate groups, and by using such small print in their menus that older customers can't read them. After enlarging the print of all its signs, one restaurant enjoyed increased sales.

DEFINITION AND MODEL OF CUSTOMER SERVICE

Defining Customers and Customer Service

First, we need to ask what is a customer. A **customer** or **client**, in this context, is an individual who receives the products or services developed by an organization. If it were not for customers and clients, no one would be available to fulfill the organization's mission. Nonprofit organizations usually deal with *clients*, whereas for-profit organizations usually deal with *customers*.

Customers can be categorized as external and internal. *Internal customers* refer to those inside an organization who require the products or services from another unit of the organization. *External customers* come from outside the organization and pay for the services and products they receive.

Customer service, sometimes called *customer relations*, has been identified as one of the most significant measures of organizational outcomes—and one that applies plenty of communication knowledge and skills. If customers do not like the product, they won't buy it. Thus, cash flow will decrease, the company's reserves will be depleted, and soon it will be out of business. If clients like the service provided by someone else better, the original organization will have no clients to serve and will see no financial or service return on their expenses or efforts.

Models of Customer Service

Models of customer service have emerged in many different forms but have primarily described organizations in terms of being **operations-centered** versus **client-centered organizations**. In recent years, a radical shift has occurred, in which organizations are moving away from an operations-centered focus toward a client-centered focus. A comparison of key elements from an older operations-centered organization and a newer client-centered organization reveals the nature of this shift (Alessandra, 1997; Moran, Harris, & Moran, 2007):

	Operations-Centered Organization	Customer/Client-Centered Element Organization
Attitude	How can we sell our product?	How can we help our clients?
Outlook	Serves the corporation	Serves the client
Concerns	Makes things easy for the client; procedures	Makes things easy for employees; procedures provide protection and are client friendly
Sales focus	Product features	Customer benefits
Economic downturn	Cuts costs	Demonstrates advantages

When organizations direct their orientation toward customer service, the results include increased sales, new customers, and decreased complaints. The examples cited at the beginning of the chapter offer proof of these effects.

In studies of all kinds of companies, researchers have uncovered a number of communication issues that lie at the root of customer relations problems and thus cause unnecessary waste and difficulty. These customer service gaps include (Zeithaml, Parasuraman, & Berry, 1990):

1. Lack of interaction between management and customers (often too many tall chart layers)
2. Lack of upward communication from contact person to management (lack of teamwork in the system)
3. Lack of employee clarity and policy in doing customer service
4. Poor hiring choice for customer service job

The need for clear communication and adequate training is essential, not only in implementing policies but also in establishing an organization's client-centered focus. That philosophy must be understood and communicated before the entire organization can be expected to practice customer-oriented behaviors.

COMMUNICATING TO ENHANCE CUSTOMER SERVICE

At the core of improved customer service is an understanding of what customers really expect. Put simply, customers want to feel comfortable and welcome, and they want to be able to find what they need. For example, people shopping for children's clothing don't want to have to go through the men's section to find them. Your ability to understand customer service needs will enhance your value to future organizations. In addition to understanding your customers' needs, you must be able to communicate with them. **Customer-centered communication** will be the focus of the following sections, which outline strategies for improving skills in this area.

Discovering Customer Needs

Researchers have established major categories of customer needs, many of which are specific needs for appropriate communication (Rogers, 2003; *San Diego Manual*, 2000; Underhill, 1999). Consider these needs:

1. *Welcoming statements.* Communication that welcomes customers into an office, a store, or other facility is a good start to meeting crucial customer needs.

Customer-centered communication involves promptness and attention. Keeping others waiting or ignoring customer needs is ineffective.

2. *Self-help information.* Customers often do not have enough information from signs and price tags to make needed decisions on their own. Signage should be abundant and easy to read.

3. *Responsiveness to requests for help.* Clients typically want personal help at critical stages of their decision making, and they expect that help to be efficient, knowledgeable, and even caring. In addition, customers don't want to have wait long to get help. When asked how long they have been waiting, most customers believe up to three times more minutes than is the case—so three minutes seem like ten.

4. *Location and parking.* Customers expect convenience when doing business, which has to do with location, safety, and access to parking. Difficulty in these areas will likely create a negative perception (Case 14.1).

5. *Respect and dignity.* Finally, customers want to be treated with respect and dignity. This desire becomes apparent upon reviewing the results of studies reporting the most common customer complaints. Their biggest complaints are as follows:

   • Being treated with apathy
   • Passing the buck

Case 14.1

Adding Lights in the Parking Lot

The chief executive officer (CEO) of a chain of food and drug stores in Texas had a decision to make: he believed that the lighting in store parking lots should be so bright that customers could "read newspapers in the parking lot at midnight," if they so desired. Given the costs of doing so, however, the company's board of directors was less enthusiastic. After all, the lighting not only had to be installed but also maintained on an ongoing basis.

What factors other than the costs of installing and maintaining the lighting should be considered in making this decision? In particular, what costs may be involved in not having lighting? What would you decide?

Source: Adapted from Zeithaml, Parasuraman, and Berry (1990).

Case 14.2

Would You Buy a Used Car from This Company?

CarMax has reinvented car sales by providing its customers with a large selection, helpful technology, and no haggling. First, the customer is encouraged to browse through kiosks that contain information such as pictures, prices, and car specifications. While the customer does a test drive, a computer completes the paperwork for a car loan and enters the state's motor vehicle data bank to transfer the title and license. After the test drive, the customer receives CarMax's written offer on a trade-in, which is good regardless of whether he or she buys a car. Within an hour, the customer has everything that is needed, including a written thirty-day guarantee with an extended warranty available.

What kinds of research about customer needs do you think went into developing CarMax's sales program? What other services might you add to meet additional customer needs?

Source: Adapted from Heil, Parker, and Stephens (1997).

- Receiving the wrong information
- Being patronized (or worse, stereotyped)

To avoid receiving complaints like these, organizations must do a better job of identifying customer needs. See Case 14.2 for an example of an organization that seems to have accomplished that goal.

Developing Client-Centered Communication Skills

A good beginning to client-center communication skills involves coupling listening skills (Chapter 4) with integrity responses that show you understand what someone is saying. Many of these communications skills can be summarized by the Chinese characters that comprise the verb *to listen* provide interesting insight into this skill (see Figure 4.1).

PARAPHRASING THE CUSTOMER'S MESSAGE   Providing feedback to another person by paraphrasing what he or she has said offers an accuracy check of the message and also demonstrates your awareness of his or her feelings. Your paraphrase of a customer's message should therefore include both elements: content and emotion. A corporate CEO accented this point, saying, "I would say that listening to the other person's emotions may be the most important thing I've learned in twenty years of business."

To paraphrase your understanding of what someone has said involves several related communication skills:

- Give the person your undivided attention.
- Respond during conversation with positive nonverbal behaviors, such as agreement behaviors. Avoid blocking behaviors, such as crossing your arms or leaning away from the person speaking.
- Ask clarifying questions in a relaxed, nonconfrontational way.

ENGAGING IN THE CONVERSATION   The turn taking that characterizes conversation means that you will have an opportunity to speak as well. For instance, you may need to tell your customers about company policy, mitigating circumstances, or other factors involved in your dealings with them. In doing so, identify facts and clarify incidents, explaining when and how something occurred. Refer to notes you may have prepared and take notes during the conversation, as needed. Finally, monitor the give-and-take of the conversation. You should not overwhelm your customers, but you should not allow them to dominate you.

Guidelines for engaging in the conversation that come from executive coaching sessions include the following:

1. *Show friendly interest.* People respond to positive, affirming behaviors with eye contact and attentive posture.
2. *Identify an area of interest.* Look for something interesting in the other person's message.
3. *Judge content, not delivery.* Don't let the speaker's mannerisms distract you from the message's point.
4. *Maintain emotional control.* Even if you might disagree with someone, avoid emotional or defensive responses.
5. *Listen for ideas, not isolated facts and details.* Try to see the "big picture" rather than get mired down in details and minutiae.

AVOIDING LISTENING DISTRACTERS   The need to avoid distractions has been mentioned several times now. The fact is, many of us listen poorly because we are easily distracted. A source of major distraction is the client and his or her habits and mannerisms. Among these are fidgeting, perhaps with the hair or fingernails; talking too loud or too soft or too fast or too slow; not making eye contact; and wearing unusual clothing or body objects.

Our tendency toward distraction can also be explained by our ability to think faster than we can speak. The average person can think at a rate of 500 words a minute, but the average speaker talks at only 175 words a minute. It is therefore not surprising that our minds wander while we're listening to others talk. You can evaluate your customer service skills by completing the assessment in Skills at Work 14.1.

Developing Customer-Centered Messages

The words we use make a difference in communicating our messages. Some words and phrases automatically turn people off, for a number of reasons. Some of the most common *irritators* we hear are these well-worn phrases:

EXAMPLES

"I'm not authorized to ..."

"You can't ..."

"You will have to ..."

"It's not our policy to ..."

"I'm new here."

"You should have ..."

"All we can do is ..."

"Why did you call?"

"Too bad."

SKILLS AT WORK 14.1
Customer Service Assessment

The statements below all describe listening behaviors. Respond to each statement by choosing one of these answers:

> 1 = Always   2 = Frequently
> 3 = Sometimes   4 = Seldom
> 5 = Never

Write your answer for each statement on the line provided. After you've responded to the statements, add your total.

_____ **1.** I think about my own speaking performance during an interaction, which results in my missing some of what the speaker says.

_____ **2.** I allow my mind to wander away from what the speaker is talking about.

_____ **3.** I try to simplify what I hear by omitting details.

_____ **4.** I focus on particular details of what a speaker is saying instead of the general meaning he or she is trying to communicate.

_____ **5.** I allow my attitudes toward the topic or speaker to influence my evaluation of the message.

_____ **6.** I hear what I expect to hear, instead of what is actually being said.

_____ **7.** I listen passively, letting the speaker do the work while I relax.

_____ **8.** I listen to what others say, but I don't feel what they are feeling.

_____ **9.** I evaluate what the speaker is saying before trying to understand the meaning intended.

_____ **10.** I listen to the literal meaning that a speaker communicates, ignoring any hidden or underlying meanings.

_____ **Total Score**

If your score was 30 or higher, you have better than average listening skills; if your score was below 30, you have lower than average listening skills. What skills do you need to work on to improve your customer service score?

Avoiding these irritating expressions, and others like them, is a good start toward developing customer-centered messages. When customers are upset or distracted, they may not hear what you are saying. So, here are some other examples of what to say instead of these irritators:

EXAMPLES

Bad: "I only work here." (Suggests you are irresponsible or disinterested in resolving the problem)

Better: "Let me see what I can do."

Bad: "You did it the wrong way." (Makes customer feel belittled and frustrated for having wasted time.)

Better: "This part of the form is tricky. I've overlooked this kind of thing myself. Let's see how we can fix it."

Bad: "I'm not permitted or authorized to ..." (Suggests you are incompetent or unwilling to help.)

Better: "This is complicated because of board policy and accounting regulations. Let's look again at the problem and see if there is anything you can do."

Obviously, the idea is to show a "can do" attitude in responding to the customer. This demonstrates understanding while moving toward a solution. Ultimately, the customer may be at fault or need to do something differently. That's not a reason to insult the customer, however, or to make the rest of his or her experience a negative one. If you can pleasantly indicate what to do, most people will do it.

Remember that your customers are coming from outside your organization, so they are not familiar with its procedures and processes. They are entering a new zone. Help them navigate by communicating with a positive attitude and providing the information they need.

Recovering from Losses and Mistakes

Some of the most sensitive cases of providing customer service involve customers who want organizational mistakes and failures to be corrected. In some of these cases, it will not be possible to satisfy customer expectations. Regardless, you should approach situations involving loss and mistakes with these guidelines in mind (*San Diego Manual*, 2000):

1. Show genuine concern and clarify what the person has said.
2. Apologize when appropriate.
3. Solve problems fairly, and keep your promises.
4. Thank the customer.
5. If possible, offer some sort of compensation.

Handling Requests

The strategy for handling requests is based on the notion of appreciating customers and empathizing with their needs while following company policy when you cannot comply. However, when you can comply, do everything you can. Several guidelines can help you determine the appropriate way to respond:

1. Be sure you understand the request.
2. Be sure the information you provide is accurate.
3. Do make promises or give potentially false or misleading answers.
4. Tell the customer clearly what *you* can do and what *he or she* can do.
5. When you have to say no, show empathy. Explain why you cannot comply, expressing regret in your vocal tone.

Dealing with Angry Customers

The most dreaded situation for providing customer service involves dealing with angry people. Sometimes, people come into your office angry; other times, you have to tell them things that make them angry. Either way, avoid either erecting a "wall" between you and the angry person— for instance, ignoring, minimizing, or denying what he or she says. Instead, try to understand the reasons for the customer's upset, and then apply strategies we've noted.

Customers get angry as a result of lack of information, perceived loss, or personality differences. A customer who has been denied needed information or who has not been informed of policies or procedures will likely become angry. In providing information, however, consider that what may sound like a routine practice to you may sound like a foreign language to a customer. Also, some customers dislike the idea of experiencing real or imagined loss. Loss of control, money down the drain, wasted time, and bad experiences all represent loss of one sort or another to the customer.

Finally, there is the personality factor. Some people are chronically angry for any number of reasons. The behaviors of angry or upset customers vary. Some customers are loud and demanding and try to make you angry. Others are looking to place blame, whether on an individual or an organization. Customers may also be uncooperative and downright threatening, making remarks such as "I'll tell your boss if you don't do this for me," "You'll hear from my lawyer," and "You'll never see me or my family here again."

Remember, except for the chronically angry customer, there is often a reason for the upset. If you can uncover that reason through effective communication, you can likely diffuse the problem. In working with an angry, dissatisfied customer, here are some best practices (Alessandra, 1997; EPA, 2001; Impact Learning, 2001):

1. *Give the customer your full attention.* Make sure the customer knows right from the start that he or she is being listened to and taken seriously. Show that you are trying to understand—for instance, "What I hear you saying is ..." or "Let me see if I have this down ..." When customer grievances are pursued actively and efficiently, it's possible to turn angry customers into satisfied ones.

2. *Acknowledge and discover the source of the customer's dissatisfaction.* Recognize the client's anger and frustration by saying things like "This must not feel too good to you" and "You must be experiencing a lot of feelings about now." Then try to find out why he or she feels this way. You might say "Help me understand why you feel this way" or ask "What is the main reason you are experiencing the problem?"

3. *Apologize for the problem.* Be sincere in expressing your regret, and offer compensation if you can (something quick and consumable, if possible).

4. *Work together to make a plan to meet the customer's expectations.* Set goals, identify the actions to be taken, and set a timeline for completion.

Communicating over customer complaints works best by seeking first to understand the problem and then to calmly recommend solutions.

In the real world of customer service, customers aren't always met with such understanding and initiative. Case 14.3 presents an all-too-common example of poor customer service.

Talking on the Telephone

A great deal of customer service involves talking to customers on the telephone as additional opportunities to solve their problems and enhance your organization's image. Here are several best practices for good telephone skills:

1. Answer in three rings or less.
2. Identify who you are by stating your name.
3. Use a friendly, nonmonotone voice.
4. Tell the customer what action you will take and when.
5. Before putting someone on hold, ask for his or her permission to do so. *Never* keep someone on hold for more than 45 seconds without returning and apologizing.
6. Return phone calls promptly, even if only to say that you are still gathering information and will report later.

Case 14.3

The Real Cost of a Coke

After picking up her food at the drive-through takeout window of a local hamburger restaurant, a woman checked what she received and discovered that she was missing a medium-sized Coke. Frustrated but determined, she parked the car and walked inside the restaurant. After waiting in line nearly ten minutes for service during the busy lunch hour, she finally had the chance to explain what had happened and request the missing Coke. The worker she spoke to looked at her with a blank expression and then said, "I need to get my manager."

After several more minutes, the manager emerged and stood behind the counter, leaning against it with his arms crossed, a serious look on his face. Once again, the woman explained what had happened and asked if she could get the missing Coke. The manager responded, "I need to see your receipt." The woman looked in her purse, thinking she might have jammed the receipt in there when she got change. Not finding it, she explained that the receipt must have been in the bag with the food, which was in the car. The manager said again, "I need to see your receipt. That's company policy."

After several minutes of verbal scuffling, the customer left empty-handed. The manager turned to his employees with a satisfied look, as if to say, "I really showed her."

Think about what that Coke cost from an organizational standpoint. The original order was around $15. With repeat business, annual sales for this single customer would be over $500.

Assuming the customer tells others about her negative experience, the loss of annual sales will be even higher.

What mistakes did the employees of the hamburger restaurant make along the way in providing service to this customer? What training would you recommend to address these errors?

By the way, the wholesale value of the Coke and the cup was 20 cents!

By employing good telephone skills, you can help address a customer's needs and enhance your organization's image as well.

Check what you have learned about providing quality customer service by reviewing the myths presented in Skills at Work 14.2. Review the relevant sections of text if your own understanding needs improvement in any of these areas.

SKILLS AT WORK 14.2
Common Customer Service Myths

Do you "buy into" any of these myths about providing quality customer service?

MYTH 1. "We are providing great service."

Perception is the key to unlocking this myth. Even if people seem generally satisfied, even pleased with the service being provided, there is always room for improvement.

MYTH 2. "If customers don't like it, they can go elsewhere."

Holding this attitude is precisely what gets companies in trouble. Informed customers today will go elsewhere if their needs are not met.

MYTH 3. "We're required to say no sometimes, which means we can't always provide high quality customer service."

Providing quality service is not about saying yes to everything but about learning how to process customers' needs and complaints in a way that makes them feel understood.

MYTH 4. "You can't satisfy customers with conflicting objectives."

You can only do what legal and organizational guidelines allow, but that's no excuse for not doing all you can in terms of being warm, caring, friendly, accurate, and responsive.

Source: Adapted from *San Diego Manual* (2000).

CHANGING THE ORGANIZATIONAL CULTURE TO ENHANCE CUSTOMER SERVICE

Some of the problems with providing good customer service communication can be traced to the organization itself. When clearly thought out policies are not in place, training and procedures to resolve customer problems may be hard to come by, or when supervisors may not support customer initiatives, it becomes easy to see a need for organizational culture to enhance these points.

Ultimately, providing quality customer service must be a value that the entire organization embraces. Implementing change can be accomplished but may be difficult (see Appendix C for change management). The first step, regardless, must be to communicate the organization's philosophy as the stimulus behind the cycle of change.

Creating a Cycle of Change

The organization's customer-centered orientation must be realized from the upper hierarchy of the organizational culture down to all its employees. Experience shows that unless everyone buys into the concept, it simply will fail. Beyond that, we suggest directions to implement organizational change (EPA, 2001; *San Diego Manual*, 2000):

1. *Set service goals.* Desired outcomes may include increased revenue, improved responsiveness and efficiency, reduced complaints, and so on. Once desired outcomes have been

---

WEB AT WORK 14.1
Customer Service Communication

As a review of this list of websites will show, training is a key element of improving customer service communication:

- **www.enterprisemedia.com** Sells training videos.
- **www.teldoc.com** An interactive site; allows you to test your "customer service IQ."
- **www.workforceinc.com/customers. htm** Offers businesses customer service training.
- **www.saleshelp.com/guestservices/ destinations/sdqframe2.htm** A specific approach to customer service training.
- **www.learnbywire.com** Focuses on telephone service.
- **www.epa.gov/customerservice/ training.htm** A page from the Environmental Protection Agency about its customer service training policy.

- **www.customer-service.com** An extensive resource with much good information.
- **http://eai.ebizq.net/crm** Great information, especially regarding lingo used on the Web; also has information on systems management and e-business.
- **www.zdnet.com** Articles published by zdnet with a unique perspective on business technologies.
- **www.bosbbb.org/services/ complaints.asp** Useful customer service and handling complaint information.
- **www.bbb.org/alerts/article.asp? ID=373** Information from the Better Business Bureau about handling complaints.
- **www.customerservicetraining.net** An overview of how to understand customer service.

Source: Adapted from Leshicar (2003).

determined, they should be clearly stated and communicated. Figure 14.1 illustrates an approach used by a restaurant to evaluate the customer service it provides throughout a typical dining experience.

2. *Measure the outcomes related to the goals.* By developing **outcomes measures**, data points can highlight success or failure in these areas. Common measures of customer service include customer satisfaction indices/surveys, records of complaints and claims, sales records, profit level, repeat business, customer attrition rate, and simple customer count. Once set, outcomes should be easy to obtain through routine electronic data traffic flow analysis or other means to capture such data. These results then should be communicated.

3. *List what the organization has learned from measuring these outcomes.* What did the research indicate?

4. *Implement policies and provide training to make change.* Training is vital to making the adjustments needed for this cycle of change to work—specifically, training in customer service communication skills (Service Quality Institute, 2001).

To learn more about training and other areas of customer service communication, access the websites listed in Web at Work 14.1.

MANAGING SALES PRESENTATIONS IN THE WORKPLACE

The field of sales, or what this chapter calls **sales communication**, is a popular blend of academics and experience. From an academic perspective, various disciplines contribute to the field of

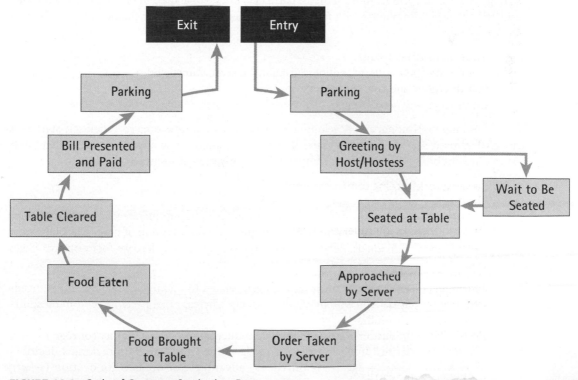

FIGURE 14.1 Cycle of Customer Service in a Restaurant

sales communication, such as communication theory, interpersonal communication, persuasion theory, marketing, and organizational behavior. From an experience perspective, sales entrepreneurs, trainers, and motivational speakers have shared a wealth of information in books, seminars, and DVDs, often based on selected success stories as well as their own background.

As you read the material in this chapter, you will recognize both of these perspectives. You also will recognize that sales communication extends the principles involved in persuasion by applying them in the unique context of the workplace. For instance, salespeople must convert changes in attitudes, beliefs, values, and behaviors into a specific outcome: sales. That outcome will be assessed using data from sales revenues, number of returns, number of new clients/customers, number of lost clients/customers, and related growth measures. Sales communication addresses issues of adoption, continuance, discontinuance of service, readoption, customer adaptation, and so on.

Most future managers will have the need to sell, be it a product or service or a proposal or concept. That makes an understanding of sales communication a vital skill.

PRINCIPLES OF SALES COMMUNICATION

In order to apply strategies for effective sales communication, it is of primary importance to comprehend the principles that provide sales foundations. The following key principles describe these sales foundations.

Motivation

The salesperson's **motivation** is a good place to start this discussion of principles because successful selling is rooted in personal motivation. In particular, salespeople need to be highly self-motivated and self-managed. Employers look for these qualities in salespeople or the potential to develop these qualities:

- Time management skills
- Communication skills: friendliness, listening, conversational ability
- Self-discipline and goal-setting ability
- Confidence and perseverance

Finding, motivating, and developing individuals who can become so-called self-starters is the goal of many sales-training seminars. Many trainers suggest that anyone can sell—that salespeople are not born but made. To accomplish this, motivation is essential.

Adopting Innovations

Everett Rogers (2003) was a leading academic researcher in a unique area of communication studies called **diffusion of innovations**. These studies trace the adoption of new technologies (or innovations) across individuals, networks, and large systems units. Here we focus on five stages related specifically to a customer's decision making.

1. *Knowledge.* The customer must have a need related to making a purchase. Some needs stem from dissatisfaction with previous products, whereas other needs arise from recognizing desirable new products.
2. *Persuasion.* The customer or client seeks to reduce his or her uncertainty (or *cognitive dissonance*, as described in Chapter 13). To help reduce uncertainty in making a decision, three kinds of knowledge are required: (a) advantages of the new innovation (*what*), (b) how-to knowledge (*how*), and (3) principles knowledge (*why*). Sources you may find

helpful for this uncertainty reduction data include benchmark information (what other organizations have done in a similar situation) and peer-group input.

3. *Decision.* Here, the customer or client must adopt or reject purchase of the innovation. A *product trial* might be offered, in which the client gets to try out the innovation for a short time to evaluate its usefulness without incurring any of the risks involved in purchasing it. Not surprisingly, product trials have proven remarkably effective in converting to sales. In those situations when the sale is not made and the innovation is rejected, several types of rejection are possible: *Active rejection* consists of considering whether to adopt an innovation but then deciding not to, and *passive rejection* consists of never actually considering adoption.

4. *Implementation.* Assuming the customer or client has chosen to adopt the innovation, the task at this stage is to make the product or service fit the client's needs. Perhaps additional equipment must be installed and training must be conducted. Providing access to training and technical advice through Web sites or other means of communication is a good way to help the client readily adapt. In addition, encouraging *reinvention*—in which the product is modified for multiple uses or is customized for the client's unique situation—is also effective at this stage. In this case, customers make the innovation their own when they reinvent it and make it routinely part of their regular operations.

5. *Confirmation.* After making the decision to adopt, the customer or client may experience *buyer's remorse*, in which cognitive dissonance sets in. When provided with needed reassurance and information, the customer is likely to continue with the innovation. Otherwise, *replacement discontinuance*, which involves looking for something better, or *disenchantment discontinuance*, which involves dissatisfaction may set in.

Sales Communication with a Marketing Viewpoint

A common misconception is that *marketing* and *selling* are the same things. Although it is true that selling is a part of marketing, **marketing** involves a much broader set of strategic concerns. Your understanding of at least the basics of marketing will make your sales communication efforts more effective. In addition, having a broad view of marketing will help you frame sales communication in the context of training and applications.

The following sections will look at common marketing practices, the fundamentals of marketing strategy, and the nature of integrated marketing (based on Kaplan, 2001; Kotler, 1999; Liraz, 1999; Pophal, 2000; Rogers, 2003).

COMMON MARKETING PRINCIPLES Philosophies about what makes for successful marketing are often stated as one-line phrases in companies' advertisements and training materials. However, many of these "best practices" are essentially intuitive and are not necessarily supported with hard evidence regarding their effectiveness. The following practices, however, have significantly more researcher support (as cited above):

- Provide high-quality and service.
- Meet customer expectations.
- Offer lower prices.
- Show continuous product improvement.
- Show product innovation.
- Enter high-growth markets.
- Develop a detailed marketing plan: should include data analysis and competitive pricing.

FUNDAMENTALS OF MARKETING STRATEGY   Developing a marketing plan or strategy is considered fundamental to achieving desired outcomes. These steps typically shape a development plan:

1. *Conduct audience research.* To determine customer needs, as indicated earlier, analyze these types of information:
   - Demographics and psychographics
   - Customer wants (such as more convenience, better quality, quicker service)
   - Trends (that is, shifts in tastes, lifestyles, economics)
2. *Identify competitive advantages.* Consider the following:
   - Does your product or service have a lower price?
   - Is it better than what the competition offers?
   - Is it compatible with other products or services?
   - Is it easy to try out and use?
3. *Do target marketing.* Select specific markets and promote your product or service to them.
4. *Make a "marketing mix."* Determine the combination of the 6 Ps in meeting a sales objective:
   - Product: the product or service and its characteristics
   - Price: base price plus discounts, payment period, allowances
   - Promotion: sales, advertising, Twitter, Facebook, blogs
   - Place: outlets, inventories, transportation, locations
   - Packaging
   - Public readiness: is this product right for this time and this audience?
5. *Evaluate marketing performance.* Analyze how well your customers were served:
   - Have sales (customer and volume) increased?
   - Were promotions timely?
   - Did the advertising reach the intended audience?

INTEGRATED MARKETING COMMUNICATION   There is a growing awareness that in marketing the right hand does not know what the left hand is doing. In fact, most large companies use different departments or employ outside firms to handle such diverse areas as advertising, public relations, Web and social media development, sales promotion, training for customer service among employees, and so on. When so many groups are responsible for these assorted functions, performance often suffers in terms of the balance, emphasis, and timing of strategic marketing factors. Consequently, a sales prospect might get the wrong contact information at the wrong time, or a customer may receive contradictory explanations.

Thus, the theory behind **integrated marketing communication** is to encourage a unified systems approach. By holding frequent meetings, connecting leaders and staff, and seeing the "big picture" with unity in mind, organizations can overcome the problems that often result from not having a unified marketing focus. As O'Hair, O'Rourke, and O'Hair (2001) point out, the goal of an integrated marketing system is to synthesize all ideas, actions, and plans from diverse groups in order to combine everyone's talents and deliver a better final product.

Relationship Selling

Often referred to in the literature as **relationship selling**, this approach represents a shift away from product-driven sales to customer-driven sales. Influenced by the customer-service paradigm (presented earlier in this chapter), this approach emphasizes interpersonal communication

The relationship-selling approach emphasizes interpersonal communication and a focus on the customer, not the product.

and a customer focus over a product focus (Streetwise tips, 2001). The key elements to relationship selling are (1) the role of the salesperson as a solution-focused consultant; (2) the need to listen and demonstrate empathy; and (3) the importance of developing friendships.

SALESPERSON'S ROLE   The selling of solutions, not products, is a major aspect of relationship selling. That is, the salesperson's role is to help the customer identify problems and then solve them. Thus, a salesperson is seen as a valuable resource for understanding the customer's needs and providing creative and workable solutions. Many companies currently embrace this approach, as illustrated by IBM's commitment to customer service and MetLife's willingness to develop extensive consultative proposals for potential customers.

This innovative emphasis on relationship selling represents a transformation in the world of sales. No longer is the salesperson a confronter or high-powered manipulator who uses scripts and guilt tactics in an approach often called *hard selling*. Rather, he or she is an interpersonal consultant whose focus is the customer's needs and objectives. As a consultant, the salesperson is encouraged to think as an insider and to make available to the client the tools he or she has that will service the problem. Consequently, interpersonal communication becomes invaluable in applying this approach—the salesperson listens first and talks less in order to understand the problem before pointing out solutions.

DEVELOPING FRIENDSHIPS   According to many relationship-selling approaches, the salesperson-client relationship does not end with closing the sale but continues through friendship that can lead to continued business. To build that sort of relationship, the salesperson must establish his or her credibility, knowledge, trust, and sociability early on. Case 14.4 illustrates the benefits realized from the relationship-selling approach and the value of building trust, in particular.

Case 14.4

The Benefits of Relationship Selling

Examples abound of companies that encourage its sales staff to build relationships with their customers and clients. The company advises salespeople to take their time in getting to know each customer and understand his or her unique needs. They are told that several visits and patient efforts make trust more likely.

The effectiveness of developing this type of salesperson-customer relationship is astounding: The average closing rate is over 50 percent for MetLife salespeople and reaches 80 percent for the top-producing salespeople in the organization. In addition to increased earnings, what else might salespeople enjoy about the relationship approach to selling? What would you enjoy about this approach to selling?

STRATEGIES FOR EFFECTIVE SALES COMMUNICATION

No single model necessarily represents effective sales communication. Given the number of organizations and publications dedicated to sales training, quite the opposite seems to be true. The websites listed in Web at Work 14.2 demonstrate the variety of organizations involved in this field.

Using information from research and personal experience, the rest of this chapter presents some of the most common sales communication strategies (Pophal, 2000; Rogers, 2003; Wechsler, 2001).

Establishing a Knowledge Basis

The beginning ingredient for excellence in sales is knowledge. The **knowledge basis** that informs a successful salesperson is substantial and includes knowledge in these four areas: (1) product knowledge (affects your credibility and reputation), (2) organizational knowledge (the company's

WEB AT WORK 14.2
Sales Training

Access these websites for more information about sales training:

- **www.businesstown.com/sales/face.asp** Provides links to other Web pages that give informal information about sales, particularly business sales.
- **www.systema.com/process.html** Is linked to an advertisement for a

business training service but has interesting information about sales.

- **www.businessknowhow.com/marketing/winslspres.htm** Shows ten tips for excellence in sales. Newsletter coming soon that offers business advice.

Source: Based on Leshicar (2003).

Sales communication involves not only product knowledge, but also forming an information relationship that solves a customer's problem.

values, history, what they stand for), and (3) benchmarks (knowing what else is out there and how you compare).

Finding Potential Customers and Clients

Finding **potential customers and clients**, sometimes referred to as *prospecting*, can involve any number of strategies: demographic analysis, trend analysis, current events studies, and networking, to name a few. Data containing potential customers' names and addresses can be purchased from marketing sources. A Web search will turn up most of the major list suppliers. Marketing data can be sorted to match your needs, as for instance by region, purchasing typologies, and demographics. Referrals and previous company contacts make up another rich client list.

In addition, you should be aware of what experts in the sales field have identified as the two greatest barriers to finding prospects: time management and fear of rejection.

Time Management and Resilience

It might seem surprising to suggest that one of the "strategies" of effective sales communication lies within yourself. However, the literature identifies the fundamental importance of self-discipline. That implies goal setting and managing one's time in a way to stay on schedule.

Related to managing one's time is resilience—persevering when things get tough. Everyone worries some time or another about being rejected, a common barrier to resilience. However, most experts agree that it helps to replace rejection with positive alternative metaphors such as "moving forward" or "each no means closer to a yes." As one sales professional reported, "I hate starting those calls, but once I make the first one, I enjoy the rest of the morning."

The actual percentage of rejection depends on the industry, the salesperson's level of experience, and the performance of the economy at that particular time. Even so, in setting your own sales goals and before seeking potential customers, calculate two factors:

1. The percentage of calls or other forms of contact that result in appointments
2. The percentage of appointments that materialize into closed sales

Of course, you may need to factor in lost appointments, returns of merchandise, and other variables. But the basic idea is to determine how much customer contact is needed to meet your goals. For example, if it takes 5 calls to make 1 appointment and it takes 4 appointments to make 1 sale, then you must make 20 calls to yield 1 sale. If your weekly goal is to make 5 sales, then you must make 100 calls. Although e-mail blasts or media sources usually yield lower percentages, the sheer volume of those sources can be useful to make initial contacts. The old motivational phrase, "Plan the work and work the plan," is fitting here.

Conducting Sales Interviews

The **sales interview** is really a form of persuasive speaking. This unique form can be described as five steps.

STEP 1: UNDERSTAND THE CUSTOMER'S BACKGROUND Before engaging in the sales interview, you should conduct the research necessary to understand the customer's key personnel and decision-making processes. Find the answers to these questions before the actual interview:

- Who is attending the meeting?
- Who makes the sales decision? How is the decision made?
- What is the meeting length?
- What is the physical arrangement of the setting of the meeting?

STEP 2: MAKE THE INTRODUCTION For obvious reasons, the client may experience anxiety or uncertainty going into the sales interview. Perhaps he or she has had bad experiences with other products, with poor customer service, or even with your organization. The customer's chief concerns probably includes these questions about you and your organization (Wechsler, 2001):

- Who is this person?
- What is this company?
- Why are they here today?
- What can they do for me?
- How long will this take?

Your job in initiating contact is to put aside these potential fears while also introducing yourself and the product. Establishing your credibility is essential here. Therefore, the introduction actually serves to build trust and rapport before moving into the product demonstration phase. You can achieve these goals by preparing a carefully worded message that anticipates these client questions, such as this one:

EXAMPLE

"Thank you for the chance to meet with you today. You are probably wondering just who I am, what my company does, why it is important to you, and what we are going to talk about. My goal today is to briefly share what my company does and my background, and then spend the majority of our time getting to know more about you, your company, your needs, and how we might be of service to you. Okay?" (Wechsler, 2001)

After making this statement, share your brief introduction and then be ready to transition into Step 3.

STEP 3: ESTABLISH THE NEED   In communication situations with limited opportunity for feedback (such as traditional mass media communications), a one-way, downward communication model requires the spokesperson to develop a powerful argument to convince listeners of their existing needs or to create new needs. In relationship sales communication, the salesperson uses a highly interpersonal approach to pinpoint the customer's needs.

One relationship selling approach, the *SPIN* selling method, creates these categories of questions that elicit the client's needs (Kotler, 1999; Wechsler, 2001):

1. *Situational questions.* Questions such as "How many of these do you typically use in a month?" explore the client's current situation. Aspects of that situation worth questioning are quality, quantity, vendor, style, price point, and length and depth of relationship.

2. *Problem questions.* Ask the client about his or her positive and negative experiences to determine why he or she purchased the product before and what options he or she may want in the future. For instance, ask "What do you like best about it?" to inquire about service, quality, policy, selection, and relationship. After finding out what the customer likes, move on to his or her dislikes by asking "What do you like least about it?"

3. *Implication questions.* If you have identified difficulties or problems, follow up by asking specifically how those problems affect the organization—for instance, "How does this problem affect productivity?"

4. *Need-payoff questions.* These questions request information about the usefulness of a solution you plan to propose. You can begin generally with a question like "What would you want in a new system?" or ask a specific question such as "How much would you save if we could reduce errors by 80 percent?" Still another follow-up to the need-payoff question moves toward the solution phase of the interview and asks specifically, "What could a company like ours do to compete for or win your business?"

STEP 4: PRESENT THE SOLUTION   As with any problem-solving sequence, the solution that is ultimately reached must (1) solve their needs or problem, and (2) offer benefits that have a relative advantage over a competitor's solution. You can accomplish all of these functions by following a model such as the popular approach of taking this initiative is called *AIDA*, an acronym that is defined by these elements:

1. *Attention.* Get the client's attention, show an overview of the product.
2. *Interest.* Create interest by demonstrating how the product works, its features, and how it satisfies a need.

3. *Desire.* Create motivation by showing the client exactly how the product will satisfy his or her need and enhance his or her operation. In creating desire, identify the product's benefits, or *competitive edge*, including the following:
   - Has a lower price
   - Will reduce other costs
   - Is more dependable
   - Is user-friendly
   - Is more convenient
   - Provides faster service
   - Offers enhanced image or reputation
   - Is accessible
   - Comes with a guarantee
   - Provide testimonials to back up your presentation
4. *Action.* Show the client how to purchase and install the product.

Your delivery of the sales presentation should be extemporaneous and lively. You will find visual aids especially helpful. Another delivery idea to secure commitment is to invite the customer to hold or touch the product.

STEP 5: ASK FOR A COMMITMENT   A common mistake among salespeople is to make a great presentation, yet never ask for a commitment (or as traditional sales trainers say, "Close the sale"). Thus, the final phase of the sales interview is to ask for a commitment. Wechsler (2001, p. 4) underscores the importance of this phase in this way: "I earned the right to ask the prospect to commit to me. I started asking people direct, non-manipulative questions about finalizing the sales process. My sales and income literally quadrupled overnight!"

Sales training suggests following two rules at this point. First, ask the client an obligating question—for example, "Mr. Smith, would this system solve the problems you have indicated?" Second, sit back and listen. If the answer is "yes," then thank the customer and move ahead with the purchase decision. If the answer is "no" or "maybe," then politely ask for an explanation—for instance, "May I ask what your objection is?"—and then answer the objection. You may find that the customer has unanswered questions or has not understood some point.

HANDLING OBJECTIONS AND ANSWERING QUESTIONS   If you can determine what the customer's objection is, then you might have the opportunity to turn a "no" into a "yes." The skills valuable in answering objections are to stay rational, not to take anything personally, and to be respectful and positive toward the customer. Avoid challenging or arguing with him or her. Rather, provide direct, solution-focused answers to his or her questions. As much as possible, connect the benefits of purchasing your product or service with meeting the client's needs.

In some situations, you may need to help the client overcome his or her tendency to procrastinate. Be assertive without being pushy. In still other situations, it may be wise to bring the presentation to a close and ask for the opportunity to amend your proposal and present it again.

Skills at Work 14.3 provides some common examples of customer objections and questions and asks you to recommend how best to deal with them. Also review the information in Chapter 5 on managing conflict.

SKILLS AT WORK 14.3
Handling Customer Objections and Questions

Imagine yourself as a seasoned salesperson. You have had years of experience in sales communication. How would you handle each of the following customer objections or questions?

1. CUSTOMER: "I don't know if this is something we should do right now. We have a lot going on."
   SALESPERSON: "May I ask what you seem to be unsure about?" *After the customer answers this question, ask for his or her commitment again.*

2. CUSTOMER: "We would need the newest model, for sure. We really wouldn't have any use for the older product line at this point."
   SALESPERSON: "We'd be happy to deliver that new model whenever you need it. I can put a rush on the delivery, if you'd like." *Do whatever it takes to meet the customer's needs: put in a special order, add a rush delivery, extend the warranty, and so on.*

3. CUSTOMER: "Wow! Your price is too high" Or "I can buy the same thing for $2.50 a unit less."
   SALESPERSON: "I can appreciate your concern. Can you tell me why you feel it is too high?" *See if there is some feature the customer wants that you can emphasize about your product.* Alternatively, "If Brand X is the same as my product, you probably should buy brand X. But let's look at them both and see if there are any value differences." *Show the customer that differences in value may be worth more than the outright cost difference.*

4. CUSTOMER: "I need to think it over. I'll get back to you soon."
   SALESPERSON: "I'm sure you have a good reason. What about the decision do you need to think about? Can I answer any questions for you?" *Try to keep the dialogue going without being pushy. Show the customer that your primary goal is to address his or her needs.*

Source: Adapted from *San Diego Manual* (2000).

In Perspective

Sales communication and customer service are related areas of communication application in business and in the professions. In fact customer service is one of the most significant measures of organizational outcomes. Models of customer service primarily describe organizations in terms of being operations-centered versus client-centered organizations. In recent years, a radical shift has occurred, moving away from an operations-centered focus toward a client-centered focus.

A number of communication issues underlie customer relations problems and thus cause unnecessary waste and difficulty. These customer service gaps range from a lack of interaction between management and customers to inadequate communication across departments. At the core of improved customer service is an understanding of what customers really expect. In addition to understanding customers' needs, it is important to be able to communicate with them using customer-centered communication approaches, including developing client-centered listening skills, developing customer-centered messages, recovering from losses and mistakes, handling requests, dealing with angry customers, and talking on the telephone.

Quality customer service must be a value that is embraced by the entire organization. Implementing change can be accomplished but may be difficult. To begin, the organization's philosophy must be communicated as the stimulus behind the cycle of change.

The key principles that underlie successful sales communication include the salesperson's motivation, diffusion of innovations, relationship selling, and marketing. Finding, motivating, and developing individuals who can become so-called *self-starters* is the goal of many sales-training seminars. Research on the diffusion of innovations traces the adoption of new technologies (or innovations) across individuals, networks, and large systems units. The approach known as relationship selling represents a shift away from product-driven sales to customer-driven sales.

Your understanding of at least the basics of marketing will make your sales communication efforts more effective. The importance of developing a marketing plan or strategy is fundamental to achieving desired outcomes. Most large companies use different departments or employ outside firms to handle such diverse areas as advertising, public relations, and sales promotion. The theory behind integrated marketing communication is to encourage a unified systems approach.

No single model represents effective sales communication, but several common strategies have been found effective. The beginning ingredient for excellence in sales is knowledge. The successful salesperson is informed by a knowledge basis that comprises product knowledge, organizational knowledge, benchmark comparisons, and an organizational plan.

Finding potential customers and clients, sometimes referred to as *prospecting*, can involve any number of methods. In addition, you should be aware of what experts have identified as the two greatest barriers to finding prospects: time management and fear of rejection.

The sales interview is really a form of persuasive speaking. Given the uniqueness of sales communication, a sales interview should include these five steps: (1) understand the customer's background, (2) make the introduction, (3) establish the need, (4) present the solution, and (5) ask for a commitment.

The skills valuable in handling customers' objections and answering their questions are to stay rational, not to take anything personally, and to be respectful and positive toward the customer. As much as possible, connect the benefits of purchasing your product or service with meeting the client's needs.

Discussion Questions

1. Why is it important to communicate an organization's customer service philosophy throughout the entire organization?
2. How is a client-centered organization different from an operations-centered organization?
3. If you were to create a customer service training program, what would you include? Why?
4. Review the information in this chapter about reasons for customer complaints and anger. Which of these have you experienced? Give examples to support your answer. How could improved communication have helped customer service in each of these situations?
5. List the characteristics that make someone a *self-starter*. In other words, what ranges of qualities are needed to be self-motivated and self-managed?
6. Compare and contrast relationship selling and so-called hard selling. What are the advantages and disadvantages from the customer's or client's perspective? What about from the salesperson's perspective?
7. The relationship-selling approach requires that you be a consultant/problem solver for your client. How can you play that role and yet represent your own company's best interests, too? Are those roles compatible? Why?
8. What is involved in creating and then maintaining a knowledge basis? For instance, what would you have to learn upon getting your first sales job—say, selling overnight shipping services for a small-sized company? What information might change and require periodic updating? How might your own goals change after you've been in this position for awhile?
9. What is the relationship between selling and marketing? What knowledge about marketing helps one to be a successful salesperson? Why?

Exercises

1. Individually or with a team from your class, interview the manager of a company or organization whose product or service is made available to the public. Ask him or her to share views on what makes good customer/client service—his or her own views and those of the company or organization. Share what you find out in report.

2. With several other members of your class, go to retail stores and restaurants in your area to shop or eat. Record your experiences in interacting with store and restaurant personnel. For instance, are you greeted when you enter? Are personnel attentive to you? Can they answer questions or offer information about their product or service? How would you rate each store or restaurant's quality of customer service? Why is this the case?

3. Search the Internet for sources of information about customer service training. Visit several websites and summarize each approach to customer service. Specifically, what philosophy may underlie each approach?

4. Give the customer service assessment in Skills at Work 14.1 to four or five people you know. After reviewing each person's score, consider whether you feel it accurately reflects his or her listening skills. What suggestions would you give each person about listening to and interacting with others?

5. Call three companies or organizations to discuss their product or service, and observe the telephone skills practiced by the people you talk to. In each case, what is the tone of voice? How helpful and specific is the information provided? If you are on hold, or are referred to other numbers, how long and how many times?

6. List in one minute all the examples of sales positions that you can think of. How many did you come up with? Next, compare lists with several classmates. How many did they come up with? What sales positions did you all think of? What are some of the most unique positions to have made one of the lists?

7. Conduct an Internet search for information about sales communication using these suggested key words: sales, sales communication, marketing communication, or others. What information comes up with each search?

8. With a small group of classmates, review the elements of the SPIN model and discuss how it could be applied in a specific organization. Role-play a scenario in which a salesperson interviews a customer by asking the appropriate types of questions to gain commitment.

9. With a team of classmates, visit five or six stores or other businesses to observe salespeople in action. What principles of sales communication do you see being applied? What strategies do you observe? What problems do you see in any of these areas? Report your findings to the entire class.

10. With several classmates, create and then role-play three or four situations involving a salesperson's handling of customer objections or questions. To get started, perhaps use some of the problems you observed in completing Exercise 4 or the examples from Skills at Work 14.1.

References

Alessandra, T. (1997). Customer-driven services for executives. The Phoenix executive briefing series. Teleconference, Abilene Christian University.

Environmental Protection Agency. (EPA). (2001) Customer service training program. Available online: epa.gov/customerservice/training.htm.

Harris, P. R., Moran, R. T., & Moran, S. V. (2007). *Managing cultural differences.* 6th ed. New York: Elsevier.

Heil, G., Parker, T., & Stephens, D. C. (1997). *One size fits one: Building relationships one customer and one employee at a time.* New York: Van Nostrand Reinhold.

Impact Learning (2001). Getting to the heart of the consumer. Available online: www.impactlearning.com/CRM-training/Customer-Service-Training/cs_course_outline.html.

Kaplan, D. (2001). Lunch or golf? Available online: kaplanmarketing.com/html/article.html.

Kotler, P. (1999). *How to create, win, and dominate markets.* New York: Free Press.

Leshicar, E. (2003). Business websites: Research directed for this text. Abilene Christian University, Abilene, TX.

Liraz, M. (1999). How is your market doing lately? In *Managing a small business.* Available online: bizmove.com/msb/marketing.htm.

National Public Radio (NPR) (2000). Customer service in business. Program during morning segment of daily newscast, February 10.

O'Hair, H. D., O'Rourke, J. S., & O'Hair, M. J. (2001). *Business communication: A framework for success.* Cincinnati: South-Western.

Pophal, L. (2000). Marketing plans work: 10 tips to make it happen. *Communication World,* October–November, pp. 22–24.

Rogers, E. M. (2003). *Diffusion of innovations.* 4th ed. New York: Free Press.

San Diego Manual. (2000). County of San Diego. Available online: www.sdapcd.co.sandiego.ca/train/custserv.pfd.

Service Quality Institute (2001). Customer service. Available online: www.customer-service.com/culture.cfm.

Streetwise tips on face-to-face selling (2001). Available online: businesstown.com/sales/face.

Underhill, P. (1999). *Why we buy: The science of shopping.* New York: Simon and Schuster.

Wechsler, W. (2001). *The six steps to excellence in selling.* Available online: totalselling.com.

Zeithaml, V. A., Parasuraman, A., & Berry, L. L. (1990). *Delivering quality service.* New York: Free Press.

EPILOGUE

What Can You Do with a Communication Major?

Far and away the best prize that life offers is the chance to work hard at work worth doing.

THEODORE ROOSEVELT

BENEFITS OF THEORY AND SKILLS

Based on what you have read in this book and discussed in your class, you should have begun to develop a number of important skills. At this point, consider how you can put those skills to work in your business and professional life. I hope that your knowledge of communication will help you develop better messages and present them more purposefully. In addition, the skills involved in good communication may help you be more accurate in other tasks, too.

Improving your communication skills will help you develop healthy relationships. As discussed in Chapter 1, communication is not merely a matter of technique. Certainly, the skills needed to create and manage messages are important. However, understanding and managing relationships is also a vital part of the total communication package.

Communication abilities will also help you create an effective leadership style. The information on group and organizational communication—and, for that matter, on areas of interpersonal/intercultural communication—is designed to help you become more effective in working with groups. To understand the dimensions of leadership and credibility will move you toward improving your unique style in leading groups.

Business and professional communication will also help you develop a more effective persuasive style. Think of ways to make your ideas clear, to be assertive, and to present information persuasively. With your purpose clearly in mind, know that various resources are available to help you in communication.

What you have learned about communication will help you develop an effective decision-making approach. One of the themes in the book has been to emphasize the need for a problem/solution orientation. Many people are hampered in decision making because they lack analytical skills. That is, they become stymied and incapable of moving through critical points in decision making.

Finally, your knowledge of interpersonal communication will help you develop a better interpersonal communication style. It's important to examine your own habits and patterns relating to people, right down to the emphases you place on words, your use of silence, and the like. By creatively thinking through the issues discussed in this text, you will have begun experimenting with your own communication style.

JOB CATEGORIES

Account executive

Advertising agency account executive

Airline flight attendant

Art gallery assistant

Art institute public relations/recruiting officer

Bankers association research associate

Beverage distributor/public relations specialist

Booking agent

Bookstore owner/manager

Broadcasting floor manager

Business manager

Cable television company sales

Campus activity coordinator

College teacher

Computer company personnel specialist

Computer company training specialist

Corporate communication training

Corporate purchasing agent

Cosmetics company promotion director

Data-processing manager

Department store buyer

Designer

Director of Chamber of Commerce

Director of conventions

Director of highway safety

Director of humanities council

Director of medical education center

Director of tourism

Elected official

Field surveyor for marketing research company

Food chain distribution manager

Food management

Food store account executive

Forensics coach for university

Graduate student in counseling

High school speech/theater teacher

Historical commission director

Hospital volunteer membership coordinator

Hotel management and manager for marketing communication

Hotel placement coordinator

Human development laboratory trainer

Human rights officer for development center

Industrial information specialist

Information specialist

Insurance claims adjuster

Insurance representative

CAREERS IN BUSINESS AND PROFESSIONAL COMMUNICATION

Think of communication skills as facilitating a number of career choices. Many jobs involve face-to-face communication, and still more involve analyzing issues and breaking down information. Jobs that involve administration, leadership, and organizational concerns are but a few areas in which communication majors can find their skills especially utilized. Some of the top jobs in recent listings have been related to communication, including corporate training and telemarketing positions.

Jobs today are moving toward information specialties. Individuals are needed who are good at working with people and who have important skills in critical thinking, decision making, and forming good relationships.

Since the marketplace changes rapidly, the job categories considered traditional today may not even exist tomorrow, as in the jobs shown in the job categories list. This makes it difficult for educators to prepare people for specific job categories. The better approach is to develop a core set of skills needed in life. You, the individual, are the constant. It is the job that changes.

JOB CATEGORIES

Insurance underwriting

Internal newsletter editor

International student coordinator

Investment company operations manager

Law firm recruiter

Liaison for foreign dignitaries for Chamber of Commerce

Lobbyist

Manager in automobile manufacturing

Manager of university career placement

Market analyst

Marketing coordinator for shopping mall

Marriage counselor

Mediator

Medical center publications editor

Mental health agency director

Military officer

Military recruitment

National sorority chapter consultant

Nonprofit organization communication director

Paralegal assistant

Power company training specialist

Private school fund-raiser

Production manager

Public information officer

Public opinion researcher

Public relations assistant in business firm

Public relations officer of hospital

Public relations representative

Publishing company editor

Publishing company traffic manager

Real estate investment company researcher

Red Cross Bank methods analyst

Research company sales trainer

Residence hall director

Retail store manager

Salesperson director of corporate communication

Speech writer in state government

Sports information officer

Staff member of community service agency

Staff writer for regional monthly magazine

State employees labor negotiator

State public relations assistant

State tourism bureau director

Stockbroker

Survey research consultant

Symphony orchestra relations

Telephone company manager of organizational development

Theater business manager

If you have the skills that can cut across almost any work situation, then you may be at a tremendous advantage for getting a job. Your knowledge of communication will help you prepare for any and all future opportunities.

The list of jobs comes from a survey of communication graduates from universities and colleges around the United States. Over two hundred job categories were discovered in this survey, which was conducted by a major publishing company. Use this list to stimulate your thinking about the future and what your skills as a communicator can do to enhance that future.

FINAL WORDS

Some important national leaders have reminded us of the importance of having an education that is not just job oriented. Too many students see college simply as a ticket to a job upon graduation. This view is shortsighted.

Today's society is changing much more quickly than a list of job categories. But the kind of education that has staying power is the kind that is founded on critical thinking, independence, and autonomy—in short, being a lifelong earner and being able to stand on your own two feet. A college education that gives students the ability to write well, to speak well, and to think well is one that can help them achieve ultimate success in life as well as in work.

Communications giant AT&T tracked the progress of nearly four hundred of its managers over a twenty-year period, according to Allen Splete, president of the Council of Independent Colleges, and found that liberal arts graduates enjoyed greater upward mobility than any other group. The study found that more than twice as many liberal arts graduates moved into middle or upper management as did graduates from other degree categories. These findings demonstrate the critical demand for people who are self-starters and who can help others in what is now a nationwide movement for self-renewal in the workplace.

Communication can be a beginning point and, when properly nourished, can provide a head start in responding to this critical need. General Motors' chair Roger Smith has said, "In an environment of rapid and constant change, we need people who can think of new strategies, as well as new ways of carrying out the old ones. The same mental processes can be acquired and sharpened in the study of liberal arts." John Gardner, former secretary of Health, Education, and Welfare and founder of Common Cause, also recommends the liberal arts: "Tomorrow's leaders must sooner or later climb out of the trenches of specialization and rise above the boundaries that separate the very segments of society. Only as generalists can they cope with the diversity of problems and multiple constituencies that contemporary leaders face." Andrew Wolfe, head of the Corporate Council on the Liberal Arts, compares a liberal arts graduate to a long-distance runner, succeeding despite obstacles and difficulty. Allen Splete concludes that the kind of education we are talking about emphasizes communication skills, analytical skills, and an understanding of the social sciences and humanities.

Earning a degree in communication is indeed making an investment in your life. It will pay dividends over the course of your lifetime in terms of corporate, personal, and family benefits. That is an outstanding return!

APPENDIX A

Communication Style in the Workplace

WHAT IS COMMUNICATION STYLE?

Everyone has a communication style. That means the way you communicate, such as how you process information. Some people get right to the point, while some take the time to chat and visit. Some people are serious and objective, while some are more emotional and demonstrative. Finally, some people focus entirely on themselves and what they are saying, whereas some observe others and pay attention to the effects of what they are saying.

These brief examples indicate how each communicator uniquely organizes information, internally processing that information, and presenting that information to others. Yet communication experts suggest that there are certain types of styles that, as you learn them, can help sharpen your communication skills and make you more valuable.

In his book *Working with Emotional Intelligence*, as well as in related materials, Daniel Goleman (1992) suggests that social style and relationship/communication ability are indeed highly valued commodities in the workplace. "There is a way to be smart," declares Goleman, "that is not IQ tested nor does it show on your transcript." Emotional intelligence (EI) involves these unspoken criteria for professional roles and job skills:

- Listening and oral communication
- Adaptability and creative responses to setback and obstacles
- Personal management
- Group and interpersonal effectiveness, cooperation, and teamwork
- Ability to negotiate disagreements
- Organizational effectiveness, desire to contribute, leadership potential
- Achievement drive, commitment
- Initiative and optimism

Goleman has observed the tangible effects of having strong EI. For instance, during downsizing, high-EI people are rarely laid off. Moreover, higher productivity results when sales staff have high EI levels, not just technical skills.

UNDERSTANDING COMMUNICATION STYLE

Communication style can be measured using a number of social and communication indices. We will review several of the many dozens available in the context of business and professional communication. These kinds of assessment devices are extremely useful for employees as well as for students and for clients in consulting. Once an individual learns his or her primary, secondary, and lesser-used styles, he or she can manage his or her communication behavior.

Social style and its twin, communication style, are based on research that clusters observations of human interaction in significant groupings. Scholars then evaluate these patterns of behaviors and develop underlying themes about them. Instruments that fit this description include the DISC model, the Myers-Briggs Type Indicator, the Thomas-Kilman Conflict Styles Instrument, and the Putnam-Wilson Conflict Styles Instrument. Many of these instruments have their roots in the pioneering work of Carl Jung and other personality theorists. And while there are differences among social-style indicators, researchers and practitioners have identified commonalities.

Darling's Social Style Model

John Darling (1985) originated a social style instrument (which was developed further by the Wilson Learning Company) that examines the qualities of assertive and responsive behaviors. Since its publication in scholarly journals, this approach has been acknowledged for its author's insights and fruitful discussion. Although the work is a starting point to discuss social and communication style, it has undergone change in its adaptation (that is, new words, adjusted concepts, and a new measuring assessment tool). A simplified version for this text is adapted from their work and applied here to help you understand and develop your personal style.

TYPES OF SOCIAL STYLES   Most style indicators begin with two dimensions, which are presented as two different axes on a graph. The *x*-axis represents low- or high-assertive behavior regarding a task or project—that is, how others view a person's communication and behavior as directive, even forceful. The *y*-axis identifies low and high emotional responsiveness—that is, how much a person communicates (high) or holds back and controls (low) his or her emotional responses to ideas and to people.

As the axes cross, they create four quadrants, which represent the four possible combinations of high and low assertiveness and high and low emotional responsiveness (see Figure A.1). Those four combinations, or styles, are as follows:

1. *Competitor.* Characterized by high task assertiveness and low emotional responsiveness. Strengths include the following:
   - Task oriented
   - Brief, factual, to the point

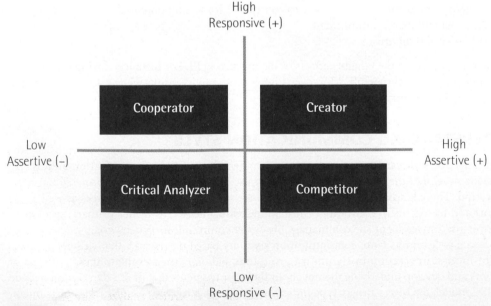

FIGURE A.1   Model of Social Styles

- Pragmatic
- Decisive
- Result oriented
- Candid
- Objective
- Competitive in a win-lose scenario

2. *Creator.* Characterized by high task assertiveness and high emotional responsiveness. Strengths include the following:
   - "Big picture" perspective
   - Fresh, novel viewpoint
   - Risk taker, spontaneous
   - Persuasive, good communicator
   - Inspirational, motivational
   - Decisive
   - Imaginative
   - Friendly, enthusiastic, outgoing

3. *Cooperator.* Characterized by low task assertiveness and high emotional responsiveness. Strengths include the following:
   - Sympathetic, sensitive
   - Trusting
   - Cooperative
   - Loyal, caring
   - Supportive
   - Diplomatic
   - Easygoing, patient
   - Respectful

4. *Critical analyzer.* Characterized by low task assertiveness and low emotional responsiveness. Strengths include the following:
   - Precise
   - Deliberate
   - Systematic
   - Information gathering
   - Industrious, well organized
   - Objective
   - Logical, serious
   - Critical, prudent

ANALYSIS OF SOCIAL STYLES   Each of these four styles is effective in specific situations. For instance, at times, the determination of the competitor style is really important. At other times, the creator's vision and imagination inspire people. The critical analyzer style's precision is exactly what's needed in some situations, yet in others, it's refreshing to be with an easy-going cooperator.

Conversely, each style is ineffective in certain situations—for both the individual and for others around him or her. The competitor's task orientation and determination may come across as being overcontrolling and uncaring. The creator's imagination and "can do" attitude may appear unrealistic or lacking discipline. The supportive, easygoing style of the cooperator may be seen as permissive or overconforming, and the precision of the critical analyzer may be perceived as inflexibility.

Cooperator Style

☐ Sympathetic, sensitive
☐ Trusting
☐ Cooperative
☐ Loyal, caring
☐ Supportive
☐ Diplomatic
☐ Easygoing, patient
☐ Respectful

Total Score ———————
Divide by 8 ———————
Percentage Score ———————

Creator Style

☐ "Big picture" perspective
☐ Fresh, novel viewpoint
☐ Risk taker, spontaneous
☐ Persuasive, good communicator
☐ Inspirational, motivational
☐ Decisive
☐ Imaginative
☐ Friendly, enthusiastic, outgoing

Total Score ———————
Divide by 8 ———————
Percentage Score ———————

Critical Analyzer Style

☐ Precise
☐ Deliberate
☐ Systematic
☐ Information, gathering
☐ Information, well organized
☐ Objective
☐ Logical, serious
☐ Critical, prudent

Total Score ———————
Divide by 8 ———————
Percentage Score ———————

Competitor Style

☐ Task oriented
☐ Brief, factual, to the point
☐ Pragmatic
☐ Decisive
☐ Result oriented
☐ Candid
☐ Objective
☐ Competitive in a win/lose scenario

Total Score ———————
Divide by 8 ———————
Percentage Score ———————

FIGURE A.2 Self-Assessment of Social Style   *Source:* Keywords adapted from Darling (1985). The scoring model and methods were developed for this text.

ASSESSING YOUR SOCIAL STYLE   To assess your social and communication style using this model, complete Figure A.2. Each of the four boxes identifies one of the four styles: competitor, creator, cooperator, and critical analyzer. For each style, there is a set of adjectives presented as a checklist. Simply check each adjective that you believe applies to you—that is, it describes what you see in yourself or what you perceive others see in you. To obtain your score, add up the number of items you have checked and divide that number by 8. Then multiply by 100 to obtain a percentage. Record these numbers as shown in the figure.

After you have completed Figure A.2 (that is, you have determined scores for all four sections), chart the information on Figure A.3 by indicating your style scores as percentages, from Figure A.2 and then marking the percentage. Your "Primary" style is that for which you obtained the highest score, your "Secondary" style is that for which you obtained the second-highest score,

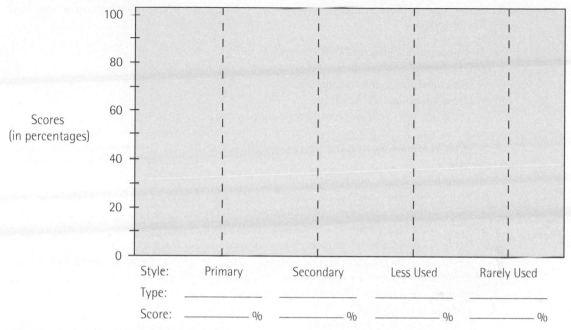

FIGURE A.3 Graph of Social Style Assessment

and so on. Enter the appropriate information for each of the four categories. Then connect the plotted points to create a graphed line.

To determine whether you see yourself as others do, ask a coworker, spouse, or friend to complete Figure A.2 based on how they perceive you. Then compare other people's scores with your own.

ADAPTING YOUR STYLE TO OTHERS As noted earlier, each of the four styles has advantages and disadvantages. By knowing your style and its relative strengths and weaknesses, you can adapt your behavior to leverage the positive aspects of that style (Darling, 1985). This isn't to say that you shouldn't be you but rather that you should realize the possible and negative side effects of your natural style. Consider these guidelines:

1. A *competitor* needs to pay attention and be less goal oriented. Thus, he or she needs to be more approachable.
2. A *creator* needs to hold back and be less impulsive. Thus, he or she needs to be more level-headed.
3. A *cooperator* needs to speed up, try new things, and be more goal directed. His or her slow pace makes others want to move more rapidly.
4. A *critical analyzer* needs to move on and avoid the paralysis that can come from too much analysis. There is a time to decide.

COMMUNICATING WITH PEOPLE WITH OTHER STYLES You can enhance your social style by managing its indicators, as just described. And when you perceive another person to be of a particular style, you can adapt and match that style. As always, respect for each person's style is important. Here are some suggestions for communicating with people who have other social styles:

1. To communicate effectively with *competitors*:
   - Be punctual.
   - Get to the point; don't waste time.
   - Use main points and key facts.
   - Use linear organization (first, second, third), and stay on the topic.
   - Keywords: *factual, logic, right, truth, explain, data, evidence, no-nonsense approach, efficiency, moving quickly, timing, practical, hard work, determination, promptness, decide.*
2. To communicate effectively with *creators*:
   - Plan social time.
   - Show enthusiasm, energy, and excitement.
   - Refer to the "big picture."
   - Refer to main ideas, but summary and paraphrase also work well.
   - Keywords: *"big picture," "can do" attitude, vision, future, energetic, get going, fun, relating to ideas, correlation, dreams, intuition, feel good, go for it.*
3. To communicate effectively with *cooperators*:
   - Listen and be genuine.
   - Show cooperation and support.
   - Relax; don't be in a hurry; speak softly.
   - Encourage the expression of ideas and don't judge.
   - Keywords: *support, team, cooperation, safety, honest, good-faith effort, trust, sincerity, genuine, low pressure, no hurry, easy going, relaxing, touch, helpful, kind.*
4. To communicate effectively with a *critical analyzer*:
   - Be on time.
   - Share a lot of details; know your proposal extremely well.
   - Identify pros and cons; use benchmark comparisons; show advantages and low risks.
   - Determine action steps and make plans; follow up in writing.
   - Keywords: *logic, analysis, little risk, safety, planning, doing in advance, research, database, measures, evaluation, strict, detailed notes, written confirmation, systematic, cause-and-effect.*

Smalley's Animal Metaphors

Gary Smalley's books and films present helpful strategies for understanding the personalities of the people we are close to. Though intended primarily for spouses and close others, these strategies can be applied to work associates and organizational life, too.

Smalley (1999) has cleverly identified four animal types, or personalities, that are similar to Darling's four social styles:

- The *lion* is bold and assertive like the competitor.
- The *otter* is fun loving and similar to the creator.
- The *golden retriever* is cooperative and sensitive to the feelings and needs of others, much like the cooperator.
- The *beaver* matches the critical analyzer, working with great precision and detail.

Lion Style		Otter Style	
Tasks charge	Competitive	Tasks risks	Promoter
Determined	Decision maker	Visionary	Enjoys change
Assertive	Leader	Motivator	Creative
Firm	Goal driven	Energetic	Group oriented
Bold	Self-reliant	Fun loving	Mines easily
Purposeful	Enjoys challenges	Likes variety	Avoids detail
Enterprising	Adventurous	Very verbal	Optimistic
"Let's do it now."		"Trust me, it will work out."	
Total Score ————		**Total Score** ————	
Total × 2 ————		**Total × 2** ————	

Golden Retriever Style		Beaver Style	
Loyal	Adaptable	Deliberate	Discerning
Nondemanding	Sympathetic	Controlled	Detailed
Even keel	Thoughtful	Reserved	Analytical
Avoids conflict	Nurturing	Predictable	Inquisitive
Enjoys routine	Patient	Practical	Precise
Dislikes change	Tolerant	Orderly	Persistent
Good listener	Deep relationships	Factual	Scheduled
"Let's keep things the way they are."		"How was it done in the past?"	
Total Score ————		**Total Score** ————	
Total × 2 ————		**Total × 2** ————	

FIGURE A.4   Self-Assessment of Personality Style   *Source:* Based on Smalley (1999)

ASSESSING YOUR STYLE   To assess your style using this approach involves using another checklist (see Figure A.4). This time, you will circle the adjectives that apply to you. Within each of the four boxes (or animal categories), you will count the number of items circled and multiply by 2. After calculating a raw score for each box, you will compare the scores to see in which area you scored the highest, next highest, and so on. Your highest score indicates your primary style and so on.

Other Models of Communication Styles

As stated at the outset of this appendix, there are dozens of models of social and communication style. To familiarize yourself with some of the most commonly referenced models, see Figure A.5, which compares these models across common elements.

Types	1	2	3	4
Which Way Model	My Way	Our Way	Your Way	No, Low Way
Darling's Social-Style Indicators	Competitor	Creator	Cooperator	Critical Analyzer
Conflict	Win/Lose	Win-Win	Lose-Win	Lose-Lose
DISC Style	Driver	Interactor	Interactor	Cautious, Steady
Thomas-Kilman Conflict Styles Instrument	Competitive	Collaborative	Accommodating	Avoiding
Putnam-Wilson Conflict Styles Instrument	Control	Solution-oriented		Non-confrontational
Blake & Mouton	High Productivity/	High Productivity/	Low Productivity/	Low Productivity/
Managerial Grid	Low People	High People	High People	Low People
Carl Jung	Thinker	Intuitor	Feeler	Sensor
Smalley's Animal-Style Metaphors	Lion	Otter	Golden Retriever	Beaver

FIGURE A.5   Comparison of Models of Communication Styles

References and Readings

Darling, J. R. (1985). Managing up in academe: The role of social style. *Texas Tech Journal of Education, 12,* no. 2.

Goleman, D. (1998). *Working with emotional intelligence.* New York: Bantam.

Richmond, V. P. (1990). Communication in the classroom: Power and motivation. *Communication Education, 39,* 181–195.

Smalley, G. (1999). *Keys to loving relationships.* [Film series]. Yukon, OK: Smalley Enterprises.

Station, T. (2000). Are you in your right mind? *American Way,* November 1, pp. 151–158.

APPENDIX B

Changes in Organizational Cultures

Effecting change in an organizational culture involves two major steps: (1) defining the target of the change effort (*what*) and (2) identifying the appropriate method of creating change (*how*). This appendix is organized according to these steps.

STEP 1: DEFINING THE TARGET OF THE CHANGE EFFORT

The elements of organizational culture that may need change fall into several categories, ranging from new formation (such as a new unit or a new company) to adjustments (such as changing a job description). Specific types of needs are identified in the following sections (Arthur Andersen, 1998).

Design Needs

Change is sometimes needed to resolve for overall design questions, which are often related to major development.

EXAMPLES

- Defining a new organization, division, or department
- Re-engineering a new process of producing a product or service
- Designing new positions to produce a good or service

Ownership and Location Needs

Some situations call for change because of changes in ownership and/or location.

EXAMPLES

- Acquisitions, mergers, consolidations
- Changes of location
- Modification of leadership resulting in changes of reporting to authority and team ownership of projects

A brief case will illustrate this type of need: A small oil company was bought out by another small company in Texas. Not only was the headquarters relocated, but employee roles changed along with systems, budgets, and so on. A cultural issue that affected employee morale was that the new owners established a fairly formal dress code, which was contrary to the more casual atmosphere of the previously independent company. Employees of that company felt insulted when they were told that they had to dress up more.

Economic Needs

Some changes are demanded because of increasing economic or market pressures. Survival even of large companies and organizations may depend on adaptation to these economic conditions:

EXAMPLES

- Market tastes change.
- Customer service needs change.
- Increased competition for goods or services is provided, including globalization.
- Increased productivity is needed.
- Cycle and process time needs to be reduced.
- Error rates need improvement.
- Cost pressures demand cost reductions, including downsizing of the workforce or reductions in products and services.
- Rapid growth involves upsizing and quantity of products and services as well as the addition of new products and services.

Technology Needs

Technology sometimes changes so quickly that an organization must face the prospect of not having newer technology. Without upgrades in technology, an organization can experience problems with poor quality, poor efficiency, and poor image. For example, the steel industry in the United States did not upgrade its technology significantly during the increased global competition and highly competitive decades of the late twentieth century. Consequently, it lost huge market shares to the more technically advanced steel industries in Japan, Canada, and Germany.

Human Resource Needs

The need for change may originate in human resource issues.

EXAMPLES

- Job alignment and retrofitting of an employee for a particular niche in the organization
- Ergonomic needs, such as safety improvement, removal of potential damage to health, and improvements in work-flow processing that benefit employee morale
- Pay structure and other benefits that realign an organization appropriately
- Need for employee self-esteem, achievement, responsibility, and growth

Communication Process Needs

Many communication functions contribute to an organization's mission, goals, product and service outcomes, employee satisfaction levels, and community and customer service satisfaction. Changes are sometimes needed because of one or more of the following concerns:

EXAMPLES

- Insufficient and incomplete information between management and employees
- Lack of understanding between people or between divisions
- Lack of understanding of the organization's focus: mission, purpose, values, and goals
- Employee orientation and training for new processes
- Decision making
- Team building
- Motivation and influence for innovations and changes
- Interview communication for hiring, evaluation, reprimand, and dismissal
- Conduct of group meetings

Environmental Needs

Environmental needs include changes in the immediate or broader community and within customers.

EXAMPLES

- Societal attitudes and demands for change
- Customer demands
- Changes in suppliers
- Changes in delivery systems

Figure B.1 on the next page provides a useful tool for assessing the existing qualities of an organization's culture.

STEP 2: IDENTIFYING THE APPROPRIATE METHOD OF CREATING CHANGE

In a certain sense, this entire book provides resources for change in that it considers the role of communication in the workplace and how improving communication can result in improved outcomes. The following sections identify specific methods of effecting change.

Leader-Directed Model

The *leader-directed model* of change involves the executive leadership dictating change and expecting employees to follow. The real strength of this model is its effectiveness in situations involving emergencies, dire conditions, and other impediments to seeking input. In addition, many employees are willing to cooperate and to do what is good for the organization. Under some circumstances, following this model is necessary—for instance, as the result of a lawsuit, a legal mandate, a board of director's mandate, or mandates from stockholders or corporate headquarters. In sum, when implemented with care and concern, the leader-directed model can accomplish change quickly.

This approach has several disadvantages, however. One is the potential for erosion of morale over time, especially if this approach is used repeatedly. A second disadvantage is that

Cultural Variable		Feedback Style						
Leadership and communication style	Authoritarian, closed, elite	1	2	3	4	5		Open, high participation
Social relationships	Unnecessary, only lines of responsibility	1	2	3	4	5		Networking for authority, morale, and productivity
Ethnocentrism	Competitive toward others	1	2	3	4	5		Cooperative, open to groups
Thought patterns	Linear, sequential	1	2	3	4	5		Picturelike
Role behaviors	Roles highly defined by Leadership	1	2	3	4	5		Roles defined by employees
Cultural space	Tight control of territoriality, determined by desk size, etc.	1	2	3	4	5		Status not determined by desk size, etc.
Cultural time	Task oriented, promptness	1	2	3	4	5		People emphasized
Touch	Low touch	1	2	3	4	5		High touch
Dress	Insistence on proper dress, uniformity of dress	1	2	3	4	5		Little restriction on dress style
Rewards/recognition	Individual performance	1	2	3	4	5		Group performance
Decision making	Centralized	1	2	3	4	5		Decentralized
Political climate	High power, dominant	1	2	3	4	5		Low power, low intensity
Values toward	Theory X: People are lazy	1	2	3	4	5		Theory Y: People are capable
World view	High fatalism	1	2	3	4	5		Low fatalism
Themes	Success through hard work	1	2	3	4	5		Motivation and creativity lead to success
High/low context	Information implicit	1	2	3	4	5		Information explicit

FIGURE B.1   Analyzing Organizational Culture

employees' zeal for change will likely be reduced or missing because they will not feel ownership of or responsibility for the decision. Third, following the leader-directed approach can increase the implementation cycle time. Users who are affected by the change will slow down, experience confusion, and show dissatisfaction—all of which waste time.

Group-Input Model

The *group-input model* seeks information for conducting a problem analysis and identifying a solution. For instance, ad-hoc and blue ribbon committees can make recommendations. Outside consultants can supply advice for change. Large-group meetings can offer leadership proposals, but small focus groups can modify, expand, and offer direction. Surveys and feedback can identify attitudes and behaviors that will provide evidence in making decisions.

This approach has the advantages of allowing broader input and producing greater satisfaction. Disadvantages include the time lapse and the extent of human and financial resources involved.

Education and Training Model

In the *education and training model*, the information manager in charge of organizational change uses all the resources available to make changes through education and training. This model recognizes that people adjust to new ideas over time and offers a reasonable opportunity for employees to learn. Through education and skill development, people invest in change.

The steps involved in implementing the education and training approach are as follows:

1. Develop team members who share the beliefs of the team leader regarding the mission, purpose, goals, and values of education and training. The team can then become a planning group and help shape the training program.
2. Describe and identify the change. As stated earlier, determine specifically who and what is affected. Define the outcomes and determine how to measure them so as to determine completion. Then, plan action goals and steps to achieve those outcomes.
3. Do a cultural analysis of the systemic forces that are operating within the organization's culture. Ask these questions:
   - What are the resources?
   - What are the strengths, weaknesses, opportunities, and threats (that is, a SWOT analysis)?
   - What are the overall driving and resisting forces of the culture?
4. Prepare and communicate the case.
5. Develop concrete action steps to follow and evaluate how well they work.

A brief case will illustrate how people can buy into a program of change with the appropriate training: Years ago, when I first started using technology in my university teaching and in my consulting and training, training in the use of technology was encouraged but not required. I participated in the training, and it showed me how to change my skills. That, in turn, shaped my attitude and made me excited about using the new technology.

Organizational Metaphor Model

The *organizational metaphor model* also takes place over time and is strategically developed, similarly to the two previously discussed models. The metaphor model assumes that every organization has key metaphors (such as slogans, phrases, and keywords) that define its identity and convey that identity to others. By changing the central metaphors, you can change the system as well as outsiders' perception of it.

Of course, the changes in metaphors must be accompanied by changes in actions, too. For instance, in the mid-1980s, when Ford adopted a quality metaphor ("At Ford, Quality Is Job 1"), it also made design changes (introducing the Taurus), communication changes (increasing employee input), and structural leadership changes (developing managers and supervisors who listened and used participatory leadership styles).

Words really do matter, however. The communication discipline has long been aware of the power of word pictures for persuasion and inspiration. Recently, the literature on organizational culture has discovered the most significant codes that organize reality for members of organizations. That is, research by noted cognitive scientists such as John Grinder (1985) in the field of neurolinguistic programming (NLP) has extensively applied the auditory, visual, and kinesthetic metaphors that anchor learning and inspire change.

Researchers have found a number of metaphors to be effective in communicating identity and change in organizations. This section contains not only the categories of organizational metaphors but also examples adapted from the original research of Christine Fischer (2000), whose survey of some 500 employees from crosssections of job categories in a large medical center resulted in a rich set of illustrations of organizational metaphors.

ORGANIZATIONAL IDENTITY METAPHORS

1. *Family.* "Some people here really care about each other." "My department is like a family left to care for itself without a safety net."
2. *Extended family.* "The organization is my anchor. It has seen me grow old and age and still leaves its door open for me."
3. *Community.* "A big city." "The organization is like a big city with everyone involved in their areas but coming together often for the good of the whole." "A small city with different branches of the government, some run by honest, hard-working people, some run by people who think the organization owes them something."

ORGANIZATIONAL CHANGE METAPHORS

1. *Too much change.* "Too many changes here, not stable. You never know what is going to happen next."
2. *A herd of elephants.* "There are many strong individuals here. They can nurture or they can panic."
3. *Winds of a tornado.* "The changes here cause upheaval in the lives of staff both personally and professionally. In some areas the winds barely touched the ground, but in other areas massive destruction took place."
4. *Survival.* "Our employer is like a fortress and by working together we can survive, severe competition." "We are like a huge clumsy dinosaur trying not to be extinct. I need to survive somehow, and I may have to trample some people in the process."
5. *Journey.* "A car on a long road trip has long stretches of smooth road with occasional twists and turns and an occasional flat tire." "A tractor pulling a hayride keeps breaking down, and sometimes people fall off but all in a fun ride." "Like a hayride, it's a big, slow-moving machine."

ORGANIZATIONAL COMPETITION, POWER, AND CONFLICT METAPHORS

1. *Lack of common goals.* "Sometimes people don't have the same goals and we work against each other."
2. *Control.* "Like a slave ship, only certain people benefit from everyone's hard work." "We are the galley ship powered by the rowing of slaves. The people who keep this organization going have no voice in decisions or direction, they are only told to work harder."
3. *Weathering one storm after another.* "A ship on the ocean riding the waves of change and those of us in the hold are feeling the greatest turbulence."
4. *A ladder in need of repair.* "No one cares about the lower rungs."
5. *A dictatorship.* "My way or the highway. Don't let the door hit you on the way out."
6. *Conflicts.* "A boiling stew. Disorganization. Conflicts within and without."

ORGANIZATIONAL STRATEGY METAPHORS

1. *Vision.* "A ship without a captain. We are going in circles."
2. *Bad to worse.* "Out of the frying pan into the fire."
3. *Confusion.* "The right hand doesn't know what the left hand is doing."
4. *Survival.* "Moving to put out fires but doing little to prevent them."

ORGANIZATIONAL PRACTICES METAPHORS

1. *Financial waste.* "Time is money." "Penny smart, dollar stupid." "A man who breaks up the foundation of his house because he needs to remodel the inside of the house."
2. *Efficiency.* "Dinosaur, move ever so slowly. Cling to the outdated because it is the way it has always done things."

ORGANIZATIONAL HIERARCHY METAPHORS

1. *Too many chefs.* "Too many chefs and not enough cooks. Too many managers don't actually do enough, whereas the workers are fewer and fewer and constantly overworked and understaffed."
2. *Beehive.* "A beehive where everyone thinks they are the Queen Bee."
3. *Fiefdom.* "Too many departments, divisions, etc., each with its own king, courtiers, and each with its own agenda."

CASE EXAMPLES OF ORGANIZATIONAL CHANGE

Ford Motor Company

Ford, mentioned earlier, experienced a drop in sales by the early to mid-1980s and was determined to make a major turnaround. After making changes, Ford rose to the number one spot in sales revenues for American-made cars and stayed in that position for a period of time.

How did this happen? By adopting a quality metaphor ("At Ford, Quality Is Job 1"), Ford made these changes:

- Major design changes, introducing the Taurus
- Significant communication changes, employing teams, feedback, and employee input
- Structural leadership changes, developing managers and supervisors who listened and used participatory leadership styles
- Role restructuring, offering early retirement and buyouts for leaders and workers who simply could not adjust to the other changes

Sears versus Wal-Mart

In the 1970s and 1980s, Sears saw itself in a shrinking market and adjusted its mission through a hands-off approach. It discontinued producing a catalog by the late 1980s/early 1990s and hunkered down in a fortress mentality.

During somewhat the same period, Sam Walton built a retail empire by seeing the huge market segment left untouched by Sears and J. C. Penney. Walton saw small-town people who wanted low-priced merchandise (Charan & Tichy, 1998). He applied the principles of vision and mission, customer service, team building, communication, relationship development, quick inventory turns, less inventory stock, and less wasted time. Walmart continues to be a megacompany.

Nike

Nike's success took off with the Air Jordan basketball shoe, but sales collapsed when the fad cooled and Jordan became injured and retired. Upon analyzing the plummet, Nike segmented its audience and created footwear products for a variety of populations and sports, not just basketball. The results were an annual sales growth rate of 39 percent and profits of 41 percent between 1995 and 1997. Now, just about anything connected with sports can be bought with a Nike brand (Charan & Tichy, 1998).

References and Readings

Arthur Andersen Consulting Group. (1998). *Change management series.* Dallas, TX: Anderson Change Management.

Charan, R., & Tichy, N. (1998). *Every business can be a growth business.* New York: Anchor.

Fischer, C. M. (2000). Exploring meaning creation: Use of metaphorical analysis to investigate organizational change. Paper presented to the National Communication Association, Seattle.

Grinder, J. (1985). *Neurolinguistic programming.* Boulder, CO: People Press.

APPENDIX C

Communication Networks in the Workplace

At its core, organizational communication is relational. People talk with others about various topics. To describe the pattern of who talks with whom is to define *communication networks* within organizations. The discovery of groups of individuals who frequently communicate with each other is not new in communication research, but its application to organizational research has enormous consequences. To best understand the social nature of communication flow within organizational cultures, we will first examine basic concepts about network analysis.

NETWORK ANALYSIS AND INFORMATION ROLES

Network Analysis

Network analysis refers to the informal interaction patterns observed among members of organizations. When looking at informal, rather than formal, communication patterns, this study in communication is called *network analysis*. The visual network models that best represent these interaction patterns are called *sociograms* or, using more colloquial language, *"office connections," "office cliques," "office rumor mill,"* or *"the grapevine."* In fact, one criticism of early management theory was that it ignored the importance of communication networks as powerful sources of organizational influence.

Information and Influence Roles in Networks

Network analysis identifies the individuals who communicate frequently or who serve as "pipelines," passing information from one person to another. The following roles and group identities all serve as vital sources in managing the information flow within a network:

1. *Links* comprise pairs of individuals who share information one way (from one to the other) or two ways (in a mutual communication relationship).
2. *Cliques* are groups that communicate frequently and share information. To the degree that clique members feel cohesive, they not only influence each other but also have the potential to stimulate productivity or kill it. For example, office workers may motivate each other toward high productivity or they may resist innovations.
3. A *bridge* passes information from the clique he or she is a member of across the boundaries directly to another clique.
4. A *liaison* links two or more cliques but is not a member of any one clique.
5. A *gatekeeper* opens or closes off information to individuals within a clique, acting as a valve for information flow. In playing this role, a gatekeeper can prevent information overload, screen irrelevant information, and facilitate vital information to increase the clique's efficiency.
6. An *opinion leader* is the person to whom others in the network go for information and advice. Leaders are usually sought because of their competence, sociability, and trustworthiness.
7. *Isolates* do not pass information and generally are outside the mainstream cliques. Isolates may be high in communication-avoidance behaviors, likely prefer working alone, and may suffer from diminished peer confidence and little social attraction.

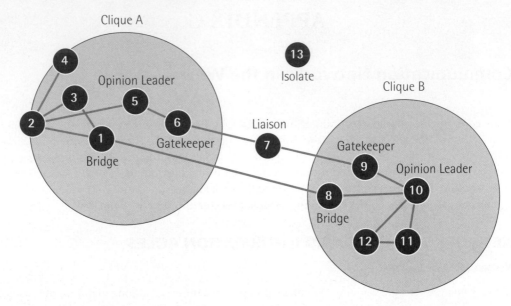

FIGURE C.1 Simplified Network Analysis

A simplified network analysis showing these various communication roles is depicted in Figure C.1. The two cliques, A and B, are determined by who talks most frequently with whom. As shown in the figure, liaison 7 passes information through gatekeepers 6 and 9 into their respective cliques, A and B. Opinion leaders 5 and 10 influence their respective groups with interpretation and advice. Clique A is more interactive than clique B. For whatever reason, person 4 is out of the information loop in clique A. Person 13 is an isolate.

A different type of network analysis blends a variety of positional roles with informal roles. In this enhanced version, it is possible to observe sources of ideas, the direction of influence flow, and friendships—all superimposed on a map of formal organizational roles (see Figure C.2). These interlocking roles can reveal much about an organizational culture.

Rumor Transmission

The idea that information flows in an interpersonal, informal network carries additional significance when we consider the nature of rumor transmission. Classic investigations in corporations have revealed that in normal business situations, the informal "grapevine" is between 75 and 95 percent correct. Certainly, that 5 to 25 percent error can be vital to the truth of the story.

Davis (1973, p. 46) reports an incident that illustrates the rumor accuracy issue:

> I recall, for instance, one grapevine story about a welder marrying the general manager's daughter that was true with regard to his getting married, the date, the church and other details. The one wrong fact in the report was that the girl was not the general manager's daughter, but merely had the same last name. Yet this one fact made the whole story erroneous—even though the rest of it was correct.

Many managers would gladly "prune" the ugly growth of the proverbial grapevine. Experts in this field underscore the fact that the *rumor* is the untrue portion of the message and should be

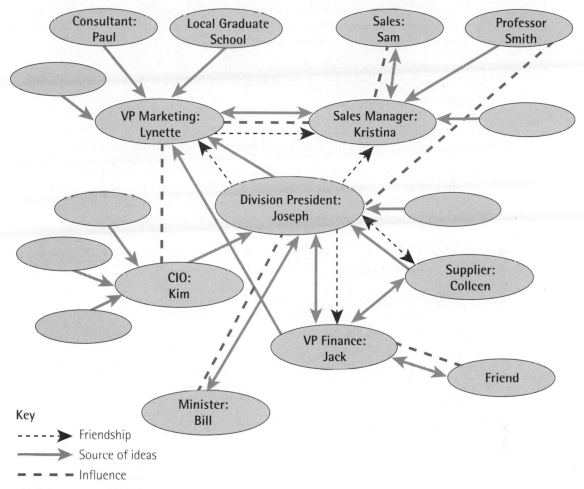

FIGURE C.2 Network Analysis Showing Influence

stopped immediately, as it may result in distorting future planning, acting on false information, or creating a false dissatisfaction scenario.

This transmission phenomenon is illustrated by the "gossip game" or "telephone game." The individual who starts the game has two chances to whisper a phrase to another individual. Then the second individual has two chances to whisper the same phrase (or the phrase that he or she heard) to a third individual, and so on. After a number of rounds, the original phrase becomes almost unrecognizable. For instance, "butterfly's nest" soon becomes something like "butter is best when it flies west."

In the same way, information spread via the grapevine can easily become distorted in these ways:

- *Leveling* is the process of taking out certain facts before passing on information.
- *Sharpening* involves selecting certain details and stretching them out of proportion.
- *Assimilation* includes inserting more facts than the original information contained.

The transmission of a rumor is usually short-lived—often, just hours or a couple of days—but the negative effects can survive for months. The initial believability of the rumor, its longevity, and its intensity and possible effects depend on several factors:

- Relevance of the rumor for individuals' sense of security or self-esteem
- The intensity with which the original rumor was told (for example, an atmosphere of urgency)
- The size of the organization (the smaller the company, the greater the impact)
- The anxiety level already present in the organization (for instance, if a few people have already been laid off, the rumor will persist that "they were only the first of hundreds")

Given the speed with which rumors can be communicated, along with the damage they can do, future managers should recognize the importance of confronting rumors directly and immediately. Organizations that have an objective source of information and a relatively speedy means of getting information back to employees are more successful in dissipating rumors.

References and Readings

Charan, R., & Tichy, N. (1998). *Every business is a growth business.* New York: Anchor.

Davis, K. (1973). The care and cultivation of the corporate grapevine. *Dun's*, July, pp. 44–47.

APPENDIX D

Written Communication in the Workplace: Reports, Proposals, Résumés, Letters, and E-mail Etiquette

IMPORTANCE OF BUSINESS AND PROFESSIONAL WRITING

Written communication for business and professional contexts is not only an expectation, but many employers complain that their employees lack necessary writing skills. This deficit results in a workplace gap, demanding more competent and knowledgeable workers. In fact, most experts agree that writing comprises over 20 percent of daily work, when we count reports, e-mails, text messages, memos, proposals, Web amendments, and the like.

REPORT WRITING

Reports can be simple forms or complex documents. Generally, reports are highly organized documents that present facts for information or call for a decision. Consider, too, that memos also follow a report patterns. Typically, reports or memos have one of two functions: (1) to inform, or (2) to analyze (called an examination report) in order to make a decision.

Strategies for Report Writing

Strategies for written presentation include several factors as you see next. Overall, however, we can state that reports typically (1) identify an issue/problem, (2) present facts to support a contention or present analysis within a problem, and (3) indicate a solution or future direction.

STICK TO FACTS, EXPERIENCES, AND OBSERVATIONS   A written report focuses on data or facts which can be qualitative or quantitative. It is not a document that demands so much essay approach as clarity, directness, and information.

IDENTIFY THE FORMALITY NEEDED   A report may be formal or informal. Know the audience. If in doubt, go more formally. However, it is rarely a good idea to use abbreviations, too many contractions, or inside information or acronyms known only to a few unless you are sure that the reader will understand what you mean. So, in referring to the American Council of Education, for instance, you are better off to state the full name rather than ACE, unless the readers know clearly the meanings.

STAY ORGANIZED   Reports or memos must not only stay with facts or produce enough information to call for a decision but also be organized in a way that readers can easily follow. Here are contrasting brief illustrations. Can you tell what makes the first illustration less compelling than the second?

> *Incorrect*: The meeting later today will consider the dimensions of curriculum and faculty. We've been round and round on this before, but we never get anywhere. So, I'm wanting us to figure where we are going, why, and what will it cost? Then, how many

faculty will we need for the project when it's all said and done. I don't know about you, but I'm hoping we'll get somewhere soon. I'm sending this to you and your chair. See you this afternoon.

Better: The agenda for the meeting at 3:00 in the conference room is to make a final conclusion on these items:

1. Curriculum
2. Faculty needed
3. Budget needed

In considering the March report, we hope to analyze the attached budget and faculty directions in making this decision by the end of the meeting which concludes at 4:30.

USE REPORT WRITING STRATEGIES   Written reports are not like other written documents, so remember the audience, the purpose, and the need for facts, and consider the formality all indicated above. Also, reports or memos typically follow patterns captured in these suggestions (Kuiper, 2009):

1. In the introduction, make clear purpose and context.
2. Indicate a main point to the document.
3. Present sufficient information so as not to leave unanswered questions.
4. Stick with the one point at a time, using numbers or bullets in readable formatting.
5. Use white space.
6. Have a strategic ending—leave a positive impression.
7. Call for action if needed—don't keep the reader guessing what you want; indicate "next steps."
8. Check and edit for spelling and grammar.

We hope you enjoyed your time in our workshop today! We would like to hear your comments concerning our written presentation. Please circle the most appropriate number for each question according to the following scale:

1 = Poor   2 = Needs Improvement   3 = Average   4 = Good   5 = Excellent

1. The written presentation had meaningful support and was well prepared.	1 2 3 4 5
2. The presentation was informative.	1 2 3 4 5
3. The materials followed a highly readable and usable format.	1 2 3 4 5
4. The activities and illustrations were relevant to the topic.	1 2 3 4 5
5. Your overall opinion of the written presentation.	1 2 3 4 5

If you rated any factors as "Needs Improvements" (2) or "Poor" (1), please provide an explanation and suggestions.

FIGURE D.1 Writing Evaluation for a Seminar or Workshop

It's worth elaborating on this final point. Most good report writing is like a briefing, addressing the key point, explaining with support, easy-to-follow formatting, and ending strongly.

PROPOSAL WRITING

Proposals are documents that ask for something to change or to happen. A proposal for a new course, a new program, a new product line, or for a new position all illustrate instances of when a proposal is necessary. Proposals usually are very detailed and, like reports, are factually oriented.

Steps in Writing Proposals

In addition to reports, the ability to write an effective proposal is a significantly important skill, one that can set future leaders apart. These steps are not necessarily linear nor are the same for every proposal, but these beginning points are worth noting. We highly recommend, also, that you use a software template in Word or from a source that also guides your topic and formatting. Like any report, you want data, good organization, white space, and to be sure to check for grammar and spelling. Authors like Yaklef (2009) believe that electronic sources have caused lazy writing, so be sure to review your work for objectivity, grammar, spelling, and an overall look of professionalism and ease of reading.

1. *Mission and Vision.* What is the reason for this proposal that stems from a deep longing or need? Why is this proposal important in light of the organization's future? How does it link with other products, programs, or services?
2. *Overview or Executive Summary.* This section presents a summary of the goals, needs, and reasons for the proposal. Most of all, this section presents the main point and objectives of the proposal and the direction of the plan, which is why it is sometimes called an executive summary.
3. *The Problem or Issues.* Understanding what this proposal addresses and why this topic is an issue becomes an important point. Like any document, you must show reasons, offer evidence, cite examples, or provide some data so the reader is compelled to note the problem.
4. *Solution or Plan.* This section presents a plan or method of resolving the problem or issue. The plan often consists of detailed lists and resources needed. The points that follow often are actually points of a plan or they stand as unique considerations.
5. *Target Market or Audience.* This section indicates demographics, strategic markets, ideal customers, and expanding markets, to name some typical subpoints in proposals that require a market.
6. *Costs.* This section shows details of expenses associated with the plan or product. Often a chart is required and/or a figure to show over time the amounts involved.
7. *Organizational Chart or Personnel Needed.* Most proposals indicate the people needed and where they fit into the organization.
8. *Revenue Projects.* In many proposals, some form of revenue or new resources are indicated, as this topic suggests.
9. *Competition.* This section reveals the competitive landscape anticipated.
10. *Future Directions.* Normally, a proposal will also suggest future directions, markets, expanded ideas in a final section in ways that do not fit the earlier part of the proposal.

BARRIERS TO EFFECTIVE WRITING

Writing Mannerisms

A number of mannerisms or bad habits can distract the reading process. Some of those distracting habits are listed here to serve as a friendly reminder to avoid them:

1. Too folksy, informal.
2. No organizational pattern that is easy to see, not just to read.
3. Not enough information or overwhelmingly too much information.
4. Unclear conclusion or direction for future next steps.
5. Using text abbreviations as if you and your best friend were writing on your phone texting each other.

Fear of Making a Mistake, So Never Starting

Real or imagined, many reports are delayed because the writer experiences some kind of apprehension. The best advice we can give is to just start. It is good advice to write anything germane to the topic you can think of and then go back and edit for support, organization, and introduction and conclusion. In other words, you do not begin with the perfect document, but you sketch the ideas and then go for the rest of what makes it good.

E-MAIL ETIQUETTE

Elements of the written communication would be incomplete without a word on rules to avoid offending people in e-mails. We will call these dos and don'ts of email etiquette (see McCombs, 2010; DeCoker, 2007).

1. Be clear as to the subject line. People like to know the topic.
2. Avoid cc and bcc unnecessarily. There is nothing worse than airing difficult issues with the boss or other coworkers until there has been a chance to resolve questions directly with the person or group involved. To unnecessarily copy others can be perceived as a power, manipulative move on your part.
3. Avoid writing in all capital letters. In text-speak, that is like shouting.
4. Avoid using symbols or abbreviating the topic of text messaging. You can appear very unprofessional and may even confuse your reader, depending on who it is.
5. When sending a message from your cell phone or portable device, note how the text may appear skewed. If the document or message is important, you may need to go to a computer to send the message in order to edit for appearance, match of logic, humor, or emotional expectations.
6. The first paragraph or sentence of the text should give an idea of what the message is about.
7. Don't forward a message without also notifying the original sender. Be careful, too, about forwarding chain letters or trivial messages—not all recipients like to have their inbox cluttered with useful material, no matter how cute you think it is. Know your reader.
8. Take care what and how you say something, since e-mail messages can have a legal implication even though they seem very informal. How is the reader thinking about what you write?
9. Think quick, clear, and organized—you have a better chance of making your point.
10. Double-check the address list. Be sure you did not in error send a message to the wrong recipient(s). If it happens to you, an apology is in order.

11. If it takes long to write an e-mail to make a point orally, then use the phone. Even better, walk to your colleague's office for a conversation and some of the interpersonal benefits that accrue.

CREATING EFFECTIVE RÉSUMÉS

A **résumé** is a summary of a person's life history regarding issues relevant to the job-selection process. In addition, your résumé serves as an example of your communication and organizational skills. You should learn how to tailor it to specific situations, to better meet the expectations of a certain position or employer. As you will learn, résumé writing follows certain social trends, so you can expect to make adjustments such as these throughout your career.

Web at Work D.1 provides information on other resources for creating résumés. In addition, using a search engine to search on the key word "résumé" may prove valuable in finding more sources.

A résumé should be organized and presented in a way that will capture the attention of those who are reviewing it and help achieve the job-selection goals of the company and the applicant. In today's marketplace, the two basic types of presentation are paper and electronic. General principles apply to both, but several differences will be noted.

GETTING STARTED   Getting started is the hardest part, so here are tips. If you're just graduating from college, or making a career change, Ream (2000) offers this advice: know yourself. Even if you are only finishing college, an inventory of your skills, likes/dislikes is important to quantify. In other words, what are your best skills? Confirm your skills with specific examples, like the time you completed a project or worked as a volunteer leader, etc. If you have strong communication skills, point out Communication or English grades. Do you like research, making presentations, being a teacher or mentor? These examples should be put together in your résumé. Also, we like to advise that you collect projects from classes or extracurricular programs or part-time jobs and assemble these as a portfolio to provide in addition to your résumé, either in a folder or in your personal website online.

WEB AT WORK D.1
Creating Résumés

Access the following websites to learn more about creating a great résumé. Be aware that some of these sites are for fee-based, professional services:

- **www.careerbuilder.com** In addition to information on creating résumés, provides information about posting résumés electronically, job listings, and other job-search advice.
- **www.provenresumes.com** Provides résumé-writing tips and information about free seminars.

- **www.resumania.com** Gives examples of real-life mistakes made in résumés and cover letters.
- **www.e-resume.net** Provides résumé-writing service; combines personalized attention with online speed.
- **www.classaresume.homestead.com** Covers résumé writing with a focus on analyzing the applicant's career field.
- **www.careerpro.com** Serves as a résumé-writing service that also offers employment counseling, outplacement services, and other job-search services.

For those who are changing careers, review your current job skills and identify the ones you enjoy or that you have excelled in conducting and feature these. Identify your critical work skills. For instance, you could examine skills such as these (Ream, 2000):

- Transferrable skills: writing, organizational skills, technical skills, communicating, and mentoring
- Analytical skills: researching, analyzing, categorizing, evaluating, and problem-solving.

This process might result in a highlight statement such as, "Ability to research, manage, and implement complex tasks while consistently meeting deadlines resulting in increased responsibility for mentoring others."

CONTENT   Résumés should contain relevant information that managers want to see. Stay focused on your abilities. Keep the objectives clear, and tailor your qualifications to the specific opportunity (Hamilton & Parker, 2001; Hutchinson & Brefka, 1997; Pontow, 2000; Ream, 2000). Furthermore, keep it short, avoid abbreviations, use a standard font and predictable layout, printed in black ink on white paper. Include your home page and video or audio materials if the job demands creative work. Use active words like "implemented, researched, advanced, increased, managed" as you simultaneously balance with specific phrases an employer is like to search for such as information career specialist, business analyst, information research professional, strategic plan developer, legal assistant, etc. (Ream, 2000). You can find a good set of format examples with Microsoft Word and go to "new document," where you can link to online templates that are easily downloaded. Most résumés generally include these categories:

1. *Personal identification.* Provide your name, phone, address, website, and e-mail at the top of each page. However, stay with a one-page résumé not to exceed two pages. Keep your personal characteristics out.
2. *Statement of objectives.* You must tailor the objective to match the job. Here, you need to use active verbs and use wording that balances key skills with the specific job opportunity, such as, "Aim to develop research and analysis for future markets in growing company where strong communication, leadership, and mentoring skills can be advanced in future management."
3. *Educational background.* In general, employers primarily want to know about your degree or degrees, including major/minors. You can include your GPA or class ranking if it is good. Also, provide a line or two under the major or minor showing what you experienced, as for instance, "Organizational communication for improving corporate cultures, intercultural communication where projects allowed presentation of cultural diversity in organizations, interpersonal communication to develop skills in relationship formation and teams building."
4. *Previous work experience.* Indicate meaningful work history, beginning with the most recent. Include dates of employment, job descriptions, and, to a lesser extent, supervisors' names.
5. *Awards and achievements.* List any significant items of recognition you have received from professional or academic organizations (without repeating the information from the "Education" section).
6. *References.* It has been traditional to provide references or contact information for individuals who can speak to your work qualifications. Most experts today, however, advise stating "Available upon request." Have a separate list. Be sure to get permission and contact information from your references in advance.

7. *Additional information.* Some résumés benefit from including information about special skills, languages spoken, equipment or software used, volunteer work, and hobbies and interests. Most employers rank memberships in social clubs and fraternities and sororities as less important. Include such information only if it may contribute to your getting the position.

STYLE AND FORMAT The conventional wisdom on writing résumés makes these suggestions for style and format:

1. *Be concise.* One page is the ideal, but two pages are acceptable. Anything longer will likely get passed over or thrown away.
2. *Recognize that language makes a difference.* Avoid using the passive voice; instead, use action words in describing your accomplishments, such as "coordinate, implemented, resolved, and planned." Also describe your performance in measurable terms, working in specific data, say, about how much you reduced the budget or improved customer satisfaction. Organize information in small sections rather than large ones. Finally, edit your spelling and grammar carefully.
3. *Attend to format.* Use standard-sized 81/2" × 11" white or off-white paper with no texture and a fine grain. Allow margins of 1" at the top and bottom and 11/2" on both sides. Use a black, standard readable font (11-point type is good) and leave plenty of space around headings. Don't use abbreviations. Don't cram material, but leave white space on the page.
4. *Specifically target the employer.* Customize each résumé to fit the expectations of the position and the employer.

For several examples of résumés, review Figures D.2 and D.3 on the following pages. Note that both are work history résumés and present similar types and amounts of information. Clearly, however, the differences in formatting distinguish the two.

Suggestions for Electronic Résumés

Because of the ease of transmission and the high cost of collecting and sorting hard-copy résumés, employers have turned to electronic methods to collect, sort, and file résumés. New graduates are finding that many companies today prefer computer-friendly scannable résumés and online résumés. These are stored as a computer file and created using word processing software and e-mail or posting on the Internet. From that point, some companies use an applicant tracking systems which scans for keywords to match your qualifications to specific job requirements. (Gunner, 2000). To maximize keyword searches, the advice given earlier also helps to remember to apply nouns rather than verbs, such as "project leader" rather than "lead a project."

Methods include attachments to e-mail messages, scanning information into a database, having an applicant complete an online résumé form, bulletin board services, news groups, and accessing a home page résumé. As noted earlier, the principles regarding good résumé writing hold true for electronic résumés, but additional guidelines must be followed to make them "computer friendly" (see *Proven Resumes*, 2010).

1. Use the "Save" or "Save As" command (if converting from another format) to save the résumé in *Plain Text* (also called *ASCII Text* or *MS-DOS* text and noted by the three-letter file extension .txt). This file type is universally acceptable. You can use Word or Adobe PDF. But, inquire as to exactly what format is needed by the company.
2. Plain Text is very basic. You may have to replace bullets with asterisks or a dash, and avoid font changes, such as bold and italic type, and it does not preserve formats such as centering

William Smith

239 E. Lake Drive, Dallas, TX 29776   214-555-5555 wsmith@igotmail.com

Objective   To develop the national sales force for an aggressive new company

Experience   2009–2011
                    National Sales Manager
                    Payless Lumber, Nashville, TN
                    • Increased sales from $50 million to $100 million.
                    • Doubled sales per representative from $5 million to $10 million.
                    • Suggested new products that increased earnings by 23%.
                    2006–2009
                    District Sales Manager
                    Smith and Barnett Bottlers, Decatur, IL
                    • Increased regional sales from $25 million to $40 million.
                    • Managed 250 sales representatives in 10 western states.
                    • Profitably implemented training course for new recruits.
                    2003–2006
                    Senior Sales Representative
                    New York Life, Southridge, SC
                    • Expanded sales team from 50 to 100 representatives.
                    • Tripled division revenues for each sales associate.
                    • Expanded sales to include mass market accounts.
                    2000–2003
                    Sales Representative
                    LitWare, Inc., Southridge, SC
                    • Expanded territorial sales by 400%.
                    • Received company's highest sales award four years in a row.
                    • Developed Excellence in Sales training course.

Education   1999–2003
                    South Lake State University, South Lake, UT
                    • B.A., Business Administration and Computer Science
                    • Graduated Summa Cum Laude

Interests   SR Board of Directors, running, gardening, carpentry, computers

Awards &   Alpha Chi, Annual Sales Club of America Outstanding Young Manager,
Affiliations   National Marketing Association of America

FIGURE D.2   Example of a Paper Résumé

CAROL ANDREWS

OBJECTIVE

To obtain entry-level coordination role in a nonprofit children's service organization.

EXPERIENCE

2008–2011

Regional Personnel Selection Manager, Big Brothers, Big Sisters, Northridge, CA

- Increased number of new volunteers by 2,396.
- Doubled number of interviews for selection from 200 to 400.
- Suggested new processes that saved 11% of recruiting budget.

2006–2008

Department Assistant Manager, Ferguson and Bardell, Northridge, CA

- Helped increase floor sales in the department store's shoe department from $250,000 to $400,000.
- Supervised two part-time student workers.
- Implemented training ideas for new recruits, speeding profitability.

2004–2006

Customer Order Representative, Fluffy Dry Cleaners, Modesto, CA

- Increased intake of orders by 21 per week.
- Expanded customer friendliness program to include 6% new customers.
- Encouraged study of reducing process time, resulting in 8% reduction.

EDUCATION

2000–2004

Northridge State University, Northridge, CA

- B.S., Major: Speech Communication, Minor: Industrial Psychology
- Graduated Cum Laude

INTERESTS

Modesto recycling service volunteer group, running, music, computers.

REFERENCES

Various academic and job-related references available upon request.

12345 MAIN STREET CAMDEN, GA 24839–6789 PHONE (403) 555-7890

FAX (403) 555-1533 E-MAIL ME@MYCOMPANY.COM

FIGURE D.3 Example of a Paper Résumé

and tabbing. To create headings, use capital letters, and to create lists, use asterisks or dashes instead of bullets.

3. Turn off the "Autoformat" function on your computer. Remove all tabs and use the space bar.
4. Use a 10- to 14-point font.
5. Set the margins at 0 and 60 characters before wrapping to a new line. Begin each new line flush left.

See Figures D.4 for an example of an electronic résumé.

In transmitting the information, send the résumé and cover letter in the same file or in the same e-mail message when possible. For more information on posting résumés, consult the resources in Web at Work at D.2 on page 368.

E-Mail Attachments

When you send a résumé as an attachment to an e-mail, be sure to have it saved as a standard Word or Adobe PDF and as a second attachment saved as a rich text format (.rtf. or .txt). This format allows flexibility for the employer in some cases, but usually you can ask ahead of time what format they prefer. Generally, you send both, but for the interview, bring your nicely formatted paper résumé.

In sending e-mail, think about issues of etiquette and avoid being too casual and presumptuous (Caudron, 2000). You are engaging in workplace communication, so your manner and style should be professional. However, many people treat an e-mail message like a text message, applying shorthand, symbols, and lowercase letters indiscriminately. Unfortunately, receivers judge the message quality by its form. If you are not familiar with common practices such as not writing in all capital letters, find a source to learn what is and is not generally acceptable. You can begin with the information presented in Skills at Work D.2 on page 368.

HOME WEB PAGE RÉSUMÉS   Creating your own Web page and making your résumé available there not only saves a lot of processing but also allows anyone to look at your résumé without committing to you in other ways. In posting your résumé on a home Web page, consider the following (Pontow, 2000):

1. Use titles and keywords. Search engines will sort by your page's title and URL and by HTML metatags in the document. The title may be the most important piece of information, since employers are more likely to search for "Communication Trainer" or "Sales Manager" than your name. Give serious thought to your selection of keywords to ensure potential viewers' success in sorting and selecting. You want them to be able to find your résumé.
2. Assist recruiters by creating additional links/pages that include ASCII and Plain Text versions of your résumé with all the HTML coding removed. This will allow recruiters to paste or transmit via e-mail more easily for processing.
3. Design your Web page résumé with hyperlinks that will take the viewer from one page or section to another. This makes it easier to scan rather than scroll through the résumé.
4. Your Web page doesn't have to be fancy, but it must be functional. If you don't feel qualified to create it yourself, get help.

EMPLOYER WEBSITES   Most companies do not take the time to search for personal websites. Rather, they expect job applicants to come to them. You can go to the website of a company you are interested in and add your résumé to their online résumé bank. To find specific companies' websites, go to Companies Online, bigbook.com, and wetfeet.com. Also check with the library for magazines and journals that specialize in describing company positions. Some companies also provide a way to e-mail your résumé.

EMILY DILLON

114 Somerset Lane
Appleton, WI 58399
(876) 555-5432 (Res.)
(876) 555-0415 (Bus.)

KEYWORD SUMMARY

speech pathologist, rehabilitation of communication disorders, early childhood education of children with disabilities, classroom modeling, therapy research and materials, CPR, Microsoft Word, PowerPoint, and Excel.

EXPERIENCE

Speech Pathologist, 2010-Present
Early Childhood Center, Appleton, WI

- Worked one-on-one with language- and speech-impaired children.
- Assisted teachers in developing classroom environment that supported language learning in all children.
- Researched and created therapy materials to target phonological processes.

Secretary, 8/08–5/10
HB Fuller Inc., Macliaon, WI

- Processed orders for shipping and receiving.
- Maintained daily calendar of shipping and receiving.
- Composed letters and memos for the plant manager.
- Copied and filed customer orders and information.

Volunteer, 6/03–7/08
Kennedy Health Care Center, Sewell, NJ

- Worked as assistant secretary in rehabilitation center.
- Processed and filed patient information.
- Scheduled appointment times for patients.
- Assisted in organizing therapy materials.
- Offered assistance and encouragement to patients as needed.

EDUCATION

University of Wisconsin, Madison, WI
Bachelor's Degree in Communication Disorders, May 2003
Master's Degree in Communication Disorders, May 2010

PROFESSIONAL AFFILIATIONS

- American Speech-Language and Hearing Association
- Wisconsin Speech-Language and Hearing Association

FIGURE D.4 Example of an Electronic Résumé

WEB AT WORK D.2
Résumé-Posting Services

For help in posting your electronic résumé, consult any of the following:

- **www.gisajob.com** An independent and free recruitment service in the United Kingdom.
- **www.jobbankusa.com** One of the Internet's largest and best-known online recruiting sites; has a state-of-the-art résumé database.
- **www.jobfolder.com** Allows users to search for a job and post a résumé free of charge.
- **www.monster.com** Offers job-search tools and career advice; can post résumés and applications.

- **www.ceweekly.com** Site of *Contract Employment Weekly,* a magazine for contractors, consultants, and temporary workers in engineering and technology.
- **http://jobsearchtech.about.com/od/ interview/Interviews.htm** Very helpful sources explaining various interview processes to expect.
- **www.socialservice.com** Advertises social service job openings and recruits social service employees; has a résumé database of job seekers throughout the United States.

SKILLS AT WORK D.2
E-Mail Do's and Don'ts

In the world of business communication, e-mail plays an ever-increasing role in ensuring the flow of information. That means it is important for you to know how to write friendly yet professional e-mails.

1. Do think about who may read your message. You will be better off handling a negative issue or addressing a third party in a face-to-face meeting.
2. Do picture the recipient's reaction to your message. How will he or she interpret your words and tone? It's easy to come across as overly harsh or abrupt in writing an e-mail.
3. Don't begin your message with criticism. By starting with a positive statement, you can only improve how your message will be received.
4. Don't send a message that you would be embarrassed to send a family member. Always remember that you cannot control the outcome or reaction of the person on the receiving end of your message.

5. Don't make your message too cryptic. Your readers shouldn't have to guess, assume, or read between the lines.
6. Do check your messages for grammatical and spelling errors. Write using complete sentences and normal punctuation. Use specialized e-mail symbols sparingly to avoid confusion.
7. Do read and reread messages before sending them. Again, e-mail can take on a too harsh tone that is not intended.
8. Do make your messages concise. Limit the length to one screen and enhance organization with the use of bullets or numbers.
9. Don't let e-mail become a substitute for in-person and phone conversations. Unless the issue is best stated in writing and needs immediate and perhaps multiperson distribution, state it in person.
10. Don't overlook the human element of communication. The message may be electronic, but the person receiving it is not.

Source: Based on McKay (2010).

However you decide to submit your résumé, make sure you follow whatever directions are provided for formatting and transmission. In addition, include a cover letter.

COVER LETTERS   A cover letter should always accompany a résumé. It provides an introduction to you and your purpose in communicating and gives an overview of your skills and experience—hopefully, encouraging the employer to look at the résumé that's been included.

In general, a cover letter should match the employer's stated job description and be addressed to a specific individual at his or her correct work address (not to "Dear committee" or "To whom it may concern"). Keep the content short (no more than one page), emphasize action words, avoid the passive voice, be specific, and use measurable outcomes. Use 11- or 12-point standard font, and print the letter on white or off-white paper—preferably, the same paper used for your résumé. Figures D.5 and D.6 provide examples of cover letters.

May 21, 2011

Mr. Stephen Jones
Acme Company
Boise, ID 12399-1239

Dear Mr. Jones:

When it comes to customer service and client relations, no doubt you receive many calls. Unfortunately, the vast majority of those calls are difficult situations, rude criticism, and anonymous callers. When I worked at various jobs during school and served other organizations during high school and college, I faced similar circumstances, ranging from serving customers at J.C. Penney's ordering department to the leadership roles I held in college organizations.

One reason I am sending my résumé to you is to become part of an assertive team to manage customer and client relationships. My experience has prepared me for this role. Although challenging at times, these experiences have taught mental toughness that sustains my interest in this rigorous field. Specifically, the Acme Company has been a leader in client relationships, as indicated in recent newspaper reports, and thus would complement my experience and inclination.

Second, my college degree inspires continuing work in customer service. Not only did I learn persuasion, sales, interpersonal communication, team building, and intercultural communication, but I learned how to present and manage ideas. For example, my portfolios for classes represent long hours of surveys and presentations that shaped my readiness for a challenging opportunity in an aggressive company like Acme.

Not surprisingly, you likely have many opportunities to interview candidates for the position. I am a candidate that has been ready for this kind of role even since childhood, when being on a winning soccer team and being my high school's student body treasurer sharpened my mental focus and teamwork shaped my interpersonal interest. During college and by working over the years as I put myself through school, these experiences have readied me to be part of a professional team.

Therefore, may I have an interview time with you soon? Our mutual interests and preparation appear solidly in place for a fascinating visit.

Sincerely,

Jennifer Frei
123 Scott Place, Austin, TX 55378–1234
e-mail: jaf11a@aus.com • phone: (252) 555-8202 • fax: (252) 555-8212

FIGURE D.5   Example of a Cover Letter from a Recent College Graduate Seeking Initial Employment

Doulette Communication Consultants

Matthew McFly • 915.679.1985 • mattmc@doulette.com

February 21, 2012

Ms. Jeanine Smith, Vice-President
Corporate Strategy Division, Brown Associates
129 North Twenty-Second Street
Des Moines, IA 59200–1456

Dear Ms. Smith:

Thank you again for the phone visit to discuss the position of Director of the Corporate Strategy Division of Brown Associates. For a number of reasons, the fit between me and Brown Associates, our mutual interests, and my experiences and training make this position seems promising.

Serving the past four years as Associate Director of Doulette has initiated the importance of strategic planning and organizational development. For seven of the last eight major projects, I have been privileged to work with a team to develop strategy based on our internal surveys of employees and executive feedback. The results have led to an astonishing quality improvement rating for those projects of 18%, 22%, and 31%, respectively. The entire process has taught me how to structure proposals and move forward to lead a team.

From this and other experiences and education, the past few years have launched my personal desire to have the opportunity to grow with a dynamic company, building on additional training beyond my university degree in communication. Training and continuing education in conflict management, customer relations policies, legal protocols for consulting and strategic planning for nonprofit organizations are the more formal courses that link directly with the position you have described at Brown Associates.

Furthermore, the challenge of developing organizations in concert with your team's goals seems a clear fit with my mission and personal vision. For some time, I have been interested in making a long-term commitment to an organization that identifies the problem solving, team development, and client relationships expressed at Brown Associates. For that reason alone, I find this position especially stimulating, and I hope a fit for us both.

A further visit about the position would be delightful. Feel free to call or e-mail, or visit my personal website at mattmac.com.

Sincerely,

Matthew McFly
Associate Director for Communication Consulting

FIGURE D.6   Example of a Cover Letter from an Experienced Professional Seeking a Position Change

WEB AT WORK D.3
Writing Cover Letters

If you need assistance in developing a cover letter, access these Internet sources, most of which offer fee-based services:

- **www.resume-helper.com** Provides consultation to determine direction, focus, and content of résumé and cover letter.
- **www.cjs-services.com** A service for writing résumés and cover letters; also some job links.
- **www.careerassist.com** Provides templates, examples, and critiques of résumés and cover letters; also provides interviewing guide.

- **www.resumania.com** Gives examples of real-life mistakes made in résumés and cover letters.
- **www.careerlab.com** Offers information to individuals and companies about a wide variety of cover letters, not just for job seeking.
- **www.jobsmart.org** Discusses what makes a good cover letter; also provides examples and additional resources.
- **http://www.collegegrad.com/job/jobinterviewtechnique.shtml** Great suggestions for new graduates regarding interview techniques.

SKILLS AT WORK D.3
Writing a Letter of Recommendation—and an Example

If you haven't already, you will no doubt at some point have to ask someone for a letter of recommendation. You will also likely write some of these in your professional career. In either case, here's what to look for:

1. ***A good recommendation is personal.*** Many people make the mistake of asking someone for a recommendation because of the person's prestige or position rather than because of their personal relationship. Someone who doesn't know you will find it impossible to write anything personal, and that will be apparent to all who read the letter. Human resource workers will look more favorably on a recommendation from, say, a professor who knows you well than a dean who barely knows your name.

2. ***A good recommendation compares you to others.*** Descriptive words such as *extraordinary*, *exceptional*, *hard working*, and *quick minded* have frequently found their way into letters of recommendation to the point that they have been overused and now lack real meaning. Someone who is considering hiring you would rather read a letter that compares you to others who have completed the same degree program or worked in the same position.

3. ***A good recommendation tells a story.*** Again, rather than rely on overused language and dry descriptions of an applicant's qualities and experience, a good letter of recommendation tells a story. A specifically insightful story that demonstrates your character or abilities can be quite persuasive.

4. ***A good recommendation focuses on your ability to perform.*** Although a recommendation can address many aspects of an individual, the main focus should be on ability to perform. That may mean the individual's scholastic ability to complete difficult assignments, perseverance in creating change, or ability to manage tasks and lead people. In addition to asking your professors and

(Continued)

SKILLS AT WORK D.3 *(Continued)*
Writing a Letter of Recommendation—and an Example

employers for letters of recommendation, also ask friends, clergy, and community leaders—anyone who can comment on your ability to get things done.

5. ***A good recommendation will contain some negative comments.*** A letter of recommendation that is singularly positive may lack credibility. By balancing your positive qualities with small character flaws and areas in need of improvement, the person writing your recommendation will strengthen his or her remarks.

Here is an example of a recommendation letter (names omitted):

The purpose of this letter is to recommend _____ for your internship. Having him this semester as a student has called my attention to his high competency and quality. As you can see below, he stands out among other senior students in several ways. Let me point out several qualities and examples of this high-quality student.

First, _____ is focused, diligent, timely, persevering, and clearly a quality learner. For instance, in our course on multinational organizational communication, _____'s team produced an outstanding project, complete with interview data, quantitative survey data, analysis, and excellent PowerPoint design. All this effort also was accomplished with precise oral communication and written communication skills.

Furthermore, he is a cooperative team player. His collegiality is seen in the hard work motivating his team to perform with high quality effort, which resulted in one of the top projects in the class as they worked with a software company making consulting and training recommendations. In fact, the company they used for their product praised the team and _____ for one of the best insight analyses they have seen in the last several years.

Without question, _____ is a capable leader while revealing statistical, qualitative, and technical skills. Moreover, his team building talents are highly commendable. I highly recommend him.

Web at Work D.3 lists some websites of services that can assist with writing effective cover letters. And Skills at Work D.3 addresses another type of correspondence that is often involved in employment applications: the letter of recommendation.

References

Caudron, S. (2000). Virtual manners. *Workforce, 79,* no. 2, 31–34.

DeCoker, G. (2007). Advice for a rookie staff member. *Chronicle of Higher Education, 54*(4), C1–C4. Retrieved from Academic Search Complete database.

Gunner, M. (2000). Give your resume the electronic edge. *Black Issues in Higher Education, 17*(10), 98. Retrieved from Academic Search Complete database.

Hansen, M. D. (1999). E-mail: What you should and shouldn't say. *Professional Safety, 44,* no. 8, 9.

Kuiper, S. (2009). *Contemporary business report writing.* 4th ed. Mason, Ohio: South-Western Cengage Learning.

McCombs, B. (2010). Email etiquette. *Canadian Journal of Rural Medicine, 15*(1), 36–37. Retrieved from Academic Search Complete database.

Pontow, R. (2000). Resumes and electronic resume writing. Available online: www.provenresumes.com/reswkshps/electronic/electrespg1.html.

Proven Resumes (2010). http://www.provenresumes.com/reswkshps/electronic/scnres.html.

Ream, R. (2000). Rules for electronic resumes. *Information Today, 17*(8), 24. Retrieved from Academic Search Complete database.

Résumé writing. (2000). Tips on writing and formatting electronic résumés. Available online: www.career-builder.com.

Yaklef, A. (2009). We have always been virtual: Writing, institutions, and technology! *Space and Culture, 12,* 76. DOI: 10.1177/1206331208327442.

APPENDIX E

Speech Evaluation Forms

Included in this appendix are two speech evaluation forms. Use them in evaluating others or in considering the factors that will be used in evaluating your presentations.

Name _____   Topic _____

Outline Method _____

Organization   _____ / 20 points
- [ ] Purpose statement clearly stated
- [ ] Thesis statement clearly stated
- [ ] Functional parts of the outline labeled
- [ ] Use of outline symbols consistent

Writing   _____ / 10 points
- [ ] Writing clearly identifies the central theme of the speech
- [ ] Speech content contained in the outline
- [ ] Verbal citations noted in the outline
- [ ] Transitions clearly stated and labeled

Preparedness   _____ / 10 points
- [ ] Complete sentences used to state main ideas
- [ ] Key words/phrases used to state subpoints
- [ ] Contains no mistakes in grammar, spelling, and punctuation
- [ ] Neatly typed, double-spaced, and on regulation paper
- [ ] Follows additional instructor requirements

Bibliography   _____ / 10 points
- [ ] At least three sources provided
- [ ] Sources typed in correct style
- [ ] Sources are current and relevant to the topic

                                                    TOTAL _____ / 50 points

FIGURE E.1   Outline Evaluation Form

Name _____   Topic _____

Speech Type/Number _____

Audience Analysis/Topic Choice   _____ / 10 points
- ☐ Clear and specific
- ☐ Interesting
- ☐ Appropriate

Introduction   _____ / 10 points
- ☐ Gained attention
- ☐ Provided reason to listen
- ☐ Clear thesis statement
- ☐ Preview of major points

Body   _____ / 20 points
- ☐ Adequate information
- ☐ Key ideas explained
- ☐ Credible source material
- ☐ Three sources used and cited properly

Organization   _____ / 10 points
- ☐ Clear organization pattern
- ☐ Clear transitions
- ☐ Major points easily identified

Conclusion   _____ / 10 points
- ☐ Summarized main theme
- ☐ Reviewed major points
- ☐ Creative/Clincher

Language   _____ / 10 points
- ☐ Clear, concise, correct
- ☐ Colorful, creative
- ☐ Helped listener to visualize

Delivery   _____ / 25 points
- ☐ Adequate eye contact
- ☐ Vocal variety and emphasis
- ☐ Appropriate nonverbal support
- ☐ General effectiveness

Time (score all or nothing)   _____ / 5 points

                                        TOTAL _____ / 100 points

FIGURE E.2   Speech Evaluation Form

GLOSSARY

Active listening Involves making responses that show you understand what someone is saying; goes beyond the physical act of hearing to include communication skills such as providing feedback and paraphrasing, turn taking, and demonstrating responsiveness through eye contact and other nonverbal behaviors.

Affinity-seeking communication Refers to developing connection or establishing bonds in relating to others on the job.

Approaches to negotiation Include the principled negotiation model, the concept of positional conflict management, and the description of successful negotiator qualities. *See also* Negotiation.

Assertiveness skills Ability to state your expectations as you work toward achieving goals.

Attitude An evaluation of something; a feeling about whether it's good or bad, useful or not useful; a predisposition of people to respond in positive and negative ways.

Audience analysis An examination of the traits that characterize the members of a specific audience, including their knowledge, attitudes, values, motives, beliefs, demographics, and the occasion for the gathering.

Audience commitment The principle that committing to action, even slightly, predicts an attitude alignment consistent with the initial modification.

Audience profile The result of an audience analysis; identifies the key traits of the group.

Behaviors Actions; may involve adoption or avoidance.

Beliefs Represent perceived truths; for instance, in an individual's integrity or even in fate.

Blocking behaviors Behaviors that erect barriers to group communication; include hidden agendas, rigid communication, overconforming communication, special pleading, pulling rank, interrupting, and defensive communication.

Bodily delivery The behaviors that affect the delivery of a message, such as eye contact, facial expressions, and posture or stance. *See also* Delivery.

Body The section of a speech that presents the main points and support materials; proves or amplifies the thesis. *See also* Main points; Support; Thesis statement.

Body movements Nonverbal behaviors such as gestures and posture that provide meaning in communication; the study of communication and body movements is called *kinesics*. *See also* Eye movements; Facial expressions; Nonverbal communication.

Causes of conflict In the workplace, include having different goals, different methods of reaching goals, scarce resources, relationship differences, unequal power distribution, unclear role expectations, different values, and face-saving. *See also* Conflict.

Centralized networks A communication network in which information is passed among group members through a central person or persons; examples include the wheel and the chain networks. *See also* Communication networks.

Channel The medium or means through which information flows within a system; usually interpersonal or mediated.

Character The audience's perception of the speaker's trustworthiness.

Charisma The audience's perception of the speaker's enthusiasm for the audience, the occasion, and the message itself.

Clarity The quality of language that is comprehended because of its directness, simplicity, and concreteness.

Client *See* Customer/Client.

Client-centered organizations *See* Operations-centered versus client-centered organizations.

Cognitive dissonance The inner conflict that is felt when an individual's beliefs, perceptions of behaviors, or attitudes do not align.

Communication apprehension An individual's fear of real or anticipated communication in a one-to-one setting, small group, meeting, or public presentation.

Communication climate Those conditions in the immediate communication context that influence the feeling of acceptance and other emotions regarding the relationship.

Communication competencies The set of knowledge and skills needed for effective business and professional communication; four major categories include organizational understanding, interpersonal communication, group and team communication, and public speaking.

Communication immediacy Refers to a feeling of nearness or closeness in talking and listening.

Communication model A visual representation of the components and process of communication; common types include actional, interactional, and transactional.

Communication networks The channels of communication available to small groups; the means by which group members have access to one another. *See also* Centralized networks; Decentralized networks; Virtual networks.

Communication omission Filtering out or eliminating significant information in relating ideas to others in business and professional settings.

Competence The audience's perception of the speaker's expertise.

Complaint or grievance interview An interview that's conducted to air complaints and grievances in the workplace.

Computer-mediated group communication An approach to information exchange in which the leader or a committee of team members develops a website or electronic bulletin board that members use to work through problems and solutions collectively.

Conclusion The closing of a speech; its functions are to summarize main ideas, bring things to a close, and motivate the audience.

Confidence The speaker's self-assuredness in presenting his or her message to the audience.

Conflict Occurs when two or more people clash over an issue about which they have different beliefs or values. *See also* Causes of conflict; Conflict communication styles; Organizational conflict; Theories of conflict; Types of conflict.

Conflict communication styles Approaches to managing conflict; five basic styles are competition, collaboration, accommodation, avoidance, and compromise. *See also* Conflict.

Connections and transitions Words and phrases that connect the introduction with the body and the body with the conclusion and that lead the audience

from idea to idea within the body of the speech; techniques include using enumeration, providing transitions, asking questions, and previewing and reviewing. *See also* Body; Conclusion; Introduction.

Connotation Refers to the feelings that words suggest as meaning.

Context The physical location or setting in which the message is delivered.

Contingency leadership Sometimes called *situational leadership*; adapts communication style to the situational information needs and maturity levels of employees; involves matching a sender's style with a receiver's needs.

Co-orientation The audience's perception of the speaker's similarity with their values, attitudes, and beliefs.

Cover letter A type of job-search correspondence that introduces the applicant and gives an overview of his or her skills and experience; should always accompany a résumé.

Credibility The audience's perception of the speaker's believability; determined by his or her competence, character, charisma, and co-orientation.

Cultural adaptation The process of moving to new surroundings, engaging in new roles, and experiencing major changes.

Cultural diversity Differences in group loyalty, ethnic or national origin, religious belief or practice, gender or sexual preference, and economics. *See also* Culture.

Culture The shared set of beliefs, attitudes, customs, rules, activities, and communication patterns that characterize an identifiable group of people.

Culture shock The stress related to entering, living, and adapting to a new culture.

Customer/Client An individual who receives the products or services developed by an organization.

Customer-centered communication Messages that suggest helpfulness and that make customers feel comfortable and welcome.

Customer service An organization's orientation to the needs of clients or customers, particularly compared to its orientation to its own needs.

Cycle of conflict The perpetual pattern that results from avoiding conflict; in general, the longer the cycle, the worse the conflict. *See also* Conflict; Theories of conflict.

Decentralized networks Communication networks in which information passes randomly among group members, not exclusively through a centrally placed individual or gatekeeper; examples include open-channel (or circle) and all-channel networks. *See also* Communication networks.

Delivery The use of vocal qualities and bodily qualities to present a message to an audience. *See also* Bodily delivery; Vocal delivery.

Delphi technique An approach to brainstorming in which group members share ideas through e-mail or other communication without actually meeting.

Demographics A group's makeup in terms of factors such as age, gender, education, income, occupation, family and marital status, residence, and culture.

Denotation Refers to the dictionary meanings of words.

Diffusion of innovation The process by which new technologies (or innovations) are adopted across individuals, networks, and large systems units.

Disciplinary interview An interview that's conducted to address employee behavior for which the major outcome is to reprimand. *See also* Interview.

Employment selection interview An interview between a prospective employee and an organizational representative that's designed to screen the prospective employee for an organizational role or position. *See also* Interview.

Ethnocentrism A sense of egotism and selfishness about a person's own culture, whereby he or she elevates that culture to a status above all other cultures. *See also* Culture.

Evidence The support material in a persuasive presentation; what is provided to prove the thesis. *See also* Support; Thesis statement.

Exit interview An interview that's conducted when an employee is preparing to leave an organization for the purpose of gathering informative feedback that will help the organization improve. *See also* Interview.

Expectations Point to self-fulfilling predictions of how people will respond; performance is typically consistent with expectations.

Extemporaneous delivery A method of delivery that involves speaking from notes or an outline that contains keywords, phrases, and ideas. *See also* Delivery; Outline.

Eye movements Nonverbal behaviors such as making eye contact that provide meaning in communication; the study of eye movements is called *oculesics*. *See also* Body movements; Nonverbal communication.

Facial expressions Nonverbal behaviors such as smiling that provide meaning in communication; universal facial expressions include those that depict anger, disgust, fear, happiness, sadness, and surprise. *See also* Body movements; Nonverbal communication.

Fallacies in reasoning Errors or weaknesses in reasoning; common types are quotations from nonauthorities, insufficient use of cases, observations, or signs, faulty reasoning from analogy or causation, hasty generalization, false dilemma, attacking the person, bandwagon technique, "two wrongs do not make a right," appeal to tradition, and faulty correlation.

Fear appeal A message that links some inherent danger, threat, or harm with a course of action, attitude, or belief.

Foundations of speaking The basic skills and knowledge needed to be an effective business and professional communicator; include credibility, confidence, and consultation about the audience. *See* Audience analysis; Confidence; Credibility.

Functions of nonverbal communication The four major functions are to complement, to contradict, to regulate, and to substitute. *See also* Nonverbal communication.

Functions of teams Purposes that satisfy organizational as well as personal needs; include the need for information, knowledge, and innovation; the need for self-directed leadership; and the need for individual achievement and satisfaction. *See also* Small group or team; Team.

Gender differences Cultural differences in expectations of men's and women's communication and other behaviors.

Group communication Communication among the members of a small group or team. *See also* Small group or team; Team.

Group discussions Communication among members of a small group or team; three steps include initiating the discussion, developing problem-solving strategies, and initiating a conclusion. *See also* Small group or team; Team.

Group interview An interview in which a group of interviewers may talk with a single interviewee or a single interviewer may talk with a group of interviewees. *See also* Interview.

High-context cultures *See* Low-context and high-context cultures.

Human relations perspective The view that employees work harder in response to leadership attention; strategies focus on ways to enhance employee attitudes and projects that engage a positive outlook among employees.

Human resources perspective The view that companies can increase productivity and improve morale by highlighting motivation and helping individuals reach their potential in terms of accomplishments and self-worth; leadership is expected to leverage the giftedness of educated employees.

Impromptu delivery A delivery method that involves speaking without any specific preparation. *See also* Delivery.

Inclusion language Language that conveys connection, reliance, trust, empathy, and belonging; goes beyond word choice to include conversational habits and nonverbal behavior; does not exclude groups.

Information sharing The exchange of information among members of an organization. *See also* Communication.

Information-gathering interview An interview that's conducted to gather information; fact-finding meetings to assess situations, events, and persons. *See also* Interview.

Informative presentations Presentations that are intended to provide new information, to reinforce previously known information, and/or to clarify understanding and reduce uncertainty; for example, oral reports, news releases and briefings, speeches of introduction, and longer informative speeches. *See also* News release or briefing; Oral report; Speech of introduction.

In-groups and out-groups In-groups include people who match our own identities or share our beliefs, values, language, religion, and so on; out-groups include those who are perceived as different from us and the people with whom we strongly identify.

Inoculation The practice of building up the audience's resistance to other messages (which will likely be heard later) by convincing them of the value of another message; sometimes called *counterpositional resistance.*

Integrated marketing communication An approach to marketing that's intended to pull together diverse areas such as advertising, marketing theory, and customer service; a systems approach to marketing. *See also* Marketing.

Intercultural communication The specialized segment of communication studies that considers the relationship between culture and language; provides insight into how perceived differences affect communication in the workplace. *See also* Culture; Strategies for intercultural communication.

Interpersonal attributions Qualities people assign to others (often in the absence of facts) to create consistent and holistic narratives about them; used to interpret what is observed about people's behavior.

Interpersonal communication Communication between individuals; usually face-to-face but can be mediated (such as telephone or e-mail).

Interpersonal perceptions How we categorize others based on our perceptions of them. *See also* Interpersonal attributions.

Interview A highly focused communication event in which groups of two or more gather for a specific exchange of information. *See also* Interview structure; Types of questions.

Interview structure Commonly involves four phases the introduction, the questions, the closing, and the follow-up. *See also* Interview.

Introduction The beginning of a presentation; its functions are to get the audience's attention, build rapport with them, orient them toward the purpose and thesis, and identify unusual words, as needed. *See also* Purpose statement; Thesis statement

Introductory speech *See* Speech of introduction.

Keyword speaking outline An outline containing key words and phrases that guide the speaker through an extemporaneous speech. *See also* Extemporaneous delivery; Outline.

Knowledge basis The collective knowledge that informs a successful salesperson; includes product knowledge, organizational knowledge, benchmark comparisons, and organizational plan.

Language style The choices of words and structures a speaker makes; elements include vividness, clarity, relational language, and connotation versus denotation. *See also* Clarity; Connotation; Denotation; Relational language; Vividness.

Leadership and management approaches Paradigms of leadership or organizational designs; significant approaches include traditional, relational, cultural, and network.

Letter of application *See* Cover letter.

Life-cycle model A model of teams that identifies the various phases they go through that determine their focus and level of productivity; phases include forming, storming, norming, performing, and superperforming. *See also* Team.

Logical fallacies *See* Fallacies in reasoning.

Low-context and high-context cultures Low-context cultures rely on having explicit and complete information; high-context cultures provide little overt information but rather expect members to gather information from the context.

Main points The key ideas that will amplify or prove the thesis statement; comprise the body of the presentation. *See also* Body; Thesis statement.

Manuscript delivery A method of delivery in which the speech is written out in its entirety and read aloud to the audience. *See also* Delivery.

Marketing The strategic plan for promoting, selling, and distributing a product or service.

Media interview An interview that's conducted with one or members of the media, such as a television reporter. *See also* Interview.

Memorized delivery A delivery method in which the speech is written out, word for word, but the speaker commits the entire speech to memory. *See also* Delivery.

Message The information exchanged through communication; can be verbal or nonverbal.

Message filtering The process of revealing or denying information to individuals and groups; may result from poor information flow, faulty listening, or inadequate communication training or communication flow policy.

Message order The principle that the arrangement of points in a message affects its overall persuasive impact; also that the order in which two messages or two speakers are heard affects their overall impact.

Motivation The salesperson's incentive or drive to sell; a primary quality of *self-starters*.

Negotiation The process by which two parties who hold opposite positions over some desired resource find a common position. *See also* Approaches to negotiation; Negotiation styles.

Negotiation styles Individual styles of managing conflict and negotiation; four styles are intuitive, normative, factual, and analytical. *See also* Conflict communication styles.

Networks *See* Communication networks.

News release or briefing An oral report that's intended to announce problems, crises, innovations, or future plans; may be preplanned or impromptu. *See also* Oral report.

Noise Interference with the message interaction process; may be physical or psychological.

Nonverbal communication Communication without words; behaviors that are interpreted to have meaning; examples include eye movements, facial expressions, body movements, and vocal utterances. *See also* Body movements; Eye movements; Facial expressions.

Objects and clothing Nonverbal behaviors such as wearing formal clothing and having body piercings that provide meaning in communication; that meaning may be intentional or unintentional; the study of objects and clothing is called *objectics*. *See also* Nonverbal communication.

Occasion The reason for a communication event.

Operations-centered versus client-centered organizations Operations-centered organizations focus on serving their own needs (for instance, selling their products); client-centered organizations focus on serving their clients' needs (for instance, helping clients solve problems).

Oral report An informative presentation that is usually shorter than a speech, lasting around ten minutes; presents more detail than a news release or briefing and is based on more research; often involves the use of visual aids. *See also* Informative presentations; News release or briefing; Visual aids.

Organizational communication Relevant information flowing between employees, between various units, and between management and employees.

Organizational conflict Occurs when policies, decisions, or directional shifts create resistance between individuals who feel others are blocking their efforts or those of their group.

Organizational culture The unique set of factors that creates the context of a given workplace; include commonly accepted attitudes, beliefs, behaviors, language, roles, procedures/rituals, scope/space, relationships, rewards, and values.

Organizational design The plan for the body of a speech; involves creating an outline and choosing an organizational pattern. *See also* Body; Organizational patterns; Outline.

Organizational patterns Logical structures used to arrange the main points within the body of the speech; for informative presentations, include topical, spatial, chronological, cause-to-effect and effect-to-cause, and known-to-unknown; for persuasive presentations, include problem/solution, proposition/proof, and motivational sequence. *See also* Body; Informative presentations; Persuasive presentations.

Outcomes The tangible results of an activity such as teamwork or training; must be observable and measurable to be useful in evaluating effectiveness.

Outcomes measures Means of evaluating the results of specific outcomes.

Out-groups *See* In-groups and out-groups.

Outline A plan that reflects the hierarchy of the main points, subpoints, subsubpoints, and so on within a speech using a designated set of symbols.

Parliamentary procedure A quasi-legal set of rules that guide formal, large-group decision making.

Participants Those individuals or groups who interact and interpret information in an organizational culture; the sender and the receiver in communication. *See also* Organizational culture.

Performance appraisal interview An interview between an employee and his or her manager or supervisor that's conducted to review past work performance; usually follows a formal, standard procedure. *See also* Interview.

Personal and organizational space The socially appropriate amount of space between people, depending on their status and relationship; organizational space comprises the furnishings and architectural designs that influence perception and interaction.

Persuasive presentations Presentations that are intended to change or reinforce audience attitudes, values, beliefs, or behaviors.

Potential customers and clients The concept of prospecting, or developing, potential customers for a product or service; may involve strategies such as demographic analysis, trend analysis, current events studies, and networking.

PowerPoint™ presentations Computer-generated slides used to present key words and graphics during a speech; a common type of high-technology visual aid. *See also* Visual aids.

Prejudice Occurs when people have preconceived attitudes toward the members of a particular cultural group, leading to bias, unfairness, intolerance, and even injustice.

Presentational skills The set of language style and delivery skills that underlie effective public presentations. *See also* Delivery; Language style.

Public presentations Speeches delivered to large groups of people; can take a variety of forms, such as informative speeches, briefings, formal reports, transfers of technical information, spontaneous reports, inspirational messages, and persuasive speeches. *See also* Informative presentations; News release or briefing; Oral report; Persuasive presentations.

Purpose statement A complete sentence that describes what a presentation is intended to accomplish; general purposes are to inform, to persuade, to entertain, and to inspire.

Qualities of successful teams Characteristics that enhance the functioning of teams; include communicating vision and mission; communicating strategic goals and activities; communicating expectations; communicating commitment and norms; communicating with senior leadership; and communicating significant amounts of information. *See also* Small group or team; Team.

Quality control circles (QCCs) Small groups that function by acquiring information and implementing meaningful changes in organizations through regular employee feedback; a concept that emerged from the larger movement known as total quality management (TQM). *See also* Total quality management.

Question-sequencing patterns Four basic patterns are used in interviewing the funnel, the inverted funnel, the hourglass, and the diamond. *See also* Interview; Interview structure; Types of questions.

Relational language Language that links the speaker with the audience, such as *we* and *us*; creates common ground.

Relationship maintenance The activities and attitudes that develop and support interpersonal relationships.

Relationship selling A customer-driven approach to sales that emphasizes interpersonal communication and a customer focus over a product focus.

Résumé A summary of a person's life history regarding issues relevant to the job-selection process; typically includes a job or professional objective, educational background, work-related experience, awards and honors received, and other relevant personal information; may be paper or electronic.

Rules governing nonverbal communication Directives that are understood in light of the cultural context of the situation and because people have been socialized into that culture; often called *norms*. *See also* Culture; Nonverbal communication.

Sales communication Persuasive messages designed to sell or market a product or service.

Sales interview An interview between a salesperson and a potential customer or client for the purpose of selling a product or service; a form of persuasive presentation. *See* Interview; Persuasive presentations.

Satisfaction outcomes Activities of a small group or team that are related to personal fulfillment and member interaction. *See also* Outcomes; Small group or team.

Scientific management perspective The view that employees are pieces of an engine or parts of an industrial whole and as such are treated as economic objects without deference to individual attitudes, feelings, values, and needs; concepts include time and motion, motivation, structure, span of control, and organizational charts.

Selectivity principle The principle that people choose to listen to ideas and messages that reinforce what they already know, believe, or like.

Small group or team Consisting of three to fifteen members (or an average of between six and eight) focused on a specific task or function; may be called a *task force*, *project group*, or *product team*. *See also* Team.

Small-group leadership styles Approaches to convey management and information in small groups and teams; three styles are highly directive, participatory, and negligent (or laissez-faire). *See also* Small group or team.

Social exchange theory The view that people tend to evaluate relationships by taking into account a ratio of their rewards to their costs.

Social judgment theory A view that suggests how people come to evaluate information, form a position, and can then be moved to form a new position.

Speech foundations *See* Foundations of speaking.

Speech of introduction A brief informative presentation that's intended to identify an upcoming speaker for the audience. *See also* Informative presentations.

Stereotyping Having a set mental picture of a particular group and arbitrarily attributing the traits of that group to someone who belongs to it.

Strategies for intercultural communication Means of managing cultural diversity, including searching for common ground, adapting to low- and high-context cultures, adapting to group and individual cultures, adapting to task and people orientations, adapting to cultural hierarchy, adjusting linearity, understanding nonverbal interactions, avoiding hasty generalizations, and engaging in cultural adaptation. *See also* Cultural adaptation; Intercultural communication; Low- and high-context cultures; Task-oriented and people-oriented cultures.

Support Information that proves or backs up the main points of a speech, such as cases, examples, statistics, and quotations; the sources of support material should be cited orally during the speech. *See also* Main points.

Systems communication perspective The view that each component within a system (such as an organization, department, or team) affects other components; leaders are expected to blend a concern for people with a concern for tasks; borrows from the foundations of systems theory.

Task outcomes Activities of a small group or team that are related to achievement of a goal or purpose. *See also* Outcomes.

Task-oriented and people-oriented cultures In task-oriented cultures, the focus is on doing one's job and its respective accountabilities and responsibilities; in people-oriented cultures, the focus is on people and personal relationships.

Team A structured entity within a larger organization, sharing a mission and goals. *See also* Small group or team.

Team norms Expectations of personal commitment and rules for operation shared among team members. *See also* Team.

Telephone interview An interview that's conducted over the telephone, not face-to-face. *See also* Interview.

Theories of conflict Four basic theories are phase theory, conflict avoidance theory (a cycle theory), the chilling effect theory (a cycle theory), and escalation theory. *See also* Conflict; Cycle of conflict.

Thesis statement The main assertion that will be made in a speech; usually stated in a single sentence.

Timing Nonverbal behaviors such as being punctual that provide meaning to communication; the study of time and communication is called *chronemics*. *See also* Nonverbal communication.

Topic selection The process by which a general subject is identified and continually narrowed so as to fit the audience and occasion. *See also* Audience analysis; Occasion.

Total quality management (TQM) Refers to a movement that drives productivity and morale through adherence to values, customer service and market-driven responses, and continuous improvement as a means of achieving organizational success.

Touch Nonverbal behaviors such as hugging that provide meaning in communication; the study of touch and communication is called *haptics*. *See also* Nonverbal communication.

Transitions *See* Connections and transitions.

Types of conflict Range from simple disagreements to outright hostility; four categories are disagreements, misplaced conflicts, nonsubstantive conflicts, and substantive conflicts. *See also* Conflict.

Types of questions The questions asked during the question phase of an interview can be categorized as closed questions, open-ended questions, hypothetical open-ended questions, probing questions, third-party questions, and leading, loaded, and illegal questions. *See also* Interview; Interview structure.

Types of reasoning Logical structures used to organize information in a speech; include cause-and-effect reasoning, reasoning from sign, reasoning from analogy, specific-to-general reasoning, and reasoning from classification. *See also* Fallacies in reasoning.

Values Enduring standards or ideals of what is worthwhile and not worthwhile; may be specific to an individual or shared by the members of an entire culture.

Verbal skills Present efficient ways of handling verbal interaction in terms of how we arrange words in messages and the vocal emphasis we apply to those messages.

Videoconference interview An interview that's conducted via a satellite downlink or multimedia technology. *See also* Interview.

Virtual networks Communication networks that use technology to provide group members with access to one another; allow instantaneous sharing of information without being in the same physical place. *See also* Communication networks.

Visual aids Visually appealing support materials used in presenting a speech; for instance, diagrams, models, overhead transparencies, and PowerPoint™ presentations. *See also* PowerPoint™ presentations.

Vividness The quality of language that conveys a sense of movement and excitement; elements include colorful language, metaphors, and narratives.

Vocal characteristics Nonverbal behaviors comprising qualities of voice that provide meaning in communication; for example, accent, volume, pitch, and rate and the utterances that accompany words. *See also* Nonverbal communication.

Vocal delivery The voice qualities that affect the delivery of a message, such as pitch, rate, volume, and pause.

Workplace communication Interaction between people, either face-to-face or mediated, in which meanings and understanding are created so as to further the tasks and relationships of the organization.

INDEX

PHOTO CREDITS